The Parisian Worlds of Frédéric Chopin

The Parisian Worlds of
Frédéric Chopin

WILLIAM G. ATWOOD

YALE UNIVERSITY PRESS

NEW HAVEN AND LONDON

Designed by Thomas Whitridge.
Set in Monotype Fournier by Ink, Inc. New York.
Printed in the United States of America.

Library of Congress Cataloging-in-Publication Data
Atwood, William G., 1932–
The Parisian worlds of Frédéric Chopin / William G. Atwood.   p.   cm.
Includes bibliographical references and index.
ISBN 0–300–07773–4 (alk. paper)
1. Chopin, Frédéric, 1810–1849. 2. Paris (France)—Social life and customs. 3. Music—France—
Paris—19th century. I. Title.
ML410.C54A78   1999   786.2´092—dc21   [B]   99–27886 CIP

A catalogue record for this book is available from the British Library.

The paper in this book meets the guidelines for permanence and durability of the Committee on
Production Guidelines for Book Longevity of the Council on Library Resources.

10   9   8   7   6   5   4   3   2   1

For David Balthrop
with the deepest gratitude and the highest esteem

Contents

CHAPTER I

Paris à la Galignani

An Anglo-Italian Guide to the French Capital
for the English-Speaking Tourist

THE PARIS THAT CHOPIN ENTERED for the first time in 1831 had the equivocal distinction of being both the cultural mecca and political scourge of Europe. At that time artists, writers, and musicians from Europe, America, and more distant corners of the globe flocked there for inspiration, experience, and the potential accolades of the "civilized" world's most sophisticated populace. At the same time the city had become an anathema to every crowned head in Europe, none of whom could forget how its new "citizen king," Louis-Philippe, and his renegade father had betrayed their aristocratic heritage to abet the cause of the revolutionary rabble in 1789. Many at first refused to recognize the new monarch's authority, while those who did never completely overcame their mistrust of him. Nor did they trust his subjects. After all it was a mere sixteen years since these erstwhile minions of Napoléon had raided their realms and plundered the wealth of the entire continent.

Notwithstanding their ambivalent attitudes, most Europeans (and their transatlantic cousins in the United States of America) conceded that Paris was the most glorious city in the world. If some Americans had reservations about the Parisians' morals, few doubted the grandeur of their city. In the previous century Benjamin Franklin and Thomas Jefferson had extolled its beauty, but it remained for the English, the Frenchman's eternal bête noire, to turn this admiration into adulation during the following century.

"Paris as a city and as a capital is certainly far superior to London," wrote Colonel Thomas Raikes, an English expatriate in Paris during the 1830s and 1840s. "There is an air of ancient grandeur in the monuments, the palaces, the hotels of the nobility, the long avenues and the spacious quays, the gardens and the statues which must strike every foreigner with admiration."[1]

The colonel's enthusiasm brings to mind the old saying, "Paris is where all good Englishmen go when they die." Actually in the early nineteenth century most tried to get there sooner. And many did, especially after 1815 when the Duke of Wellington dispatched Napoléon to the island of St. Helena and bought himself a fine town house on the rue Faubourg Saint-Honoré.² The price had to be right since the owner, Napoléon's sister, Princess Pauline Borghese, was understandably anxious to get out of town. In the decades that followed, the tourist trade across the channel flourished as never before. Few Englishmen made the trip without a copy of *Galignani's New Paris Guide* under their arms, and those who weren't too seasick pored over it in anticipation of the pleasures that awaited them.

It was in the fall of 1831 that Chopin, with a passport from Vienna to London, stopped en route in Paris. Not until July 1837 did he finally make it to London. A week later he was back in Paris, having learned in that brief interval why the English preferred it to their own capital. Although little more than half the size of London, Paris was, as Jules Janin, put it, "the head of France…the heart of Europe."³ Taking the metaphor a step further, Théophile Gautier called the French capital the very "brain of the world."⁴

Perhaps the worst thing about Paris was getting there. For most travelers its inland situation necessitated a difficult journey over poor, often unsafe roads. To avoid this some of the English took a steamer up the Seine from Le Havre as far as Pecq, a small town four leagues west of the city. From there it was only a short trip by diligence to the capital's three stagecoach terminals—the Messageries Royales southeast of the Bourse, the Messageries Générales of MM. Laffitte and Caillard, just north of the Louvre, and a third "suburban" depot on the east side of the rue Faubourg-Saint-Denis. By this time tourists had already gotten a taste of Parisian bureaucracy at one of the city's fifty-seven barrier gates, where a green-uniformed customs agent searched their luggage for such taxable items as wine and tobacco.

From 1837 on it was possible to make the trip from Pecq by the new railroad, which deposited travelers in a Gothic waiting room filled with paintings at No. 120 rue Saint-Lazare (fig. 1.1). Only the more adventurous took this route, as it was a harrowing experience to travel at the breakneck speed of thirty miles an hour, through smoke-filled tunnels and across high, narrow viaducts. Red-hot cinders pelted the train and occasionally started fires that more than once proved fatal to passengers, who were always locked inside the coaches. As the novelist Paul de Kock bewailed, "To go on the railway! why it is to take your life in your

1.1: The first railroad terminal in Paris (shown here) was at the site of today's gare Saint-Lazare. Among the dangers of early rail travel was the practice of locking passengers inside the wooden cars, which prevented them from escaping the frequent fires that occurred when live cinders from the locomotive sprayed the roofs. Among the train's inconveniences were the lack of toilet facilities. (For Chopin's amusement at this, see the beginning of Chapter 10.)

hands!"[5] Despite these perils, in May 1843 Chopin and George Sand went by train as far as Orléans en route to Nohant, Sand's chateau in the province of Berry. Although they encountered no misfortune, the noise gave the sensitive musician such a headache that he made most future trips there by carriage.

For those like Chopin, who preferred traveling by diligence rather than rail, fiacres (small hackney coaches) were available at the stagecoach terminals to take the daytime travelers to their destinations in Paris. The smaller two-wheeled cabriolets were cheaper but offered little protection in bad weather. Those who trusted Galignani's guidebook, though, never worried about the weather. Paris, it assured them, was a "naturally salubrious" city with none of the fogs, clouds, or "sickly sunbeams" of London.[6] Even more economical than a cabriolet were the city's 378 omnibuses, those elongated, horse-drawn carriages introduced into Paris in 1828 by their inventor, M. Omnès from Nantes. Each was painted a different color, given a fanciful feminine name (la Dame Blanche, l'Algérienne, la Béarnaise) and assigned to certain streets. They were available from 8:00 A.M. to 11:00 P.M., but for those not familiar with their routes it was easy to get lost, and anyone who ever read Mrs. Trollope or Lady Blessington knew there were parts of Paris it was best to avoid. By 1835 the omnibuses were transporting 100,000 Parisians a day around the city.

Although Paris, then as now, offered a wide selection of hotels at all prices (fire and lighting were always extra), most well-heeled English and American tourists settled into M. Meurice's City of London Hotel on the rue de Rivoli at the corner of the rue Castiglione. There one could count on an English-speaking staff, a decent English breakfast, and English newspapers. As for mail, the Meurice, like all Paris, had postal deliveries three times a day, and after 1845 messengers could readily dispatch one's telegrams from telegraph offices on both sides of the Seine.

For those who couldn't afford M. Meurice's establishment or the other luxury hotels between the rue de Rivoli and the northern boulevards, there were boarding houses. But, as Galignani's guidebook warned, many of these harbored disreputable gambling dens since King Louis-Philippe had shut down the legitimate casinos in the Palais Royal in 1836. If one planned to be in Paris any length of time, it was more economical to rent an apartment and have an upholsterer furnish it.

Once installed in suitable quarters, the visitor could set about the serious business of sightseeing. This, of course, was something Messrs. Galignani had anticipated, and their *New Guide* of 1841 contained a "List of places that must be seen by the stranger"—thirty-four in all, including public buildings, monuments, museums, libraries, parks, and churches. With surprisingly few exceptions, these sights are still available to the tourist today.

Because the guidebook of 1841 had been written the year before, it describes Paris as it was in 1840, conveniently the midpoint of Chopin's residence there. It was a city between revolutions, enjoying an era of relative calm. This is not to say, however, that those years were uneventful ones.

Politically, France was trying to cope once again with the clumsy, inefficient mechanism of constitutional monarchy. The Bourbons, imbued with the notion of their divine right to rule, had not been able to tolerate the charter imposed on them by the Allies after Napoléon's defeat. When they were eventually ousted in the July revolution of 1830, it was hoped that their Orléans cousin, the new king Louis-Philippe, had somehow managed to learn what they could never learn and forgotten what they could never forget. To the nation's disappointment, however, the new king established an oligarchical regime controlled by the *nouveau riche* middle class. It was, so to speak, a "bourgeois-cracy" that satisfied few Frenchmen, least of all Louis-Philippe, who found himself in a perpetual tug-of-war with his ministers. Toward the end of his reign, as age made him increasingly isolated and inflexible, the stage was set for another revolution in 1848. Although its instigators were again the working classes, they had progressed from the disorganized rabble of 1830 to a more sophisticated, better-educated mass aligned with revolutionary colleagues in England, Italy, and Germany. This new breed of worker had developed as a product of France's delayed industrial revolution. With the increased availability of primary education and the dissemination of cheap daily newspapers under the Orleanist regime, they had been transformed from mere urban peasants into a self-conscious social force that was to be known in the future as the proletariat. In the mid-1840s, Marx came to Paris to observe their problems, and what he saw helped to formulate his *Communist Manifesto*, published in January of 1848.

The emergence of this new social class in Paris was reflected in the art and literature of the period, which devoted increasing attention to the "common man" and "the people." In the transition from Romanticism to Realism, we see the virtual extinction of the grand genre of historical painting devoted to the glorification of kings and princes and the rise of a popular art portraying the poor—for example, in Honoré Daumier's lithographs and the canvases of Gustave Courbet and Jean-François Millet. At the same time, Louis Jacques Mandé Daguerre's new camera began to show us the ordinary "man on the street," living in a world of stark reality without the contrived idealizations of the Romantic painters.

In a similar vein, both drama and literature began to choose their protagonists from the lower strata of society; among them, the impoverished young artists and their unwashed grisettes in *Scènes de la Vie de Bohème* and the humbly born courtesan of *La Dame aux Camélias*. Novelists like George Sand drew attention to the many social inequities of the period, while would-be reformers like Eugène Sue and Victor Hugo spoke out against the inhumane victimization of the masses. At the same time, social prophets of the era, Charles Fourier, Auguste Comte, and the Saint-Simonians were devising utopian communities intended to mitigate, if not erase, the socioeconomic ills of the world. Even the

Catholic church began to take a more liberal stance. At Notre-Dame, priests like the abbé Lacordaire preached with new evangelical fervor about the equality of men. Others like the abbé Lamennais and the philosopher Pierre Leroux (two of George Sand's spiritual gurus), felt that the church was not going far enough and urged more radical social action—even when it brought them into conflict with the sacred dogmas of Catholicism. In their view, social justice outweighed theological abstractions. The pope cried heresy, but they stuck to their beliefs. For Leroux the price was ostracism and poverty; for Lamennais, excommunication.

Soon this newly awakened social consciousness expanded to embrace not only the working classes but also those who suffered exploitation and oppression, including women, children, the sick, and the handicapped. Hospital conditions were improved, and prison reforms instituted. For the first time criminals were viewed as victims of their environment, and efforts were made to rehabilitate them. But the magnitude of these artistic, social, and politico-economic changes failed to rouse the aging Louis-Philippe, who by then had turned over the reins of government to his brilliant but backward-looking prime minister, François Guizot. On a soggy February morning in 1848, a rained-out banquet of government protesters unexpectedly ignited the tinder of revolution that was to bring down the July monarchy. Amid the ashes of this conflagration, a number of rabid Republicans and proto-communists tried to revamp the socioeconomic structure of the nation. Among them were George Sand and several of Chopin's compatriots who belonged to a leftist group known as the Polish "Reds."

The political extremism of these radical groups, however, frightened the less progressive population in the provinces into voting a conservative government back into power. Shortly afterward France would elect a Bonaparte to become its president. Four years later the *vox populi* of the new republic had been silenced under the dictatorship of Louis-Napoléon's second empire. "*Plus ça change, plus ça reste la même chose!*" This familiar phrase ("The more things change, the more they stay the same") is said to have been coined by Alphonse Karr, a satirical journalist of the period.

If France seemed to be going in political circles from 1830 to 1850, Paris, by contrast, was making steady progress in the direction of civic improvement. Much of this was due to M. Claude Berthelot de Rambuteau, Louis-Philippe's prefect of the Seine from 1833 to 1848. During that time he effected countless changes that were to make the city a much safer, more attractive, and healthier place in which to live.

At the beginning of 1830 there were approximately 1,200 streets in Paris, "scarcely any two being of the same dimensions or running exactly in the same direction."[7] Most were dark, narrow, and unpaved, with rivulets of sewage flowing down the middle of them. Sidewalks were rare. Even guests at the Tuileries arrived in the king's presence covered with mud just from walking from their carriages to the palace entrance. According to Chopin, Paris in 1831 had "more mud than you could imagine."[8] Thanks to M. de Rambuteau, asphalt-covered sidewalks were constructed along the wider streets, and carriageways were covered with cobblestones. Mrs. Frances Trollope, an English novelist and social observer, found that the cobblestones made for a great deal of noise and discomfort as vehicles rattled over them. She herself preferred the smooth macadamized streets of London. But then without their cobblestones, she reflected, what would Parisians use for making barricades in future revolutions?

While paving the streets, M. de Rambuteau changed their contour from a concave to a convex configuration. This allowed rainwater and refuse to flow to the sides, where he installed drains to carry them into an expanded sewer system. Unfortunately not all the drains were adequately covered, and children often fell through them into the city's labyrinthine netherworld.

Further sanitary measures taken by the prefect included ordinances requiring that all houses have gutters and that no trash be thrown in the streets except at night. The latter applied especially to the emptying of chamberpots onto the pavement, which was a common practice then. Even Louis-Philippe's sons emptied theirs into the rue de Valois when they lived in the Palais Royal. Now, under M. de Rambuteau's supervision, proprietors were obliged each morning to sweep the previous night's debris off their side of the street into the newly constructed sewer drains. These changes prevented pedestrians from getting splashed by passing carriages and allowed them to dispense with the vials of aromatic vinegar or eau-de-cologne they once held under their noses to combat the stench of the streets. Unfortunately for the poor little *gamins* who made their living by throwing wooden planks across the polluted thoroughfares for squeamish pedestrians, M. de Rambuteau's improvements caused a serious unemployment problem.

Other benefits owed to the new prefect included the erection of street signs (blue lava plaques with white lettering, attached to the corners of buildings) and the installation of gas lights along its streets, quays, and public squares. Prior to 1830 there had been almost no street lighting except for a rare oil lamp that smelled and dripped onto the heads of hapless passersby. During the Restoration homeowners had been required to keep a candle burning in their second floor windows. Even then most nighttime strollers carried their own lanterns and the more cautious carried weapons as well. It is interesting to note here that George Sand's predilection for men's clothes in the early 1830s may have stemmed not so much from any lesbian leanings as a desire to protect herself from sexual assault on the dangerous Parisian streets after dark. Besides, men's clothing was significantly cheaper than the reams of expensive fabric required to outfit a respectable lady of her time.

Not only did M. de Rambuteau improve the safety and sanitation of the city; he also beautified it. Along the boulevards and quays, he planted trees to replace those cut down for barricades in 1830. In addition, he constructed numerous fountains, including those in the place de la Concorde, the place Saint-Sulpice, the place Louvois, and the Molière fountain on the rue Richelieu.

Unfortunately the prefect's concern for economy prevented him from accomplishing as much as he might have. Knowing that the conservative Louis-Philippe didn't approve of a spendthrift government, he adopted a policy of frugality to please him. Because of this he neglected one of the city's most crying needs: broad new thoroughfares to cut across the medieval maze of narrow crooked streets that created an impossible congestion in the very heart of Paris. Not until the Second Empire would Baron Haussmann open up the choked city with his spacious, arrow-straight boulevards. Had M. de Rambuteau spent more liberally to improve the flow of traffic in Paris, Louis-Philippe's forces might have had the mobility to put down the revolution of 1848 and prevent Louis-Napoléon from ever coming to power.

As it was, Paris under the July monarchy remained a coachman's nightmare. On the Right Bank there were only two north-south throughways: the rue Saint-Denis and the rue Saint-Martin. East-west traffic had to rely on the rue Saint-Honoré in the west, while the east had no major artery until the rue de Rambuteau was put through in 1843. On the Left Bank the situation was even worse. There, the rue Saint-Jacques provided the only significant north-south passage, while no convenient east-west route existed at all. Of course there were the quays and boulevards that M. de Rambuteau had made more passable, but even there traffic was chaotic since carriages, omnibuses and horseback-riders moved where they could without adhering to designated lanes. Only the Champs Elysées (known as the avenue de Neuilly until the mid-1830s) had a high-speed central lane reserved for the royal family, diplomats, and certain government officials.

As for connections between the Right and Left Banks, Paris in 1841 could boast twenty-four bridges stretching from the Pont de Bercy in the east to the Pont de Grenelle on the west. A few of these were designed specifically as pedestrian ways, and some charged a small toll. On the Pont des Arts, for example, three sous bought one the opportunity of strolling from the Louvre to the Institut between rows of potted shrubs. Although most bridges were of stone, a solitary wooden one survived. More and more, iron was becoming an important structural element, especially in the city's five new suspension bridges. During Chopin's time, the oldest bridge in Paris was the Pont Notre-Dame (replaced in 1853 by the present Pont Notre-Dame). The most colorful of all, though, was undoubtedly the Pont Neuf, still lined by shops and crowded with bootblacks, dog shearers, and vendors of everything from toys to food. Beneath it were stalls for fishing tackle and a bevy of chattering laundresses. The equestrian statue of Henri IV at its center was of recent origin, having been cast during the early years of the Restoration out of the melted-down bronze from Napoléon's statue in the place Vendôme.

Under the bridges passed water coaches carrying passengers from one part of town to another and barges that loaded and unloaded their merchandise at the numerous ports along the Seine. During the late 1840s there was a rage for gondolas that could be rented of an evening, complete with serenading musicians and flavored ices. Along the quays were floating public baths, some of which were quite luxurious. Upstream toward the eastern part of the city where the river water was clearer and purer were several swimming schools, the choice ones being those on the île Saint-Louis's quai de Bethune and quai d'Anjou.

In the course of 1841 the population of Paris reached the one million mark. Even then it made up less than 5 percent of the population of France. At that time the city had only twelve arrondissements, nine on the Right Bank and three (the present tenth, eleventh and twelfth) on the Left Bank. Among gossips, however, there was a fictitious "thirteenth arrondissement" with a mythical *bureau de mariage*. To be "married in the thirteenth arrondissement" became a euphemism for an illicit relationship such as that between Chopin and George Sand.

Until 1840 Paris proper was bounded by the old Farmers' General wall, constructed between 1784 and 1791 more for tax purposes than defense. In 1840, however, Louis-Philippe's prime minister, Adolphe Thiers, began building new fortifications around Paris out of fear that the former anti-Napoleonic Allies (England, Prussia, Russia, and Austria) would again attack Paris over a Middle Eastern dispute involving the pasha of Egypt and the sultan of the Ottoman Empire. His fears proved to be mostly paranoid, but the fortifications were nevertheless finished and the boundaries of Paris extended to take in many former suburbs, including Passy and Montmartre.

To explore the new "Greater Paris" of this time, it was best to hire a cabriolet or a fiacre. A cabriolet cost around 1 franc, 50 centimes; a fiacre, a bit more. To judge the value of a franc in those days, it is helpful to consider that some working-class families were fortunate to make 1,000 francs a year, while a student in the Latin Quarter could enjoy the spartan pleasures of a bohemian life on an annual income of 1,200 francs. Further up the social scale, someone like Chopin, whose income might reach as much as 25,000 francs in a good year, could afford a carriage, kid gloves, expensive restaurants, seats at the Opéra, an apartment on the exclusive Chaussée d'Antin, shopping in the Palais Royal's elegant Galérie d'Orléans, and five months of leisure in the country. In short, 25,000 francs a year could buy any bachelor a very comfortable existence in Louis-Philippe's Paris. Unfortunately Chopin spent as rapidly as he earned; like 75 to 80 percent of Parisians in his day, he died poverty-stricken.

FIRST ARRONDISSEMENT

On both banks of the Seine, the arrondissements were numbered from west to east, with the first arrondissement extending from the Arc de Triomphe to the east end of the Louvre. Here, according to Messrs. Galignani, was the foremost sight in Paris, the Palace of the Tuileries and its adjacent Arc du Carrousel. Today nothing but the palace's two lateral pavillions and the garden to their west still survive. The only other public gardens in Paris then were the distant Bois de Boulogne and Bois de Vincennes on the Right Bank and the Luxembourg gardens and the Jardin des Plantes on the Left Bank.[9] The open spaces of the Champs Elysées were then being developed, but much of this terrain was still rather wild and not always safe. The Tuileries garden, the most centrally located of the city's parks, was usually crowded from early morning to dusk, when the drumbeat of the palace guard signaled its closing. On the sunny north terrace overlooking the rue de Rivoli, old men in rented chairs dozed over their rented newspapers. Below them on the graveled allées, wasp-waisted ladies in taffeta capes and velvet skirts (bulging out over the new crinoline petticoats) strolled between lilac bushes and clipped orange trees while groups of young men leaned against the marble statuary discussing the transactions of the Bourse or the latest proceedings in the Chambers. At the eastern end of the gardens, next to the palace, a large ditch separated the public grounds from those reserved for the royal family. This mutilation of the park, resented by many, was deemed necessary because of the frequent attacks on the king's life. For the same reason no one in work clothes or carrying parcels (other than books) was allowed into the garden. More as a matter of civility than security, lighted cigars were also forbidden, and according to the king's son, the Prince de Joinville, the National Guard put up a "Homeric struggle" to make strollers keep their dogs on leashes.[10]

The main entrance to the Tuileries palace was on its eastern front rather than the garden side. There, a tall iron grill separated it from the place du Carrousel with its triumphal arch erected by Napoléon in 1806. Like many of the city's public spaces then, it was an unpaved area that became a quagmire whenever it rained. Twice Chopin had to leave his carriage here when he played before the royal family. Here also Louis-Philippe often reviewed his troops. From their upstairs apartments, the royal family looked out upon a veritable slum wedged between the Arc du Carrousel and the Louvre a short distance beyond it. In this cramped little rabbit warren of alleyways and unpaved streets, a motley assortment of Bohemians, birdsellers, and working-class people were crowded together in the few dilapidated buildings that remained habitable. In the midst of it all were the weed-covered grounds of the church of Saint-Thomas-du-Louvre, strewn with the rubble of its dome, which had collapsed the previous century, killing six priests. At its eastern boundary stood the Louvre itself, rising above piles of stone and lumber assembled for the long-overdue repair of the nation's chief artistic repository. For centuries plans had been made to clean up the mess; meanwhile, Bourbons, Bonapartes, and Orléans continued to live with this royal eyesore on their doorstep.

During the July monarchy an atmosphere of informality reigned inside the palace—quite different from the strict protocol that had prevailed under the Bourbons. Louis-Philippe often carved the meat at dinner and had a penchant for showing guests the double bed where he and the queen slept. In the absence of the royal family, the public was allowed to view its apartments.

The nearby Louvre was another of Paris's royal palaces, then open to the public as an art museum every day (except Monday) from 10:00 A.M. to 4:00 P.M. Those with foreign passports were admitted free of charge. On Sundays when the admission was waived, the crowds were overwhelming. Except for the annual Salon, the Louvre exhibited no contemporary art. In compensation, however, it sheltered many a contemporary artist in the nooks and crannies of its upper floors. Their presence as squatters had been tolerated for decades because the government seemed to have neither the interest nor the means to utilize these vacant spaces in the vast structure. According to George Sand, Chopin had little interest in art but was obliged to visit the Louvre's annual Salon exhibits whenever friends like Delacroix, Henri Lehman, or Ary Scheffer had works on display.

Both the Restoration and the July monarchy failed to make any significant improvements in the Louvre. Although the exhibition rooms were fairly well maintained, the rest of the building had fallen into decay. Windows were broken and stonework damaged. In the central courtyard, abandoned excavations created "a puddle in winter and a gravel pit in summer."[11] The magnificent east facade was enclosed by "an inglorious wooden paling, fit for nothing better than to protect a bed of cabbages."[12] In reality what it did protect was a mass grave for victims of the 1830 revolution. A pyramid topped by a funerary urn had been erected in their memory, and mourners surrounded it with a collection of tasselled flags, spears, and halberds. Today I. M. Pei's glass pyramid on the west side of the Louvre provides a historical echo to its predecessor in Chopin's time.

Scattered about the first arrondissement were many of the city's most fashionable hotels, situated mainly on the rue de Rivoli, the rue Saint-Honoré, and the area around the place Vendôme. During Chopin's time the place Vendôme looked much as it does today. In 1833 the statue of Napoléon had been restored to the top of its column, where a white flag with the fleur-de-lis had flown throughout the Restoration. The many votive wreaths left each day at its base proved an ominous omen for the Orleanist monarch, whose kingdom would soon be ruled by another Bonaparte. To the east of the column, at No. 12 place Vendôme, Chopin was to die on October 17, 1849, during the first year of Louis-Napoléon's presidency.

A few blocks to the the west lay the rue Royale, which marked the boundary between central Paris and the faubourg (suburb) Saint-Honoré. At the head of this street, facing the place de la Concorde, was the church of of the Madeleine. Still unfinished in 1841, it stood, like the Louvre, amid heaps of stone blocks and other building materials. Construction had begun on this Parthenon-inspired structure in 1764. Its completion was delayed, however, by turbulent times and by successive administrations that quibbled over whether it should be a church, a theater, a banquet hall, a shrine to Napoléon, or merely another government office building. Eventually in 1842 it was completed and consecrated as a church. Seven years later, on October 30, 1849, Chopin's funeral was to take place there.

Moving westward from the rue Royale, one entered the faubourg Saint-Honoré, second only to the faubourg Saint-Germain in the aristocratic quality of its residents. Many embassies were also found here, the largest and most sumptuous belonging to the English, where *le tout Paris* gathered for Lord and Lady Granville's lavish balls. Through the king's court director of music, Ferdinando Paër, Chopin was introduced to the Granvilles, who provided him with one of his earliest entrées into Parisian society and many of his first pupils. Farther west in the place Beauvau was the embassy of the Kingdom of the Two Sicilies, ruled then by a nephew of the French queen, Marie-Amélie. Across from it, on the rue Faubourg-Saint-Honoré, stood the Elysée palace, once the home of Louis XV's mistress Mme Pompadour. Since Napoléon's abdication there in 1815, it had remained virtually unoccupied. Those who weren't put off by the building's "lonely and deserted" appearance could visit it with permission from the proper authorities. Not until Louis-Napoléon moved into it as president of the second republic did the palace again play an active role in the social and political life of Paris.

In addition to its many embassies, the faubourg Saint-Honoré also housed the headquarters of a foreign government. At No. 25 rue Faubourg du Roule, Prince Adam Czartoryski administered the affairs of the Polish government in exile from 1833 until 1843, when he moved to the Hôtel Lambert on the île Saint-Louis. Chopin was a frequent visitor to both of the Czartoryski's homes, where he often became involved in projects to aid his fellow emigrés.

North of the Madeleine and the faubourg Saint-Honoré stretched acres of empty lots sprinkled with a few recently built houses. Mrs. Trollope and her friends enjoyed wandering about the area at night, letting the dark and desolate scene stimulate their Gothic imaginations. It was in one of these new buildings, at No. 5 rue Tronchet, that Chopin took a small apartment in 1839 when he and George Sand returned from their winter in Majorca. It consisted of two rooms and a vestibule that he decorated with plain gray curtains and a shiny gray wallpaper topped by a dark green border. He chose gray because it seemed "neither commonplace nor ostentatious" and didn't look like something a grocery clerk would pick.[13] Unfortunately the northern exposure of the little flat proved too chilly for the ailing musician, who soon moved into a small pavilion at No. 16 rue Pigalle, in the city's second arrondissement.

South of the Madeleine was the place de la Concorde (or place Louis XV, as many still called it). At the beginning of the July monarchy, this most spacious of all Parisian squares remained unpaved and surrounded by deep ditches that reeked of garbage. The two Neoclassical structures along its north side had originally served as the Garde-Meuble (or furniture storehouse) of the king. By

Louis-Philippe's time the eastern building had become the Ministry of the Navy, while the other (today's Hotel Crillon) still remained a warehouse. In 1833 M. de Rambuteau undertook to transform this foul-smelling muddy plot into the grand place de la Concorde we know today. First he smoothed out its potholes and covered the entire area with asphalt. Next he filled up the ditches and converted them into gardens. Later he erected statues, fountains, and twenty gas lamps with gilded globes to illuminate the area. In the center of it all he raised the obelisk of Luxor on October 25, 1836, under the eyes of the royal family and a crowd of 150,000 spectators. The column was one of two identical obelisks given to France by Mehemet Ali, the pasha of Egypt. After spending six years and two million francs transporting the first of these bulky objects to Paris, the French government decided not to bother with the other one. Colonel Raikes found the obelisk a "very unsightly object,"[14] but most Parisians loved it. As Jules Janin commented, the more useless a monument, the dearer it is to the Frenchman's heart. Louis-Philippe liked the obelisk because it made no political statement and therefore wouldn't be torn down in future revolutions—and it has indeed survived five subsequent governments.

It was from the place de la Concorde that the annual promenade de Longchamps began. Every year during Lent, Parisian society put on its finest attire and paraded up the Champs Elysées in carriages or on horseback to the triumphal arch, then down the Saint-Germain road (today's avenue de la Grande Armée) to the racing field at Longchamps. This springtime ritual helped to fill the idle hours of the rich and provided entertainment for the poor who lined the route to watch. Prior to 1830 the Champs Elysées hadn't been developed much past the Rond Point (then called the place de l'Etoile), and it was considered a dangerous place after dark when its sole lighting came from the candles of the shopkeepers' stalls along the road. Only a decade later, the area had been landscaped with fountains, flowers, and graveled paths. Pretty little houses with gardens and even an occasional mansion started to spring up in this rural setting (fig. 1.2). Franconi's circus brought its act to the area, and Ravalet opened a riding school there. The flamboyant conductor Musard provided music for open-air dancing in the summer; in winter, Parisians flocked to the nearby Jardin d'Hiver, where they meandered around its fountain and marveled at the exotic flowers that filled its conservatory. On the allée des Veuves (today's avenue Montaigne), the gardens of the Bal Mabille were laid out with an orchestra kiosk in the center and tables scattered about in the shadows of the surrounding trees. Here the dancing was spirited, not

1.2: The Champs Elysées, Paris's most famous thoroughfare, was virtually undeveloped at the onset of Louis-Philippe's reign. Much of the deserted and overgrown land bordering it was considered dangerous after dark. Later, however, it became a popular gathering place for all elements of society, especially at Easter when the annual Promenade de Longchamps took place. On these occasions, the avenue became a fashion parade as the elegantly dressed *belles* and *grandes dames* of the city rode to and from the race track at Longchamps in their open carriages.

to say raucous, attracting grisettes and students as well as aristocrats and rich bourgeoisie. Down by the Seine along the Cours la Reine was a sinister underworld of subterranean taverns graphically portrayed by Eugène Sue in his 1842 novel, *The Mysteries of Paris.*

Past today's Rond Point, the south side of the Champs Elysées was bordered by the quiet village of Chaillot. It was on its main street, the rue de Chaillot, that Chopin spent the last summer of his life.[15] From his apartment there he had a magnificent view of the city, which was to be one of the few pleasures left to him.

At the Barrière de l'Etoile was the great triumphal arch begun by Napoléon in 1806 and finally finished by Louis-Philippe in the fall of 1835 (although the official dedication was postponed until the anniversary of the July revolution the following summer).[16] The inaugural day turned out to be rainy, and the king refused to attend for fear of a possible assassination attempt. Chopin also missed the event as he was away in Dresden visiting Maria Wodzińska, to whom he was secretly engaged. From under the arch one could look west toward Neuilly, where the royal family spent much of its time in a comfortable one-storied "chateau." The informal atmosphere of this suburban retreat provided a a more restful environment than did the oppressive rooms of the Tuileries. None of the splendid residences over which the queen presided—including Saint-Cloud, Fontainebleau, and Compiègne—delighted her more than the unpretentious little villa at Neuilly.

A short distance south of the royal compound was the Bois de Boulogne, a large wooded area where no major landscaping had yet been attempted. Apart from the duelling that occurred in its many secluded nooks, the major attractions of the bois were the horse races at Longchamps and the weekly strollers on Sunday. George Sand and her daughter enjoyed horseback riding there and were sometimes accompanied by Chopin in his carriage.

One of the chief ornaments of Paris under Louis-Philippe were the grands boulevards, which began at the Madeleine in the first arrondissement and swept in a giant arc around the north side of the city to end near the Pont d'Austerlitz east of the île Saint-Louis. Vestiges of the Farmers' General wall still bordered its two western segments, the boulevard de la Madeleine and the boulevard des Capucines. Between the remains of the wall and the boulevards was a sunken street, the rue Basse du Rempart, which could be reached from above by a staircase. Despite being dark and fetid with sewage draining into it from the upper roadway, the street still attracted banking firms like Laffitte and Blount and such residents as Balzac's one-time mistress, the Duchesse d'Abrantès; Chopin's pupil, the Baronne d'Ivry; and George Sand's confidante, the critic Gustave Planche.

SECOND ARRONDISSEMENT

The rue de la Chaussée d'Antin marked the beginning of the most fashionable of all the boulevards, the boulevard des Italiens, as well as the second arrondissement, which extended from the north side of the Tuileries up to the village of Montmartre. For Chopin this relatively small enclave was the focal point of his life in the French capital. Here he was to spend over sixteen of the last eighteen years of his life; here were the city's three opera houses, the conservatory, and most of the concert halls in which he performed. The Chaussée d'Antin where he lived from 1833 to 1839 had a reputation for being a street of nouveaux riches bankers and businessmen who gradually insinuated themselves into "society."

Under Louis-Philippe they were well ensconced and regularly swelled the ranks of those who attended the Tuileries balls. Here the "king of bankers and banker of kings," Jacques Laffitte, began his career at Perregaux's bank. Here also Alexandre Dumas felt it appropriate to install his fictitious Baron Danglars, the unscrupulous sailor-turned-financier in *The Count of Monte Cristo*. At the time Chopin moved there, he had acquired a number of aristocratic pupils (mostly ladies) who complained that his earlier apartments had too many stairs or were too dark and cramped. Naturally the social *cachet* of the Chaussée d'Antin made it a high rent district. Soon the musician found that he couldn't shoulder the costs there alone, especially after having furnished his new quarters with expensive furniture that was well beyond his means. To make ends meet, he was forced to look for a roommate. In his first apartment there, at No. 5 rue de la Chaussée d'Antin, he took in a young Polish doctor, Alexander Hoffmann, whom he had known in Warsaw. Later, when he moved farther up the street, he shared his new quarters at No. 38 with another old Warsaw friend, Jan Matuszyński, who was studying at the Paris medical school. It was while living here that the young musician began his affair with George Sand.

The rue Saint-Lazare marked the northern boundary of the Chaussée d'Antin. Two blocks to the west was the gare Saint-Lazare, which had opened in 1837. A few blocks farther toward the rue Pépinière was a district that had recently become known as "Little Poland" because of the impoverished Polish emigrés who had settled there in 1831. Because most were unskilled laborers, unable to speak French, there was a high unemployment rate among them along with an equally high crime rate. Although Chopin helped to raise money for these unfortunate victims through his participation in benefit concerts, bazaars, and organizations that sought employment for them, he seems to have had little if any personal contact with them.

Much more in keeping with his fastidious tastes was the fashionable boulevard des Italiens, which formed the southern boundary of the Chaussée d'Antin. Between its tree-lined promenades was a broad, central carriageway paved since 1837 with bituminous flagging. Gas lighting had been installed the same year, along with the first of the city's famous pissoirs, described by the Galignanis as "a welcome convenience . . . in the shape of large circular hollow pillars, placed at the edge of the pavement at suitable distances which externally serve for the purpose of bill-sticking and internally as watering places."[17] By 1841 the trees that replaced those cut down in the revolution of 1830 had grown tall enough to shade

the boulevard's many idlers, who rented wicker chairs to sit and watch the passing scene. In the early days of the July monarchy it was not uncommon to see the
king himself stroll by in an ordinary frock coat with his ever-present umbrella in
hand. Although this was the main parade ground for the Parisian dandies, people
from all walks of life came to enjoy the plethora of boutiques, restaurants, cafés,
and flower stalls that lined the boulevard.

On the north side at the rue Taitbout was the famous Café de Paris, with its red
velvet curtains, mirrored walls, and a menu that featured boned larks and fillets of
partridge. It was actually more of a club than a restaurant, with a special section
reserved for regulars like Alexandre Dumas *père*, Alfred de Musset, Dr. Véron (a
one-time director of the Opéra), and an eccentric, Baron Saint-Cricq, who pep-
pered his salad with snuff, poured ink in his coffee, and eventually wound up in an
insane asylum. Upstairs, Lord Henry Seymour had a private gymnasium where
the boulevard's aristocratic Anglophiles came to box, fence, or simply while away
the afternoon. His mother, Lady Yarmouth, who owned the building, also lived
there and saw to it that the Café de Paris closed promptly at ten o'clock every
evening so as not to disturb her sleep. Across the rue Taitbout was the Café Tortoni, most famous for its ices, although it served meals as well. Like the Café de
Paris, it had its favored clientele who entered through a back door without having
to hassle with the crowds in front. Its peak hours were noon and late at night after
the theaters had closed. During lunch, its front steps were known as "the little
Bourse" because of the traders who gathered there to discuss stock issues, railroad
shares, and international loans. Just inside the front door was a bulletin board
where dandies posted items for sale such as horses, cabriolets, and objets d'art to
pay off their gambling debts. There, in April of 1822, the seventeen-year-old
Aurore Dupin (later known as George Sand) met the baron Casimir Dudevant
and married him the following September. Next to Tortoni's was the brand new
Maison Dorée (often called the Café Hardi after its owner), less chic perhaps but a
favorite with businessmen who liked a cold lunch. It was here on a warm July
evening in 1838 that an agitated Chopin finally committed himself to his future
liaison with George Sand.[18] Still farther east was the Café Riche with portions
generous enough to satisfy the gourmand as well as the gourmet. On the south
side of the boulevard was the Café Anglais, a quiet establishment catering to an
older crowd. Its cuisine had no connection with its name, and the Galignanis conspicuously omitted it from their list of "English Eating-Houses."

Running north from the boulevard des Italiens was the rue Laffitte, which led

1.3 The baron James de Rothschild was one of the leading financial and social figures in Paris under the July monarchy. His charming and cultivated wife, Betty, as well as their daughter, Charlotte, became pupils of Chopin's, and the baron himself provided occasional financial assistance to the chronically insolvent musician.

up to the church of Notre-Dame de Lorette. Like the Chaussée d'Antin, it too was a street of rich financiers. At No. 15 was the palatial home of Baron James de Rothschild, whose wife and daughter were pupils of Chopin (fig. 1.3); nearby were the banking houses of Jacques Laffitte and Co. and Ferrier-Laffitte and Co. On the same street was the Hôtel de France, where George Sand was living when she met Chopin in 1836. That same year construction on the church of Notre-Dame de Lorette was completed. Thackeray found its interior gaudy, but most Parisians were more concerned with what went on outside rather than inside the church. The land around it had been exploited by speculators in the last years of the Restoration. Once they started selling off the empty lots, the area quickly became populated with members of the artistic, literary, and theatrical worlds, not to mention an even greater number of ladies with no visible means of support. They were, as it soon became apparent, "kept women," or high-class street walkers, to whom Nestor Roqueplan applied the sobriquet "Lorette." Their presence made "respectable" inhabitants feel that the church had become "more a boudoir to our Lord than a temple to God."[19] It was in this neighborhood that Chopin and George Sand spent most of their nine years together, first in the rue Pigalle, and later in the square d'Orléans, on the corner of the rue Taitbout and the rue Saint-Lazare.[20]

The first of these residences at No. 16 rue Pigalle consisted of two small garden pavilions set behind a larger structure facing the street. Sand moved there in the fall of 1839 just after their return from Majorca, but Chopin didn't join her until the next year. For the sake of propriety, the novelist and her daughter, Solange, shared one of the pavilions while her son, Maurice, occupied the other with Chopin. To provide a further air of respectability, Sand removed her collection of Giorgone nudes from Chopin's quarters so as not to offend his young female pupils. Although Balzac has given us a detailed description of Sand's pavilion (carved oak furniture, Chinese vases, and Delacroix paintings), we know little about her lover's rooms. Probably they were furnished with the same gray curtains, red sofa, and white slipcovers that had graced his rue Tronchet apartment. As for the square d'Orléans, it was (and still is) a spacious residential complex centered around a beautiful courtyard with a fountain. At the time the musician and novelist moved into it, their neighbors reflected the artistic bent of the quarter (often called "The New Athens"). Among them were the pianists Frederick Kalkbrenner, Charles Valentin Alkan, and Pierre Zimmerman, all of whom performed at various times in concerts with Chopin. Also living there were the ballerina Marie Taglioni and the sculptor Jean-Pierre Dantan, who specialized in bronze caricatures of his contemporaries.

On a hill high above this area was the rustic village of Montmartre with its cow pastures, gypsum quarries (from which plaster of Paris was made), and famous windmills that ground the local corn (fig. 1.4). Besides its bucolic charm and panoramic views, Montmartre had the advantage of being a very economical place to live. For this reason the impecunious Berlioz moved to its heights in 1833 with his new bride, the English actress Harriet Smithson. At that time, Berlioz and Chopin were *en rapport* despite the great difference in their musical tastes. Twice, in 1833 and 1834, Chopin assisted Berlioz in the latter's concerts, and on several occasions he visited the young married couple in their new home. Undoubtedly Chopin and the Berliozes also ran into each other below Montmartre along the short rue Lepeletier, where the city's Académie Royale de Musique (generally known as the "Opéra") was located. Two narrow passages filled with shops connected the new house to the boulevards—hardly a dignified entrance to one of the city's most prestigious cultural establishments.

On the south side of the boulevard, almost in line with the Opéra, stood the new Salle Favart, tucked away in a cramped enclosure behind a row of expensive shops. During Chopin's early years in Paris, the Salle Favart housed the Italian

1.4 On several occasions Chopin came to visit the newly wed Hector Berlioz and his bride, the English actress Harriet Smithson, on the heights of Montmartre, a semi-rural Parisian suburb. At the base of its western slope was the cemetery of Montmartre, where George Sand buried her mother in 1837 and where many of Chopin's Polish friends were later interred.

Opéra, which he preferred to the city's other two operatic companies. Twice he participated in charity concerts given there, one for the benefit of Harriet Smithson and the other to raise money for the city's indigent Polish emigrés. In 1838 a fire destroyed the building, which was reconstructed two years later as a home for the city's Opéra Comique. Its new quarters boasted one of the first systems of air-conditioning known to the modern world. The machinery for this was driven by horses in the basement and passed air over ice, which was forced up through pipes into the hall. In winter the same pipes were used for conducting heat through the building.

On returning to the boulevards and proceeding east, one came to the boulevard Montmartre, where the Jockey Club was located. Modeled on mens' clubs popular in London at the time, the club had been founded in 1833 to foster the new passion for horse racing in France. Appropriately there was a pair of jockey scales just inside the entrance, while upstairs in a room overlooking the boulevard members were once said to play billiards on horseback. Cigar smoking was limited to the reading room, but snuff boxes were found on every desk and table throughout the club. Gambling often went on until five o'clock in the morning.

South of the boulevard on the rue Richelieu was the Hôtel-des Princes, which according to Thackeray served the best *table d'hôte* of any hostelry in Paris— although he complained that it was overpriced. For the successful composer Giacomo Meyerbeer, to whom money was no object, it provided a comfortable pied-à-terre while his productions were in rehearsal at the Opéra. Further down the same street was Chopin's publisher, Maurice Schlesinger, whose music shop was considered the largest and handsomest in Europe.

At the southern end of the rue Richelieu was the the Palais Royal, built for Cardinal Richelieu in the seventeenth century and later home to Louis-Philippe throughout the Restoration and the first year of his reign. After the Orléans family moved to the Tuileries in 1831, their former apartments housed foreign dignitaries but could be viewed by the public every Sunday from 1:00 to 4:00 P.M. The renowned Théâtre Français adjoined the palace on its southwest side. There Chopin spent many an evening, laughing at Mlle Mars's portrayal of a saucy ingenue, listening to the impassioned Rachel declaim the lines of Corneille and Racine, or watching spellbound as Marie Dorval made one of her emotional appearances in the Romantic dramas of Dumas or Hugo.

Besides the Théâtre Français, the Palais Royal's other attractions included its many shops, restaurants, and cafés. According to the perpetually debt-ridden Henri Murger (author of *Scènes de la Vie de Bohème*, which inspired Puccini's opera *La Bohème*), the Palais Royal was a place where you ran into everybody— especially your creditors (fig. 1.5). Chopin also loved to shop and eat there. During his summers at George Sand's chateau, he pestered friends in the city to pick up shirts, back-scratchers, and other items for him in its arcades. Among the palace's restaurants were Véry, Véfour (still operating today) and Les Trois Frères Provenceaux, three of the city's best gastronomical establishments with suitably astronomical prices. On a more modest level was the Café des Aveugles, where a working-class clientele downed its simple fare to the accompaniment of a band of blind musicians.

For many years the two foremost attractions of the Palais Royal had been prostitution and gambling. During the eighteen years that Chopin lived in Paris,

1.5 The Palais Royal, originally built for Cardinal Richelieu, became the home of the Orléans family until 1831 when the new king, Louis-Philippe, moved into the Tuileries. During the Restoration and the early years of the July monarchy, this spacious palace had also been a notorious center of gambling and prostitution, as well as the haunt of writers and publishers described in Balzac's *Lost Illusions*. In Chopin's later years, it acquired a more tranquil atmosphere as its arcades became filled with respectable boutiques and restaurants.

the number of prostitutes registered with the municipal authorities rose from 3,527 in 1831 to 4,202 shortly after his death in 1849. They ranged in age from precocious eleven-year-olds to mature seductresses in their fifties. Those who had lost their physical charms often turned from the streets to the houses of prostitution, where they became "madames."

For those addicted to gambling, there was little glamour to be found in the Palais Royal's casinos, or "pleasure pits" as Balzac described them. They were bare and tawdry, with greasy wallpaper and dirty splintered floors. Yet every evening these bleak rooms were "teeming with spectators and players: indigent old men who shuffle along there to find warmth; tormented faces belonging to those whose orgies began in wine and will end up in the Seine."[21] It was a world of frenzied pleasures and quiet desperation. On December 31, 1836, when Louis-Philippe closed the gaming houses in the Palais Royal, the prostitutes went elsewhere and society took to the boulevards for their entertainment. From then on, the Palais Royal assumed an air of indolent calm that characterizes it to this day.

Returning once more to the grand boulevards along the rue Valois one would have passed the concert hall of Henri Pape at the corner of the rue des Bon Enfans. There Chopin once performed a two-piano version for eight hands of Beethoven's seventh symphony with his pupil Adolf Gutmann and two neighbors from the square d'Orléans, Pierre-Joseph-Guillaume Zimmermann and Charles Henri Valentin Morhange (known as "Alkan"). Despite the skills of the performers, one of the reviewers considered the arrangement a travesty of the great composer's work. Farther north, on the rue Vivienne, was the Bourse, where Baron James de Rothschild could be seen leaning against the same column every day assessing the fluctuations of the stock market (fig. 1.6). Opposite the west entrance of the Bourse, at the Théâtre de Vaudeville, audiences often neglected the drama onstage to stare up at the box of Alphonsine Plessis, the wan lady of the camellias. Her brief affair with Alexandre Dumas *fils* would one day be portrayed on that very stage for the teary-eyed pleasure of future theatergoers.

Back on the boulevard Montmartre, shops were more numerous if not as recherché as on the boulevard des Italiens. There the "carriage trade," which usually arose around midday, did most of its shopping in the afternoon. At that hour the boulevard became filled with the ostrich feather bonnets and cashmere shawls of elegant ladies who emerged from carriages emblazoned with family crests. What they couldn't find along the boulevards, they searched for in the city's enclosed passages, forerunners of our present-day shopping malls. Off the boulevard Montmartre was the passage des Panoramas, constructed in 1808 by the American Robert Fulton, a year after he launched the first successful steamship on New York's Hudson river. Directly across from it on the north side of the boulevard, the similar but less chic passage Jouffroy had been erected on land where Rossini once lived. Farther east on the boulevard, the popular Théâtre Variétés attracted crowds eager to see performances of the scandalous new can-can during Carnival. A brief side excursion north along the rue Faubourg Montmartre led one to the rue Cadet. There at No. 9 the piano manufacturer and music publisher Camille Pleyel established a concert hall where Chopin made his Paris debut on February 26, 1832. As Pleyel's business acumen brought him more and more profits, he moved his hall farther north to larger

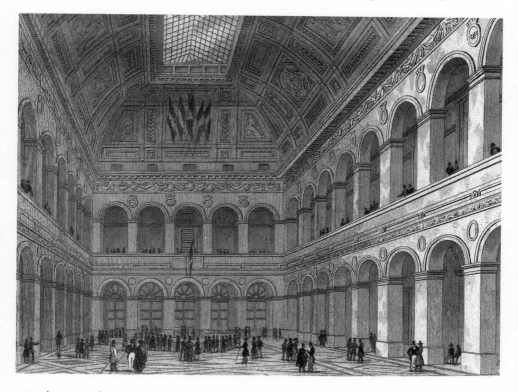

1.6 In the Bourse, the Paris stock market, the number of shares traded daily more than tripled during the July monarchy. On almost any weekday, baron James de Rothschild could be found there, leaning against his favorite column and managing the affairs of his family's vast financial network, which he shared with his four brothers in Frankfurt, London, Vienna, and Naples.

quarters at No. 22 rue Rochechouart. Here, on February 16, 1848, Chopin made his last appearance on the Parisian stage in a performance that was acclaimed as "without equal in our earthly realm."[22]

East of the rue Montmartre lay the next link in the chain of Paris's grands boulevards, the boulevard Poissonière. On its south side there still stands a six-story building at No. 27, where Chopin first lived when he arrived in Paris during the fall of 1831 (fig. 1.7). From his top-floor apartment, he had enviable views of the city: to the north rose the heights of Montmartre, while south, across the Seine, the dome of the Panthéon towered over the surrounding Latin Quarter. A further advantage of his picturesque aerie was its proximity to the Paris Conservatory, located only a

(Fabrique de tapis de M. Sallandrouze.)   (Bazar de l'Industrie.)

1.7 Chopin's first apartment in Paris was located at No. 27 boulevard Poissonière, on the top floor of the Bazar de l'Industrie, at the far right of this picture.

block north on the rue Bergère. Here Chopin made many friends who were invaluable to him in his musical career. On at least four occasions, he performed in the building's beautiful red and gold concert hall.

Just west of the Conservatory was the narrow, mews-like Cité Bergère, to which Chopin moved in 1832. His second-floor apartment there (at No. 4 Cité Bergère) was dark and gloomy, but the frail musician, already afflicted with tuberculosis, was only too glad to be rid of the exhausting climb up those endless stairs on the boulevard Poissonière. Climbing the social ladder, however, was quite a different matter. "I have been introduced all around the highest circles! I hobnob with ambassadors, princes and ministers," he wrote an old friend back in Poland.[23] Clearly a better address was necessary, and in 1833 Chopin settled into the fashionable Chaussée d'Antin.

THIRD ARRONDISSEMENT

Proceeding east into the third arrondissement, any stroller who passed Eugène Scribe's Gymnase theater on the boulevard Bonne-Nouvelle was sure to find one of his new vaudevilles or dramas on its boards. For Chopin the city's plethora of theaters became one of his greatest delights in Paris. As a child he and his younger sister, Emilia, often entertained family and friends with their amateur playwriting and acting. Even as an adult, the musician was noted for his comic impersonations of stuffy Englishmen or boorish Germans. Certainly he enjoyed a good vaudeville as much as anyone. His real respect for M. Scribe, however, stemmed from the author's opera libretti rather than his stage plays.

South of the boulevard were more shopping passages, including the passage du Saumon, the longest in Paris. In it was the Rocher de Cancale restaurant, which Chopin considered "the most grandiose in all Paris."24 Also in this arrondissement was the place des Victoires, the center of the newspaper district. Branching off from it to the northeast was the rue de Mail, where the Erard family had established a small concert hall at No. 14 to provide a showcase for the pianos they manufactured. Liszt was especially fond of their instruments, while Chopin preferred the lighter touch and softer tone of those made by Pleyel. Nevertheless Chopin performed twice at the Salle Erard, presumably on their pianos.

FOURTH ARRONDISSEMENT

The fourth arrondissement, which hugged the Seine, offered little of interest to Chopin, although he undoubtedly passed through it often to visit Prince and Princess Czartoryski after they moved to the île Saint-Louis. On these visits, he may well have crossed the rue des Prêtres-Saint-Germain-l'Auxerrois, where the offices of the *Journal des Débats* was located. For years his friend Hector Berlioz served as music critic for the paper.

FIFTH ARRONDISSEMENT

North and east of the fourth arrondissement lay the fifth, bisected by the boulevards Saint-Denis and Saint-Martin, which clearly lacked the *bon ton* of the western boulevards. For this reason Chopin seldom ventured into the area except for an occasional visit to the Théâtre Porte-Saint-Martin, where productions of the popular new "Romantic drama" were frequent. At the eastern end of the boulevard was the Chateau d'Eau, one of the many fountains supplying the city with water. Just north of this, Daguerre's Diorama had been a popular attraction until fire destroyed it in

1839. Next door to the Diorama was the Wauxhall d'Eté, an amusement park modeled after those in London with concert and dance halls, reading and smoking rooms, as well as compact little gardens for strolling. There, in 1833, Paganini slipped in under cover of darkness to hear Chopin play a glitzy operatic transcription for eight hands and two pianos with Franz Liszt and the Herz brothers.

SIXTH ARRONDISSEMENT

At the boulevard du Temple, one took a southerly turn into the sixth arrondissement, where the most lively of Paris's entertainment districts was located. It was often called "the boulevard of crime" because of the innumerable atrocities committed in the melodramas staged by its ten theaters. Other attractions here included cafés like the exotic Jardin Turc, coffee houses, taverns, wax museums, and open-air food shops. At night the boulevard glowed with lights and swarmed with strolling musicians, dancers, jugglers, magicians, storytellers, and pickpockets. Few of the Parisian elite were to be seen here, except those who liked to go "slumming." Snobs called it "the Indies" because it was so far from the civilized life of the city.

SEVENTH ARRONDISSEMENT

In Chopin's time, the seventh arrondissement coincided roughly with the area known as the Marais. Once an aristocratic enclave in the seventeenth century, it had become a shabby district of lower-middle-class residents under Louis-Philippe. Many fine old houses still stood as reminders of the quarter's former grandeur, but the great families that once inhabited them were gone. At the southern edge of the arrondissement was the newly renovated Hôtel de Ville, where the prefect of the Seine, M. de Rambuteau, occupied spacious apartments that he had created for himself at the city's expense. The reconstruction took three years and nearly quadrupled the size of the building. Here M. de Rambuteau received the elite of Paris on Saturday evenings, giving lavish receptions with up to five thousand guests at a time. For a party celebrating the marriage of the duc and duchesse d'Orléans (the French crown prince and his bride), Chopin claimed that the prefect issued no fewer than fifteen thousand tickets.[25]

EIGHTH ARRONDISSEMENT

The eighth arrondissement, one of the largest in the city, took in most of the Right Bank east of the place de la Bastille. The latter for many years was generally referred to as the place de l'Eléphant because of the huge wood and plaster

1.8 The fountain of the elephant in the place de la Bastille was started under Napoléon but never finished. By Chopin's time, it had fallen into ruin. In 1840 the Orleanist government replaced it with today's "July Column" to commemorate those fallen in the revolution of 1830.

elephant that Napoléon had placed there in 1808. It was the model for a future eighty-foot-tall bronze elephant intended to straddle the Canal Saint-Martin while spouting water from its trunk (fig. 1.8). The project, however, never materialized, and the makeshift mammal gradually deteriorated in its basin of water, having become a haven for rats and street urchins. In 1831, on the base intended for the elephant, Louis-Philippe laid the first stone of the July column, a monument to those who died in the 1830 revolution.

East from the place de la Bastille and north along the quays of the Canal Saint-Martin stretched large working-class neighborhoods. These enclaves fascinated Karl Marx in the 1840s but were generally feared by the Parisian bourgeoisie as breeding grounds of cholera and revolution.

At the easternmost extremity of this arrondissement, in a semi-rural area that had been annexed to the city only in 1841, lay the cemetery of Père Lachaise. Here on October 30, 1849, Chopin's body was laid to rest after his heart had been removed and returned to Warsaw. Of the three major cemeteries of Paris, it was the newest and most prestigious. During the reign of Louis XIV, the land that it was to occupy had belonged to Père Lachaise, the king's confessor. After the suppression of the Jesuits in 1790 the property reverted to the state, and in May 1804 it was acquired by a certain Nicolas Frochot, who decided to make a cemetery of it in compliance with Napoléon's edict that all burial grounds be moved outside the city walls. To provide his enterprise with a touch of class, Frochot had the bodies of Molière and La Fontaine, as well as Héloise and Abélard, transferred to his new burial ground. By 1841, thirteen thousand people had been interred there, and the rue de la Roquette, leading from the place de la Bastille to the cemetery, was lined by gravestone shops interspersed with vendors of wreaths and flowers. The spaciousness and tranquillity of this green oasis drew many Parisians there for a restful stroll on pleasant summer evenings. Although the cemetery possessed a potters' field, most of those who came to rest in M. Frochot's plots were "people of quality." Père Lachaise, in Dumas's words, was the only place "worthy of receiving the mortal remains of a Parisian family: only there could a well-bred corpse feel at home."[26] Victor Hugo expressed himself even more succinctly: "To be buried in Père Lachaise is like having mahogany furniture."[27] Chopin, who was so delighted with "the exquisite mahogany furniture" of his Paris apartment, may well have agreed, since he chose to be buried there.[28] Even Napoléon, while in exile on the island of Saint Helena, expressed a similar desire, although Fate ultimately consigned his remains to the crypt of the Invalides. Of course, not everyone held such an exalted opinion of this posh stopover on the way to Judgment Day. Mrs. Trollope, with typical Anglo-Saxon practicality, failed to see the point of scrambling for social status after death and lamented that in Père Lachaise "wealth, rank and pride heap decorations over the worthless clay, striving vainly to conceal its nothingness."[29] Few Parisians, however, shared her feelings. In 1841, omnibuses continued to run every five minutes between Père Lachaise and the place du Carrousel.

A small fragment of the eighth arrondissement extended west of the place de la Bastille into the Marais. Salient among its past glories was the beautiful red-brick place Royal (now the place des Vosges), with its white stone trim. To the imaginative Gérard de Nerval, it resembled an august parliamentary court decked out in crimson and ermine robes. Here Victor Hugo held court at No. 6, while the actress Rachel presided over No. 9.

NINTH ARRONDISSEMENT

The ninth arrondissement consisted of the île Saint-Louis, the île de la Cité, and a narrow strip of the Right Bank adjacent to them. Just upstream from the île Saint-Louis was a third island, known as the île Louviers. For centuries this unpopulated plot had been used to store firewood, but in 1841 it was in the process of being joined to the Right Bank, and houses were starting to be built there.

The île Saint-Louis was claimed by some to be the most virtuous part of Paris in the 1840s. Not a prostitute was to be seen on its streets, although a hashish club did flourish for a while on the quai d'Anjou. The island was primarily a residential area with a number of fine seventeenth- and eighteenth-century structures. Among these was the exquisite Hôtel Lambert, which Chopin's good friends, Prince and Princess Czartoryski, converted (in 1842) from a military warehouse to the social and political hub of the city's Polish colony. A short way down the island's quai d'Anjou, Baudelaire rented an apartment at No. 17, and Daumier moved into a house at No. 9.

If the île Saint-Louis represented the epitome of virtue at this time, the neighboring île de la Cité was one of the most vice-ridden districts of Paris then. Between the spire of Sainte-Chapelle and the towers of Notre-Dame was one of the city's worst slums. Narrow, crooked streets dating back to the Middle Ages were bordered by five- and six-story tenements that shut out the sunlight, forcing the occupants to keep an oil lamp burning all day during the winter months. In his novel *The Mysteries of Paris,* Eugène Sue has left us a vivid account of this quarter, which became home to some of the most destitute of Polish emigrés. "Wretched houses, with scarcely a window and...staircases, so steep that they could only be ascended by the aid of ropes fastened to the damp walls by iron hooks; the lower stories of some of these houses were occupied by sellers of charcoal, tripemen or vendors of impure meat."[30] This was an area of thieves, prostitutes, and ex-convicts, who spent their evenings in smoke-filled taverns called *tapis francs* or in bawdy dance halls like the Prado where the women came cheap. As Sue observed, the latter even danced without hats, a sure sign of low life in those days.

At the southern boundary of this unsavory area was the morgue. An average day filled it with eight to twelve bodies dredged up from the Seine—some murdered, others the victims of their own despair. To retrieve these corpses, a chain net had been strung across the river downstream at Saint-Cloud. During the cholera epidemics that devastated Paris in the 1830s and 1840s, carts piled high with the dead filled the quay alongside the morgue. Many had come only a short way from the Hôtel Dieu, the city's oldest hospital, just across the street from the morgue. In 1840 the Hôtel Dieu had 1,500 beds and cared for 11,000 patients a year. Its large complex of buildings stretched from the south side of the Parvis Notre-Dame down to the quay. There portions of it bridged the smaller arm of the Seine to connect up with additional facilities on the Left Bank.

Dominating the île de la Cité was the cathedral of Notre-Dame, one of the oldest, most historic, and most beautiful churches in all Europe and yet strangely unappreciated by Parisians in the mid-nineteenth century. By 1845 the south choir was already in ruins, while the rest of the huge Gothic structure was crumbling away at such an alarming rate that a group of concerned citizens (including Victor Hugo and the painter Jean-Auguste-Dominique Ingres) demanded that the government take steps to prevent its complete disintegration. Prosper Mérimée, who was inspector general of historical monuments in France then, appointed his friend, Eugène Viollet-le-Duc, to take charge of the task. To him we owe the preservation of Notre-Dame—although he has often been criticized for having done more remodelling than restoring. Be that as it may, Viollet-le-Duc was greatly admired in this century by Frank Lloyd Wright, who once gave his son a copy of the architect's *Discourses* with the admonition, "In these volumes you will find all the architectural schooling you will ever need."[31]

In addition to his work on Notre-Dame, Viollet-le-Duc restored the exquisite Sainte-Chapelle in 1841. It had originally been built by Saint Louis to house such holy relics as the blood of Christ, the milk of the Virgin, the swaddling clothes of the infant Jesus, and Moses' rod. During the early part of Louis-Philippe's reign, it had been used to store flour and later served as a repository for old government records. At one point the state even put it up for sale but found no bidders!

TENTH ARRONDISSEMENT

The three remaining arrondissements on the Left Bank occupied a much smaller geographic area than those across the Seine. Culturally and socially, however, they were of equal importance. The tenth or westernmost arrondissement included the "noble faubourg" of Saint-Germain, so called because of the aristocratic society that lived there. This may well have been Chopin's favorite part of Paris. Certainly he spent innumerable evenings in its salons, where his impromptu performances at the piano made him a popular guest. Because there were no concert halls in the faubourg, however, he never played in public there. Occasionally, though, he took part in informal musicales at embassies, private residences, or—as on one occasion in 1836—in a girls' finishing school on the rue de Lille.[32]

Most of the area's residents belonged to the prerevolutionary ancien régime and were still loyal to the deposed Bourbon dynasty. For them Louis-Philippe was a usurper even though he actually belonged to a branch of the Bourbon family, descended from Louis XIV's younger brother Philippe, duc d'Orléans. They refused to participate in the court life of the new monarchy rather than rub shoulders with the era's nouveaux-riches, who might have financial clout but no taste or manners. The novels of Balzac and Stendhal have preserved the titled world of the faubourg Saint-Germain where M. le Marquis de **** and Mme la comtesse de **** inhabit their splendid townhouses in disdainful isolation, protected by a walled *cour d'honneur* on the front and an enclosed garden on the back. At a Tuileries ball, Louis-Philippe once complained that it was easier to entice the English nobility across the Channel than to get the aristocracy of Saint-Germain across the Seine.

Except for Balzac's fictional social climbers (and their real-life models), most Parisians found little of interest in the quiet streets of the "noble faubourg," which lacked restaurants, theaters, or other places of amusement. The fact that the high walls of the quartier's grand *hôtels particuliers* sheltered some of the oldest and most distinguished families of France had no relevance to their lives. Few could even begin to imagine the opulence hidden behind "these dull-faced mansions."[33] At that time most of the faubourg's great houses were still in private hands. A few, however, were let out. Chateaubriand, for example, rented quarters in the Hôtel Clermont-Tonnerre on the rue du Bac, while the king's sister, Mme Adélaïde, leased the Hôtel Matignon, in the rue de Varennes, to a rich American, Colonel Thorn. A few of the houses no longer served as residences, having been converted into government ministries or foreign embassies. Among the most magnificent of these, the Palais Bourbon on the quai d'Orsay across from the place de la Concorde, housed the Chamber of Deputies. Delacroix had recently painted the murals in its Salle du Roi and was working on others in the library.

In the rue de Grenelle, several large mansions had been connected to form the ministry of the interior, where the city's main telegraph office was located. Three subsidiary offices were established elsewhere in the city with antennae rising above the towers of Saint-Sulpice, Saint-Eustache, and Montmartre's tiny church of Saint-Pierre (overshadowed today by the soaring Basilica of Sacre-Coeur just east of it). Other mansions in the faubourg Saint-Germain had been converted to new uses like the Hôtel Biron, which had been turned into a girl's boarding school by the sisters of the Sacred Heart. Among its alumnae were Liszt's mistress, the Comtesse d'Agoult (briefly attracted to Chopin), and Eugénie de Montijo, the future empress of Napoléon III. In another convent, the Abbaye-aux-Bois, on the southern outskirts of the "noble faubourg," the aging Mme Récamier passed her last years. There, with her devoted admirer Chateaubriand, she held a literary salon often referred to as "the foyer of the Academy," to which so many of her guests were elected.

The Academy itself (or rather, the five academies of the French Institute) was housed in the Palais de l'Institut at the northeast corner of the tenth arrondissement on the quay opposite the Louvre. There the "immortals" of France met weekly to hear learned papers, discuss learned subjects, and quibble over which of their learned colleagues deserved admission. When Berlioz, forever short of funds, was elected to the Academy, he considered the honor a "myth" but relished the annual stipend of 1,500 francs it offered. To the west of the Institut, on the quai Malaquai, was the new Ecole Royale des Beaux-Arts, an eclectic mixture of Renaissance and Gothic styles finished in 1839. At that time George Sand's son, Maurice, was considering a career in art but rather than sending him there she placed him under the tutelage of Delacroix, who was an intimate of the Chopin-Sand ménage.

Farther west the quai Voltaire became a sort of recherché flea market for Parisian connoisseurs of the arts. Mrs. Trollope and Lady Blessington loved to shop there for rare books, engravings, and *objets de vertu*, while the royal family browsed its contents for Louis XV pieces to fill their palaces. Progressing downstream along the Seine was the quai d'Orsay, lined with curiosity shops full of amber vases, diamond-studded watches, and gilt-headed canes. It was in one of these shops that Balzac's Raphael in the *Peau de Chagrin* found the ass's skin that was to destroy him.

Occupying most of the western part of the tenth arrondissement were the Invalides and the Ecole Militaire. In December 1840, Chopin joined the crowds who thronged the Esplanade des Invalides to witness the return of Napoléon's remains, which now rest under the dome of that church. The Invalides was a hospital for retired soldiers, mostly veterans of the Napoleonic campaigns who affectionately placed statues of the emperor in their little garden plots. By then the neighboring Ecole Militaire had been converted from a school into barracks for four thousand soldiers from various branches of the army. On its west side, sloping down toward the Seine, was the vast tree-lined Champs de Mars, a frequent site of military reviews, horse races, and special celebrations like the king's birthday and the anniversary of the July revolution.

The avenue de Saxe, named for George Sand's great grandfather, led from the Ecole Militaire to the place de Breteuil where the artesian well of Grenelle had just been completed (in 1841). It took nine years to drill and yielded four thousand liters of water a minute under such force that it could supply a six-floor building with running water (fig. 1.9). Previously the city's main source of water had come from a tributary of the Marne by way of the Ourcq and Saint-Martin canals. From these canals, it was piped to fountains and hydrants on both the Right and Left Banks. Those who didn't care to fetch their own water could hire one of the city's twenty thousand water carriers to bring the precious liquid to their door in large horse-drawn barrels. Most of these men were sturdy Auvergne peasants who, for a few sous, would haul their buckets up to your floor and splash their way across foyer and salon to deposit it in your kitchen or water closet. In Mrs. Trollope's opinion, the money lavished on the grand monuments of Paris would have been better spent on plumbing, a luxury much more common in London than on the continent. For the Parisian who lacked the domestic convenience of a water closet, there were the public baths, two of the most popular being the floating Bains Vigier (on the Seine below the Tuileries) and the Bains Chinois on the boulevard des Italiens, where the Sicilian composer, Bellini, had a pied à terre during his years in Paris (fig. 1.10).

ELEVENTH ARRONDISSEMENT

The eleventh arrondissement was centered around the recently enlarged and remodeled Palais de Luxembourg in the middle of the Left Bank (fig. 1.11). Inside the Luxembourg were the Chamber of Peers, the Court of Peers, and an art gallery devoted to the works of contemporary artists. The new south front of the palace, finished in 1841, looked out on a lovely garden, which rivaled that of the Tuileries in size and beauty while being more serene. Adjoining the palace on the west was the smaller and older Petit Palais de Luxembourg, where Chopin once performed in a concert given by the duc Decazes, who was then chief justice of the Court of Peers.

To the northeast of the Luxembourg palace was the Odéon, one of the few theaters on the Left Bank. It could seat up to 1,600 people and counted a host of directors who, in sixty years, had little success drawing crowds away from the city's principal entertainment districts across the Seine. From 1840 on it became a

1.9 The artesian well of Grenelle was located in what is today the place de Breteuil, just south of the Invalides. It took over seven years to dig. At the time of its completion in 1841, water from it could reach the highest story of any house in Paris. The 130-foot column shown here was torn down in 1903 and replaced by a monument to Louis Pasteur.

1.10 Les Bains Vigier (*left*) were among the many public baths in Paris. Because of their location, adjacent to the Tuileries garden, the Vigier Baths attracted a particularly *soigné* clientele. Besides these floating establishments on the Seine, Paris had many other public baths located on both the Right and Left Banks. Some, like the Chinese Baths on the boulevard des Italiens, provided residential apartments, one of which was inhabited for awhile by Chopin's friend, the Italian composer Vincenzo Bellini.

1.11 The Luxembourg palace under Louis-Philippe housed the Chamber of Peers, the Court of Peers, and a museum of "modern" art. Its gardens often served as trysting places for the aristocratic ladies of Saint-Germain. The low building to the left of the Luxembourg, known as the petit Luxembourg, was occupied by the chief justice of the Court of Peers, the duc Decazes. Chopin once played in a concert there in 1836. Note the telegraph antennae on the towers of the church of Saint-Sulpice, just behind the petit Luxembourg.

second stage for the Comédie Française. There, only a month after Chopin's death, George Sand produced her first successful play, a stage adaptation of her novel *François le Champi*.

In this part of the eleventh arrondissement lived many of Paris's authors and critics, including Charles-Augustin Sainte-Beuve and Jules Janin. Although the Café Risbeck in the place de l'Odéon was a rendezvous for many of these literati, the Café Pinson, on the rue de l'Ancienne Comédie, attracted others like Honoré Balzac and George Sand. Close by, the Café de la Rotonde was a favorite haunt for young bohemians like Charles Baudelaire and Gustave Courbet, as well as doctors and medical students from the nearby Ecole de Médecine, including, in all probability, Chopin's roommate in the Chaussée d'Antin, Dr. Jan Matuszyński.

Just east of the Ecole de Médecine, across what is now the boulevard Saint-Michel, was the Hôtel Cluny, which belonged to a M. du Sommerard until it was purchased by the city in 1844 and opened to the public as a museum. In the opinion of the British Colonel Raikes, its "worm-eaten furniture" and "rusty snuffers" were hardly worth a visit.[34] What a shame, he complained, that M. du Sommerard had spent his money so foolishly. Today the Hôtel Cluny houses one of the finest collections of medieval art and artifacts in the world.

TWELFTH ARRONDISSEMENT

East of the Hôtel Cluny runs the rue Saint-Jacques, which separated the eleventh from the twelfth arrondissements. It cut through the Latin Quarter, so named for its scholars who, in medieval times, spoke and wrote Latin in their classrooms. To this day it remains the area where many of the city's educational institutions are still located. Most of its schools were clustered around the eighteenth-century Panthéon, which had originally been constructed as a church to Sainte Geneviève, the patron saint of Paris. Among them were such institutions as the Sorbonne (more or less in ruins under the July monarchy), the Collège de France, the polytechnical and law schools, and the Collège Henri IV, attended by the king's sons. The southern end of the boulevard Saint-Jacques was intersected by a ring of boulevards enclosing the Left Bank of the city. Geographically they were analogous to those on the Right Bank, but very different in character. Their lack of bustling shops, cafés, and crowded theaters gave them a semi-rural aspect compared to their equivalents across the Seine. At night, however, the *guingettes* (taverns) of the area came to life with singing and dancing. The best known of these, La Grande Chaumière, on the boulevard Montparnasse at the rue d'Enfer, sat in a garden of acacia and lime trees, surrounded by thatched-roofed cabins. Beyond the dance floor, banked with flowers, an assortment of games and rides were available, including seesaws, wooden horses on wheels, and slides called "Russian mountains" with sand piles at their base to catch the screaming merrymakers. By day, the main attractions in this part of town were the public executions at the place Saint-Jacques or excursions to Versailles on the new railroad, which left from the avenue du Maine near today's gare Montparnasse.[35] In 1830 Thiers once called railroads toys for the curious; by 1841 they were rapidly becoming an accepted fact of life.

Proceeding east along the boulevard Saint Jacques, one crossed the river Bièvre (now filled in), a shallow muddy stream polluted by toxic chemicals from the Gobelins factory, famous for its tapestries and Savonnerie rugs. This

1.12 The amphitheater in the Jardin des Plantes was used for public lectures on scientific topics like comparative anatomy and chemistry, given by such contemporary authorities as Baron Cuvier and Joseph-Louis Gay-Lussac. Berlioz found Gay-Lussac's discussion of electricity fascinating. But Chopin, who once attended a scientific congress in Berlin, was bored by such events and no doubt avoided them in Paris.

portion of the twelfth arrondissement, known as the faubourg Saint-Marcel, was an impoverished, crime-ridden district, grimly portrayed in Hugo's *Les Misérables* and Sue's *Mysteries of Paris*. It was once said that more money could be found in a single house in the faubourg Saint-Honoré than in the entire faubourg Saint-Marcel. Running diagonally along the southern portion of the faubourg was the boulevard de l'Hôpital, which led past the Hôpital Salpêtrière (for insane and indigent women) to the Seine, where the new gare d'Orléans (today's gare d'Austerlitz) had just opened in 1838. It was from here that Chopin took his first train trip.

Just north of the gare d'Orléans was the Jardin des Plantes, full of diversions for tourist and resident alike. In 1844 Chopin took his sister there when she was visiting Paris. Neither felt it was as impressive as the botanical gardens in Warsaw, which were laid out on a picturesque slope overlooking the Vistula river. During the musician's trip to Majorca with George Sand in 1838, the exotic flora of the island, "palm trees, cedars, cacti, olive trees, orange and lemon trees, aloes, figs, [and] pomegranates," reminded him of everything "the Jardin des Plantes has in its greenhouses."[36] Besides botanical specimens the garden possessed what Heine called a "zoological Pantheon...of beasts."[37] By 1836 its menagerie already included two elephants, a giraffe, and an orangutan, to which anacondas, ostriches, zebras, lions, tigers, leopards, panthers, hyenas, and an Andean condor were soon added. Elsewhere on its grounds were research laboratories, a gallery of comparative anatomy, a phrenological display, an amphitheater for public lectures, and a library of natural history (fig. 1.12).

At the west end of the Jardin des Plantes was the Hôpital de la Pitié, where Lucile Louvet, the prototype of Mimi in Puccini's opera *La Bohème* was to die in 1848. Across the street from La Pitié stood the prison of Sainte-Pélagie, filled with journalists and political opponents of the July monarchy. Living conditions in the prison were generally tolerable and often quite comfortable. Many of the inmates enjoyed well-furnished private rooms; others doubled up for companionship or were quartered in dormitories that could hold as many as forty prisoners.

A few blocks north, on the rue des Fosses Saint-Bernard, was another prison, the Hôtel de Bazancourt, facetiously referred to as the "Hôtel des Haricots" (or house of beans), a corruption of the name of General Darricau, who established it. Many prominent literary people, including Balzac, Dumas *père,* and Sue did time there for skipping their National Guard duty. Under Louis-Philippe, whose power relied heavily on the support of that middle-class militia, this was a serious offense. For several years to come the National Guard continued to support him, but Paris was never a city to tolerate either mediocrity or stagnation. Louis-Philippe symbolized both and his reign was to be short-lived. By 1848, revolution had forced both the king and Chopin to seek refuge in England, while the Galignanis scrambled to make drastic revisions in their next year's *Paris Guide.*

CHAPTER 2

Polish Parisians

A People in Exile

"*OH, GOD, DO YOU EXIST?* . . . Haven't you had enough of the Muscovites' crimes?—Or is it—can it be—You yourself are a Russian!" This hysterical outburst was written by Chopin on hearing that Warsaw had fallen to the czar's troops early in September 1831. During the hours that followed, the musician filled his journal with frenzied lamentations over the imagined fate of loved ones left behind in Poland. "My poor father, he must be starving and can't find a scrap of food for mother!—my sisters, have probably fallen prey to the uncontrolled rage of the Russian soldiers. . . . Are the Muscovites now rulers of the whole world? . . . Oh! If only I could have killed just one of them . . . but no, here am I, doing nothing, idling away my time, sighing and pouring out my despair on the piano! . . . My God, Oh my God! Make the earth tremble and swallow up the wicked around us. May the French suffer all the torments of Hell for not coming to our aid."[1]

At the time Chopin unleashed this agonized tirade, he was in Stuttgart en route from Vienna to London with plans to stop for awhile in Paris. There he hoped to obtain a residency permit, even though Czar Nicholas I (as titular king of Poland) had forbidden any of his Polish subjects to settle there. If the French rejected Chopin's request, he would have to move on to London, which was his authorized destination. To add to his anxiety, his passport was to expire in just one month's time, so he had to act quickly. In spite of his anger at the French, he wanted to remain in Paris. He was after all half-French, his father having been born in the Vosge district of northeastern France. Furthermore he spoke the language well, albeit with occasional lapses and a slight Polish accent. Above all, he longed to live in Paris because it had become the leading musical center of Europe since the recent deaths of Schubert and Beethoven in Vienna. Among his papers, Chopin carried a letter of introduction to Ferdinand Paër, the director of music at the court of Louis-Philippe.

Unlike the new king and his advisors, many Frenchmen were sympathetic to the plight of the Poles. Among them were Victor Hugo, the poet Pierre-Jean de Béranger, and several members of the French Chambers who had condemned Russia's brutal repression of the Polish insurrection. On September 15, when news of Warsaw's surrender reached Paris, crowds marched on the Russian embassy, smashing windows and crying "Down with the Russians," "Vengeance," "War with Russia," and "Long live the Poles."[2] The American Samuel F. B. Morse, who was in Paris then, wrote, "The news of the fall of Warsaw is now agitating Paris.... About three o'clock our servant told us that there was fighting at the Palais Royal [where the new king, Louis-Philippe lived].... There was evident agitation in the multitudes that filled the sidewalks.... The shops began to shut, and every now and then the drum was heard beating to arms. The troops were assembling and bodies of infantry and cavalry were moving through the various streets"(fig. 2.1).[3]

Two days later, Morse called on General Lafayette, who had already met with some of the first Polish emigrés. When the American asked if there was any hope for Poland, the general replied, "Oh, yes! Their cause is not yet desperate; their army is safe but the conduct of France, and more especially England, has been most pusillanimous and culpable."[4] Meanwhile the disorders continued, with many rioters crying, "Down with Louis-Philippe!" Street lamps were smashed, gunshops looted, and barricades erected out of sawed-off trees and overturned vehicles. Eventually the National Guard was called out to restore order, but not until five people had been killed and 152 wounded.

In the early months of 1831, some time before the Russians finally quelled the Warsaw uprising, the Poles had already established a legation in Paris with the hope of acquiring financial and military aid from the French. Unfortunately it was headed by the seventy-two-year-old general Karol Kniaziewicz, "a glorious souvenir" from the past with little knowledge of the French language or the art of diplomacy.[5] Besides its feeble leadership, the legation had the further disadvantage of not being recognized by the Orleanist government. Despite Lafayette's claim that all France supported the Poles, a number of its politicians were quite hostile to them. General Sebastiani, one of Louis-Philippe's ministers, praised the Russians for restoring "order" to Warsaw, while Adolphe Thiers, later prime minister of France, considered the Poles mere "adventurers." Prince Talleyrand's niece, the duchesse de Dino, had an equally low opinion of them. "What a host of miserable creatures," she exclaimed. "It is natural to want to

2.1 Samuel F. B. Morse was an art student
living in Paris when the first Polish emigrés began arriving there in 1831. Because
of his friendship with General Lafayette,
Morse assisted him in his efforts to aid the
new exiles and helped to form fund-raising committees for their benefit in both
Paris and the United States.

shelter them, but it must be admitted that in the present state of France they can
only be a new element of disorder."[6] Many years earlier, in her youth, the
duchess (then Princess Dorothea of Courland), had been passionately in love
with the Polish prince Adam Jerzy Czartoryski, but for political reasons was
forced to marry Prince Talleyrand's nephew—whom she eventually abandoned
for his uncle.

In a more tactful expression of the government's views, the duc de Mortemart
pleaded that France had not yet recovered from its own revolution (of 1830) and
was therefore not in any condition to help the Poles. The prime minister, Casimir
Périer, also opposed aid to the Poles on the chauvinistic grounds that the Frenchman's wealth and blood should be expended on his own fellowmen rather than
foreigners. The undeniable relief felt by the bankers and financiers of the
Orleanist regime on hearing of the Poles' defeat was clearly evident in the
marked rise of stock prices on the Paris Bourse.

One of the few officials in the Orleanist government genuinely sympathetic to
the Polish cause was General Lafayette, head of the National Guard (fig. 2.2).
Early in January 1831, the general gathered all the pro-Polish elements in Paris
together in a Central Franco-Polish Committee, headed by himself and his son-
in-law, Louis de Lasteyrie. Because Lafayette had fought alongside Washington
in the American Revolution, he was able to rally the support of a group of Paris's

2.2 The marquis de Lafayette was a French general and statesman who had formerly fought alongside the Polish general Kościuszko in the American Revolution. Because of this, he was highly sympathetic to the plight of Polish exiles like Chopin, who were seeking refuge in Paris during the 1830s. Thanks to his efforts, financial aid and job opportunities were made available to many of these unfortunate victims.

2.3 James Fenimore Cooper. Like Samuel F. B. Morse, Cooper was living in Paris at the time of the great Polish emigration to that city in 1831. He also collaborated with Lafayette in raising money to ease the lot of these displaced people. Because of the crowded conditions in Paris, many were given assistance to cross the Atlantic and find new homes for themselves in the United States.

colony of Americans. Although small in number, it showed great concern for the displaced Poles and induced the United States to welcome many of them to its shores. Samuel F. B. Morse, who had met Lafayette and painted his portrait five years earlier, now sought out the elderly hero and took rooms near his home on the faubourg Saint-Honoré's rue d'Anjou. Just across the river, on the Left Bank's rue Saint-Dominique, the American novelist James Fenimore Cooper headed up a committee of his countrymen to solicit contributions on behalf of the Poles (fig. 2.3). The parallel between their own recent fight for independence and that of Poland elicited a large outpouring of funds from Americans on both sides of the Atlantic.

Because of the cholera epidemic that had spread from eastern Europe into France that fall, many of the Polish exiles seeking asylum in France were placed in quarantine before being allowed into the country. Among the first arrivals were several young radical friends of Chopin's from Warsaw, including Joachim

Lelewel (a historian and former professor at Wilno University) and Maurycy Mochnacki (a Romantic writer and literary critic). During his last year in Warsaw, Chopin often joined them and their comrades in the city's coffee houses, where they discussed plans for the coming insurrection against Russia. Because the little group was under surveillance by the czar's spies, their conversations and Chopin's association with them were regularly reported to the Russian authorities. Although the frail young musician took no part in their plotting, the grand duke Constantine, commander in chief of the Polish army, suspected him of being a conspirator. "It is only effete young men and some young rascals who are patriots," he told his brother, Czar Nicholas I.[7]

For the rest of 1831 and well into the following year, Poles continued to pour into Paris. Their preference for France stemmed from the fact that the Polish aristocracy had long regarded the French language and culture as definitive marks of a civilized society. "For Paris boasts her frequent change of fashion / And what the French invent is Poland's passion," Adam Mickiewicz wrote in his epic poem *Pan Tadeusz*.[8] Clearly the Poles were accustomed to a French ambience and felt at home in it. Their ties to France were further strengthened by the gratitude many felt toward Napoléon for reestablishing a Polish state (the Duchy of Warsaw) in 1807 and the camaraderie established by the participation of Polish troops in Bonaparte's armies.

To the discomfiture of the July monarchy, the allure of Paris was so great that by November 1831 Chopin commented, "The number of Poles here is inconceivable."[9] Since his recent arrival in Paris he had already run into many old friends from Warsaw, including Lelewel, Mochnacki, and a number of other emigrés who were to exert a significant influence on his life there. One of these, Prince Walenty Radziwiłł, introduced him to the baron James de Rothschild whose wife, Betty, and daughter, Charlotte, soon became his pupils. Other distinguished emigrés like the Komars invited him to dinner as did their daughter, the countess Delfina Potocka, a great beauty who sang sublimely (fig. 2.4). Among the many men who fell under the spell of her charms was Chopin himself, who became her piano teacher and (according to one of his pupils) her lover as well.

Still other compatriots whom Chopin encountered during his first months in Paris included Count Plater (whose daughter, Pauline, was also one of his pupils) and Count Grzymała, a former soldier under Napoléon twice imprisoned by the Russians. In Paris the latter made an enviable living playing the stock market, which enabled him to lead the life of a cultivated boulevardier. Seventeen

2.4 Countess Delfina Potocka (née Komar), a Polish emigrée separated from her husband, became notorious for her numerous love affairs, the most famous being with the Polish poet, Zygmunt Krasiński, who inspired Chopin to set four of his poems to music. An excellent singer and pianist, Delfina studied for a time with Chopin and may well have had a brief affair with him, although proof of this is controversial. There can be no doubt, however, about Mme Potocka's deep affection for her teacher. She was present at his bedside the night he died, having played and sung for him shortly before he lost consciousness.

years older than Chopin, he became an avuncular advisor to the young musician and an unwitting pawn in George Sand's campaign to win the latter's affections. Closer to Chopin's age were several of his fellow students from the Warsaw conservatory (Antoni Orłowski, Wojciech Sowiński, and Julian Fontana), who tried with little success to establish musical careers in Paris. Of these, Fontana was to develop the closest relationship with Chopin, even though the latter imposed on him endlessly to copy his manuscripts and placate his publishers in the disputes he had with them. Over the following years, the Polish colony in Paris rose from a few hundred to several thousand persons. For Chopin they were to form a sustaining link to the homeland he would never see again.

While the early emigrés included members of the Polish aristocracy and middle class, most of them came from the lower classes and arrived destitute with little or no means of support. In general this impoverished element settled into an enclave west of today's gare Saint-Lazare, called "little Poland"—"a filthy jumble of hovels and shacks, the wretched abode of ragpickers, scrap collectors and immigrants."[10] Many were illiterate and required the services of public letter writers or "scriveners," who thrived in the district. Others collected in a crime-ridden ghetto on the île de la Cité. Reluctantly the prime minister, Casimir Périer, gave them a modest subsidy.

To many Parisians the newcomers were heroes; for others, they were a danger-

2.5 Maurycy Mochnacki, a friend of
Chopin's in his youth, was a journalist
for Warsaw's *Kuryer Polski*, in which he
wrote favorable reviews of the musician's last concerts there. Later in Paris,
Mochnacki's radical political views alienated him from the more conservative
groups of emigrés to which Chopin
belonged. (Courtesy of Dr. Janusz
Cizek)

ous lot of revolutionaries typified by Chopin's friends, Lelewel and Mochnacki
(fig. 2.5). In his novel *Cousine Bette,* Balzac describes the fears many Parisians felt
toward these migrants from the vast plains of eastern Europe. They were a primitive, unstable race of malcontents "who want to set Europe on fire . . . to ruin trade
and businessmen, . . . ferocious animals not really to be classed as belonging to the
human race at all. These Poles don't realize what times we live in. We're not bar-
barians any more!"[11]

Others, equally naive, imagined the Poles to be strange creatures with Oriental faces, dressed in bizarre Asiatic outfits. Naturally the theaters, quick to exploit
the public's expectations, staged productions with Polish themes, calculated to
gratify the Parisians' love of the exotic. Patriotic Polish songs (invariably mis-
spelled and mispronounced) were sung in the entr'actes of dramas. On the boulevard du Temple, the Franconi brothers whipped up an extravaganza in their vast
Cirque Olympique, entitled "The Poles, Events Out of Their History." While
Chopin complained that the production was rife with phony Polish-sounding
names, he noted that "the public rushed to the theater in a frenzy to marvel over
the costumes."[12] No doubt they were spectacular, reflecting what Balzac called
the Poles' "Oriental taste for magnificence."[13]

Even in the more sophisticated circles of Paris, an obsession with the new Polish emigrés was evident. Daniel François Auber's latest cantata, entitled "Song of

the Poles," drew crowds to the city's concert halls, while a new musical concoction called "The Fall of Warsaw" was presented at the Opéra-Comique. Soon Parisian music journals were reviewing concerts by such Polish virtuosi as Chopin and his friends Julian Fontana, Wojciech Sowiński, and Antoni Orłowski. The visiting violinist Charles Lipinski (billed as a rival of Paganini) performed to great acclaim, while lesser entertainers such as the guitarist Szczpanowski and the touring Kontski family appealed more to the curious than the connoisseur. In the salons of the faubourgs Saint-Germain and Saint-Honoré, the Polish Polonaise enjoyed a considerable vogue, as did the mazurka, which rivaled the polka and the can-can among the city's *jeunesse dorée*.

One of the strongest bonds between the Polish refugees and their French hosts was the Roman Catholic faith. For both, the Russian Orthodox Church was a form of apostasy. Because of this, many who supported the Polish cause were clergymen like the abbés Lamennais and Lacordaire as well as comte Charles de Montalembert, an active lay leader in the church. All three men condemned the anticlericalism of the July government and saw the Poles as defenders of religion as well as liberty. For Lacordaire, Roman Catholic Poland represented the altar on which that liberty had been sacrificed in 1831. This theme of Poland's martyrdom would soon give rise to the Poles' concept of their messianic role as the "Christ of Nations." In Montalembert's view, the 1830 insurrection represented the first step in their divine obligation to redeem mankind from the forces of evil. Rome, however, saw things differently. From the Vatican, the ultraconservative Pope Gregory XVI condemned the Polish uprising as a disruption of the social order of Europe and praised the czar's repression of it.

Ironically this Romantic notion of the Poles as God's chosen instrument to purge the world of evil was destined to split the exiled Polish community in two. Many young radicals like Lelewel and Mochnacki interpreted it as a mandate to continue their struggle for freedom against not only Russia but all despotic regimes wherever they existed. They linked the restoration of freedom in Poland to a liberation of all victims of tyranny throughout Europe and the rest of the world. As a step toward this goal, some formed military legions to fight for the oppressed in Northern Italy and the Middle East, while others joined underground revolutionary societies like the Carbonari.

By contrast the conservative emigrés bided their time, hoping to revive the kingdom of Poland through diplomatic negotiations. In Paris this group was represented by men like count Ludwik Plater and Bronisław Niemojowski, the last

2.6 Joachim Lelewel was another of
Chopin's early friends in Warsaw who
shared his musical interests; in 1826 he
published a musical bibliography.
During the uprising of 1830, Lelewel
fought against the Russians and later
fled to Paris after his country's defeat.
In France his activities with the leftist
Polish "Reds" soon led to his expul-
sion. He is remembered today principally as a historian. (Courtesy of Dr.
Janusz Cizek)

president of the national government in Warsaw. Simultaneously in London,
men like Prince Adam Czartoryski and Julian Ursyn Niemcewicz were attempting to secure support from the English government. For the most part, these men
were members of the aristocracy and landed gentry who hoped to reestablish a
constitutional monarchy in Poland. At the same time their younger radical compatriots believed, with an almost Jacobinic ardor, in Poland's resurrection as a
peoples' republic. In time the latter came to be called the "Reds" and the former,
the "Whites." Unlike the impetuous Reds who demanded immediate action, the
Whites foresaw a long period of exile before the Poles regained their independence. As the aging count Plater told Niemcewicz, "Poland will not perish—ever,
but we shall never see it again."[14]

Early in November 1831, the emigrés set up their own committee in Paris,
apart from Lafayette's central Franco-Polish committee. Soon it was taken over
by the Reds with Lelewel as president and Mochnacki as secretary (fig. 2.6). The
French government eyed it suspiciously, fearing the intentions of its leftist leaders. Less than a year later Louis-Philippe, at the instigation of the Russian ambassador Pozzo di Borgo, expelled Lelewel. Following this event, most Poles rallied
around Czartoryski, who by 1833 had settled permanently in Paris.

Strangely enough, Prince Adam Jerzy Czartoryski (later known as "the
uncrowned king of Poland") had grown up at the Russian court, where he lived

on intimate terms with the imperial family (fig. 2.7).[15] He was related by marriage to the dowager czarina Maria Feodorovna, whose son, Alexander I, appointed him Russia's minister of foreign affairs and even allowed his empress, the czarina Elizabeth, to have an affair with him. Not until 1810 when Czartoryski, like most Poles, fell under Napoléon's spell, did a strain develop in his relations with the czar. After the "Congress" Kingdom of Poland was formed in 1815, Czartoryski served as one of its senators and remained a staunch advocate of Russian-Polish cooperation until the revolution of 1830. Although he deplored the Polish uprising as "the height of folly" (because of insufficient forces and bad timing), he reluctantly assumed leadership of it and fought side by side with his countrymen on the battlefields.[16] After the fall of Warsaw he went to London, hoping for aid to renew the struggle. There the Russian ambassador's wife, Princess Lieven, condemned the prime minister, Lord Grey, for receiving a "criminal." Frustrated, Czartoryski left for France to join Niemcewicz, then head of the Polish legation in Paris. At age seventy-five, Niemcewicz still enjoyed considerable prestige among the emigrés for his literary fame as well as his dedication to the cause of freedom. But time had taken its toll on the poet, who was now entering exile for the fourth time.[17] Old and exhausted, the former hero had become sentimental, indecisive, and weak-willed— in short, "a political nonentity."[18]

Czartoryski himself, although still vigorous, was already sixty-one when Warsaw fell in 1831. Both he and Niemcewicz, knowing that the reconstruction of a new Polish state would require a great deal of time, worked to provide the emigré community with sufficient amenities to make their long exile comfortable and productive. Among the cultural organizations they founded was the Polish Literary Society, which Chopin joined in January 1833. Later the composer contributed the handsome sum of over 200 francs to the Polish Polytechnical Society, a sort of placement bureau for unemployed refugees. Around the same time, Princess Czartoryska established the Polish Ladies' Benevolent Society, which raised money through concerts and a yearly Christmas bazaar. At these events valuable objets d'art (including needlework by the queen and princesses, paintings by Delacroix, and handwritten manuscripts by George Sand) were offered for sale (fig. 2.8). Chopin not only performed at one of the princess's concerts, he also provided occasional background music for the crowds that came to browse at her bazaars. Through these charitable projects, Mme Czartoryska was able to raise substantial sums for her impoverished compatriots. Unfortunately, not all the princess's benevolent endeavors achieved comparable results. On April 3,

2.7 Prince Adam Jerzy Czartoryski has often been described as "king" of the Polish exiles in Paris. He headed up the conservative or "White" political faction of the emigrés, who hoped to regain their homeland through diplomatic negotiations rather than military force. Such views appealed to Chopin more than those of the hot-headed Mochnacki and Lelewel.

2.8 Princess Anna Czartoryska. While Prince Czartoryski was concerned primarily with negotiating for the return of the Poles to their homeland, Princess Czartoryska devoted herself to improving the quality of their lives in exile. It was she (often with Chopin's help) who established many of the cultural and charitable organizations that ameliorated the conditions under which the Polish colony was forced to live. (2.7 and 2.8 courtesy of Dr. Janusz Cizek)

1840, she sponsored a production of von Flotow's opera *La Duchesse de Guise,* in which several bona fide "princesses and duchesses" took minor roles.[19] Afterward Jules de Castellane invited the cast to his home for dinner and a fancy-dress ball where everyone came in Polish costumes. Although the proceeds from the evening came to 30,000 francs (duly turned over to indigent Poles), the total cost of the lavish production amounted to 100,000 francs, leaving Mme Czartoryska and her sponsors to make up the difference out of their own purses.

Other cultural projects of the Polish colony included organizations devoted to history, statistics, and Polish studies, as well as Polish-language schools and residences for orphans and the aged. On November 24, 1838, the Polish library was signed into existence at Ludwik Plater's home on the rue de Londres. It opened on March 24, 1839, and still exists today at No. 6 quai d'Orléans on the île Saint-Louis, where much of the research for this book was done. Earlier the Poles had already founded a number of literary and political journals to serve their community. Many of these could be found in the reading room of the Polish Club on the rue Godot de Mauroy, just north of the Grand Boulevards.

Faithfully each year the Poles commemorated the November uprising, initially in the Church of Saint-Louis d'Antin (not far from the Right Bank's "Little Poland"), and later in the Left Bank's church of Saint-Germain-des-Prés, where the heart of Poland's seventeenth-century Polish king, Jan Kazimierz, still rests. The main parish church for most of the aristocratic emigrés, however, was Saint-Roch, near the Tuileries, often attended by the queen, Marie-Amélie. During the early years of the emigration, father Alexander Jełowicki (who ministered to Chopin in his last hours) founded a Polish Catholic mission in the Church of the Assumption (near the northeast corner of the place de la Concorde) which eventually became known as "the Polish church."

In 1843 Prince and Princess Czartoryski moved from the faubourg Saint-Honoré's rue de Roule to the palatial Hôtel Lambert at the eastern end of the île-Saint-Louis. Although the princess once complained to Lafayette that France's betrayal of the Poles had caused the loss of her husband's vast fortune, the family was far from destitute. In their new home they entertained on a grand scale, drawing guests not only from the Polish colony but also from the elite of *le tout Paris*. Receptions, dinners, balls, and concerts (often with Chopin's participation) were frequently held in the splendid LeBrun Salon, with its frescoed ceiling, marble sculpture, medallioned walls, and parquet floors (fig. 2.9). Much of the Hôtel Lambert's grandeur at this time was the work of Eugène Delacroix, who contributed to the renovation of the seventeenth-century mansion. Formerly it had belonged to a contractor of military bedding, who had allowed the sumptuous edifice to fall into a state of neglect, stuffed with cots, mattresses, pillows, and blankets.

At the frequent social gatherings in the newly renovated Hôtel Lambert, the duchesse de Dino found Prince Czartoryski a "languid" host. Quite the opposite, Princess Czartoryska displayed an indefatigable energy in her many roles as chatelaine of an opulent household, advisor to her beleaguered husband, fundraiser for innumerable charities, and a perpetual source of inspiration to the struggling Polish colony in Paris. The courage and strength that carried her through these stormy years aroused the admiration even of her enemies. No doubt Mme Czartoryska's incessant activity on behalf of her fellow-emigrés helped her forget the past. Even the socialist-minded George Sand (who never shared Chopin's fondness for aristocratic society) had great respect for Mme Czartoryska. Besides writing an article on her for the Parisian journal *Le Siècle*,

2.9 The Hôtel Lambert's exquisite Galerie LeBrun, shown here as a *salon de conversation* during a ball, served in more serene moments as a *salon de musique* where Chopin and his pupils, among others, often performed.

Sand helped tend the stalls at her annual bazaars for the benefit of Polish refugees (fig. 2.10). At one such event, the novelist tried to sell Baron Rothschild an expensive bottle of perfume. When he balked, she continued to badger him until he finally made her a proposition. If she would give him her autograph, he would sell it and donate half the profits to the Polish cause. After a moment's hesitation, she agreed, scribbled a note on a scrap of paper and handed it to him. From a nearby stall Heinrich Heine watched as the financier read what George had written. Suddenly he saw the baron turn pale and falter. Rushing over to him, Heine caught a glimpse of the note in his hand which read, "Receipt for 10,000 francs to aid Polish exiles in need, George Sand." Although the story is probably apocryphal, the princess rewarded Mme Sand for her efforts with an antique silver bracelet that had long been a treasured heirloom in her family.

As for the Czartoryskis' gala soirées at the Hôtel Lambert, guests remembered

2.10 Mme Anna Czartoryska hosted many fund-raising bazaars for the Polish emigrés, such as the one shown here. At a similar event in 1847, Chopin wrote George Sand's daughter, "Already the sale has brought in nearly 20,000 francs. There were many beautiful things there...Delacroix executed a small Christ that drew much admiration" (Chopin, *Correspondance*, 3:317).

them principally for three things: their lavishness, their noisiness, and the great diversity of those present. Certainly the opulence of the parties came as no surprise, considering the splendor of the Hôtel Lambert and the wealth of the Czartoryskis (fig. 2.11). In regard to the noise, it may well have been due to the reverberations of the mansion's marble interior—or a boisterous addiction to the Bordeaux grape, which the Parisian bon vivant, Barbey d'Aurevilly, found common among the Polish emigrés. As for the heterogeneity of those who attended these soirées, it was as striking as it was stimulating. Unlike patrons of many Parisian salons, the Hôtel Lambert's guests were not confined to people of

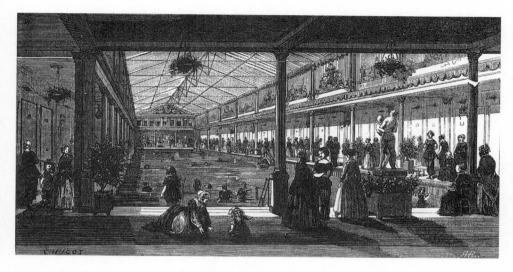

2.11 In an era when safe water was a precious commodity, the extraordinary luxury of a private swimming pool reflects the enormous wealth the Czartoryskis enjoyed, even in exile. When George Sand's daughter, Solange, arrived for the hashish parties at the île Saint-Louis's Hôtel Pimodan, Théophile Gautier noted that her hair was often still wet, no doubt from swimming in the pool shown here at the neighboring Hôtel Lambert.

any social class or special interest such as music, literature, or politics. And because the Czartoryskis (along with Chopin) were among the few Poles to find favor with the Orleanist court, members of the royal family could be spotted from time to time at their soirées. The cordiality between the Czartoryskis and the Tuileries was limited, however, due to Louis-Philippe's fundamental distrust of the Poles.

Despite the varied background of their guests, most of those circulating about the Czartoryskis' salon were either Polish or aristocratic; many, like Count Walewski (Napoléon's half-Polish natural son) and Prince Poniatowski, a great-nephew of the late Polish king Stanislas Poniatowski, were both. Each winter, these two noblemen attracted the attention of all Paris as they raced their splendid sleighs at top speed along the city's snow-packed boulevards. Equally racy in his own way was the Polish count Ignacy Gurowski, who lived for a time under the "protection" of his homosexual lover, Astolphe de Custine. The latter, a dilettantish writer, delighted the Polish colony with his book *La Russie,* a travelogue highly critical of the Russians. For many years Custine seems to have been smitten by Chopin, to whom he continually wrote seductive letters inviting him to his Paris apartment or his country house in Montmorency.

Often the notorious clamor of the Hôtel Lambert gave way to an attentive silence during the princess's many musicales. There, on select occasions, Chopin or one of his pupils treated the company to an impromptu performance. Among these students was the half-Polish Marie Kalergis, a towering six-foot goddess whose flamboyant affairs with Liszt, Musset, Gautier, and the future emperor Napoléon III provided perpetual gossip for *le tout Paris*. Delfina Potocka, another colorful student of Chopin's who performed occasionally at these musicales, was regarded by Count Apponyi as a "very beautiful woman with a lot of wit although not especially brilliant."[20] Mme Potocka was a gifted pianist with an extraordinary singing voice, which put her in great demand at the city's best salons. Equally in demand were her romantic favors. Among her lovers she counted the comte de Flahaut, the duc d'Orléans, and the Polish poet Zygmunt Krasiński. Whether Chopin was also one of this privileged coterie has been contested by biographers for the past 150 years. Certainly he felt a great affection for her. In 1847, more than a decade after their supposed affair in the Chaussée d'Antin, Chopin wrote his family, "You know how I love her."[21] At that time he had just broken up with George Sand, and Delfina was urging him to come to Nice with her for the winter. Before his final Paris concert in February 1848, he held a rehearsal at her apartment, and the following year, when he was too weak to venture out of his quarters in Chaillot, she came to sing for him. That fall, as he lay dying in the place Vendôme, she rushed from Nice to be with him during his last moments. At his request she again sang for him, this time—according to those present—with tears flowing down her cheeks.

Still another of Chopin's pupils who not only appeared in the Czartoryskis' salon but also often stayed in the Hôtel Lambert as a guest was Princess Marcellina Czartoryska (née Radziwiłł), the wife of Prince Adam's nephew, Alexander. According to Berlioz, the princess was "a musician of wide knowledge and exemplary taste and a distinguished pianist."[22] Her renditions of Chopin's works were generally considered closer to the composer's own interpretation of them than those of any of his other pupils. In addition to talent, Princess Marcellina was blessed with beauty and a warm, generous disposition. Delacroix confessed he could fall hopelessly in love with her, and Chopin once described her as "goodness itself."[23] It was through Princess Marcellina's efforts that Chopin's sister was able to obtain a passport for Paris to comfort her brother in the last weeks of his life. Mme Czartoryska herself took rooms in the place Vendôme to be near her dying teacher and played some of his favorite Mozart works for him on his deathbed.

Through his association with the large emigré population in Paris, Chopin inevitably became involved in their mutual efforts to sustain each other in those days of adversity. According to many sources, his compositions provided a great souce of inspiration for his displaced countrymen. Undoubtedly his use of traditional Polish musical forms like the polonaise and the mazurka roused nationalistic sentiments and a sense of cohesiveness among those Poles scattered across Europe and the New World. For them his music evoked memories of a Poland most would never see again. While some took solace in these memories, others found them a source of strength in their continuing struggle for freedom. Although Chopin's music undoubtedly came to him intuitively rather than through any consciously patriotic design, it served all the same to symbolize the will of the Polish people to survive. Those who overemphasize its nationalistic features, however, tend to lose sight of its essentially universal nature.

Apart from the inspirational effect of his music, Chopin aided his countrymen in many other ways. Not only did he contribute his time and money to Princess Czartoryska's Benevolent Society and General Bem's Polytechnical Society; he also helped his comrades on a more personal level. Even when he could ill afford it, he lent money to those in need like Antoni Wodziński, whose sister, Maria, had once been his fiancée. (Later, when the young man failed to repay him, he mused philosophically that reneging on debts was a typical Polish trait.) Through his musical connections, he worked to get a publisher for his former music teacher at the Warsaw Conservatory, sought theatrical engagements for visiting Polish dancers, traveled to Rouen to perform in a benefit concert for an old conservatory classmate, and accepted indigent emigrés as pupils for whatever they could pay him.

During his liaison with George Sand, Chopin managed to interest her in Polish culture, especially its literary aspects. On their return from Majorca in 1839, she became absorbed in the works of the Polish-Lithuanian poet Adam Mickiewicz and wrote an essay for the *Revue des Deux Mondes* comparing him with Byron and Goethe. This, in Chopin's words, was "a great boon to the French intelligentsia as well as to Mickiewicz's finances."[24] The following year, Alexander Chodźko, a friend of Chopin's who taught Oriental studies at the Collège de France, arranged for Mickiewicz's appointment to the school's new chair of Slavonic literature. Naturally Sand was anxious to attend his lectures and encouraged Chopin to accompany her.

Although Chopin appreciated Mickiewicz's poems enough to set several of them to music, he had little enthusiasm for the poet's lectures, which combined a militant mysticism with a penchant for socialism and revolution. The great difference in the two men's temperaments kept them from ever being close friends. Apart from Chopin's music, Mickiewicz had little respect for the composer, whom he saw as a passive, parasitical individual, a "moral vampire" who had become Sand's "evil genius" and would eventually destroy her.[25]

The focal point of the course that Mickiewicz conducted at the Collège de France from 1840 to 1844 was his messianic vision of Poland as the Christ of nations, destined to suffer and die for the political and social redemption of the rest of the world. This theme was to be taken up by most of the Polish poets of that era. Although Lithuanian by birth, Mickiewicz grew up in a cultural environment that was Polish and began formulating his concept of Poland's messianic role in history well before the November uprising of 1830 (fig. 2.12). In 1823 he was a member of a liberal anti-Russian group of university students who regarded Poland as a victim of czarist tyranny. At that time he started work on a long poetic drama entitled *Dziady* (Forefathers' eve), which dealt with the Polish tradition of a communion between the living and the dead on All Souls' Day. In it he prophesied the coming of a great man who would lift Poland up and guide it toward "the Way, the Truth and the Light." In short the latter was to be a messiah who would deliver not only the Poles but all oppressed peoples from their suffering. This messianic vision was a grandiose concept, at once a luminous revelation and a shadowy enigma. As such it appealed to the Romantic mood of the times that perceived Poland—on the misty reaches of eastern Europe—as a land shrouded in Oriental exoticism and peopled by a race of Tartars whose ancestors rode across the steppes of Asia with Genghis Khan and Tamerlane. For the Polish emigrés themselves, the notion of a messianic mission sustained their faith in a better world to come and helped them endure the deprivation and loneliness of exile. In his poetic masterpiece *Pan Tadeusz*, Mickiewicz expresses the great sense of desolation felt by those driven from their homeland: "My country, thou art like good health; I never knew till now how I yearn for thee."[26]

Like Chopin's music, the spiritual concept of Polish messianism brought solace to many of the emigrés. At the same time, it served as a stimulus to others like Mickiewicz, who felt that the fulfillment of Poland's divine role as the savior of humanity demanded the effort of every one of its sons. Far from being a privilege

2.12 Adam Mickiewicz, of Polish-Lithuanian descent, is generally considered the nineteenth century's greatest poet in the Polish language. During the 1830s and 1840s when he lived in Paris, he was in frequent contact with Chopin and George Sand. Although he and Sand formed a mutual admiration society based on their common literary and political interests, a state of antagonism, bordering on animosity, existed between Chopin and the poet. (Courtesy of Dr. Janusz Cizek)

restricted to the rich and aristocratic classes, it was a calling bestowed on the poor and humble as well. Along with young radicals like Lelewel and Mochnacki, Mickiewicz felt that the failure of the Warsaw uprising had been due to the refusal of the nobility and the landed gentry to recruit the help of the peasantry. This, he claimed, was contrary to the innately egalitarian spirit of the Polish nation, which had a tradition of electing its kings rather than submitting to the despotism of a hereditary dynasty. "The Pole is a natural democrat and Republican," he wrote.[27] With such views it was inevitable that he should side with the liberal "Red" emigrés rather than the aristocratic "Whites" of the Hôtel Lambert.

Strangely enough, Mickiewicz, this champion of liberty, had been drawn to France by his great admiration for its autocratic emperor, Napoléon. This seeming paradox stemmed from the Pole's belief in the spiritual influence of the dead on the living. Because Napoléon had freed the Poles from foreign subjugation in 1807 (by establishing the duchy of Warsaw), Mickiewicz came to regard his spirit as one of liberation. In his eyes, the ambitious Corsican appeared to be a divinely inspired leader whom God had bestowed on the French. This, he felt, made France worthy of being included in his messianic vision as the "Sword of Action" to Poland's "Shield of Faith." In time, though, Mickiewicz became disillusioned with France and complained bitterly that Lamennais had been "the only Frenchman who has sincerely wept for us."[28] Yet even after he lost his faith in France, he retained his trust in the watchful care of Napoléon's spirit over the Poles.

In December 1840 Mickiewicz had a vision of a stranger coming to him in a cart from Lithuania. This unknown man, he concluded, was the bearer of Napoléon's spirit, destined to bring salvation to Poland and all mankind. Not long afterward, when he had brought his wife home from an asylum following one of her mental breakdowns, the man in his vision appeared on the doorstep of their house in Paris. He was Andzej Towiański, a member of Lithuania's lesser nobility and a mystic devoted to the teachings of Saint Martin and Emanuel Swedenborg. After reading their works, Towiański felt called to bring spiritual regeneration first to the Poles and later, through them, to the rest of the world. Earlier in life he had conceived an intense adulation of Napoléon, whom he now pictured on the right hand of God, seeking once again to conquer the world, albeit this time in a spiritual rather than military fashion. En route to Paris, Towiański stopped to visit many of the sites of Napoléon's victories, reaching the city only days before the interment of his hero's remains in the Invalides. Like Mickiewicz, he too was subject to visions and had recently abandoned his wife and children after a dream in which he saw a lady with a white glove pointing toward France. Although Towiański himself was not Jewish, his quasi-religious philosophy was heavily influenced by the mysteries of the Jewish cabala, and he predicted that the ultimate salvation of humanity would be brought about by three new "Israels" composed of the Jews, the French, and the Slavs.

Certainly there was an obvious parallel between the ancient diaspora of the Jews and the recent dispersion of the Poles in 1831. Both peoples shared the conviction that their suffering was a prelude to the coming of a savior. Perhaps it was this correlation of Jewish and Polish themes in Towiański's message that intrigued Mickiewicz, whose wife was a baptized Jew and belonged to a Judeo-Christian sect known as the Frankists. Its founder, Jacob Frank (1726–91), was a Jewish spice merchant's apprentice who decided, during a trip to the Middle East, that he had a higher calling in life: that of the world's long-awaited messiah. Soon he gathered together a number of adherents over whom he exerted a charismatic, almost hypnotic influence. At their meetings, the Frankists often disrobed and indulged in orgiastic rites as a means of seeking out the "nakedness of truth." Both the Christian and Jewish communities of Poland condemned Frank's messianic claims and accused his followers of not only sexual license, but idolatry and witchcraft as well. Fearful of their wrath, Frank fled to Turkey, where he converted briefly to Islam.

Soon, however, he returned to Poland and founded a commune for his disciples, which included his own personal harem of twelve "consorts."

As his little band grew, Frank petitioned the Polish king, Friedrich Augustus III (a half-brother of George Sand's great-grandfather, Maurice de Saxe), to grant him a large fiefdom in east Galicia for his colony. To assure the king's coopération, he promised that his followers would convert en masse to Christianity. Once the request was granted, Friedrich Augustus demanded that all the members of Frank's sect be baptized as they had agreed. At this point, Frank ordered his followers to submit as a matter of form while secretly retaining their Jewish faith. He also prohibited them from intermarrying with gentiles for the next one hundred years. In 1759 Frank himself was baptized, with Friedrich-Augustus III named as his godfather. Following this he was elevated to the peerage and given the title of baron Frank-Dobruszki. Among others baptized then was Schlomo Schnorr (christened Luke Franciszek Wołowski), the great-grandfather of Celina Mickiewicz. In light of Frank's decree that none of his disciples marry gentiles until 1859 or later, it seems unlikely that Celina's family (who were devout Frankists) would have permitted her marriage to Mickiewicz unless they thought he was of Jewish descent, even though he had been raised a Catholic.

Although Celina seemed to have had no qualms about the marriage, Mickiewicz showed little enthusiasm for it. Perhaps he already knew of Celina's mental instability or, as some have claimed, he had once been the lover of Celina's mother, Maria Szymanowska (an outstanding pianist greatly admired by Chopin). Were such rumors true, then either guilt feelings or a lingering affection for Mme Szymanowska might have dampened Mickiewicz's ardor for her daughter.

Considering Celina's (and possibly Mickiewicz's) Frankist backgrounds, it is no wonder that they quickly fell under Towiański's spell. Not long after the mystic arrived in Paris, he gave a sermon to the Polish colony redolent with the messianism that Frank himself had preached. Under the towering nave of Notre-Dame, he announced, "You are the first to be called to take part in this great Work of God's Mercy, a Work devoted to the deliverance and spiritual progress of mankind."[29] "Poland," he continued, "is the keystone in God's Design which is unfolding for the salvation of the world."[30] Mesmerized by his oratory, Mickiewicz readily accepted Towiański's offer to cure his wife. This the Lithuanian mystic accomplished by whispering some words in her ear, after which she dropped to her knees and reached out to kiss her husband and children. Towiański then spoke to her alone for half an hour. From then on she had no further breakdowns. At this point Mickiewicz began to call Towiański "master," and in May 1842 he escorted him to the Tuileries for an audience with Louis-Philippe. Meanwhile some in the Polish colony began to suspect Towiański of being a Russian agent. A few months later, he was jailed and deported for prophesying the death of the duc d'Orléans, which later took place near his home on the very day Towiański was arrested.

In the years that followed, the mystic's influence over Mickiewicz gradually waned, and his one-time disciple embarked on a new phase of his life. During this period Mickiewicz abandoned his poetry ("Perish, my songs; arise, my actions," he proclaimed) and began to formulate the religious and political goals that he would pursue for the rest of his life.[31] In his lectures at the Collège de France from 1840 to 1844, Mickiewicz expressed his great reverence for Napoléon's political and military genius and his growing conviction that militant actions as well as mystical visions were necessary if Poland's messianic role as the savior of nations was to become a reality. The dreamer was turning into an activist who no longer shunned the use of force that had proved so effective in the hands of radical socialists and revolutionaries like the Carbonari. After all, weren't his goals the same as theirs? Weren't they both striving for the liberation of the oppressed? This unexpected transformation of the poet into a fiery freedom fighter alarmed Louis-Philippe, who had recently jailed Napoléon's nephew for twice attempting to overthrow his regime. In 1844 the Orleanist government dismissed Mickiewicz from the Collège de France on the grounds that his teachings were inflammatory and seditious. This failed to silence him, however, and four years later when Louis-Philippe was routed from his throne, Mickiewicz founded a Republican journal, *La Tribune des Peuples*, with such radical contributors as the Russian anarchist Mikhail Bakunin and the Italian revolutionary Guiseppe Mazzini—both of whom happened to be in correspondence with George Sand. In his last years, Mickiewicz busied himself with the cause of freedom in Italy and Turkey, where he organized Polish legions to fight against the Austrians and the Russians. He died in 1855 during the Crimean War after having failed to establish a Jewish legion in Turkey.

Among other emigré poets who preached the theme of Polish messianism were Juliusz Słowacki (1809–49) and Zygmunt Krasiński (1812–59), who, together with Mickiewicz, make up the "Prophetic Trinity" of Polish poetry. Słowacki, "the epitome of a melancholy Romantic," was a sickly, introverted dreamer who bitterly resented Mickiewicz's physical strength and poetic gifts

2.13 One of the triumvirate of great Polish Romantic poets, Juliusz Słowacki was a morbid, introspective individual, given to delusional fantasies toward the end of his life. At one time he and Chopin had been in love with the same girl, Maria Wodzińska, who spurned them both. Although the two men had some social contact in Paris during the early years of their exile, Słowacki later accused Chopin of being a peacock, to which the musician responded by calling the poet a numskull. (Courtesy of Dr. Janusz Cizek)

(fig. 2.13).[32] Consumed with a desire to outstrip his rival, he often failed to recognize his own unique talent; his poem, *In Switzerland,* is considered by many critics to be "the supreme love poem in the Polish language."[33] It was inspired by Maria Wodzińska, with whom Chopin had an unhappy love affair. Although Słowacki became a recluse in later life, he mingled socially with his fellow Poles during the early years of their exile in Paris and once recalled a boring evening at some friends that was finally livened up when Chopin got drunk and began to improvise at the piano. Despite his enjoyment of Chopin's playing, Słowacki was critical of the composer for "wasting his talent 'caressing the nerves of the French aristocracy' instead of sowing rebellion with his music."[34]

Like Mickiewicz, Słowacki fell under the influence of Towiański; two of his greatest works, *The Genesis of the Spirit* and *The King Spirit,* bear evidence of the Lithuanian mystic's messianic beliefs. Poland, for Słowacki, was a distilled incarnation of all the suffering it had endured. Because of this, it was destined to become the "King Spirit," or savior of the universe, capable of transforming mortals into transcendent beings equal to the angels on high. So deeply did Słowacki immerse himself in this mystical milieu that his fragile psyche began to take on a Christ complex. During a trip to the Holy Land, he once spent a whole night in the savior's sepulchre, where he envisioned himself redeeming humanity through his own self-sacrifice. "Transfigured" by his contact with Towiański, Słowacki gradually withdrew from society and, at the time of his death, firmly believed himself to be a prophet. Both he and Chopin were to die of tuberculosis in the same year, 1849.

The third member of the nineteenth-century triumverate of Polish poets, Zygmunt Krasiński (1812–59), was the son of one of Napoléon's Polish generals and a Radziwiłł princess. Perhaps the most cosmopolitan of this poetic trinity, Krasiński was also the most pessimistic in his view of Poland's future—mainly because he felt that the generation to which he belonged lacked any real determination and moral strength. His own weak constitution probably enhanced the sense of defeatism that pervaded his outlook. In contrast to his frail physique, however, Krasiński possessed a remarkably robust libido. Among his many "heavenly angels" (as he called his mistresses) was Chopin's friend and pupil Delfina Potocka. His rich and aristocratic wife, Eliza Branicka, was also a friend of Chopin's and the sister of another of his pupils, Countess Katarzyna Branicka. In Krasiński's major work, the apocalyptic *Non-Divine Comedy,* he portrays a cataclysmic conflict between a weak and decadent aristocracy and the proletariat of the future. To his despair, he foresaw the victory of the proletariat and the triumph of socialism, which he predicted would lead to the eventual disintegration of all civilized society and a complete loss of individual freedom. Amazingly he prophesied a Russian empire remarkably like that created by the Bolsheviks in 1917.

Chopin, who seems to have had little concern and less comprehension of such complex philosophical arguments, never felt any real affinity with these three poetic giants of his time. More compatible with his own personal lyricism were the poets Stefan Witwicki and the "Ukrainian nightingale" Józef Bohdan Zaleski, both of whom were companions of his youth from Warsaw.[35] Until his death in 1847, Witwicki retained close ties with Chopin, whom he saw frequently in Paris. On several occasions, he even endured the tiring journey to Sand's chateau for the sake of the musician's company. In the case of Zaleski, Chopin's longstanding attachment was further strengthened when the poet married one of his Polish pupils, Zofia Rozengardt, in 1845. As a wedding gift for them, he wrote his only known religious piece, a "Veni Creator" (never published) for choir and organ. Although the bond between Chopin and the Zaleskis seems to have been cordial, it fell short of genuine camaraderie—perhaps because Mme Zaleska found her teacher a touchy and temperamental person, difficult to get along with. She had come to study with him when she was only nineteen years old. Still very much under the bourgeois influence of her parents, who ran a restaurant in Warsaw, the naive girl was put off by Chopin's icy sophistication.

> You cannot imagine a person who can be colder and more indifferent to everything around him. There is a strange mixture in his character: vain and proud, loving luxury and yet disinterested and incapable of sacrificing the smallest part of his own will or caprice for all the luxury in the world. He is polite to excess, and yet there is so much irony, so much spite hidden inside it. Woe betide the person who allows himself to be taken in. He has an extraordinarily keen eye, and will catch the smallest absurdity and mock it wonderfully. He is heavily endowed with wit and common sense, but then he often has wild, unpleasant moments when he is evil and angry, when he breaks chairs and stamps his feet. He can be as petulant as a spoiled child, bullying his pupils and being very cold with his friends. Those are usually days of suffering, physical exhaustion or quarrels with Madame Sand.[36]

The fact that Witwicki and Zaleski didn't mount the pulpit of Polish messianism and utter thundering pronouncements about impending doom or millennial bliss was a relief to Chopin. Little by little the tone of moral superiority among those who preached Poland's Christ-like role in history was beginning to irritate many Frenchmen once sympathetic to the Polish cause. Indeed, the Romantic concept of Polish messianism seemed increasingly irrelevant to an industrialized society searching for a more practical and immediate solution to the socioeconomic disruptions confronting it. For the Polish "Reds," this solution had come to mean participation on an international level in the class conflicts destined to supplant the petty, outdated political feuds of national and ethnic groups. This was to be the militant message of Sand's "Father Communism," which the "Reds" were quick to embrace. Soon they would be joined by a number of the "Whites," including men like General Bem who began to collaborate with Russian revolutionary groups. On November 29, 1847, Marx and Engels attended a Paris meeting of Polish workers celebrating the anniversary of the 1830 Warsaw uprising. By then even Czartoryski was beginning to abandon his conciliatory efforts and encourage uprisings of Poles in Cracow, Posnania, and Galicia. Later he would urge his countrymen to join the fight for Italian independence against Austria, a longtime foe of Poland.

By 1848, with revolutions erupting all over Europe, the Poles felt their day had come. On March 10, the French provisional government formed a Polish revolutionary legion. The group was created ostensibly to liberate the Poles from Russian domination, although some claimed its real purpose was get the worst hotheads out of France and allow the new provisional government time to stabilize itself. As the acknowledged head of that government, Alphonse-Marie-Louis Lamartine notified Russia, Prussia, and Austria that the current status of Poland jeopardized their relations with the new French republic. He refused to declare war on Russia, though, a move that pushed many of the emigrés into the radical camp. On May 15, during a discussion of the Polish problem in the National Assembly, a mob invaded the Chamber, declared the assembly dissolved, and announced a new socialist-dominated government. Their attempted coup was quickly suppressed, but few Poles now had any faith in the Hôtel Lambert's ability to reestablish a kingdom of Poland through diplomatic channels. At this point most preferred a republic to a constitutional monarchy anyway. With the growing conviction that only a general overthrow of the old order in Europe could ensure Poland's liberation, more and more of the Poles flung themselves willy-nilly into the latest of the ubiquitous revolutions that consumed the European continent that year. In Sardinia, Hungary, and Lombardy they fought against the Austrians; in Sicily, against the King of Naples; and in Transylvania and Turkey, against the czar of Russia.

Alarmed by the defection of so many Polish Whites to the Red cause, Lamartine accused the emigrés of fomenting "turbulence and anarchy" and denounced them as the most dangerous of all foreigners in Paris.[37] This remark was to cost him their support in the first presidential elections of the new republic, held that December. Instead the Poles rallied around his rival, Louis-Napoléon, who won by an overwhelming margin. For the most part the emigrés welcomed the new president. But those who expected him to follow in the footsteps of his uncle and befriend their cause were soon disappointed. Not until the end of World War I was Poland finally restored to the map of Europe, ironically under the leadership of a musical heir to Chopin, the great pianist and composer Ignace Jan Paderewski.

From Citizen-King to Prince-President

France as a "Bourgeois-cracy"

*W*HEN CHOPIN CROSSED INTO FRANCE FROM STUTTGART in the fall of 1831, he passed through the Vosges region, where his father was born and where the Chopin family had lived for generations. His grandfather, François, had been a wheelwright and later a wine grower in the village of Marainville. There he and his wife raised three children—a son, Nicolas, who was to be the father of Frédéric, and two daughters. In 1787, Nicolas, at the age of sixteen, immigrated to Poland, where he remained for the rest of his life. Subsequently he lost all contact with the family he left behind, possibly because turbulent events in France and Poland impaired communications or perhaps because he preferred to forget his peasant origins once he had risen to the more prestigious ranks of tutor and professor in his adopted country. Whatever the reason, his son Frédéric seemed unaware that his journey to Paris had taken him within a few miles of his two aunts, Anne (Mme Joseph Thomas) and Marguerite (Mme Nicolas Bastien). Both were to die in 1845 without ever having met their famous nephew.

In all probability, the twenty-one-year-old musician was also unaware of the political instability of the nation he had just entered. As Chopin neared Paris, he was to encounter a city still reeling from the previous year's revolution. Thanks to the influence of General Lafayette, for whom most Frenchmen had the utmost respect, the nation came to be governed by an insecure Bourbon prince, Louis-Philippe, duc d'Orléans, a man thoroughly distrusted throughout the courts of Europe.

Ironically the July monarchy was able to survive the hostile forces that opposed it thanks to the uprising of Chopin's countrymen against their Russian oppressors in November 1830. At that time Czar Nicholas had massed troops along the western border of Poland with the intention of marching on France to overthrow Louis-Philippe and restore the Bourbons to their "legitimate" throne.

Fate, however, was marching to a different drummer, which decreed that Warsaw should fall to the Russians, while Paris was spared to become a refuge for many Polish exiles in the years that followed.

"THE BEST OF ALL REPUBLICS"

The French revolution of 1830 was to bring Louis-Philippe power but not popularity. He rose to the throne "in three days over barricades and broken pavements," just as he was to fall from it eighteen years later—again "in three days over barricades and broken pavements." Louis-Philippe was, in fact, known as the "king of the barricades" to his fellow monarchs, who considered him an interloper without any claim to legitimacy. Although his predecessor, Charles X, still believed in the divine right of kings, most postrevolutionary Frenchmen had abandoned this notion as an anachronism in their time. By 1830, men like General Lafayette and Alexis de Tocqueville had become staunch advocates of the republican form of government as practiced in the new United States of America. They had serious doubts, however, about the ability of their countrymen to accept a democratic system so at odds with the hierarchical structure of French society in the nineteenth century. For this reason Lafayette abandoned his dream of a republican France after the fall of Charles X and proposed instead a constitutional monarchy in which the duc d'Orléans would be placed on "a throne surrounded by republican traditions."[1] But many who had manned the barricades in the recent struggle envisioned a return to the democratic principles of 1789. For them another constitutional monarchy represented a negation of all they had fought for. To allay their fears, Lafayette assured them that with Louis-Philippe as their new king, France would prove to be "the best of all republics." Then, in a dramatic scene on the balcony of the Hôtel de Ville, he embraced the future monarch before a large crowd assembled below. Amid an ecstatic outburst of "Vive le duc d'Orléans" and "Vive le Général Lafayette," the July monarchy was born.

On August 9, in a simple ceremony at the Palais Bourbon, the former duc d'Orléans became "King of the French" (rather than "King of France"), a title he chose to emphasize the bond between himself and his subjects. Later he liked to boast that the legitimacy of his throne was derived from "the people" when, in fact, it had been handed to him by an aristocratic general—with a reluctant nod from the working classes, who bore the brunt of the glorious three-day revolution. Lafayette's compromise succeeded because the nation's dominant middle class, fed up with the Bourbons and frightened by the Republicans, found Louis-

Philippe an acceptable combination of royal renegade and lukewarm liberal. If few Frenchmen objected, few were pleased.

In acquiescing to Lafayette's "best of all republics," the French had in fact merely agreed to disagree. Once the barricades were taken down and a semblance of order restored, the political squabbling began. England was the first state to recognize the new government, while the absolute monarchies of Russia, Prussia, and Austria delayed their approval for some time. Ironically, of all the nations in Europe, France itself was the only one that never really endorsed the new regime.

"TO REIGN VS. TO RULE"

At the time of the 1830 revolution, there were four main political factions in France: the Legitimists (also known as Royalists or Carlists), who supported the deposed Bourbon dynasty and wore black ribbons in their gray hats; the Bonapartists, who hoped to see Napoléon's son, the duc de Reichstadt, occupy the throne some day and sported red flowers in their buttonholes; the Orleanists, or *juste-milieu,* who supported Louis-Philippe (with varying degrees of enthusiasm) and appeared, like the king, in dark-colored frock coats or a National Guard uniform; and finally the Republicans, who wore white vests, coats with wide lapels, and round hats called *bousingots,* which were shaped like a truncated cone and decorated with a tricolor cockade.

Of these four groups, the least organized were the Bonapartists, many of whose members finally threw in their lot with the Orleanists. The Legitimists and Republicans, on the other hand, retained a strong animosity toward the July monarchy. The Legitimists refused the king and queen their titles, referring to them simply as M. Philippe and Mme Amélie. One particularly bellicose Carlist, M. Berryer, even tried to run the royal couple down with his cabriolet as they strolled near the Arc du Carrousel. Although he failed, he received a hero's welcome in the salons of Saint-Germain. The Republicans (drawn from a broad spectrum of society) were divided into the moderates, who were content to pursue their goals within the framework of the new monarchy, and the extremists, who by 1848 had become either socialists or disciples of the new "communism." Most of the seven assassination attempts on Louis-Philippe during his reign were instigated by agitators from extremist Republican groups.

Soon after the July Days, the Orleanists split into a right wing led by François Guizot and Casimir Périer and a left wing under the leadership of the banker

Jacques Laffitte and the marquis de Lafayette. For the next ten years, this two-party system created a state of political flux in France: seventeen cabinets succeeded one another rapidly, with each lasting an average of about seven months. Even Chopin, who generally distanced himself from politics, quickly sensed the precarious state of the Orleanist government and described the new king as "that fool whose regime just hangs in there by a mere thread."[2] Not until the Soult-Guizot government, organized in October 1840, did the country experience any significant political continuity. By then Louis-Philippe, who had grown increasingly conservative, finally found a minister with whom he could get along: François Guizot, a Protestant professor and historian with considerable intellect but little humor. For eight years Guizot was the effective head of government, while the old Napoleonic general Soult remained its official prime minister. This arrangement pleased the king, but prompted his astute queen to warn him that Guizot was "a crab with tenacious claws which cling fast to the rock of power. One will never get rid of him without getting rid of the rock."[3]

At the beginning of his reign, Louis-Philippe felt constrained to adopt a liberal image in deference to those who had brought him to power. Accordingly he chose Laffitte to head his first cabinet and made Lafayette commander-in-chief of the National Guard. By March 1831, Laffitte fell because of his inability to control the rioting of Republican rebels. He was succeeded by the more conservative Casimir Périer, a man every bit as determined to rule as the king himself. Almost immediately Louis-Philippe locked horns with his new prime minister, who in turn locked him out of the council chamber. Only when Périer died in the cholera epidemic of 1832 did Louis-Philippe regain full control of the government.

In June of that year more riots instigated by the Republicans pushed the king further to the right, in the direction already taken by Périer. On the whole, though, 1832 proved to be a good year for the Orleanist regime. With the death of the duc de Reichstadt and the successful suppression of the duchesse de Berri's attempt to place her son, Henri V, on the throne, the Bonapartist and Legitimist causes suffered severe setbacks. Only the Republicans still posed any real threat to Louis-Philippe's survival.

Périer's successor, the pliable General Soult, allowed the king significant latitude in pursuing a course he now called "conservative liberalism," which was designed primarily to benefit the aristocracy and the rich bourgeoisie. By 1834 many liberal-minded Frenchmen who once had supported the Orleanist regime began to voice their discontent. When the government reacted by tightening restrictions on the right of free assembly, riots broke out among the working classes in Lyon and Paris. Young revolutionaries gathered outside the iron grill of the Tuileries, brandishing knives and hurling threats at the royal family.

The following year Giuseppe Maria Fieschi's attempt to assassinate the king led to further repressive measures. Among these were the so-called September Laws, enacted to stifle the press, whose attacks on the king and his ministers were blamed for stirring up the public. Liberals like Alphonse-Marie-Louis de Prat Lamartine and Pierre-Paul Royer-Collard felt the government's reaction was excessive, but outside of France it greatly enhanced Louis-Philippe's image. "I always thought he [Louis-Philippe] was a mischief-maker," wrote the Austrian chancellor Prince Metternich, "but now I see that he is indeed a king."[4]

From the distance of Vienna, Louis-Philippe may have appeared kingly enough, but at home he found himself in another power struggle with his latest prime minister, the rigid and authoritarian Achille-Charles-Léonce de Broglie. When the opportunity came to dismiss him in February 1836, Louis-Philippe welcomed in his place the young and enthusiastic Adolphe Thiers, a man whose intense ambition made him seem a willing pawn for the king's political ends (fig. 3.1). One of Thiers's first objectives in office was to make a suitable marriage for the heir to the throne, the duc d'Orléans. He was to fail, however, because Europe's monarchs remained distrustful of the upstart Orleanist regime. To improve French prestige and regain the military glory that the nation had enjoyed under his late hero, Napoléon, Thiers tried to involve France in Spain's civil war as an ally of the beleaguered Queen Isabella. Had he succeeded, Chopin and George Sand might well have found a better reception among the Majorcans on their journey there in 1838–39. Louis-Philippe, however, would have no part of such war-mongering and forced the prime minister's resignation. Angry and frustrated, Thiers swung toward the political left and adopted as his motto, "The king reigns but does not rule."

The subsequent marriage of the duc d'Orléans to the Princesse Hélène of Mecklenberg-Schwerin in May 1837 was an auspicious event for the Orleanist family and excited great furor in Paris. "All over the city," Chopin wrote, "there are nothing but parties, balls and banquets.... The new princess delights every-one. She is praised not only for her beauty but her good sense."[5] When she gave birth to a son the following year the future of the dynasty seemed secure, but the present continued to bring new challenges to Louis-Philippe's authority.

In March 1839 the mercurial Thiers returned to plague him. Bellicose as ever,

3.1 The fiery and impetuous Adolphe Thiers was the prime minister whom Louis-Philippe feared and detested above all others. His liberal policies alienated members of the ancien régime aristocracy as well. As the comte de Castellane observed, "He has nothing ... to compensate for his unattractive face and his glasses" (Castellane, *Journal*, 3:114). Besides being a politician, Thiers was a highly respected historian. At Nohant during the summer of 1845, Chopin kept a volume of his works on his desk (probably Thiers's history of the French Revolution).

the aggressive prime minister tried again to drag Louis-Philippe into war, this time against the sultan of the Ottoman Empire, who was being attacked by the pasha of Egypt, Mehemet Ali (donor of the obelisk in the place de la Concorde). His policy was to put France in conflict with Russia, England, Austria, and Prussia, who backed the sultan. In anticipation of an attack by these allied forces, Thiers began to erect fortifications around the perimeter of Paris. Shortly afterward, another attempt on Louis-Philippe's life in September of that year convinced the king that he had more to fear from within than without. Neither he nor France was in a mood for war, and on October 29, Thiers resigned once more, disgusted with the monarch whose pacifism he derided as "Crowned Inertia."

This final departure of Thiers marked the beginning of a prolonged period of political harmony, when France was to prosper under the leadership of Guizot, a man very similar in outlook to the king (fig. 3.2). For once Louis-Philippe was content to let his prime minister rule, knowing that he would act in a manner consistent with his own policies. Both men found a common ground in their authoritarian view of government. For Guizot there were two things indispensable in managing a nation: reason and the cannon. Little in his outward demeanor, though, suggested the man of iron within. "Thin and pale, with an emaciated-looking face and a finely-drawn mouth, Guizot had eyes veiled with sadness."[6] He also had a rich powerful speaking voice that made the actress Rachel long to have him as a leading man in one of her tragedies. Under Guizot, the Middle Eastern conflict was resolved, and France had hopes of resuming its position in the European family of nations.

3.2 The scholarly, arch-conservative François Guizot was Louis-Philippe's most valued prime minister, even though his policies were to cause the fall of the July monarchy in 1848. At that time, Guizot followed the king in his flight to London. During the Easter season of that year, Chopin visited the exiled prime minister in his new English home.

During the "peace and abundance" of the Guizot years, the streets of Paris remained virtually free of barricades, and there were only two attempts on the king's life. One had to be myopic, however, not to detect the social and political discontent that was brewing in the wings of what Heine called this "bourgeois comedy." Sue, Hugo, and Sand voiced this discontent in their novels, and journalists filled their columns with it. Still the king and his prime minister, enthralled by the harmony of their relationship, remained oblivious to the fact that their days were numbered—either because of their own short-sightedness or because, as Balzac put it, the French were "too intelligent to let any government get firmly into the saddle."[7] Whatever the case, the fall of the July monarchy in 1848 came not from a minister who challenged the king's right to rule, but from the people who took away his right to reign.

"THE NAPOLÉON OF PEACE"

The populist image that Louis-Philippe tried to create among his subjects never fooled the rest of Europe, which still viewed him as a reckless firebrand intent on destabilizing the status quo sanctified by the Congress of Vienna in 1815. During his first years on the throne, the suspicion of other European leaders put the king in the ambiguous position of playing the bourgeois liberal at home and the Bourbon cousin abroad. To stay in power he had to pat the head of the French worker to whom he owed his crown, scratch the back of the French middle class who maintained him in power, and extend the myriad hands of a Tibetan deity to the hostile monarchs who threatened to unseat him. Except for England, where the Magna Carta had long since sown the seeds of constitutional monarchy, Europe was ruled by autocrats who regarded "the king of the barricades" as a serious menace to their authority. Nor did Louis-Philippe inspire much confidence among the French, who felt that the inconsistency of his domestic and international positions reflected a lack of integrity. In the end, the July monarch was to lose the trust of his subjects without ever having gained the respect of his fellow rulers.

Early in his reign, Louis-Philippe recognized the precariousness of his position both at home and abroad. As king of a nation beset by internal social and political dissension, he shunned any foreign entanglements until he could command a more unified support from the splenetic Frenchmen he was struggling to govern. Toward this end, he adopted a foreign policy designed to avoid confrontations with outside powers whenever possible. The bankers who supported him—Baron James de Rothschild, Alejandro María Aguado, and Baron Adolphe d'Eichthal— encouraged his pacifistic tendencies for fear that the outbreak of war would interrupt the intricate network of international channels through which their businesses operated. Louis-Philippe's conciliatory policy, moreover, was one particularly suited to the times when revolution rather than war posed a greater threat to many European rulers. The year 1830 was particularly rife with revolution: the French revolution in July, the Belgian rebellion against Dutch rule on August 25, and the Polish uprising against the Russian czar on November 30. Although the first of these had brought Louis-Philippe to power, he strove to distance himself from the other two. With Belgium, however, it was hard to avoid involvement, considering that it sat on the northern border of France and had a large French-speaking population. Charles-Maurice de Talleyrand-Périgord, who was ambassador to England at the time, called a five-power conference in London to discuss the situation. The debate lasted nearly three years, which gave the wily ambassador ample time to reflect on his course of action. (Being the consummate diplomat that he was, he had a horror of hasty decisions: never follow your first impulse, he once cautioned; it is invariably generous.)

Holland's invasion of Belgium in August 1831 finally pushed Louis-Philippe to send in troops. With the conquest of Antwerp that December, Belgium finally achieved its independence. Four months earlier Louis-Philippe's eldest daughter, Princesse Louise, had married the newly elected Belgian king, Leopold of Saxe-Coburg-Gotha, an uncle of Queen Victoria. By this shrewd bit of diplomacy, France's "citizen-king" had allied himself with both the thrones of Belgium and

England as well as the court of Saxe-Coburg-Gotha, one of the most prestigious marriage markets for European royalty of the time.

As for the Polish problem, Louis-Philippe tried his best to ignore it for fear of antagonizing the formidable Czar Nicholas I. The plight of the Poles, he claimed, was an internal problem of the Russian state. In December 1830 the czar ordered all Russians and Poles to leave France. Those who defied him, as Chopin did the following year, were subject to imprisonment if they ever returned to Russian-occupied territory. This decree, as well as Chopin's infatuation with Paris, deterred the Polish musician from ever going back to his native land— even when he was offered the post of court pianist at Saint Petersburg, which would have granted him immunity to any political reprisals. Subsequent attempts by the Italian states to throw off the Austrian yoke met with similar indifference from Louis-Philippe, as did Thiers's attempt to draw him into the Middle East crisis of 1840.

In 1844 French relations with England became severely strained when Mr. Pritchard, a Protestant missionary acting as British consul to the French protectorate of Tahiti, was arrested and expelled from the island for stirring up anti-French feeling. Briefly threats of war were hurled back and forth until both sides finally decided Mr. Pritchard wasn't worth all the fuss. In October of that year Louis-Philippe and his youngest son, the duc de Montpensier, visited their "dear cousins" Queen Victoria and Prince Albert, who gave them a most cordial reception. Besides finding the French king lively and sagacious, Victoria was delighted to learn that "He wishes Tahiti '*au fond de la mer* (to go to the bottom of the sea).'"[8]

Two years later, in 1846, the winds off the Channel had once more grown chilly as a result of the so-called Spanish marriages. At that time Louis-Philippe hoped to form an alliance with Spain by marrying the duc de Montpensier to the infanta Maria Luisa Fernanda, sister of the Spanish queen, Isabella II. This plan alarmed the English, who feared that Spain would fall under French domination should the still-single Isabella leave the throne to her sister. As a result, Queen Victoria demanded that the wedding be deferred until Isabella had married and produced an heir. When the young queen was later engaged to the effeminate duke of Cadiz, Louis-Philippe decided not to wait for an heir (which the presumably impotent duke could never sire); instead he arranged for both Isabella and her sister to be married in a joint ceremony on October 10, 1846.

The day after their double wedding, Chopin wrote his family that the French minister of public instruction, M. Salvandy, had sent Alexandre Dumas and others to record "the ceremonies of the two marriages and the events surrounding them."[9] "The young queen is quite fat," he added, repeating the gossip of the Parisian salons where everyone was "carrying on about the gifts the duc de Mont[pensier] was supposed to have given his bride."[10] Chopin's particular interest in the affair probably stemmed from his introduction to the Spanish queen's mother, Maria Cristina, when he played before her at the Tuileries five years earlier.

As might be expected, Louis-Philippe's scheme to place his descendants on the Spanish throne aroused the ire of Queen Victoria, who removed his portrait from Windsor. In the end, however, nobody went to war. After all, hot, arid Spain with its treasury depleted and its land decimated by the Carlist wars was— like Mr. Pritchard—simply not worth the fuss.

"THE RESPECT OF ASSASSINS"

To many of his subjects Louis-Philippe's pacifist policies deprived France of one of the most beloved elements of its national character: military glory. Not even the humiliating defeat at Waterloo could erase from their memories the power and prestige, the pomp and panoply of the Napoleonic empire. Louis-Philippe understood this and allowed the Bonapartists considerable freedom in pursuing their cult of the emperor. Worshipping the past, though, did nothing to enliven the present. The July monarch's legacy of "peace and abundance" failed to provide the exhilaration demanded by the volatile Gallic spirit. "France is intensely bored," Lamartine observed long before the revolution of 1848. He was not alone in foreseeing the great cataclysm that would eventually destroy the Orleanist regime. When it came about, most were less surprised by the suddenness of the regime's collapse than by the length of its survival.

From the beginning, Louis-Philippe's popular base was limited. His reign was marked by endless journalistic attacks, riots, and assassination attempts, which kept the nation's courts and prisons filled with anti-government offenders. In theory the king's adherents (the *juste-milieu* or Centrists) seemed the ideal party to deliver the "Liberty and Order" promised by the new regime since its middle-of-the-road position should have kept these two ideals from degenerating into leftist anarchy on the one hand or rightist repression on the other. But despite some success at first, anti-government demonstrations soon became an almost daily occurrence. In September 1831, for example, when news of the fall of Warsaw reached Paris, the rioting that followed had to be quelled by the army and the

National Guard. Chopin, who arrived in Paris shortly afterward, gave a first-hand account of the economic and political unrest in the city: "The lower classes are angry and ready to use whatever means necessary to escape their terrible poverty. Unfortunately the government keeps a close eye on them and the mounted police break up any gathering no matter how small."[11] To the beset monarch, it was beginning to appear as if the principles of liberty and order were mutually exclusive.

The year 1832 brought more plots against the king, one by Royalists, who planned to invade the Tuileries during a court ball, and another by conspirators operating out of the towers of Notre-Dame. In June bloody riots broke out at the funeral of the Republican General Lamarque; red flags fluttered in the breeze and a state of martial law was declared. When calm finally returned, eight hundred Parisians were dead or wounded and the Republican cause severely compromised. Later that year the death of Napoléon's son, the duke of Reichstadt, left the Bonapartists in disarray.

All this augured well for the July monarchy. Louis-Philippe seemed to have weathered the storm when on November 19, 1832, he was nearly struck down by an assassin's bullet on the Pont Royal, just outside the Tuileries. It was fired by a law student, Louis Bergeron, and became the first of seven attempts on his life.

In 1833 the only attacks made against the king were printed ones. Violence, however, erupted in April of the following year when the Italian Carbonaro, Giuseppe Mazzini, led a workers' revolt in Lyon. This triggered a sympathetic manifestation in Paris a few days later. Two thousand to three thousand of those involved in the Lyon and Paris riots were arrested, and approximately one hundred of them were brought to trial in May 1835. Despite the presence of troops to control disorders, fist fights broke out in the courtroom, and the legality of the trials was questioned by supporters of both the left and the right. Women were not allowed to attend the proceedings, although one of the "boys" in the visitors' gallery turned out to be George Sand, whose lover at the time, Michel de Bourges, was a lawyer for the defense (fig. 3.3).

Hardly had the uproar of this so-called monster trial died down than all Paris was stunned on July 28, 1835, by the second and most vicious of all the attempts on the king's life. During the celebration of the fifth anniversary of the July revolution, the Italian anarchist Joseph Fieschi and four accomplices opened fire on Louis-Philippe as he, his sons, and a number of government and military officials paraded down the boulevard du Temple. One of the bullets grazed the king's

3.3 The interior of the Chamber of Peers in the Luxembourg Palace. It was in the palace's Court of Peers that the "Monster" trial of anti-government workers was held in May 1835.

forehead, while his horse was struck in the neck. Altogether forty-two people were either killed or injured by Fieschi's notorious "infernal machine," a contraption that consisted of twenty-five rifles rigged to fire simultaneously. The king's courage during this ordeal won him the admiration of most Parisians and greatly increased his popularity. The ensuing September Laws of 1835, however, designed to weaken Republican opposition by restricting the press and theater, brought new protests. Following Fieschi's trial and execution, opportunists profited from the occasion by putting the assassin's one-eyed mistress on exhibition at the cashier's counter of a Paris restaurant, where the public paid a fee to view her.

In 1836 Louis-Philippe's carriage was fired on twice (in June and December) by assailants named Alibaud and Meunier, respectively. Both missed their mark, but the king was sufficiently unsettled to equip his future carriages with a cast iron lining. Although Alibaud was executed, Meunier's sentence was commuted to exile in the United States, where the royal family sent him financial support! With so much unrest in Paris that year, Louis-Napoléon's attempted coup in far-off Strasbourg on October 30 seemed comparatively harmless, and he too was dispatched to the United States on the promise that he would never return to France.

Following a period of relative calm, more Republican riots racked Paris in 1839 and 1840, when a fifth attempt on Louis-Philippe's life was undertaken by a worker named Darmès, who fired at his carriage on the quai des Tuileries.

Not until 1846, however, the year Louis-Napoléon escaped from Ham and a bad harvest plunged the nation into recession, did significant signs of unrest reappear. On April 16 a former *garde-général* of the forest of Fontainebleau, Pierre Lecomte, fired on the king there. Then, on July 29, a worker named Joseph Henry aimed an unsuccessful shot at the king while he stood on a balcony of the Tuileries during a commemoration of the July Days. In a game effort to make light of the situation, Louis-Philippe quipped that it always seemed to be open season on him. Later, though, he complained bitterly that he had never been respected during his reign except by assassins.[12]

"THE MAN BENEATH THE CROWN"

Strictly speaking, Louis-Philippe was never crowned; that is to say, he never went through a formal coronation like his predecessor, Charles X. It was only in a figurative sense that he accepted the crown before the Chamber of Deputies on August 9, 1830. None of his portraits show him wearing a crown, and on the rare occasion when a crown does appear, it rests on a table near him as if he were the protector rather than the possessor of it. For France's "citizen king," an umbrella took the place of a scepter, and a toupee that of a crown. What then, we might ask, was the nature of the man beneath the toupee?

Louis-Philippe, who came to the throne as a compromise, went through life as a contradiction. Born of royal blood, he was to represent the very quintessence of everything bourgeois. He looked "more like a shopkeeper from the Marais than a sovereign of a great country" and exhibited tastes that were ordinary and unimaginative.[13] If he were ever overthrown, Victor Hugo remarked, his natural tendencies would qualify him to take up the trade of a grocer. In de Tocqueville's words, he simply lacked grandeur: "He had no flaming passions, no ruinous weaknesses, no striking vices.... He was extremely polite, but without discrimination or greatness, the politeness of a merchant rather than a prince."[14] It was only fitting that his middle-class subjects should call him their "citizen king." To cater to their idealized image of family life, Louis-Philippe stationed himself at the head of the dinner table and hacked away at the roast rather than let servants carve it. Later, as he ate, he often paid little attention to those around him until the end of the meal when, in a burst of loquaciousness, he would regale the table with anecdotes and reminiscences. Only in conversation did he seem to rise above the prosaic. Many people found him charming, even witty. Chopin's friend, the critic and dramatist Ernest Legouvé, admired his ability to tell a good story and delighted in his sparkling banter. Others, like Talleyrand's niece the duchesse de Dino, found him garrulous and boring. He was "always talking and always of himself," she complained.[15]

If the king annoyed aristocrats like Mme de Dino, he pleased most of the bourgeoisie, who would walk up to him after a dinner and thank him as casually as if he were their next-door neighbor. This, in Hugo's opinion, might have been all well and good for a backwoods president like Andrew Jackson, but certainly not for the King of the French. Many Americans, in fact, had great respect for Louis-Philippe. William Rufus King, the United States ambassador to France in 1846, praised the July monarch as "every inch a king."[16] His predecessor, Ambassador Lewis Cass, was not only an admirer but an intimate of Louis-Philippe who invited him to the palace of Saint Cloud in the fall of 1839, where Chopin played for the royal party after dinner. Because of the admiration of these ambassadors (as well as Lafayette's endorsement of him in 1830), Louis-Philippe became a "universally popular figure" in the United States—so much so that many Americans sent him gifts, including barrels of flour, Texas diamonds, rifles, cheese, apples, nuts, and even a set of false teeth.[17] Others, however, mailed him bills for services they had rendered him during his years of exile in America.

By 1847, Ambassador King's replacement, Richard Rush, showed considerably less enthusiasm for the king than did his predecessors. The French themselves, he noted, had a "special distrust of Louis-Philippe. He was said to be hypocritical, crafty, forgetting all his great duties to the nation in exclusive devotion to the interest of his family and the perpetuation of his dynasty."[18]

Certainly the king had ample cause to defend the integrity of his lineage in the face of rumors that he was not a descendent of royalty at all but the son of a Tuscan jailer. Unlikely as it might seem, this story circulated widely and found acceptance among those who could not otherwise reconcile his pedestrian presence with a regal ancestry. According to gossip, Louis-Philippe's father, the duc d'Orléans, after four years of marriage and no heir, grew obsessed with having a son. When his firstborn proved to be a girl, he secretly exchanged her for the newborn son of a jailer, Lorenzo Chiappini, in the northern Italian town of Modigliani. The girl, Maria Stella, later married an English nobleman, Lord Newborough, and after his death, a Russian baron named Ungern-Sternberg. Not until a deathbed letter from Chiappini did Maria learn of her supposed identity and make an effort to assert her claims. When she arrived in Paris for this purpose, Louis-Philippe refused to see her, and after he became king he ordered her out of the country. In the absence of any serious inquiry into the matter, her story has generally been discredited.

During his youth, Louis-Philippe exhibited the confidence of wealth and social position. The uncertainties of life under the French Revolution's Reign of Terror and the hand-to-mouth existence of an emigré, however, left him with an underlying sense of insecurity. In later years his natural exuberance had to struggle against inner, almost paranoid fears. This was especially evident in the economic sphere, where no amount of riches could ever exorcise the ghost of his impoverished exile. Although a Catholic, Louis-Philippe always adhered to that tenet of the Protestant ethic that claimed riches to be a sign of divine favor.

This and other contradictions in the July monarch's personality were most apparent when it came to matters of morality. In him, for example, the protective paterfamilias existed side by side with the unscrupulous opportunist who would stab his Bourbon relatives in the back to gain their throne. The bravery of the man on the battlefield and in the face of assassin's bullets contrasted with the cowardice of the fallen monarch who left his own grandchildren to the mercy of the mob while he fled to safety in their carriage. As de Tocqueville wrote, "He was open only to what was useful...and...believed so little in virtue that his sight was darkened."[19]

Paradoxically, the autocratic bully who tried to dominate his ministers grew up under the control of two overbearing women who were to influence him throughout life: his authoritarian governess, Mme de Genlis, and his inseparable sister, Mme Adélaïde. It was these two women who gave Louis-Philippe his relentless determination—a characteristic that few would have suspected behind the easygoing facade of the corpulent monarch with an abdomen like a shelf. Hidden within his Pickwickian frame was an active and ambitious mind. Despite Mme de Genlis's assertion that he "was completely ignorant and had no intention of remedying this defect," Louis-Philippe was far from dumb—nor was he docile.[20] As his mother-in-law, Queen Maria Carolina of Naples, remarked:

"Louis-Philippe is a man who appears outwardly to be easily influenced. Inwardly he will always seek his own benefit."[21] Certainly the one thing he wanted most in life was the throne of France. Yet long after he had achieved that goal, he retained the habits of a courtier, continually currying the favor of his fellow monarchs, who tended to withhold their approval even when they granted him their recognition. "All of you treat me like a pariah and a revolutionary," he complained to the Austrian emperor's representative in Paris.[22]

Louis-Philippe also courted bankers like Laffitte, Aguado, and Rothschild, who were often the powers behind the thrones of Europe. If anything, he had more rapport with financiers than kings and understood the language of the Bourse better than that of the court. It is not surprising that historians have labeled his era the "Reign of Money" and that Louis-Philippe has come to typify the greed and selfishness of the era's bourgeois capitalists. According to a contemporary wit, he belonged to the parish of Notre-Dame de la Bourse, presided over by Bishop Rothschild. In a similar vein, Victor Cousin, a philosopher of the time, once ventured that if someone tossed a ten sou piece into the Seine, Louis-Philippe would be the first to jump in after it. And yet this acquisitive man spent liberally of his own fortune to build or restore many of the monumental landmarks of France.

Such inconsistencies of behavior, which are petty foibles in the common man, became magnified in a personality as complex as Louis-Philippe's. Unfortunately his inability to resolve them often created the appearance of vacillation or, worse yet, duplicity—hardly qualities to foster respect and popularity.

Even at the peak of public sympathy for him (just after Fieschi's attempt on his life), Louis-Philippe failed to inspire affection. The following portrait of an unloved sovereign was written by Colonel Raikes, a longtime resident and assiduous observer of Louis-Philippe's Paris: "No monarch is more unpopular, or indeed surrounded by more enemies. There is nothing truly great in the character of this man; he has physical courage without moral courage; cunning without great talents; some head but little heart; a boundless ambition without magnanimity, ... preferring always ... the crooked to the straight path; he has no pride, it would mar his projects; he has no private vices, they would interfere with business; but he has above all that insuperable bar to all noble feeling, an inordinate love of money, which no principle can check or hypocrisy disguise. ... He might have made a thriving tradesman, but can never become a glorious king."[23]

Contrary to the fanciful rumors of his birth, the future King of the French officially came into the world on October 6, 1773, a child of the Voltairean age of reason. Typical of the times, no one bothered to christen him until he was twelve, when Louis XVI and Marie-Antoinette served as his godparents. A descendant of Louis XIV's younger brother, Philippe, duc d'Orléans, he was a distant cousin of his predecessor, Charles X. His great-great grandfather had been regent of France during Louis XV's minority, while his father, Philippe "Egalité," sided with the Republicans in the revolution of 1789 and voted for the execution of Louis XVI. Later, "Egalité" himself fell under the guillotine during the Terror of 1793. For a time Louis-Philippe fought with the Republican armies before he realized that no one of aristocratic birth could escape the vengeance of the Jacobins. Fearing the worst, he fled the country and lived as a nomad for over twenty years in Belgium, Switzerland, the United States, Cuba, England, and the Kingdom of the Two Sicilies.

In November 1809, shortly after his thirty-sixth birthday, Louis-Philippe married Princess Marie-Amélie of Bourbon-Naples, a daughter of Ferdinand IV of Naples (fig. 3.4). Few members of European royalty at that time could rival the intensity of her religious fervor or the complexity of her dynastic connections. Through her Bourbon lineage, she was descended from Louis XIV's grandson, Philip V of Spain, which made her a cousin of her new husband. On her mother's side, she was a granddaughter of Maria Theresa of Austria. With both Hapsburg and Bourbon blood in her veins, Marie-Amélie held the title of a royal highness that in the protocol of Europe's courts gave her precedence over her husband (a mere serene highness) until his accession to the French throne. Among her aunts and uncles, she could number Queen Marie-Antoinette of France, Emperor Josef II of Austria, and King Carlos IV of Spain. Her niece, Marie Caroline, duchesse de Berri, was the mother of the Legitimist pretender to the French throne, and her first cousin, the duchesse d'Angoulême (a daughter of Louis XVI) was the dauphine of the Bourbon line. Napoléon's second wife, the empress Marie-Louise, was the daughter of her first cousin, the emperor Francis II of Austria, while Queen Isabella II of Spain was the daughter of another first cousin, King Ferdinand VII. Later, through her children's marriages, Marie-Amélie acquired numerous ties with the German branch of Queen Victoria's family. Such a convoluted web of hereditary and marital relationships was to create many painful moments in her personal life as the house of Orléans came into repeated conflict with her various royal and imperial relatives.

The greatest cross that Marie-Amélie had to bear during her marriage, however, was surely the presence of her domineering sister-in-law, Mme Adélaïde,

3.4 King Louis-Philippe and Queen Marie-Amélie (*top center* and *top right*) with their eight children and the king's inseparable sister, Mme Adélaïde (*top left*). Through the marriages of his children, Louis-Philippe was able to ally himself with the reigning families of Belgium, England, Brazil, Spain, the Kingdom of the Two Sicilies, and several of the smaller German states.

who wielded an inordinate influence over Louis-Philippe. When Mme Adélaïde spoke, she expected to be heard; when she was ignored, she fainted. Her masculine aggressiveness was matched by her masculine appearance, which she tried to soften with an excessive amount of make-up, "applying every color of the rainbow to her face."[24] Because of her ruddy complexion, she was suspected of being an alcoholic, while the intimacy of her relationship with the king fueled accusations of incest. Although we can probably dismiss such allegations as mere gossip, Mme Adélaïde was undoubtedly an iron-willed woman with an unshakable devotion to her brother.

In 1814, through the generosity of Louis XVIII who chose to forgive Louis-Philippe's Jacobin past, the duc and duchesse d'Orléans were allowed to settle in Paris at the Palais Royal, which had been for generations the residence of the Orléans family. Life there, however, was soon interrupted by the return of Napoléon during the "Hundred Days." When Louis XVIII fled France, Louis-Philippe was emboldened to announce that although he would never cause the crown to tumble from his cousin's head, he would not hesitate to pick it up if it were to fall. Later, in the course of the second Restoration, civility if not cordiality prevailed between the two families until the birth of the heir to the throne, the duc de Bordeaux, in 1820. He was the posthumous son of the murdered duc de Berri, a nephew of the childless Louis XVIII. Had the newborn been a girl, the throne would have passed to the Orléans line. Sorely disappointed by the infant's gender, Louis-Philippe and his sister challenged the legitimacy of the little boy in belligerent and insulting terms.[25] Surely Marie-Amélie must have cringed at their behavior since the baby was the grandson of her favorite brother, the duke of Salerno.

To escape the hubbub of the Palais Royal and the chilly decorum of the Tuileries, the Orléans family spent much of their time at the rambling Chateau de Neuilly, only fifteen minutes west of Paris (fig. 3.5). Once the property of Napoléon's sister, Caroline Murat, it consisted of a collection of one-story buildings with beautiful gardens and a park that extended to the Seine and included the island of La Grande Jatte (later immortalized in Georges Seurat's famous painting). Acres of hay fields and potato farms surrounded the unpretentious compound.

At the outbreak of the Three Glorious Days in July 1830, the duc and duchesse d'Orléans were relaxing in the peaceful precincts of their little chateau. Alarmed by the course of events, Louis-Philippe hid in a small pavilion on the property until he felt it safe to reenter Paris, where he was to fulfill his dream of picking up the crown that had fallen from his cousin's head.

3.5 The small, one-story Chateau de Neuilly, on the outskirts of Paris, was the favorite residence of the Orleanist monarch and his family. Its cluster of modest structures in a semi-rural setting offered an atmosphere of intimacy and informality. Earlier in the century the property had belonged to Napoléon's sister, Caroline Murat.

During the early months of the July monarchy, bedlam prevailed at the Palais Royal. Crowds of grimy workmen stationed themselves about the palace as self-appointed guardians, treating the royal family with an exuberant familiarity. Several times a day Louis-Philippe was expected to appear at a window and lead the mob in a lusty rendition of the Marseillaise. Such circumstances not only compromised the dignity of the new king, but interfered with his ability to govern. Nearby in the empty Tuileries he would soon find the security and privacy he sought. Although he didn't relish the "Chateau's" gloomy atmosphere and unpleasant associations, he finally moved there on October 16, 1831. Chopin, who arrived in Paris about that time, saw the Tuileries lit up for the first time in over a year. Seven years later, on February 16, 1838, he performed there before the royal family in the Salle des Spectacles, a combined theater and concert hall located just above the royal apartments on the ground floor. In gratitude, the king presented him with a lavish silver-gilt tea service. Later, in December 1841, he would again perform at the "Chateau" in the elegant quarters of the duc and

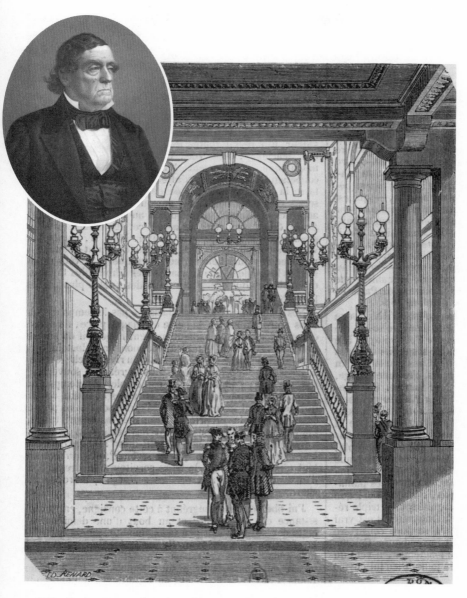

3.6 The grand staircase in the palace of Saint-Cloud with an inset of Lewis Cass, the American ambassador to France from 1836 to 1844. On October 29, 1839, Chopin and Ignace Moscheles played before the royal family and their guests at the palace of Saint-Cloud. Among the guests was Ambassador Cass, an avid Francophile who enjoyed a close rapport with Louis-Philippe.

duchesse d'Orléans, where it was de rigueur to converse in a whisper and exceedingly gauche to applaud the musicians. Although he was well received on this second occasion (the queen seemed particularly charmed by him), Chopin left in a rather grumpy mood—perhaps because his aristocratic friends in the faubourgs Saint-Germain and Saint-Honoré looked askance at his association with the usurper and his family (fig. 3.6).

During the July monarchy, it was the custom of the king and queen to give six balls a year, along with frequent concerts and gala dinners. Every other Sunday there was a reception at 8:00 in the evening. Guests usually included aristocrats, military officers, and a host of bourgeoisie, whose blue frock coats and white pants replaced the knee breeches and silk stockings of the prior regime. Much in evidence were the uniforms of the National Guardsmen, who always figured prominently on the Tuileries guest lists. Many of the guardsmen were tailors, grocers, and shopkeepers completely untutored in the art of conversation or table manners. To create a more egalitarian image, Louis-Philippe dispensed with the brilliant blue and silver livery of the Bourbons. Servants now wore black frock coats, which made them barely distinguishable from the guests in blue frock coats. Gone also were the elaborate toilettes of the Restoration ladies, now replaced by the simple bonnets and shawls worn by middle-class women of the period. Guests at these functions no longer approached the throne to be formally presented to the king and queen. Instead the royal couple strolled about accompanied by an attendant who asked each person his name (since most were unknown to their majesties). Colonel Raikes, who attended one of these "plebeian" receptions, sighed that the "days of courtly magnificence" were gone forever.[26]

At the end of such evenings, Louis-Philippe often retired to his rooms, where he would stay up until 1:00 or 2:00 in the morning, poring over dispatches, legislative bills, and other government matters. In general he slept six to seven hours a night, arising at 8:00 A.M. Often he would skip breakfast, preferring only two meals a day with frequent bowls of chicken broth to sustain him in the interim. Clothed only in a dressing gown, he liked to remain in his rooms until lunchtime, attending to correspondence and signing documents. Later in the day, he typically moved upstairs to the billiard room, which he used as an informal study and reception hall. There, seated on a bench, he perused the *London Times* (the only paper he read every day) and went over the latest official reports. Diplomats and other visitors often came for consultation. If they were accompanied by their wives, the latter retired to the adjacent Salon de Famille, where the queen and princesses bus-

3.7 A military review in the courtyard of the Tuileries between the royal apartments (*left*) and the Arc du Carrousel (*right*). On the two occasions when Chopin performed at the Tuileries, he approached the main entrance to the palace (under the dome at *left*) through this courtyard.

ied themselves with needlework and embroidery as they chatted. According to the Prince de Joinville, the women's conversation was generally soporific. But their handicraft, donated to charitable causes, drew the gratitude of Polish refugees, impoverished "Israelite Girls," and other beneficiaries of their generosity.

Naturally there were frequent variations in the daily routine of the royal family. For Louis-Philippe these included military reviews, cabinet meetings, and the official opening of the chambers (fig. 3.7). Occasions such as the anniversary of the July revolution, the king's fête day on May 1, and the dedication of public buildings and monuments demanded the presence of the rest of the family as well (fig. 3.8). These events were always feared because they provided excellent opportunities for would-be assassins. Throughout the ceremony for the erection of the obelisk of Luxor, Marie-Amélie stood protectively in front of her husband. When M. de Rambuteau, prefect of the Seine, begged her to move to one side so the crowd could see the king, she replied, "Can you guarantee me his life?"[27]

In a reign beset by internal dissension and foreign opposition, Louis-Philippe and Marie-Amélie found their greatest pleasures in their domestic life, centered

3.8 The Fêtes des Trois Glorieuses, or the celebration commemorating the three glorious days of the July revolution. In 1845 Chopin wrote an account of that year's event: "The city is to be illuminated.... The festivities will take place along the banks of the Seine: Fancily decorated boats and Venetian gondolas will pass back and forth on the river during the evening.... The Champs Elysées will be less lit-up than before, all the illumination being concentrated this time on the quays where fireworks will be displayed. They are also organizing regattas, that is, a kind of boat racing. There is no end to the ingenious things being planned as well as the precautions being taken to prevent any accidents" (Chopin, *Correspondance*, 3:206).

around their eight children. The eldest and heir to the throne was Ferdinand, duc d'Orléans, generally considered the most handsome of their five sons. He was a dashing soldier who proved his valor at the walls of Antwerp and in the mountain passes of Algeria. He was also intelligent, cultivated, and an elegant man-about-town. Only one significant defect marred this otherwise gifted and glamorous prince: he was the son of Louis-Philippe, whom most of Europe considered an unprincipled renegade sitting on an ill-gotten throne. Because of this, the duc d'Orléans's prospects for a marriage suitable to his rank were seriously compromised. Eventually, however, an acceptable alliance was contracted in 1837 with the German princess, Hélène of Mecklenberg-Schwerin.

All in all, five of Louis-Philippe's children married into the houses of the small

German principalities. Besides the duc d'Orléans, there were Princesse Marie, who wed Duke Alexander of Württemberg, and Princesse Louise, Princesse Clementine, and the duc de Nemours, who found spouses in the reigning family of Saxe-Coburg-Gotha (related to Queen Victoria, her consort, Prince Albert, and her mother, the duchess of Kent).

Marie-Amélie, a staunch Catholic, was disturbed that these German marriages brought so many Protestants into the family. From the outset she had particular reservations about Princesse Hélène, who seemed to hold herself apart from her in-laws. Louis-Philippe later came to share his wife's attitude. In May 1837, however, when *la belle* Hélène arrived in France for her wedding with the duc d'Orléans, she was received enthusiastically in all quarters. Once the young couple had established residence in the Pavillon de Marsan, the Tuileries saw a return of grandeur. Servants' liveries reappeared, as did the ancien régime court dress for men, consisting of knee breeches and silk stockings. By contrast, the king's own apartments were considered of inferior taste and less well maintained.

Princesse Louise, the second of the Orléans children, lived in the Tuileries only briefly before her marriage at Compiègne on August 9, 1832, to Queen Victoria's uncle, King Leopold of the Belgians. He was considerably older than Louise and had previously been married to Princess Charlotte (the daughter of England's George IV) before her death in childbirth. Although Louise didn't relish the marriage, she went through it with tear-filled eyes so her father could have at least one political ally on an otherwise hostile continent.

Both the duc d'Orléans and Princesse Louise held liberal views on political matters and often criticized their father for being too conservative. The younger Princesse Marie, a talented painter and sculptor, went even further and declared herself a Republican. Unfortunately she died at the age of twenty-six without fulfilling either her democratic or artistic goals. Her parents' grief was intense, although they probably never really understood her inner aspirations. Undoubtedly the greatest tragedy of Louis-Philippe's family, however, was the accidental death of the duc d'Orléans during a trip to visit his mother at Neuilly in 1842. En route the horses of his carriage got out of control, and when he tried to jump to safety, he struck his head on the pavement and died within hours. Marie-Amélie blamed herself, and for days the family couldn't tear her away from his casket (fig. 3.9).

Relations between the widowed duchesse d'Orléans and her in-laws grew even more distant after the funeral, when Louis-Philippe decided that she should not become the regent for her son, the four-year-old comte de Paris, now heir to the

3.9 The Chapel of Notre-Dame-de-la-Compassion, commemorating the death of the duc d'Or-léans, is located today next to the porte des Ternes. It was originally erected in 1843 on the site of the house where the young heir to the throne died in a carriage accident the previous year. Inside the chapel a cenotaph was erected to the memory of the duke whose body was interred at Dreux with other members of the Orléans family. The exquisite stained-glass windows of the chapel were designed by Chopin's favorite contemporary artist, Jean-Auguste-Dominique Ingres.

throne. Instead he chose his second son, the shy, introverted duc de Nemours. This was an unfortunate decision since Nemours was not well liked by the public, who mistook his withdrawn manner for arrogance. Furthermore the young duke was a political conservative, swimming against the liberal current of the times. Both the death of the duc d'Orléans and the appointment of his brother, Nemours, as regent greatly weakened the position of the monarchy at home and abroad.

Far more popular than Nemours was the exuberant Prince de Joinville, Louis-Philippe's third son who had chosen a naval rather than a military career. It was he who took charge of bringing Napoléon's remains back from St. Helena. On one of his tours of duty he met Princess Francesca, daughter of the Brazilian emperor Dom Pedro, and later married her. "Little Chica," as she was called, brought a breath of fresh air into the Tuileries. She enchanted Queen Victoria, who found her a "charming, sprightly, lively creature."[28] Equally impressed, Chopin called her the "Brazilian princess with the lovely big eyes,...the most beautiful member of the [royal] family.[29]

The English monarch was also delighted by the the the duc de Montpensier, the youngest of the Orléans children, and expressed the hope that her own son, Bertie (the Prince of Wales and later Edward VII) would take after him. Later, though, Montpensier's marriage to the Spanish infanta Maria Luisa Fernanda caused a deep rift between the French and English houses.

The remaining Orléans son, the duc d'Aumale, having inherited the enormous wealth of the Prince de Condé, became the richest of all the princes. His youthful affairs with actresses brought him considerable notoriety before he eventually married his cousin, Princess Carolina of Naples. In February 1848, when the July monarchy was overthrown, he was governor general of Algeria. By that time Louis-Philippe was nearly seventy-five and clearly showed his age. The "sagacious" man with a "wonderful memory" (as Queen Victoria described him in 1844) had gradually lapsed into a state of senile imbecility. Still as garrulous as ever, he could no longer maintain his train of thought. Furthermore, Mme Adélaïde's death the previous year had crushed his spirit. Two months afterward, when revolution broke out, it was a pathetic old man who fled Paris for the English Channel, slumped down in his carriage with a woman's black bonnet pulled over his forehead to hide the familiar pear-shaped face of the King of the French.

On his arrival in England, Queen Victoria, reconciled at last to the Spanish marriage of the duc de Montpensier, gave asylum to her *cher cousin* and his wife, putting them up in Claremont House, the former home of their son-in-law, King Leopold, during his first marriage. Guizot, the prime minister whose policies were largely to blame for the fall of the July monarchy, also took refuge in England, where Chopin visited him in April of that year.

Although Victoria and the Tories received the Orléans family cordially, Prince Albert and Lord Palmerston wanted them out of the country. Only at the insistence of Sir Robert Peel and the duke of Wellington were they allowed to stay. Over the next two and a half years, Louis-Philippe's health declined, and on August 26, 1850, he died. Later that day, before leaving on her summer vacation in Scotland, Queen Victoria instructed Lord Palmerston to decree a period of mourning for the court as befitted an abdicated king.

With the death of Louis-Philippe, the prospects of an Orleanist dynasty in France perished. Nevertheless three of his grandchildren were to wear a crown:

Princesse Clementine's son, King Ferdinand of Bulgaria, and Princesse Louise's children, King Leopold II of the Belgians and the empress Carlotta of Mexico. Ironically all three bore the name of Saxe-Coburg-Gotha rather than Orléans.

"REVOLUTION AND REPUBLIC"

In 1830 Charles X fell because of what he did; in 1848 Louis-Philippe fell because of what he didn't do. Charles with the arrogance of his Bourbon ancestry had proclaimed his fatal ordinances, which imposed severe restrictions on the liberties of his subjects. Louis-Philippe, on the other hand, lulled by the stability of Guizot's administration, became a victim of his own inertia. As age overtook him, the king allowed his conservative prime minister a free hand, confident that he would preserve the status quo. It was this passivity that cost him his throne.

In the unbroken continuum of history, it is often difficult to define the exact boundaries of an event or an era. Certainly the February revolution of 1848 was rooted in social, economic, and political circumstances that long preceded the actual outbreak of fighting. Among these was a poor harvest in 1846, which sent the price of grain soaring. "Corn and wheat are extremely expensive and poverty is everywhere," Chopin wrote his family that year.[30] Subsequent hoarding and speculation drove prices even higher. Without feed for livestock, a shortage of meat soon developed. A chain reaction then set in that had severe economic repercussions. The hardest hit by these events was the working class, which staged a series of strikes in 1847. As Alfred de Vigny noted, France was becoming polarized between those who earned and those who owned, between those who produced and those who consumed. Because the working classes were now concentrated in the larger industrial cities, they could act in a collective fashion—unlike the peasant workers of the past, who had been dispersed in remote and isolated pockets across the country.

The discontent of this new working class (now referred to by Marx as the proletariat) found a voice in liberal newspapers like Armand Marrast's *Le National*, which intensified the agitation for electoral reforms. On July 9, 1847, the first of a series of so-called reform banquets was held. In the beginning these gatherings were peaceful affairs that opened with a respectful toast to the king. Soon, however, Republican extremists infiltrated their ranks and the banquet rhetoric turned menacing. This change alarmed Guizot, who banned an upcoming dinner to be held in the Champs Elysées on February 22, 1848. The king, on the other hand, remained unperturbed and assured his prime minister that the French never indulged in revolutions during the winter.

Unfortunately Guizot's last-minute cancellation of the banquet was too late to prevent a large crowd from assembling in the Champs Elysées on the appointed morning. For a while the protestors milled about idly, but boredom soon led to drinking and carousing. When minor episodes of street fighting and vandalism broke out, the National Guard did little to check them. On the following day rioting resumed and became widespread. That evening a mob wended its way to the ministry of foreign affairs in search of Guizot. When they tried to force their way in, soldiers guarding the building opened fire. After the shooting, fifty-two dead bodies were left on the steps of the ministry. Rioting had turned into revolution.

Overnight, barricades went up all over the city, especially in the working-class quarters. Because they blocked movement about the city, the king was unable to contact and bring together those who might form a new cabinet and save his government. As the army and the National Guard began to defect to the insurgents, Emile de Girardin, editor of the influential daily *La Presse*, urged Louis-Philippe to abdicate. Marie-Amélie objected, but without military support or political backing, the king had no choice. Hastily, with protestors battering down the doors of the palace, he signed over the throne to his grandson, the comte de Paris (then only nine years old), and fled through the Tuileries garden into a hackney coach waiting outside. Undaunted by these events, the duchesse d'Orléans struggled across the place de la Concorde with the duc de Nemours and her two sons. They had hoped to reach the Chamber of Deputies and establish the claims of the young comte de Paris to the vacant throne. But cries of "Vive la république!" dashed their hopes and forced them to flee for their lives (fig. 3.10).

"This country is lost, my poor child," the duc de Morny wrote his half-sister, Emilie de Flahaut, one of Chopin's pupils. "It has been dishonored. It was a matter of who was more cowardly: the King, the princes, the Chamber, the army!"[31]

For Chopin as for the French, February 1848 was to end disastrously. Ironically the pianist had just experienced one of the greatest triumphs of his life earlier that month. On February 16, he played for the last time before the Parisian public in a brilliant concert at Pleyel's rooms on the rue Rochechouart. The much-touted event was sold out two weeks in advance. Of the three hundred tickets available, the king, the queen, and the duc de Montpensier bought thirty, which they distributed to friends at court because the official period of mourning following Princesse Adélaïde's death prevented them from attending. Unfortunately the effort demanded by this occasion left Chopin with a severe attack of "neuralgia" that incapacitated him for the next few weeks. It was during this

3.10 The funeral procession for victims of the February revolution of 1848. Here we see the cortege passing along the Grands Boulevards in front of the porte Saint-Denis on its way to the place de la Bastille. A year later Chopin's cortege was to follow this same route, continuing on from the place de la Bastille to the cemetery of Père Lachaise via the rue de la Roquette.

time, just six days after his concert, that the revolution erupted. "I was in bed during the whole commotion." he wrote George Sand's daughter, Solange.[32] By the time he was up and around on March 3, he found Paris "quiet but with a calm born of fear. . . . The shops are open but there aren't any customers.—Foreigners are waiting with their passports in hand while damage to the railroads is being repaired. In the meantime, political clubs are popping up everywhere."[33] The following day, he happened to pass George Sand on the steps of a friend's apartment. After an awkward conversation lasting only a few moments, they parted, never to see each other again.

On April 19 a gloomy Chopin, muttering that his career was over, left for England on the invitation of a Scottish pupil, Miss Jane Stirling. There he encountered many other musicians like Berlioz, who were fleeing the violent upheavals on the continent. During the fall, while traveling about Scotland, he learned that condi-

3.11 Lamartine addressing the people at the Hôtel de Ville on February 26, 1848. "The mob wanted the red flag of revolution. They tore down some red curtains at the Hôtel de Ville and waved them excitedly on poles. Lamartine... told the crowd that the red flag was associated with the guillotine, the tricolour with the victories of Napoléon" (E. L. Woodward, *French Revolutions* [Westport, Conn.: Greenwood, 1979], 167). From that day on the tricolor has remained the flag of France.

tions in Paris were still unsettled. According to the *Glasgow Saturday Post* of September 30, the rue Royale and the Grands Boulevards were all but deserted and the city's musical life virtually moribund. Alphonse Lamartine, who assumed leadership of the provisional government that year, proved to be more of a visionary than a politician (fig. 3.11). He had, in Captain Gronow's words, "too much poetry in his head for a statesman."[34] His idealism was marred by impetuousness and above all inconsistency. As Mme de Girardin put it, he kept changing his idée fixe. In an attempt to remedy the nation's unemployment problem, Lamartine instituted a program of workers' ateliers, or workshops. Among other things, these ateliers sponsored the planting of "liberty trees," which soon became so plentiful that the comtesse de Boigne claimed that Paris had begun to look like a forest. Before long these workshops became havens for radical agitators, intent on overthrowing the provisional government and establishing a socialist republic.

When the Assembly voted to close the socialist-infested ateliers, bloody riots known as the "June Days" cost the lives of twelve thousand Parisians. Atrocities committed then constitute one of the most repugnant pages in all French history. Women sold the National Guard poisoned brandy, and fire trucks were used to spray vitriol on the soldiers. General Brea was killed by insurgents after they first gouged out his eyes and cut off his legs. Another soldier had both hands hacked off and stuffed into his pockets.

This butchery was finally brought to an end by General Cavaignac, who became both a hero among the moderates and their candidate for president in the subsequent December elections. Lamartine, of course, hoped to see himself chosen as the new president once the provisional government had been dissolved (fig. 3.12). His inability to control the extremists and maintain order, however, was to cost him the support he once had. As it turned out, neither of these presidential candidates could compete with the man whose very name embodied the greatness and glory of France: Louis-Napoléon Bonaparte. After the downfall of the July monarchy, he wasted no time returning to Paris, where he announced to the Assembly his resumption of rights as a French citizen. Later in June and again in September, he won election to the Assembly.

On November 12, the new constitution of the republic was proclaimed in the place de la Concorde during a light snowfall. Here and there an occasional cry of "Vive la république!" could be heard, but for the most part the crowd was silent. By the time of the presidential elections on December 10, the reactionary mood of the provinces and the charisma of the Bonaparte name had ensured the victory of Louis-Napoléon. For his inauguration, the new president wore an appropriately Republican frock coat. But shortly afterward, while reviewing the National Guard, he changed into a general's uniform and was greeted prophetically with cries of "Vive l'Empereur!"

The first government of the new republic was a conservative one. Except for Alexandre-Auguste Ledru-Rollin, most of the leaders of the February revolution were now either in prison, exile, or retirement. Many of Louis-Napoléon's backers, however, supported him for their own ends, having the impression that he was none too bright and easily manipulated. According to Ferdinand Denis, the new president had a good heart but a feeble intellect that could do little more than plan a pleasant lunch.[35] This impression of stupidity was reinforced by his slow, hesitant French (spoken with a heavy German accent), while his habit of constantly smoking a cigarette made him seem nervous and unsure of himself.

3.12 Members of the French provisional government of 1848. Following the revolution that year, George Sand became an active propagandist for the new republic, working closely with the minister of the interior, Ledru Rollin (*far right*) and the unofficial minister of labor, her one-time lover, Louis Blanc (*far left*). Adolphe Crémieux (*sixth from left*) was a prominent Parisian lawyer of Sephardic lineage and a benefactor of the actress Rachel. He was also a social acquaintance of Chopin who occasionally dined in his home.

Either Louis-Napoléon was a cretin as Thiers assumed, or a secret drinker as others suspected. His physical appearance was equally unimposing. He had the "gracefulness of awkwardness," one of his contemporaries remarked.[36]

In the spring of 1849, Paris was again in the grips of a cholera epidemic. By April, five members of the Assembly had died, despite the containers of chlorine placed around the chamber where they met. Although 150 radical Republicans or "Reds" obtained seats in the Assembly that May, cries of "Vive l'Empereur!" greeted Louis-Napoléon on his public appearances. At the Elysée palace where the new president presided, the ambiance was conspicuously regal with so few Republicans in evidence that the duc de Morny was offered 100 ecus for each one he could spot. On February 17, 1849, the first grand ball held at the palace was described as "quite princely."[37] Aristocratic titles, forbidden by the constitution, were used to announce the guests, many of whom came from the faubourg Saint-Germain.

By October several of Louis-Napoléon's intimate coterie, including his half brother (the duc de Morny), the comte de Flahaut, and Adolphe Thiers, had begun to discuss the possibility of making him emperor. A few weeks later the prince-president dismissed his cabinet and formed a new one, headed by himself. Not even Louis-Philippe had dared to risk such a step. The Second Empire, still more than two years away, was already taking shape. As Balzac predicted with uncanny accuracy, the second republic could never last more than three years; after that France would be ruled by a dictator.

CHAPTER 4

Society and Salons

A "Who's Tout" of le Tout Paris

"*I AM LAUNCHING MYSELF* little by little into society, alas, with nothing more than a ducat in my pocket!" Chopin wrote a Polish friend in the fall of 1831, shortly after he arrived in Paris.[1] Only by selling a diamond ring that the czar of Russia had given him was Frédéric able to pay for the last leg of his journey there. But even though he was nearly broke, the young musician had a wealth of talent and at least two other assets highly esteemed by Parisians: French blood flowed through his veins, and an aura of bon ton radiated from his person. The latter, no doubt, had been acquired from his childhood contacts with the aristocratic student boarders in his parents' home.

Just as he had once delighted the salons of Warsaw, the young musician now won the admiration of Parisian society, which was charmed as much by his social grace as by his musical gifts. Back in Poland, his father grew alarmed at the endless "courtesy calls" followed by late-night soirées, suppers, and balls that seemed to be consuming his son's time and energy. In his letters, he repeatedly warned Frédéric not to tire himself out with such strenuous activities. "I know these grand affairs help you make new and valuable contacts, but what about your health?"[2] Furthermore he worried that so much attention would go to his head. "My dear boy, a young man can easily be led astray if he doesn't watch himself.... As you surely know, so-called 'high society' often proves to be quite shallow when seen close up."[3]

For many Parisians, "high society" no longer existed after the revolution of 1830, when an opportunistic bourgeoisie burst forth amid the debris of a fallen dynasty to establish itself as the dominant social and political force in a nation exhausted by decades of turbulent changes. This sudden rise to power of an untutored (and often unprincipled) middle class appalled the country's ancien régime, for whom it signaled the demise of civilized society. Few were as incensed at these events as Talleyrand's niece, the duchesse de Dino, who bewailed the state of society in Paris at the beginning of the July monarchy (fig. 4.1). "Everything," she cried, "is unrecognizable. The men spend their whole lives in the cafés, and the women have vanished. . . . The Opéra and the Italians still attract some people, but if the leading singers remain onstage, only the seamy side of society can be found in the boxes."[4] Worse yet, the "seamy side" had begun to infiltrate the city's salon world. With a mixture of amazement and regret, Mme de Dino noted that her sister-in-law, the Princesse de Poix, had gone to the duchesse d'Abrantès's Monday evenings, where she ran into Mme Victor Hugo (figs. 4.2, 4.3). To understand her consternation, it must be explained that the Princesse de Poix was a Talleyrand-Périgord, married to a Noailles. Both families belonged to France's prerevolutionary ancien régime, while Mme d'Abrantès, the widow of Napoléon's Maréchal Junot, was a member of the less esteemed Bonapartist society, whose titles were not even recognized by many of the older aristocracy. During the Restoration, it would have been inconceivable that two such ladies would be found together in the same room, and even less likely for the Princesse de Poix to be engaged tête-à-tête with the bourgeois wife of a "Romantic" writer like Hugo.

Of the many changes that accompanied the new monarchy, Mme de Dino was clearly most disturbed by those affecting *le beau monde,* that "beautiful world" of Parisian society often referred to as *le tout Paris.* Of course, that phrase was never meant to be taken literally. On the contrary, "all Paris" referred only to the fortunate few who "really mattered" out of the city's nearly one million inhabitants. Just who belonged to *le tout Paris?* In the transitional world of Louis-Philippe, where the boundaries of society were more elastic than ever before, *le tout Paris* was hard to define. Loosely speaking, it signified "our kind." As such it might be restricted to the ancien régime aristocrats of the faubourg Saint-Germain, or stretched to include the newer Napoleonic nobility of the First Empire and even the bourgeois "barons" of industry and commerce. Those with Catholic credentials naturally dominated this exclusive club, but in the increasingly secularized atmosphere of the period, even Protestants and some Jews qualified for membership.

Certainly by 1831 *le tout Paris* was expanding, although not enough to justify Mme de Dino's exaggerated reaction. Because the July revolution had lasted only three days, it could hardly be blamed for all the radical changes that she decried. In fact, some people like comte Rodolphe Apponyi were rather surprised at how little the overthrow of the Bourbons had upset society. To be sure, *le beau monde*

4.1 The duchesse de Dino, born Princess Dorothea of Courland, became the wife of Talleyrand's nephew, whom she later abandoned for Prince Talleyrand himself. Their liaison lasted until her lover's death in 1838. During that time she remained intensely loyal to the aging prince. Others, however, found her an arrogant and conniving woman who generated countless enemies in her lifetime. Her caustic and combative personality may well have stemmed from an early unrequited love affair with Chopin's close friend and compatriot, Prince Adam Czartoryski.

4.2 The duchesse d'Abrantès, widow of Marshal Junot. A well-intentioned busybody, Mme d'Abrantès dabbled in seduction (with Prince Metternich, Balzac, and others), social climbing, amateur theatricals, and modest literary ventures. A great part of her memoirs were ghostwritten by Balzac. In general she met with little success in her undertakings (least of all her financial ones) and died virtually destitute.

4.3 Mme Victor Hugo was a lady of incredible forbearance married to a philandering, egotistical, and self-righteous husband whose faults rivaled the magnitude of his talents. Eventually she formed a liaison with the literary critic Sainte-Beuve and after the birth of her fifth child, refused further conjugal relations with her husband. Despite these storms, the marriage survived until Mme Hugo's death in 1868.

had indeed been taken by surprise (between a waltz and a galop, as he noted), but a moment later when the music started up again, barely a soul had missed a step. At the Austrian embassy where Rodolphe's uncle, comte Antoine Apponyi, was ambassador, the balls continued, but in many of the nearby mansions of Saint-Germain, they did not. Because Parisian society was inextricably bound up with politics, which determined who was "in" and who was "out," the old nobility (known in political circles as "Legitimists" or "Carlists") now found themselves "out" of the new "in" world of rich middle-class *arrivistes.*

Those aristocrats who abandoned France in the wake of the 1830 revolution did so voluntarily and not because their lives were in jeopardy as in 1789. At the center of the place de la Concorde where the guillotine once stood, the peace-loving Louis-Philippe was to erect the obelisk of Luxor that cost Parisians millions of francs but not a single head. Among those Carlists who left the country, some, like François-René de Chateaubriand, returned soon after having made their political statement. For the most part the emigration of aristocrats in 1830, unlike that which occurred forty years earlier, was an interior rather than exterior one. Instead of going abroad, most merely retreated to their chateaux where, as the duchesse de Dino put it, they could "sulk to their hearts' content with an insolence which is quite impossible to believe."[5]

Mme de Dino herself preferred to switch rather than sulk. Both she and her uncle by marriage, Prince Talleyrand, decided not to let family pride stand in the way of securing an influential niche in the new order.[6] Others of similar background, however, anticipated the imminent fall of the Orleanist regime and preferred to await it in the comfort of their country homes. As it turned out, these aristocrats had underestimated the bourgeoisie, whose wealth, energy, and determination were to sustain the July monarchy for eighteen years even though they numbered less than 15 percent of its subjects. From the point of view of *le monde,* however, these pushy parvenus with neither polish nor pedigree were not of their "world." Hence they ignored them.

Throughout French history, *le monde* had consisted almost exclusively of the aristocracy, until their catastrophic reversal of fortune in 1789. At that time those who merely lost their fortunes were lucky compared to those who lost their lives. Many who survived the Terror did so, like Louis-Philippe, by fleeing the country and living in exile. Not until a quarter of a century later, after Napoléon's defeat at Waterloo and the reinstatement of the Bourbon monarchy, were these emigrés finally able to return home. There they found their social status intact but their fortunes in shambles. Insofar as he could, Louis XVIII arranged for the restitution of their property and the indemnification of their financial losses. Once again the old social order was established (at least in form if not in substance), for the harsh years of exile had left their mark. Restoration society, like the time-ravaged palace at Versailles, had lost much of its prerevolutionary lustre. Their social gatherings lacked the sparkle of the eighteenth-century salons; conversation was less piquant, clothing less elaborate, and etiquette less rigid.

One of the most striking characteristics of the emigrés who returned in 1814 was that many in their adversity had found religion. Gone was the ribald wit and licentious behavior of the previous century. Among the era's lustiest libertines then was Louis XVI's youngest brother, the comte d'Artois, later to become the sanctimonious Charles X in 1824. Surrounded by clergy and obsessed with protocol, Charles conducted court life at the Tuileries with all the solemnity of a high mass. It would be a mistake, though, to confuse the emigrés' piety with humility. The morose and humorless duchesse d'Angoulême (daughter of Louis XVI and Marie Antoinette, married to her first cousin, the son of Charles X) might humble herself before God, but never before her fellow man. This spiritual arrogance suffered a severe blow with the 1830 revolution, when the so-called Alliance of Altar and Throne was sundered, provoking a backlash of anticlericalism in the early years of Louis-Philippe's reign.

The new king, reared on Voltairean principles by his governess, Mme de Genlis, did little to oppose the irreligious mood of his subjects. This permissiveness, in the wake of his shabby maneuvers to gain the Bourbon crown, provided considerable moral ammunition for those still loyal to Charles X. Their indignation was further inflamed when the "usurper" took away their royal pensions and government offices. For some this meant permanent exile from Paris, where they could no longer afford to live; for others, however—especially the younger generation—the city's pleasures soon triumphed over their pique. It took only one bleak and boring winter in the country to draw them back to the capital.

What they saw on their return was a more liberalized society. The middle class, which now surrounded the king, had to rely on its wit and industry rather than hereditary privileges to get ahead. Under the July monarchy, the critic Jules Janin found that no matter how "great a name may be, people are obliged to regild their titles with some degree of personal merit."[7] By the beginning of 1833, enough of the old aristocracy was back in Paris for their presence to be felt.

As far as Chopin was concerned, they were distinctly superior to the motley crowd of Orleanist society. "I favor the Carlists and detest the [Louis-] Philippe crowd," he announced that January.[8]

Unfortunately those who returned at this late date discovered that many of the official plums they hoped to obtain from the new government had already been plucked by members of their own class who were foresighted enough to ally themselves with the new regime. Prince Talleyrand, for example, had become ambassador to England, while the duc de Broglie served on the king's cabinet. Others from such ancien régime families as the Noailles, Osmonds, Choiseuls, Beauvaus, Mortemarts, and Richelieus curried favor with the court by appearing regularly at the Tuileries receptions.

Not all the Legitimists who gravitated back to Paris did so with the intention of capitulating to the usurper's regime. Chateaubriand, for example, settled there to be near his beloved Mme Récamier while still remaining loyal to his equally beloved king, the titular Henri V, grandson of Charles X. Like most of the old aristocracy, Chateaubriand lived in the faubourg Saint-Germain on the Left Bank, directly across from the Tuileries palace and its gardens. For much of Paris then, the elite of this "noble faubourg" were considered a smug, self-centered society, unable to accept the realities of a changing world. The comte d'Hausonville once described this insular realm as "hemmed in to the north by the mountains of folly and on the south by the sea of ignorance, . . . separated from the land of common sense by the gulf of prejudice and from the realm of utopia by the plain of mediocrity." Through its center ran "the river of Pride."[9] By day, Saint-Germain was a quiet area free of commercial establishments; by night, its streets were often choked with carriages bringing the crème de la crème of Parisian society to some gala ball or reception. Time, though, was running out on this faded world of ancient power and privilege. The refusal of many of its inhabitants to collaborate with the July monarchy condemned them to a peripheral role in the new regime. Along with their loss of political influence, this landed aristocracy, dependent on an agrarian economy, saw their incomes plummet disastrously with the belated arrival of the industrial revolution in France. By the end of the Restoration, many of Saint-Germain's noblest scions had found themselves in financial straits with little left but their titles. "In France from now on," Balzac wrote, "there will be great names but no more great houses" (fig. 4.4).[10]

During the Restoration the scintillating social life of Saint-Germain provided

4.4 The entrance to the Hôtel de Narbonne, one of the faubourg Saint-Germain's grand *hôtels particuliers*, built on the so-called *cour-et-jardin* pattern, with a courtyard for carriages on the street side and a garden in the rear. In Chopin's time, the Hôtel de Narbonne belonged to comte Louis de Narbonne, the father-in-law of M. de Rambuteau, Louis-Philippe's prefect of the Seine.

a welcome relief to the stifling decorum of the Tuileries. The July revolution, however, darkened many of the district's most brilliant salons—some temporarily, some forever. And, as inevitably happens to the best of neighborhoods, outsiders moved in. Among them were a number of newly titled Bonapartists like the duc and duchesse de Dalmatie and the widowed duchesse de Montebello (whose son, Gustave, helped Chopin find singers for one of his early concerts in Paris). American tourists like James Fenimore Cooper rented rooms on the rue Saint-Dominique, while an unprepossessing Jewish professor named Levi set up a school for girls in the rue de Lille. Music figured prominently in the curriculum of his young charges, and on February 7, 1836, Chopin performed at a "brilliant soirée" given there.[11]

Less exclusive but still heavily aristocratic was the faubourg Saint-Honoré, across the river to the west of the place de la Concorde. Although its inhabitants had perfectly acceptable escutcheons, their pedigrees generally took up less space in the *Annuaire de la Noblesse de France* than did those of their neighbors in Saint-Germain. Many, in fact, were of foreign rather than French origin, like the Polish Prince Adam Czartoryski on the rue faubourg du Roule and the nonconformist Italian Principessa Belgiojoso, whose home on the rue d'Anjou became a haven for Carbonari, literati, and virtuosi.

Real estate outside of these select faubourgs found few aristocratic buyers except for an occasional renegade like the marquise d'Osmond, who chose to live in the dank recesses of the rue Basse des Remparts below the boulevard des Capucines. As she aptly observed, it was far more important how one lived than where one lived. In all Paris there was only one place a proper Legitimist absolutely refused to set foot: the Tuileries.

In general the lifestyles of the ancien régime nobility set them apart from their fellow Parisians as much as did their soigné addresses. At home they preferred Louis XV fauteuils to the heavy mahogany furniture so popular since Napoléon's time. Their salons exhibited a lightness and grace devoid of the heavy door hangings, dark velvet draperies, and fringed mantel cloths of their contemporaries. Most shunned the exotic "Oriental" (that is, Arabic) decor popular with the younger Romantic generation. Stained glass windows, Turkish water pipes, and the cozy little genre paintings that adorned the walls of bourgeois salons were rarely seen in the faubourg Saint-Germain, where family portraits and large historical paintings looked down on sparsely furnished rooms with glistening marble floors, often bare of carpets. The Neoclassical preferences of the Carlists, considered outmoded by 1830, carried over from the furnishings of their *hôtels privés* to their clothing. Women dressed simply in white muslin gowns with few adornments during the day. In the evening many like the duchesse de Guiche (forced to sell her diamonds after the fall of the Bourbons) dressed with equal simplicity. Elderly men still wore silk stockings with knee breeches and buckle shoes, while an occasional dowager appeared in the old hoop and pannier skirts she once wore at Versailles.

Not only inherited tastes but also economic pressures accounted for the restrained lifestyle of many aristocrats. Grand galas were seldom given. The pristine white and gold ballrooms of Saint-Germain with their sparkling chandeliers were closed down and entertaining confined to smaller private quarters, dimly lit by gas or oil lamps. Dinners now offered fewer courses, while receptions often provided the guest with no refreshment other than water. Seldom was there dancing, and then only to piano accompaniment—in contrast to the lavish balls given by the Rothschilds, where Johann Strauss sometimes conducted his latest waltzes. The spartan quality of social life in Legitimist salons was also a way of showing the rest of Paris that there was no point in trying to maintain the old standards of decorum in a city where true society had all but vanished.

With the passage of time, many of the faubourg's younger inhabitants began to flee the stifling formality of this social milieu for a gayer atmosphere in sympathetic establishments like the British and Austrian embassies. Lord and Lady Granville's salon in the former particularly appealed to those caught up in the current Anglophilic fashions of the times, while that of the Austrian comte and comtesse Apponyi drew those with a penchant for a more rigid decorum. Both provided a stimulating social life that contrasted favorably with the funereal solemnity of Carlist soirées.

It was not only loyalty to the Bourbon dynasty that bound the Legitimists together, but also a deep faith in the Catholic Church, which sanctioned the divine right of that family to rule over France. Throughout the early years of the July monarchy, when anticlericalism was prevalent, the Legitimists remained among the faithful. The churches were "the favorite resort of... the highborn," Mrs. Trollope observed in 1835.[12] At the same time Jules Janin noted that, next to the opera, Parisian society loved a beautiful religious ceremony "full of pomp and dramatic effect.... They tell you of the curate's laces, of the richness of his ornaments and the embroidery of his surplice just in the way they would speak of the shawl and dresses of some great coquette."[13] Beyond its aesthetic aspects, though, religion played a very pragmatic role in the lives of this worldly elite. As we are told in Balzac's novel, *La Duchesse de Langeais,* "Religion will always be a political necessity.... Religion, after all, is at the root of the conservative principles which enable the rich to live in peace. Religion is closely bound up with property."[14] To their chagrin, the old aristocracy learned soon after the July revolution that they would have to make do with less property and more religion.

At least they still had the opera. Certainly for the older generation, schooled on the principles of eighteenth-century rationalism, that was a much-preferred alternative to church-going. Even those without any great appreciation of music found the social compensations of the opera sufficient to make any performance a pleasure. Most of the ancien régime were also fond of the theater, where their tastes generally ran to the classics. Because of this they were seen mainly at the Comédie Française and rarely in the boulevard theaters, which offered a more pedestrian fare. Few cared for the new Romantic drama; its sensual excesses were at odds with the sedate ritual of their daily lives. Romanticism in general placed too much emphasis on the emotions to please tradition-bound Carlists. As Balzac's Claire de Beauséant warned the socially ambitious Rastignac in *Père Goriot,* "If you feel any genuine emotion, hide it like a treasure; don't ever let it be suspected or you'd be ruined."[15]

The fact that it was considered poor taste to show emotion in Legitimist circles doesn't mean that its members were devoid of feeling. On the contrary, beneath their composed facades lay dormant passions that often found expression as the July monarchy encroached more and more upon their world. Although some limited themselves to a controlled disdain, others gave vent to their anger quite blatantly. Carlist journals of the period like *Le Revenant, Les Cancans,* and *La Mode* launched venomous attacks against the royal family and the *juste milieu* that supported it. These attacks disturbed the sensitive Marie-Amélie, who felt deeply wounded that people of her own class would turn on her so viciously.

Strangely enough, no matter how offensively they behaved, these aristocratic survivors of a vanishing era remained, in Mrs. Trollope's perception, the most respected of Parisians, never subject to caricature or ridicule even by those who disagreed with them. This, like many of her assertions, contains some truth and much hyperbole. Members of the bourgeoisie who failed to penetrate the tight little circle of Saint-Germain did, in fact, criticize, mock, and insult its inhabitants. In the face of such attacks, the faubourg's hostesses guarded their guest lists with ever-increasing vigilance. As one of them explained, the most important thing to know is not when to open the door, but when to close it.

With her marvelous knack for generalization, Mrs. Trollope divided Parisians into two social groups: the *rococos,* who were inherently conservative like the Legitimists, and the *décousus,* or the "ragged," seamy side of society, which included Republicans, Romantics, and the just plain vulgar. If the décousus lacked the *savoir-faire* of the *rococos,* they were certainly more progressive in their outlook. Parisians, however, were far too colorful a lot to be portrayed in such black-

and-white terms. Somewhere between the *rococos* and the *décousus* were the *juste milieu*, which constituted the major social and political force in France under the July monarchy. In a way it was the most democratic element of the nation because it accepted almost anyone into its ranks, be they Carlists, Bonapartists, Republicans—even foreigners.

As might be expected, the Carlists were those most sought after by the *juste milieu*, which loved to bask in the reflected glory of their historic names and inhale the subtle aroma of their perfumed elegance. But noble lineage, courtly bearing, and sparkling bons mots were not essential for membership in Orleanist society. Many Bonapartists, despite their high-sounding titles of prince, duke, baron, and so forth, were of lowly origins. Often their fathers or grandfathers had been cabin boys, footmen, dyers, or barrel makers. Among the *juste milieu*'s bankers and industrialists were a number of self-made men who had accumulated more money than manners in the course of their rise to respectability. Typical of the petty bourgeoisie that filled the ranks of the National Guard, for example, were grocers, government clerks, tailors, and shopkeepers, whose muddy boots, loud voices, and dowdy wives would have been more at home in the raucous receptions of Andrew Jackson's White House than at a royal ball in the Tuileries.

This heterogeneity of Orleanist society stemmed not only from Louis-Philippe's self-proclaimed liberalism but also from a purely egocentric desire to boost his image. To prove his popularity, the king needed to surround himself with an admiring throng of courtiers, and in the vast spaces of the Tuileries, it took masses of people to create the illusion of a throng. Because most of the former Restoration court now boycotted the "Chateau," the new king had to tap whatever social reservoirs he could find to flesh out the grand salons and ballrooms of his palace. Eventually it was to be a motley assemblage of social (and not-so-social) types that made up the Orleanist "court."

At the head of this official society were the reigning king and queen. In deference to their rank, the annual *Almanach of 25,000 Addresses of the Principal Inhabitants of Paris* began its alphabetical listings with the letter *O* for Orleans and ended up with those whose surnames started with *N*. Although a great number of those recorded in the *Almanach*'s pages possessed either titles or wealth, it was sufficient just to be respectable, and many of the city's bourgeoisie found their names among the favored few. When one considers that in 1840 the 25,000 people listed made up only 2.5 percent of the Parisian population, this was truly an elite. In keeping with the international flavor of the city, many foreigners were to be found in its pages, including diplomats and a number of Polish emigrés. While friends of Chopin's like the Czartoryskis and the Platers were listed, the musician himself didn't rate a mention—although his mistress, George Sand, did. Quite a few Jewish names appeared in the *Almanach*, among them the Rothschilds, the actress Rachel, and an acquaintance of Chopin's, Céleste Morhange Marix, who taught music and sold harmoniums.

At the first reception given by the royal family in the Tuileries on October 2, 1831, it was apparent that Orleanist society was a very mixed bag. Both the throne room and its antechamber were crowded to the point of suffocation. Some complained of the poor lighting, but had it been brighter there would have been little splendor to observe. The king himself, in a frock coat and gray hat, had insisted that his hussars dress similarly for fear that their brilliant uniforms might seem too pretentious for the court of a citizen king. All in all the evening lacked dignity, and it was obvious to onlookers that the king and queen were not enjoying themselves. Six years later when Johann Strauss conducted his orchestra at the Tuileries, he was astonished at the casualness of the court. After the concert two unknown ladies approached him and began to chat; only later did he discover they were Marie-Amélie, Queen of the French, and her daughter, Queen Louise of the Belgians.

Comte Apponyi was equally amazed at the absence of decorum in the Orleanist court. At one of the Tuileries balls, he complained that "except for members of the diplomatic corps, there was virtually no one from high society present."[16] Because of poor attendance at these "galas," the court started passing out free tickets to members of the National Guard. For the duchesse de Dino, the resulting crowds were "too much of a hodge-podge to be attractive," while the comte de Castellane found the presence of ribbon clerks and tailors' sons on the dance floor a ridiculous charade of equality.[17] Even Louis-Philippe was dismayed by the shabbiness of his "court" and tried to improve its quality by seeking out foreigners with royal or aristocratic credentials. Besides members of the ruling families of Brazil and Belgium (related by marriage to his children), he actively sought out the English nobility to the point where it was said that anyone with a British accent had carte blanche at the Tuileries.

Gradually the animosity of the ancien régime toward the July monarchy began to subside, and many of the scions of Saint-Germain followed the lead of their colleagues, the duc de Noailles, the Princesse de Vaudemont, and the comte de Castellane, in seeking a rapprochement with the inhabitants of the "Chateau."

These were venerable names in Parisian society, as Chopin well knew. "You play better if the Princesse de Vaudemont...takes an interest in you," he wrote his family soon after his arrival in Paris.[18] A short while later, the comte de Castellane's daughter became one of his pupils.

During the early years of the July monarchy, there had been a number of Republicans among Louis-Philippe's supporters. Probably the most prominent of these was Alexis de Tocqueville, who for all his admiration of American democracy, was content to enjoy the monarchical ambiance of the Orleanist regime while confining his Republican sentiments to paper. Before long, however, Republicans in France had become a party "very nearly worn out among the *gens comme il faut*," according to Mrs. Trollope.[19] Even aristocratic ones like the marquis de Lafayette were no longer in vogue.

By contrast, Bonapartists became an increasingly important element in *juste milieu* society. Many had lived abroad since 1815 and were only too glad to return home once the Bourbons were gone. Others, like the comte de Molé, the duc Decazes, and Prince Talleyrand, readily accommodated to life under the restored Bourbon monarchy where they found favor and political advancement. At the time of the July revolution, most of the Bonapartists still in France shifted their allegiance to Louis-Philippe's government. Once committed to the Orleanist cause, many rose rapidly to prominent positions in the new regime. Three Napoleonic marshals became prime ministers under Louis-Philippe (Soult, Mortier, and Gérard), while General Lobau and the comte de Flahaut (two of Napoléon's aides-de-camp) became commander in chief of the National Guard and ambassador to Austria, respectively. Both Mlle Lobau and Mlle Flahaut were pupils of Chopin.

Besides Bonapartists, Republicans, renegade Carlists, the English, and other foreigners, the mélange of Orleanist society included a number of Jews who had made their names primarily in the financial and artistic worlds. Their entrée into official society reflected the increasing democratization of western Europe's industrialized nations like England, Holland, Belgium, and France. Most came from bourgeois backgrounds, although some, like the Belgian ambassador's wife, Mme Le Hon, and Liszt's mistress, the comtesse d'Agoult, had aristocratic connections. Perhaps no single element of Orleanist society was more representative of the era than its bankers, who provided the wherewithal to convert Guizot's *enrichissez-vous* from a slogan into a reality for many Frenchmen. With the exception of financiers like Laffitte and Perregaux, most Parisian bankers were Jewish, including baron James de Rothschild, baron Adolphe d'Eichthal, and Auguste Léo, all of whom had close links with Chopin. Rothschild and Léo, for example, provided the musician with loans, while Mme Rothschild and her daughter—as well as Mlle d'Eichthal—studied piano with him. To Mlles Rothschild and d'Eichthal Chopin dedicated several of his compositions, including a ballade and two sets of waltzes. Baron Rothschild himself even became a member of the two most exclusive men's clubs in Paris—the Jockey Club and its older, more traditional rival, Le Cercle de l'Union. In the artistic world, Jews like Heinrich Heine, Jacques Halévy, Henri Herz, and Giacomo Meyerbeer played a significant role in *juste milieu* society.

The prominence of the Jewish community in Louis-Philippe's Paris is impressive when one considers that Jews constituted only eight thousand out of the city's total population of nearly one million in 1840. France's acceptance of Jews, however, should not obscure the fact that anti-Semitism was still widespread throughout the country then. With rare exceptions—like Chopin's friends Adolphe Crémieux in the Chamber of Deputies and the Polish exile Franciszek Wołowski in the second republic's National Assembly—it was unusual to find Jews in elected offices. Many Frenchmen still clung to attitudes described by Balzac in his novel, *Cousin Pons,* where he refers to the "concentrated avidity," "sly cunning," and "mock humility" of the Hebrews in his time.[20]

Somehow all these disparate elements of Orleanist society managed to congeal into a cohesive body that, to quote Mrs. Trollope, exuded an air of "prosperity and satisfaction."[21] The ladies, she noted, indulged in more elaborate toilettes than did their counterparts in Saint-Germain, and tended to wear less jewelry and rouge than English women. During the day, they were never seen without their ubiquitous cashmere shawls. In the evening, they donned open-back dresses and twined artificial flowers around their ears. The more daring crowned this with a *coiffure à la girafe* (a top-knot strung with ribbons, pearls, feathers, or flowers), while the demure preferred a *coiffure à la Vierge,* with their hair combed flat and encircled by a gold chain from which a jewel or other ornament hung down over the forehead. Briefly after the July revolution, there was a craze for red, white, and blue clothing, while the "Oriental" look, based on Moroccan, Algerian, or Turkish styles, persisted throughout most of the 1830s and 1840s. To keep one's finger on the pulse of haute couture, it was necessary to view the daily Promenade de Longchamps during Holy Week, which served for years as the city's major fashion show. Ladies of *le beau monde* drove up and down the

Champs Elysées from the Place de la Concorde to the Longchamps race track, displaying their elaborate spring wardrobes that had kept seamstresses and couturiers busy for months.

In the masculine world of fashion, it was the elegant "dandies" and "lions" who set the pace, but unlike women's styles theirs were almost exclusively imported from England. The duc d'Orléans, who was noted for his sartorial taste, tried to reestablish the former elegance of the Tuileries soirées by having men dress in the grand style of the previous century, with powdered wigs, culottes, silk stockings, and buckled shoes. He even required them to wear a sheathed sword at their sides. Although most complied, some of the king's ministers, like Thiers and Dupin, refused and always appeared in the contemporary attire of blue frock coats, white cashmere trousers, and boots.

For Orleanist society, the culmination of the social season was the king's fête day on May 1. It was a time of gaiety throughout Paris, not only in the salons of the city's elite, but also on the streets, the Seine, and all the open spaces of the city like the Champs Elysées, the Tuileries garden, and the Champs de Mars. Greased poles, Punch and Judy shows, boat races, band concerts, fireworks, and torchlight parades were all part of the general revelry. At the Tuileries, there were receptions for the diplomatic corps, the clergy, members of the Chambers, officers of the military, and prominent individuals from the financial and commercial worlds. As the Prince de Joinville put it, all "came to parade before the chief of State ... and pronounce ... a series of clichés ... generally devoid of any sincerity, to which the poor [king] is forever condemned to answer with all sorts of banalities."[22]

Fortunately for those who found the Orleanist court boring and déclassé, there was a world beyond the Tuileries, that of the Parisian salons. In Carlist circles, some of these may have provided even less stimulation than the "Chateau." But for all their picayune observance of the social amenities, these salons did cultivate a purity of taste and an artfulness of conversation that won them the admiration of every level of Parisian society. The inhabitants of this exclusive world remained the symbols—if no longer the possessors—of that elusive mystique called "status." Nevertheless there were times when the air of the Carlist salons became almost too rarified to sustain life. In the less exalted atmosphere of the *juste milieu*, pleasures were less pallid, concerns more current, and the general mood more spirited.

As Arsène Houssaye (author and director of the Comédie Française in Chopin's time) noted, "the Revolution of 1830 was a revolution more of customs than of politics."[23] Although Louis-Philippe deliberately injected a more liberal tone into his government, the new charter under which he ruled was not that much different from the previous one, which Charles X strove to abrogate. Far greater were the differences between the dominant social classes of the two regimes—that is, the old aristocracy of the Restoration, socially arthritic despite all efforts to rehabilitate it, and the heterogeneous *juste milieu* society, united chiefly by the upwardly mobile goals of its adherents.

In general the Parisian salon world was run by women, although there were exceptions, such as the author-statesman François Guizot (a widower), the dandy Comte Jules de Castellane (a bachelor), and Chopin's cloying admirer, the marquis de Custine (a homosexual). In other salons like that of the politician Adolphe Thiers and the poet-novelist Charles Nodier, there were nominal hostesses—for example, Thiers's wife or her mother and Nodier's vivacious daughter, Marie. Nevertheless the tenor of such establishments was set by the host. In a few cases like the salons of the *grandes demimondaines* and Hugo's *Cénacle* of Romantic writers, those who attended were almost exclusively male. Strangely enough the three most popular salon hostesses under the July monarchy were neither Parisiennes nor even Frenchwomen: the comtesse Apponyi, Lady Granville, and the baronne de Rothschild. Precisely because they were foreigners, their salons became a neutral ground where all the city's fractious social elements could come together. These ladies, who remained outside the petty bickering of Parisian society, provided a sort of demilitarized zone for *le beau monde*.

This is not to say that these salons were entirely free of social or political bias. The Apponyis at the Austrian embassy had definite Legitimist leanings, which distanced certain liberals like Lafayette and the duc d'Orléans. The latter's brother, the Prince de Joinville, on the other hand, called it the *"premier salon"* of Paris, and Louis-Philippe himself made a point of cultivating the ambassador to curry favor with Metternich and the Austrian court. At the English embassy the Granvilles' guests were equally "upper crust" but of a more progressive bent, while the crowd at the Rothschilds always included a generous sprinkling of bourgeoisie from the *juste milieu* (fig. 4.5). Early in his Paris career, Chopin acquired introductions into all three salons.

The Austrian embassy, in keeping with its Carlist proclivities, was located in the faubourg Saint-Germain, first at No. 39 rue Saint-Dominique, and later in the Hôtel de Chatelet, at No. 127 rue de Grenelle. In the latter, a large winter garden with a vaulted glass roof provided a flower-filled setting for many of the Apponyis'

4.5 The Hôtel de Charost, at No. 39 rue du Faubourg Saint-Honoré, has housed the British embassy since 1825. It was here in Lady Granville's salon that Chopin acquired many of his first pupils in Paris. Here also the duc d'Orléans found refuge from the ostracism that he encountered in many of the Carlist salons in the faubourg Saint-Germain.

elaborate social affairs. Mme Apponyi, known affectionately as "Poney" to her friends, received regularly on Monday evenings and often gave Sunday afternoon musicales (fig. 4.6). On these occasions, "the music was delicious."[24] Rossini often seated himself at the piano to accompany such stars of the Italian Opéra as Tamburini, Rubini, and Grisi, while "Kalkbrenner, Liszt, Chopin and others provided the instrumental music."[25] In a social world of entrenched customs, Mme Apponyi's *déjeuners dansants,* or lunch dances, were a breath of fresh air. With an unflappable calm, she continued them throughout the cholera epidemic of 1832, her sole concession being to omit ice water, truffles, salads, and sorbets from her table. Not even the Republican uprising in June of that year could interrupt the routine of her salon. "The cannons boomed all evening," her husband's nephew wrote, "but in spite of that, conversation was still quite lively."[26]

4.6 The comtesse Apponyi, wife of the Austrian ambassador to Paris. Her salon was one of the most politically conservative and socially prestigious in all Paris. Her love of music attracted many of the finest musicians of the city, including Rossini, Paër, Kalkbrenner, Chopin, many singers from the Opéra and the Italian theater, and a wealth of talented amateurs like Delfina Potocka and Prince Belgiojoso.

Although neither cannons nor cholera could ruffle Mme Apponyi, intrigue could. Spawned by idleness and sparkling with wit, gossip thrived in the Parisian salons, where one of its chief purveyors was the comtesse de Flahaut. Born Margaret Elphinstone, she was the daughter of Admiral Lord Keith (to whom Napoléon surrendered after the battle of Waterloo) and wife of Talleyrand's natural son, comte Charles de Flahaut. Because her Bonapartist husband was an equerry to the duc d'Orléans, Mme de Flahaut shunned the Austrian embassy and for many years did her best to stir up trouble between the Apponyis and the Tuileries. In general she tended to put people off with her incessant talk and tactless behavior. Although the duc d'Orléans approved of her "advanced liberal views," he admitted that his "principal reason for liking her is that nobody else does."[27]

With the exception of Mme de Flahaut, many aristocratic members of the *juste milieu* were welcome at the Austrian embassy. Most of its habitués, however, were Carlists. For example, at a ball given by the Apponyis in 1832, three-quarters of those present were Legitimists. This prompted Louis-Philippe to ask Mme Apponyi not to invite anyone who didn't attend the Tuileries, to which she replied that the embassy would give no further balls rather than acquiesce to his demand. When he made a similar appeal to Lady Granville at the English embassy, she replied politely but firmly that she had no intention of changing her guest list. From then on the two ladies continued to entertain as before without further interference from the "Chateau."

According to the Maréchal de Castellane, Lady Granville gave "the most beautiful parties in Paris."[28] Particularly memorable was her ball in honor of Queen Victoria's twentieth birthday on May 24, 1839. The theme was roses, which were worn by all the ladies present. Throughout the embassy and its garden were "mountains of roses." The garden itself was covered by a tent under which a *salon de conversation* had been created, with sofas in silk and damask placed around a central table full of books and albums. The sanded paths of the garden were covered by a cloth to protect the satin ball slippers of the ladies present. Roughly two thousand guests attended, including members of both Saint-Germain and Orleanist society.

Among those who frequented Lady Granville's parties was the duc d'Orléans (fig. 4.7). Those who knew him claimed he had great charm and cultivation. Women everywhere were attracted to him, and before 1830 he was highly popular in social circles all over Paris. After his father became king, however, he found himself excluded from many of the city's Legitimist salons. Although Lady Granville continued to welcome him in the embassy, she was less forbearing with the comtesse de Flahaut, who often took shelter there, partly because she was persona non grata elsewhere and partly because she counted on the Granville's influence to get her husband appointed ambassador to England. Whether or not Lady Granville was aware of these motives, she didn't care much for the abrasive countess. "Her manner is hard," she observed. Others who knew the countess complained of her acid wit and sour disposition.[29] According to a newspaper of the time, she even looked like vinegar.

In spite of the tenuous nature of their relationship, Mme de Flahaut and Lady Granville had at least one thing in common: their intense dislike of the Talleyrand-Dino ménage. Both the comte and comtesse de Flahaut considered the duchesse de Dino a "horrid little serpent" because she had thwarted the count's bid for Prince Talleyrand's post of ambassador at the court of Saint James.[30] In Lady Granville's opinion, the unscrupulous prince was just as repulsive as his mistress. Once at a party in Paris she described him as crawling past her "like a lizard along a wall."[31] Society, of course, loved to cultivate such feuds and took great delight in bringing Lady Granville and Mme de Dino together, in the hope of sparking some fireworks. Invariably they were disappointed, as the two ladies always behaved in public with the utmost civility.

4.7 The duc d'Orléans, a handsome, dapper, and cultivated man-about-town, was a welcome habitué of the salon scene in the later years of the Restoration. His father's unsavory reputation among the Legitimists, however, limited the duke's social mobility under the July monarchy, when he became the butt of painful jokes and insults in the Carlist salons of Saint-Germain.

The fact that the Granvilles came from two of England's most aristocratic families helped solidify their social position in Paris, where Anglomania was rampant throughout the Restoration and Orleanist monarchies. Lord Granville was a Leveson-Gower and brother to the first duke of Sutherland, who owned one of the grandest houses in London with a splendid art collection, much of which formerly belonged to an ancestor of Louis-Philippe.

As for Lady Granville, she was a Cavendish whose father and brother were the dukes of Devonshire. With such family connections, the Granvilles attracted many of the English aristocracy to the Paris embassy during their tenure there. The willingness of these visitors to attend the Tuileries court delighted Louis-Philippe, who went out of his way to cultivate them. When for example the Granvilles' nephew and niece, the second duke and duchess of Sutherland, came to Paris in 1837, they were shown around the newly renovated palace of Versailles by the king and queen themselves. No doubt the Sutherlands were impressed. On the other hand, they knew how to make quite an impression themselves. Whenever they arrived in Paris, they were accompanied by such pomp that ordinary Parisians mistook their procession of carriages for those of the pope or visiting royalty. Chopin, who came to know them on these visits to the French capital, later played at an 1848 reception in their London house before Queen Victoria and Prince Albert.

Among the nonaristocratic English who made their way to the Paris embassy were William Makepeace Thackeray, who was married there on August 20, 1836, and the Irish actress Harriet Smithson, who became the wife of Hector Berlioz there in October 1833, with Franz Liszt as a witness. Unfortunately, in 1841, Lord Granville suffered a stroke and had to retire. His and his wife's departure from society was widely regretted throughout the Parisian social world.

Like the Granvilles and the Apponyis, most other foreign diplomats in Paris made little effort to mute their political preferences. The Belgian embassy, for instance, was so openly Orleanist that it became known as an annex to the Tuileries. This was partly due to the fact that the ambassador, comte Le Hon, owed his title to Louis-Philippe for arranging the marriage of Princesse Louise of Orléans to King Leopold of the Belgians. As for Mme Le Hon, she had a far more personal attachment to the Orléans family, having become the mistress of its crown prince, the duc d'Orléans. Later, when she switched her affections to the duc de Morny, Mme Le Hon constructed a private oratory next to her boudoir in honor of her royal ex-lover.

The Belgian embassy at that time was located on the Chaussée d'Antin, in a house that once belonged to Mme Récamier. The famous chaise longue on which David painted her still remained there. Like Mme Récamier, Mme Le Hon was exceedingly beautiful. Unfortunately she was also exceedingly selfish and not especially bright. Nevertheless invitations to her Saturday night dinners were as much sought after as those to Mme Apponyi's lunch dances and Lady Granville's balls. Among the Belgian nobility to be seen at Mme Le Hon's were the two Chimay princesses, one of whom claimed to be a pupil of Chopin, while the other was an illegitimate daughter of Napoléon.

Also noted for their social prestige were the embassy of the Two Sicilies in the faubourg Saint Honoré's place Beauvau and the Russian embassy (located for awhile at No. 12 place Vendôme, where Chopin later died). The embassy of the Two Sicilies was considered by the English expatriate Albert Dresden Vandam to rank with the Austrian and English embassies as one of the few really good salons in Paris. For politics as well as pleasure, Louis-Philippe often frequented the Russian embassy. There he could enjoy the delightful hospitality of the ambassador, count Pozzo di Borgo, while keeping tabs on the unpredictable Czar Nicholas I. At the Hanoverian legation, baron and baroness Stockhausen (both pupils of Chopin) often treated their guests to splendid musical evenings with performances by themselves and other artists.

Another baroness and pupil of Chopin's, Mme James de Rothschild, drew as distinguished and varied a crowd to her salon in the rue Laffitte as any to be found in the diplomatic circuit (fig. 4.8). A member of the famous banking family from Frankfurt-am-Main, Betty de Rothschild was the daughter of her husband's older brother, Salomon Rothschild, who headed the Viennese branch of the family business. She arrived in Paris in 1824 at the time of her marriage to her uncle. Their mansion, just north of the boulevard des Italiens, was one of the most luxurious in Paris, having been built for another banker, Laborde, and subsequently owned by Queen Hortense of Holland and Napoléon's minister of police, Joseph Fouché. Henri Duponchel (later director of the Paris Opéra) decorated it for them in the extravagant style of the rich bourgeoisie of the neighboring Chaussée d'Antin. Chairs embellished with bronze *dorée* caryatids and surmounted by the family's coat of arms rested on thick Oriental carpets. Between the windows, hung with gold- and silver-tasseled draperies, was a collection of paintings by Rembrandt, Reubens, Van Dyck, Hobbema, Hals, Velasquez, and Murillo. The family's 10,000-acre country estate at Ferrières, which Chopin visited in the fall of 1847, was equally rich in decor and required a staff of one hundred servants to maintain.

For many a Parisian gourmet, the greatest treasure of the Rothschild household was to be found in the kitchen: the famous chef Marie-Antonin Carême, once in the service of the prince regent of England and later employed by Talleyrand at the Congress of Vienna. In addition to Carême's sumptuous dinners for up to sixty guests, the Rothschilds also gave frequent musicales and a weekly ball. With her charm and beauty, the baronne de Rothschild lent an air of cultivation to her salon, which offset the rather boorish impression made by her husband, who had a remarkably simian face, a harsh gutteral accent, and an arrogant manner. Notwithstanding these disadvantages, James often boasted that he had never met a woman who could resist him.

Politically, Baron James was a supporter of Louis-Philippe, although in 1840 the comtesse Nesselrode claimed that the banker was, in fact, more like a viceroy if not the true king of France. Mme de Rothschild, on the contrary, liked to think of herself as a Carlist until the fall of Louis-Philippe, when she decided to become an Orleanist. Nevertheless her salon remained, for the most part, politically neutral. Even the elite of Saint-Germain solicited invitations to it, though this meant rubbing shoulders with Bonapartist peers and bourgeois businessmen. The fact that many prominent members of the literary and artistic worlds— including Chopin, Delacroix, Balzac, and Heine—gathered there made the house on the rue Laffitte one of the most cultivated rendezvous in all of Paris.

4.8 The baroness Betty de Rothschild ranked with Lady Granville and the comtesse Apponyi as one of the three most popular hostesses of the Parisian *beau monde* during the 1830s and 1840s. Because both the baroness and her daughter, Charlotte, were pupils of Chopin, her salon on the rue Laffitte became one of the musician's favorite haunts. Here as in other salons he often brought along his most talented students to perform for the pleasure of the hostess's guests.

There were so many salons in the Orleanist capital that it would be impossible to describe them all here. In their variety they covered a vast spectrum of political, social, and artistic tastes. But no matter where they were located or what type of crowd they attracted, their fundamental purpose was diversion. In Chopin's time the salon world was composed of "two thousand to three thousand people who knew each other, visited each other and having nothing else to do, cultivated their finer feelings."[32] In Tom Prideaux's words, these salons formed "an intellectual bazaar" where ideas were traded.[33] Because they were designed to fill leisure time—of which the upper classes had an abundance—it was usually possible to find one with an open door at almost any hour of the day or night. The vicomtesse de Noailles, for example, received in the morning (Saturdays only) as did the comtesse de Flahaut (Tuesdays only), whereas the comtesse Apponyi held dances at lunchtime. In the afternoons one could find the comtesse Lobau or Mme Récamier "at home" nearly every day of the week. Most salons, however, flourished in the evenings. Some received guests daily, like that of the comtesse de Castellane; others received only once a week, like those of the comtesse Le Hon (Saturdays) or the Princesse Lieven (Sundays). Such a plethora of salons inevitably led to complications in scheduling. One young bachelor, hoping to establish a literary salon, chose to receive on Sundays at midnight, the only free hour left in the city's crowded social calendar.[34]

After the July revolution, changes occurred in the fabric of society that were detrimental to salon life. First, many of the bourgeoisie who found their way into *le monde* were too busy with commercial matters to spare time for the financially unproductive pastimes of the salon. Second, as already noted, many of the old aristocracy, who were the most accomplished in the art of leisurely living, abandoned Paris for their rural estates. Third, the proliferation of English-style men's clubs in Paris drained away a good part of the male population, especially the younger men. And finally, there was what the comtesse de Castellane called the destructive influence of representative government, which drew politicians into huddles that excluded the ladies.

All of these factors seriously undermined the quality of conversation, which, after all, was the main diversion of the salons. Such conversation as persisted in the post-Restoration era dwelt more on mundane, practical matters than before. Until then, the art of turning a phrase had been all-important. People didn't pay so much attention to what you said as to how you said it. By 1830, however, the art of conversation, although declining, was certainly not dead. Mrs. Trollope, for one, admired the Frenchman's "charming talent" for "uttering trifles so that they may be mistaken for wit."[35] In its sparkling quality "French talk is very much like champagne," she bubbled.[36]

In the opinion of many a Parisian, the highest level of conversation was to be found in the salon of Mme Récamier. According to the marquis de Custine, Mme Récamier knew how to converse better than anyone in France. Alphonse de Lamartine concurred, claiming that conversation in her salon was "of an exquisite taste and courtly tone, rarely animated but of a delicious warmth that taught one the value of listening well rather than talking well."[37] At times, though, discussions there could be of such extreme refinement that they left some, like the literary critic Sainte-Beuve, quite enervated.

Invariably present at Mme Récamier's four o'clock gatherings was her love of many years, the aging and world-weary author François-René de Chateaubriand, whom Lamartine described as more meditative than talkative. One of his literary colleagues, Ernest Legouvé, liked to call him "the God of Silence."[38] According to Mme Ancelot, Chateaubriand scorned the pettiness of small talk and preferred to immerse himself in a quiet state of "perpetual self-adoration."[39] This placed such a damper on conversation that everyone at Mme Récamier's spoke softly as if someone sick were in the room. The truth was, Chateaubriand, the fluent writer, spoke only with difficulty. He was not spontaneous and had to pause between remarks to formulate what he would say next. All too often the pomposity of his utterances made him more appreciated when he didn't speak than when he did.

Certainly not everybody on the salon circuit was a polished conversationalist. Many a self-made "gentleman" of bourgeois origin had little formal schooling, which he tried to hide beneath a facade of reticence. Franz Liszt, whose education as a child prodigy had been seriously neglected, later read voluminously so he wouldn't have to suffer in silence away from the piano stool. By contrast Chopin, who had obtained an excellent education in the Warsaw Lycée where his father taught, was readily accepted in the Parisian salons as a social equal rather than a mere entertainer. Even though he never gained complete mastery of the French language, he was able to converse with the smoothness and grace of an aristocrat, a skill that Liszt always envied.

George Sand, on the other hand, like Chateaubriand, was noted for a sparseness of words despite her logorrhea on paper. In her own salon, she characteristically stood silent in front of the mantel smoking a cigar and flicking the ashes from time to time into a nearby bowl of water. (She had a phobia about starting a fire and never used ashtrays.) In other people's salons, she usually refrained from smoking but spoke little, staring instead into the fire or quietly stitching handkerchiefs.

At the other extreme were those talkers who never knew when to stop. Among these were the caustic comtesse de Flahaut and her English friend, Lady Jersey, who acquired the nickname "Silence" because she expected everyone to remain silent during her perpetual chatter. The English ambassador's wife, Lady Granville, was herself a highly excitable talker and had to be asked to moderate her voice when it got too loud. Perhaps the most long-winded prattler in all of Paris was the king himself. Naturally people tended to voice their annoyance only in private or in memoirs judiciously published after his fall. Although Louis-Philippe was acknowledged to be a delightful raconteur—brilliant, witty, and intelligent—even the most avid of courtiers learned to seek refuge from the avalanche of his royal verbiage. Dumas *père* and Balzac were also guilty of conversational incontinence, although their natural charisma, enhanced by the glitter of celebrity, allowed them to get away with it. Dumas's blustery outpourings were once compared to the noise of a hurricane, while Balzac's torrential talkathons made him a social pariah in many salons. The duchesse de Castries, after a long struggle to defend her virtue against the latter's amorous onslaught, concluded that the seductive Balzac was a far better talker than writer. There were those, however, who complained that the brash young author was not so much a sparkling conversationalist as a babbling monologist. Moreover, his incessant chatter often exceeded the boundaries of good taste. Marie Potocka, a relative of his future wife, once had to warn him about holding his tongue at Mme Apponyi's, where his risqué remarks were not always appreciated.

In some circles, though, the dubious taste of Balzac's verbal eruptions was considered less offensive than the heated rhetoric of political discussions. Despite the loquacious writer's insistence that "no salon would be complete without its politician," there were those who absolutely forbade any talk of politics under their roofs—among them Mme Merlin, the grande dame of Parisian musical salons, and comte Jules de Castellane, who staged amateur theatricals in his spacious faubourg Saint-Honoré mansion.⁴⁰ Of course, there were other salons in which politics constituted the main topic of discussion, such as that of the duchesse de Broglie, daughter of Mme de Staël and wife of one of Louis-Philippe's prime ministers. It was there that another of the king's prime ministers, François Guizot, met the Russian Princesse Lieven, who eventually became his mistress (fig. 4.9). Although deeply devoted to each other for the rest of their lives, the two never married, presumably because the princess could not endure the thought of being announced in society as plain "Mme Guizot." Consequently the couple maintained separate establishments throughout their long liaison, each creating a salon that attracted the most influential of politicians. For Mme Lieven, politics became such an obsession that she would talk about little else. As the duchesse de Dino remarked, "She must have the stir of news and conversation.... When she is alone there is nothing to do but go to sleep."⁴¹ Thanks to Guizot she was seldom alone, a situation that became of great concern to liberal politicians, who felt she wielded a dangerous degree of influence over her lover. Thiers, in fact, stopped coming to her salon, saying, "Madame, I shall be pleased to pay my respects to you when you are no longer the Minister of France."⁴²

Thiers's own salon in the rue Saint-Georges, run by his wife and her mother, Mme Dosne, catered to a left-of-center political clique whose views differed considerably from the conservative ones of Guizot and Mme Lieven. Amid its suffocating clutter of bric-a-brac there was much talk but little conversation, since Thiers seldom allowed anyone to interrupt his endless monologues.

A steady diet of political discussions naturally bored many salon-goers. At Alphonse Lamartine's Sunday receptions on the rue de l'Université, conversation frequently turned from politics to literature, which was not surprising con-

4.9 The formidable Princess Lieven was a proud and meddlesome lady, married to the czar's ambassador at the court of Saint James. According to the *London Times* of May 23, 1841, she was "an arrogant...mischievous... odious...and supercilious" person who "fancies herself a power." Later she left the prince to become the mistress of Louis-Philippe's prime minister, François Guizot. After her husband's death, she refused to marry her lover because she could not bear to give up her aristocratic title. (Courtesy of Dr. Janusz Cizek)

sidering that the host was better known as a poet than a statesman throughout most of Louis-Philippe's reign. The great man, however, was not always poetic, and could frequently be heard to "swear like a ragpicker."[43] Although his salon was located in the select faubourg Saint-Germain, it was neither opulent nor tasteful. On the contrary, guests described it as poorly furnished, messy, and full of dogs and cats. Known for his sartorial elegance, Lamartine seems to have spent more on his clothes than his house. At the time of his death, over two hundred pairs of shoes and an equal number of waistcoats were found in his closets.

Across the river off the Champs Elysées was the salon of Mme Emile de Girardin, where conversation also centered around political and literary subjects, with more emphasis on the world of letters. Like George Sand, Mme de Girardin took a masculine nom de plume, the "Vicomte de Launay," for the articles she published in her husband's newspaper, *La Presse.* A number of the literati who attended her salon also contributed to *La Presse,* including Balzac, Hugo, Sue, Lamartine, and Dumas. In her youth, when elocutionary prowess rivaled the art of conversation, the precocious Mme de Girardin (née Delphine Gay) made the rounds of Restoration salons, giving dramatic readings and reciting poetry, much of which she had composed herself. "Endowed with uncommon literary, poetical and intellectual gifts," she was touted as nothing less than all "nine muses rolled into one" (fig. 4.10).[44] Considering that a number of her rivals had a repertoire of prepared monologues that could last two hours or more (some could even improvise on a given topic in either poetry or prose), Delphine's abilities must surely have been of Olympian dimensions.

The young girl's physical assets were equally impressive. Blond, blue-eyed, and beautiful (although a little large of frame), Delphine admitted that the praise she received may have been due more to her looks than her talent. Perhaps her greatest asset was her ambitious mother, Sophie Gay, who shamelessly exploited the child's abilities for the sake of gaining access to a social world that would otherwise have excluded them. After Delphine's marriage to the newspaper magnate Emile de Girardin, she became a journalist, playwright, and one of the city's leading hostesses. In her salon she acquired the reputation of being a formidable conversationalist. "Two hours of talking [with Mme de Girardin] left you as stiff and sore as a boxing match," one of her guests remarked.[45]

Other literary salons devoted to readings and recitations included those of Victor Hugo and Charles Nodier. In the eyes of "Society," neither could claim much distinction. They didn't attract an aristocratic following and weren't presided over by an officially recognized *grande dame*. Worst of all, they bore the stigma of being "Romantic," which implied that their guests were rowdy, vulgar, and devoid of any respect for traditional values. In such salons, almost everyone dressed unconventionally (with a penchant for medieval or Renaissance garb), lolled about on sofas, put their feet on tables, smoked cigars, and wore their hats indoors. Charles Dickens once visited Hugo in the place Royale and found not only the crowd but the salon itself "a most romantic show ... like a chapter out of one of his own books."[46] It was full of antique armor, tapestries, coffers, and canopied thrones, forming a decorative collage typical of the era. There, readings of Romantic poetry, plays, and other literary genres were received with exaggerated solemnity. The crowd grew intense, its drawn faces often giving way to tears of anguish or smiles of ecstasy. Silence reigned except in moments of extreme transport, when guests would burst out with cryptic cries of "Cathedral," "Ogive," or "Pyramid" to express the sublimity of their feelings.

Not far away in the library of the old Arsenal just south of the place de la Bastille was the salon of the writer Charles Nodier. Although he was occasionally called "the poet of vampires" due to the macabre nature of his Romantic works, the mood of his Sunday night gatherings was far more bouyant than the strained exhaltation of an evening at Hugo's. After readings by authors like de

4.10 Mme Emile de Girardin (née Delphine Gay) became one of the leading feminine authors during the July monarchy. Like George Sand, she used a masculine nom de plume, the vicomte de Launay. Her diverse talents found expression in journalism, poetry, and playwriting. But the scope of her work was limited, according to Lamartine, who described her as a bird confined to the "gilded cage" of the Parisian salons.

Musset, Merimée, de Vigny, and Sainte-Beuve, Nodier's guests relaxed with lighthearted conversation, card playing, and dancing.

In the dimly lit salon of Mme Récamier, darkened by heavy draperies that were always pulled even in the middle of the afternoon, the fiery actress Rachel gave stirring recitations and Chateaubriand read passages from his final opus, *Memories from beyond the Tomb*. As the title implies, the work was rather lugubrious, a natural outgrowth of the author's morose personality. Mme Récamier once claimed that Chateaubriand was "unhappy about living but would be equally unhappy about dying" (fig. 4.11).[47] Late in life, as his fame became eclipsed by younger writers, the melancholy septuagenarian assumed that he had become deaf because he no longer heard people talking about him.

In some salons the passion for drama went beyond mere readings and recitations to the presentation of elaborate theatrical productions. One of these was Balzac's elusive amour, the haughty comtesse de Castries, who gave a private performance of Alfred de Musset's *Caprice* years before it was ever accepted on the public stage. In her youth the white-skinned, titian-haired beauty had mesmerized Balzac when he first met her in the salon of Olympe Pélissier, one of the era's "grand horizonals" who later married Rossini. At that time, Mme de Castries "literally dimmed the light of the candles" whenever she entered a room.[48] Life, however, had not been kind to her; a riding accident left her crippled, and an unhappy marriage forced her into the arms of Prince Metternich's son, by whom

4.11 François-Auguste-René de Chateaubriand. Like Talleyrand and the duchesse de Dino, Chateaubriand and Mme Récamier found solace in each other's company during their final years. Being tone deaf, Chateaubriand could hardly appreciate Chopin's music. He did, however, profess to be jealous of George Sand's early novels.

she had an illegitimate child. Even though she later rose to the rank of duchess in 1848, the title-conscious Balzac lost interest in the once-beautiful countess, whom age had made as "hideous as a corpse."[49]

Although other Parisian hostesses like the duchesse d'Abrantès, widow of Napoléon's marshal Andoche Junot, indulged in amateur dramatics, none could rival the comte Jules de Castellane, who took the matter seriously enough to build a theater for his productions in the garden of his faubourg Saint-Honoré mansion. There he gave elaborate performances of vaudevilles, comedies, opéras comiques, and at times, even grand operas and ballets. In general the parts were taken by prominent social figures of the day, who had varying degrees of dramatic talent. Many a Parisian *grande dame* vied for a leading role. Among the male actors was Chopin's great admirer, the mincing marquis de Custine, whom the actress Marie Dorval once called *"monsieur en jupon"* (milord in skirts). Unfortunately the marquis had a speech impediment that provided unwelcome comic relief in his most solemn moments. For Castellane's more serious enterprises, he often called on professional actors and singers. Rachel's brother and sister sometimes appeared there, but the great actress herself seldom displayed her talents gratuitously.

Even though few of the city's salons went so far as to give entire operas or ballets, some form of musical entertainment was common in most of them. At Rossini's Italian-styled villa in Passy (built on land granted him by the municipality of Paris), one could always find "good music" and "excellent macaroni."[50]

When the ebullient host sat down at the piano to play, his mobile face and supple body movements led the expatriate Lady Morgan to consider him as fine an actor as a composer. According to François Auber, director of the Paris Conservatory, when Rossini's fingers raced across the keyboard one could almost see the ivories smoke. For many a guest, however, the main attraction at the Rossini salon was the composer's second wife, Olympe Pélissier, whose exquisite beauty had once drawn to her boudoir such libidinous literati as Eugène Sue and Honoré Balzac.

Among Chopin's neighbors in the square d'Orléans was the pianist Friedrich Kalkbrenner, whose salon offered some of the best musical fare to be found in the city. Although he was an excellent technician, many Romantics felt that his pedantic playing lacked "feeling." Nevertheless he acquired enough devotees to make him so vain and pompous that a contemporary exclaimed, "My God, how he is going to bore the cherubims on high" when he dies.[51] Still, Orleanist society flocked to Kalkbrenner's salon and invited him to perform in theirs. He was particularly in demand as an accompanist—except at the Austrian embassy, where Mme Apponyi complained he had the habit of charging ahead as if attacking a sonata, leaving the bewildered singer behind in great despair. Chopin, on the other hand, was always welcomed at Mme Apponyi's frequent musicales. "You are immediately considered to have great talent if you have been heard at the English or Austrian embassies," the young Pole learned during his first months in Paris.[52]

Rather slighted by history, the comtesse Merlin on the rue de Bondy was claimed by many Parisians to provide the finest music of any salon in Paris. The fact that she could draw a crowd to her home, so far from the fashionable haunts of society, is proof of the excellent fare she offered. Even the tone-deaf Chateaubriand would journey out to her musical evenings, where he would stifle a yawn during the opening measures of an aria before falling fast asleep by the middle of it. Among the artists on Mme Merlin's programs were Liszt and Paganini; often Rossini accompanied the singers, which invariably included Mme Merlin herself. Although she once had a splendid voice, social considerations precluded any professional exploitation of it. In general her life was dominated by two things: her love of music and a morbid fear of growing old. As age encroached, she plucked out her white hairs with an obsessiveness that left her nearly bald and persisted in afflicting her guests with a voice long past its prime. Friends also noted that the older she got the more décolleté were her dresses and the louder her bravuras. Despite these failings, her "charming concerts followed by very agreeable suppers" remained a celebrated feature on the Parisian scene.[53]

Where there was music one often found dancing, a social diversion that has always been as contagious as it is controversial. Worldly though they were, Parisian salon-goers never danced during Lent or in times of mourning. After the 1830 revolution, Saint-Germain went into a state of self-perpetuated mourning, first for the fall of the Bourbon dynasty, then for the imprisonment of the duchesse de Berri, and later for the death of Charles X. As a result, few ballrooms in the "noble faubourg" ever rang with the music and laughter they once knew in happier days. What dancing there was occurred in an informal, often impromptu manner. The Carlists' moratorium on gala balls in the early years of the July monarchy was hailed by the Legitimist journal *La Mode* as "truly heroic." Such heroism didn't appeal to everyone, though, and many of the faubourg's younger generation escaped to the dance halls in the Champs Elysées. There they brushed against their grooms and valets, spinning and skipping their way through the latest waltzes and polkas, or gawked at the high-kicking queens of the demimonde, showing off the salacious new can-can.

The rare balls that did take place in Saint-Germain were given mostly by outsiders. At the Austrian embassy, the dazzling Hungarian costumes of comte Apponyi and his nephew attracted as much attention on the dance floor as did the elaborate toilettes of the ladies. Probably the most extravagant of the faubourg's balls, though, were the fancy-dress galas given by the rich American Colonel Thorn in the opulent Hôtel Matignon. To ensure that his meticulously planned evenings wouldn't suffer any interruption, he locked the gates of his mansion from 10:00 P.M. to 3:00 A.M. so guests couldn't arrive late or leave early. Less decorous than Colonel Thorn's lavish entertainments were the ostentatious affairs of the Russian Prince Tufiakin, which attracted an *outré* assortment of artists, courtesans, and actresses to the usually restricted faubourg.

In Orleanist circles, dancing could be a dull and decorous ritual at the Tuileries or a giddy whirl in the dance halls of Musard or Jullien. Often it was a simple spur-of-the-moment affair like those at Charles Nodier's salon, where guests would roll up the carpet for a rousing polka accompanied by his daughter, Marie, at the piano. On the night of February 21, 1848, the last of the Orleanist balls took place. It was given by the new Belgian ambassador and his Polish wife, the prince and princesse de Ligne—on the Champs Elysées. Toward midnight the ominous sound of cavalry marching down the avenue signaled the end of the July monarchy. Soon the lights of the refurbished Elysée palace were to illuminate the glittering balls of the nation's new President, Prince Louis-Napoléon Bonaparte.

Strangely enough in a city noted for its fastidious gourmets, food was a rather insignificant feature in most Parisian salons of the 1830s and 1840s. There were, of course, the midnight suppers at a ball, lunch at Mme Apponyi's *déjeuners dansants*, and the magnificent banquets by chef Carême at the Rothschilds. Yet in many salons no food or drink was served at all. This was particularly true of Legitimist salons, where such economies were a necessity. Often, however, refreshments weren't served because the "open house" nature of most salons made it impossible to predict how many people would drop by on a given day or night. In some cases dinners for a select number of guests might precede an "at home," particularly when a concert or theatrical event was planned. Such dinners generally began early, around five o'clock, with ten to fifteen courses, including as many as six hors d'oeuvres, two soups, and four entrees. No one was expected to eat everything; instead guests merely sampled what they wanted from the many dishes offered them. Although cheese was served at every meal, proper ladies (who always wore gloves at the table) were offered daintier dishes like *crème fraîche*, sweetmeats, or cookies. To protect their large white cravats, men swathed themselves in napkins at the dinner table. Although eating slowly was deemed a virtue, it was, in fact, a social necessity in view of the great importance attached to maintaining conversation throughout the meal. At the end of dinner, finger bowls were expected to be used for rinsing the mouth and nostrils as well as the hands.

In the majority of salons, refreshments tended to be sparse, and late-comers often found nothing left by the time they arrived. The prefect of the Seine, M. de Rambuteau, loved to serve tricolor ices, while the prosaic Mme Lamartine provided only cold tea and little else. At Victor Hugo's, food was seldom served except when the author was campaigning for election to the Academy and could scarcely risk sending potential supporters home on an empty stomach. "Spiritual" nourishment, of course, was always available there in the form of communion with the "master."

Somewhere in virtually every Parisian salon there was a card table for the amusement of the guests. At the Tuileries, Louis-Philippe could frequently be seen playing his favorite game of whist. Lord Granville was also fond of whist and gambled heavily at it. Afterward he would keep Lady Granville up for hours at night, recounting each of his plays. Mme Halévy, the wife of the composer, was another heavy gambler whose late-night games became so boisterous that her husband finally called the police to break them up so he could get some work done. The tenor Rubini was equally addicted to cards. When asked to sing one night at a soirée, he refused to leave the whist table and performed the requested aria while continuing his game.

At George Sand's salon in the square d'Orléans, the favorite game was billiards. Because her billiard table occupied so much space, Chopin's piano had to be shoved into a tiny side room. Far from being offended, the musician loved retreating to the little music room to escape his mistress's guests, which often included a scruffy assortment of actors, bohemians, militant socialists, and boorish provincials who spat on the floor.

Sophie Gay liked to have her guests entertain each other by telling ghost stories, while other hostesses encouraged group participation in *tableaux vivants* or games of charades. By today's standards such pastimes may seem puerile. But even contemporary "jet-setters" would probably have enjoyed the comtesse Merlin's musical charades, where "more often went on than met the eye."[54]

Undoubtedly the most challenging games played in the Parisian salons of the July monarchy were those of self-advancement. Although most participants were reluctant to admit it, we know from the novels of Balzac, Dumas, and Stendhal that these were viciously competitive games with extremely high stakes. Because of the intrinsically social aspect of the salons, they were inevitably the breeding ground of climbers intent on making advantageous contacts and ingratiating the "right" people. For those eager to play the game, it was necessary to get onto the playing field, that is, to gain access to the salon of someone already in society. Only a few—like the American Colonel Thorn—could start at the top with sponsors from the finest of the ancien régime families. For many a humble shopkeeper, artisan, or government clerk in Louis-Philippe's National Guard, the game began with an invitation to the Tuileries. The effect was like a balloon ride into the social stratosphere, which left some giddy and others terrified. Those truly determined, though, didn't rest until they had risen into the empyrean of Saint-Germain. To achieve this was a feat that only the most wily of social cosmonauts could accomplish. Even Mme de Flahaut and the duchesse de Dino, for all their intrigues, failed, as did the Bonapartists with all their titles. Nor could the rich financiers and industrialists of the Chaussée d'Antin do any better with all their bloated bankrolls. For such aspirants the only access to ancien régime society was through the portals of the embassy salons, which served as strategic operation centers for anyone concerned with social climbing.

Even Louis-Philippe himself used the embassy salons for his own political gain, hoping to improve his international clout with such powers as Austria,

4.12 This portrait of Mme Récamier was sketched shortly after she died from cholera in the epidemic of 1849. On her deathbed she was attended by Dr. Cruveilhier, who later the same year cared for Chopin during his last hours.

England, and Russia. The game of political advancement, in fact, rivaled that of social climbing in most salons outside the faubourg Saint-Germain. At the Tuileries, of course, it was the chief pastime.

In Mme Récamier's salon, a genteel form of intellectual sparring was the name of the game, which the participants conducted with all the solemnity of a religious ritual. Arsène Houssaye once compared these afternoon gatherings of the faithful to "a daily mass" with Chateaubriand as God and Mme Récamier as the Holy Virgin (fig. 4.12). The boys' choir, he added, was made up of those campaigning for election to the Academy.[55]

For the younger Romantic writers anxious to advance their literary careers, the altar to worship at was Victor Hugo's salon in the place Royale. They "flatter him from morning to night and revere him like a God," comte Apponyi wrote. All this, he added, makes the great author "vain and fatuous beyond all belief."[56] The marquis de Custine had a more subtle technique to ensure the success of his writing: he invited the critics to his salon, where he cajoled them into giving him good reviews. Some, however, proved recalcitrant, among them Sainte-Beuve, who called the home of the marquis and his male lover a veritable Sodom and Gomorrah.

Like Custine, the comtesse d'Agoult also had difficulty playing the literary game because of her sexual indiscretions. While still married, she tried to seduce Chopin, prior to eloping with Franz Liszt, by whom she had three illegitimate children. After the breakup of her liaison with Liszt, the comtesse found herself an outcast in Saint-Germain, when she returned to create a new life for herself under the masculine nom de plume Daniel Stern. Her liberal politics and feminist views (consciously copied from George Sand) were to brand her new salon "the House of Democracy" and thoroughly alienated her ancien-régime neighbors.[57]

Clearly "getting ahead" was one of the most popular diversions in the Parisian salons during Chopin's time. One might almost say it was society's main preoccupation. This jockeying for position, whether social, political, or artistic, closely resembles what has lately been called "gamesmanship." Perhaps no one captured its spirit better than Mme Merlin when she quipped, "I love to play innocent games with people who aren't."[58]

CHAPTER 5

Pox Britannica

The Great Epidemic of Anglomania

When you happen to be going along the boulevards, stop at the shop of my tailor,
Dautrement, and ask him to make me a pair of gray pants. Pick out a dark shade
of fabric suitable for winter, very soft, tight-fitting and without any stripes. An
Englishman like you knows what's fashionable these days.
                    —Frédéric Chopin, October 3, 1839[1]

*L*A MANCHE, OR "THE SLEEVE," as the French refer to the English
Channel, has long represented the great gulf that lies between the Gallic and
Anglo-Saxon temperaments. When the Normans breached that strait in 1066, the
waters closed after them as swiftly as had the Red Sea behind Moses, leaving
Britain as insular as ever. Of course one still sees residua of the Norman conquest
in the physical features of certain Englishmen, as well as the use of common lati-
nate words like "domicile" and "pedagogue"—not to mention others where the
French has become more fractured like "Marylebone" and "Bar-le-Duc."

Later cultural exchanges across the Channel often occurred in a similar manner, that is, from the clash of hostile armies, as in the Hundred Years' War. Characteristically, the great epidemic of Anglomania that plagued France in the nineteenth century began in the wake of hostilities between two countries that had
been at odds since 1776, when the French supported the rebellion of the American colonies against Great Britain. Later, in retaliation, the English gave shelter
to many of the French aristocrats driven across the Channel by the revolution of
1789. Not until 1802 with the Treaty of Amiens did the two nations resolve their
differences to the immense delight of the English, who swept across the Channel
in hordes to enjoy the joie de vivre of the French capital for the first time in over
a quarter of a century. They were received by the Parisians with open arms, for
the pleasure was mutual. Once more the fires of friendship were rekindled in the
centuries-old love-hate relationship between the two nations.

Along with the English came the first of the French emigrés who had fled their own country during its devastating Reign of Terror. In their exile they had learned to drink tea instead of *café* and attend routs (or *raouts*) instead of *bals*. They also learned to eat "crackers," "buns," "muffins," "plumcake," and "ginger-bread," which they shamelessly introduced into the sacred domain of French gastronomy. In their dress and manners they came to accept Beau Brummell as their god of fashion. This period of mutual admiration between the French and the English was soon cut short by Napoléon's bellicose imperialism, which put an end to any further cross-Channel intercourse. Even then English words, customs, and mannerisms succeeded in penetrating the British blockade of the French coast.

By 1814, with the defeat of Napoléon and the restoration of the Bourbons, the blockade was lifted and a new wave of emigrés returned to find the English and their Allies camped out on the Champs Elysées. The chauvinistic mood of the Empire had turned sour, leaving the French in a receptive mood to outside influences. Both the new king, Louis XVIII, and his brother the comte d'Artois (later Charles X) had spent considerable time in England. They, as well as many members of their exiled court, came back imbued with Anglo-Saxon tastes and manners. This affinity for things English was especially evident among the male emigrés, who were more exposed to the world abroad than were their protected wives and daughters. Many had acquired a fluency in the language, visited the men's clubs, adopted the local style of dress, and taken a fancy to the vigorous outdoor pleasures of the English country gentleman. In France social life was generally dominated by women, unlike in England, where it was common for men to lead an independent life apart from the drawing rooms of their spouses. In an attempt to recreate this masculine independence, the returning Frenchman adopted the pose of a "dandy" or social "lion," which at times propelled liberation from feminine society into open disdain of it.

The word "dandy" was said to have originated in Scotland during the late eighteenth century as an affectionate diminutive of "Andrew." That prototypical "dandy Andy" came to represent the quintessence of fashion in his time. In a letter of Lord Byron's dated July 25, 1813, the term "dandy" was first applied to the "bucks" or "beaux" of Regency England. Soon afterward, "dandyism" spread across the Channel, where it become especially popular among idle young aristocrats bored with the sterile social life of the Restoration. By 1830 Musset, Balzac, and Stendhal were beginning to portray the dandy in their writings, and in October 1832 he first appeared on the French stage in a play called *The Dandy* by Ancelot and Léon.

If the origin of the word remains nebulous, the definition of it is even more so. The dandy was basically a young man of elegance and sophistication. Beyond these basic attributes, the dandy could be anything from an effeminate fop to the most rugged of sportsmen. Some spent their days parading up and down the boulevards with rouged and powdered faces, shaved eyebrows, and a simpering gait. Others galloped at breakneck speed down the Champs Elysées from a racing meet in the Bois de Boulogne to a boxing match at Lord Henry Seymour's gymnasium. But whatever he did, the dandy, be he macho or mincing, did it with an English flair.

Although most dandies were rich and aristocratic, such qualifications were not required of all. Certainly it took a great deal of money to spend twenty-four hours a day doing the right thing in the right clothes at the right place. Anyone adept in the art of sponging, though, could reduce the cost to as little as 15,000 to 20,000 francs a year. Chopin, who earned roughly 2,000 francs a month from teaching (with some additional profits from his compositions and an occasional concert) was therefore able to maintain the lifestyle of a dandy, albeit on a marginal level. As he complained to a friend in Warsaw, his carriage and kid gloves alone ate up most of his income. From a financial point of view, it was certainly a great advantage to be a bachelor as most dandies were. "A bachelor," Balzac pointed out, "can live in a cozy mezzanine. Society doesn't expect him to spread himself. He can manage on one servant and devote all his money to his enjoyments. The only appearances he has to keep up are his tailor's concern."[2] Although there is no reason to think that Balzac had Chopin in mind when he wrote this, his description provides a typical portrait of the young musician during his early days in Paris.

Other dandies who had to earn their own money like Chopin included the novelist Eugène Sue and Dr. Louis-Désiré Véron, a one-time doctor who sold patent medicines, ran the Paris Opéra, and managed several literary and political journals. All of these enterprises reaped him large profits except for the practice of medicine. In general, most dandies came from the city's *jeunesse dorée* (gilded youth) and belonged to wealthy, often titled families like the "king of fashion" himself, the comte d'Orsay. Also belonging to this privileged set were the duc de Morny (son of Queen Hortense of Holland and the comte de Flahaut), the Prince de la Moskowa (Marshal Ney's son), comte Demidoff (future husband of Princesse Mathilde Bonaparte), comte Walewski (Napoléon's son by the Polish Maria Walewska), and two of the Orleanist princes, the duc d'Orléans and the duc de Nemours. Of course there had to be some bona fide English dandies

5.1 A trio of 1838 dandies dressed for the evening with top hats, cravats (black at night as opposed to white for daytime wear), single- and double-breasted waistcoats, redingotes of varying length, straight or tapered trousers (often strapped under the foot), and soft leather shoes or low boots.

among the crowd like Colonel Thomas Raikes and Captain Rees Howell Gronow. The fact that their titles weren't aristocratic didn't matter because they themselves were authentically British.

What exactly was involved in "playing the dandy"? For many it was a light-hearted matter, pursued merely for the fun of it—just another of those amusing salon games so popular all over Paris. For some, however, it was a compulsion based on profound psychological disturbances. The first prerequisite for playing the dandy was to look the part. Because dandies considered themselves an exceptional breed endowed with a Brahman-like superiority, it was essential to stand out from the crowd. In Paris this meant dressing like an Englishman (fig. 5.1). Until 1848 the man of fashion was almost always seen in a "redingote" (the French corruption of an English riding coat). In the 1830s such coats typically had enormous sleeves and a voluminous collar extending up to the ears. Its pinched waist required plumpish dandies to wear a corset for the sake of presenting a fashionable silhouette. Favorite colors for a redingote tended to be drab shades of gray, green, or brown, euphemistically described as "London smoke," "Green tea," or "English bronze." A bright vest or *gilet* of silk, satin, or velvet, adorned with gold chains and trinkets, relieved the somber tones of the redingote. The brilliance of these waistcoats delighted Balzac, who once bought thirty-one of them in a single month with the intention of collecting a total of 365, one for each day of the year. Trousers offered the dandy less of an opportunity for self-expression. The three preferred styles were skin-tight leggings with a strap under the foot; very loose, full trousers like those of a cossack; or pants that fitted closely over the thighs and then flared out into an "elephant foot" below the knees. Cravats (which went out of style after 1840) were almost always white and of an incredible amplitude, requiring yards of material, wound several times around the neck. Following Beau Brummell's lead, French dandies began to stiffen their cravats with starch, which made it extremely difficult to turn the head. At the height of the cravat's popularity, an Italian opened a school in Paris to teach the dandy how to ensheath himself properly in these monstrous mummycloths. For footwear, varnished English riding boots with spurs were the vogue at all hours of the day whether the dandy knew how to ride or not. One was never seen without them, even at soirées and balls where the true French *gentilhomme* wore soft leather slippers to spare his hostess's fine Savonnerie carpets and parquet floors. By day the dandy carried a walking stick and at night, a gold or ivory-knobbed cane. Yellow gloves, top hat, and a monocle completed his ensemble and informed the world that he belonged to the ultra-smart band of elitists known among Parisians as "the yellow-gloved brigade."

When that dandy of dandies, the comte d'Orsay, moved to London with his mistress, Lady Blessington, he could see at once that his English finery no longer made him stand out from the rest of society. He was forced therefore to look for other ways to assert his individuality. First of all he discarded the white cravat that he had worn in Paris. Instead, he began fastening the top of his shirts with stickpins of diamonds or colored jewels and took to wearing pantaloons of sky-blue silk. "In his tilbury...he looked like some gorgeous dragon-fly skimming through the air."[3] By London standards this was a bit sissified, but at least it set him apart from the pack, which was the goal of all dandies.

The fact that many cultivated and productive people, particularly those in the arts, were considered dandies reflects the dual nature of Parisian dandyism. There were those whom Prévost calls *les dandys de bon ton,* which included men like Chopin, Delacroix, Mérimée, Stendhal, and de Vigny—stylish young men-about-town in their leisure time but with a serious side to their character. Far from being vacuous poseurs obsessed with the trivia of image-building, they were people of substance who didn't need to hide behind a facade of inconsequential absurdities. They contributed to society and enriched it with their work, in contrast to their parasitic counterparts, whom Prévost called *les dandys ridicules*. While the latter prospered during the Restoration, the bourgeois climate of the July monarchy was less sympathetic toward their foppish self-indulgence, and by 1840 they began to disappear. *Les dandys de bon ton,* however, survived because their dandyism served merely to embellish the man of substance within. For the *dandys ridicules,* there was no man within. Their lives were a vacuum that, by the laws of nature, should have collapsed spontaneously had they not found some way to fill up the void of their existence. To do this required an art as ephemeral as that of the medieval alchemist. Ultimately neither the dandy nor the alchemist was ever able to produce something noble out of something base.

Nevertheless the *dandy ridicule* deserves credit for perfecting the complex art of giving idleness the appearance of activity. He was, in fact, the veritable picture of perpetual motion. Getting dressed of a morning, for instance, was a frenzied ritual, often with a tailor in attendance. This was typically followed by a visit to his mistress or (of equal importance) a horse dealer, where he inspected the latest imports from England. On these occasions he rode with an English saddle on a mount duly registered in a "stud book." Otherwise he drove a light, two-wheeled tilbury (which he called a "centaur," being a combination of man and horse). Invariably he was accompanied by his groom (always called "John," whatever his real name might be). *Déjeuner* or lunch followed, at a fashionable boulevard restaurant like Tortoni's or with guests *chez soi,* where an elegant simplicity *à l'anglaise* was the custom. Tablecloths were shunned, as was anything typically French like wine, champagne, truffles, or patés. Instead, fresh eggs and vegetables, greens, rice, berries, and soda water were served.

The afternoon was often given over to *le sport,* which might consist of pigeon shooting in the galleries of the Tivoli Gardens (modeled after New House at Battersea, London), or a workout at Lord Seymour's gym, where wrestling, fencing, and boxing were the favorite pastimes. Frequently the dandy would ride out to the Bois de Boulogne beside his mistress's carriage to watch or even participate in the races of the "gentlemen riders" there. Most likely he would put down a considerable amount of money on the horses, for it was very "smart" to bet at the races. All *les snobs* did. Later he might stroll in and out of the fashionable shops along the boulevard des Italiens before dressing for dinner (fig. 5.2).

In the evening, the dandy ridicule frequently changed his white cravat for a black silk one and doused himself in English toilet water. Gallic at heart, he could not resist the pleasures of French cuisine for his main meal of the day. If he were

5.2 The north side of the boulevard des Italiens. The tall, arched windows on the ground floor of the central building belong to one of the city's most exclusive eateries, the elegant Maison Dorée, located conveniently near Chopin's Chaussée d'Antin apartments. Here in the summer of 1838, the confused and indecisive musician had dinner with a Polish friend and confidante, count Grzymała, to decide whether he should or shouldn't submit to George Sand's advances. To the left of the Maison Dorée is the Café Tortoni, where in 1822 George Sand first met her husband, the baron Casimir Dudevant.

eating out he probably had no choice; even English hostesses usually had French cooks, as did the so-called Café Anglais. Although Paris had a number of "English eating houses," they were not sufficiently chic to attract the dandy. After dinner the restless young buck would wander from theater to theater with his eyes focused more on the boxes than the stage. At the Opéra, it was considered bourgeois to appear before the first intermission. If one came earlier it was to dawdle in the *foyer de danse,* where svelte ballerinas provided more titillation than did plump prima donnas (fig. 5.3).

Only after dark did the true dandy really come to life. At the theater and the opera, as well as at the soirées, balls, and diplomatic receptions that followed, he revealed himself in his most quintessential form (fig. 5.4). His behavior in these

5.3 In the Salon de Danse at the Paris Opéra,
Parisian dandies loved to congregate before a
performance to admire the young ballerinas (or
figurantes) limbering up before a performance.
Here, in a Gavarni sketch, we see a *figurante* who
seems to be casting a suspicious eye on her
admirers—possibly from previous experience
with such individuals.

settings was typically disdainful and insolent to everyone around him, especially women. In their presence he purposely kept his hat on, blew cigar smoke into their faces, and took great delight in bringing up subjects considered unsuitable in mixed company. On such occasions he talked loudly in an affected English accent, pretended to be bored by everything, and yawned frequently to prove it. At all costs the dandy refrained from admiring anything; enthusiasm was the hallmark of inferiority. At the Opéra, Berlioz noted that the yellow-gloved dandy "applauds slowly, almost noiselessly ... for the eyes only. He thereby says to the whole house, 'Look! I condescend to applaud.'"[4] This blasé attitude, along with a glacial expression (English reserve forbade the display of emotion), were essential to the dandy's Anglophilic image. When Julien Sorel, in Stendhal's *The Red and the Black,* dropped his "air of impenetrable frigidity ... he no longer looked English."[5] Yet although the dandy purposely avoided expressing his likes, he was quite vocal about his dislikes, the chief of which were "Work, Utility, Nature, Woman, Progress and Democracy"—in short, everything that the middle class idealized.[6] Comfortably secluded from all these irritations of life, the dandy finished the day at his club, where he whiled away the wee hours of the morning with his aristocratic friends in such masculine pursuits as smoking, drinking, and gambling.

5.4 A scene in the Parisian dance palace, the Ranelagh, modeled after the Ranelagh Gardens in Chelsea, London. The original building was constructed in 1784 in an open area that was then part of the Bois de Boulogne. Subsequently the site was incorporated into the suburb of Passy. The structure shown here was erected in 1834. Other similar English-styled amusement centers in Paris then included the Vauxhall (where Chopin performed on two occasions) and the Tivoli Gardens.

Closely related to the dandy during the Louis-Philippe era was the social "lion," although it is not clear whether he was a mere variant of the dandy or a species in his own right. Some say that lions were a new breed that had distinguished themselves by some outstanding act, while others claim they were simply an overblown version of your run-of-the-mill dandy. For Delphine de Girardin, the distinction between the two was simple: a dandy was a man who wanted to be noticed; a lion was one who *was* noticed. Not to be outdone, a few women patterned themselves after the Paris lions and became known as *lionnes* (lionesses). They were typically aggressive, independent of their husbands, and fond of such macho pleasures as shooting, riding, and gambling. Jules Janin and Balzac describe them as dressing lavishly and having a taste for gothic decor with rapiers, spears, shields, and cuirasses hanging from the walls of their salons.

Except for the lionesses (who were relatively few in number), most Parisiennes remained more French than English in their habits. Although the *coiffure à l'anglaise,* with long ringlets of hair falling down over the shoulders from beneath a tulle bonnet, was popular for awhile, most women's clothes and hairstyles were created by Parisian couturiers and coiffeurs. Mme Sauvinet on the boulevard des Italiens was one of the city's leading dressmakers under the July monarchy, but by the late 1840s her preeminence had been challenged by the young Englishman Charles Frederick Worth, who came to dominate women's fashions in Paris and abroad for the rest of the century. This perennial passion of Frenchwomen for being well dressed made haute couture the one item in Paris that cost more than in London at a time when the English capital was considered the most expensive city in Europe. (Chopin, for one, fumed at the outrageous prices he encountered on his two visits to London in 1837 and 1848.) Even though the chic Parisienne might wear the finest of French fashions as she toured the city's elegant boutiques, she made a point of carrying the English *Quarterly Review* under her arm like a stylish accessory, as essential to her image as the proper gloves or hat.

Because many French women failed to share the Frenchman's Anglophilic tastes, a number of the latter sought wives from across the Channel. As a result, English brides became something of a status symbol, even though they were not deemed very attractive by French standards. Compared to petite Parisian beauties, their tall, gangly figures earned them the sobriquet of *asperges* (asparagus stalks). In addition they were considered far too "exalted and melancholy, cold and unnatural" to please such impassioned Frenchmen as Alfred de Musset.[7]

5.5 Among the many English brides of
Frenchmen in Chopin's time was the
Anglo-Irish actress Harriet Smithson,
who married Hector Berlioz at the
British embassy in October 1833 with
Liszt as a witness.

Nevertheless English brides remained in great demand, no doubt because
Britain, a more prosperous nation than France at the time, had a greater selection
of rich heiresses. The German composer Richard Wagner, for one, suspected
that the wealth of the English accounted for much of the Anglophilia so prevalent in France then. And as early as 1835, Colonel Raikes was struck by the number of advertisements in the newspapers for an English wife with a fortune.
Among Frenchmen who married into money were the comte de Flahaut, the
comte d'Orsay, and Napoléon's illegitimate son, the comte Walewski. All too
often, however, these marriages brought no monetary reward, as in the case of
Lamartine, de Vigny, and Chopin's friend, the dramatist-critic Ernest Legouvé.
Poor Berlioz, in fact, received nothing but a dowry of debts from his first wife,
the actress Harriet Smithson (fig. 5.5).

Because so many of the English flocked to France during the Restoration and
the July monarchy, few Frenchmen had to bother crossing the Channel to find
their brides. The low cost of living on the continent attracted many tourists as
well as "distressed gentlefolk" like Beau Brummell, whose meager incomes could
buy them a better life in France than in England. Naturally after Wellington's
victory at Waterloo in 1815, anti-British sentiment ran high, as it did in 1840 when

England joined other European powers in an alliance against France over a political crisis in the Ottoman Empire. In August of that year, Parisians went so far as to attack the carriage of the English ambassador, Lord Granville, and in December newspapers advised the English not to appear in public during ceremonies for the return of Napoléon's remains.

Apart from these few incidents, the tempestuous romance between the French and the English continued to such an extent that Colonel Raikes claimed Paris had practically become a British colony. This onslaught of the English was particularly visible in the stagecoach terminals, where Thackeray described the hubbub of their arrival. As diligences from the Channel pulled into the courtyard, a great uproar would break out, with horns blasting, postilions screaming, porters scrambling, and hotel agents crying out the names of their clients. In the midst of all this chaos, Thackeray would simply shout "Meurice!" whereupon a young man emerged from the crowd and whisked him off to the British tourist's favorite pied-à-terre in Paris, the Hôtel Meurice.

Among the rich English arrivals were prominent aristocrats like the duke of Hamilton, Sir Henry Bulwer (brother of the novelist Edward George Bulwer-Lytton), and Lord Hertford (owner and restorer of the comte d'Artois's "folly," Bagatelle, in the Bois de Boulogne). The poor were typically nameless yet numerous enough to have charity balls given for their relief. Somewhere between the affluent and the penurious were students like Lindsay Sloper and Jane Stirling, both of whom took piano lessons with Chopin; Thackeray, who came to study painting with baron Antoine-Jean Gros; and Fanny Kemble's sister Adelaide, anxious to perfect her technique in the art of bel canto singing (fig. 5.6). When one adds to these expatriates the hordes of tourists who visited Paris each year, there were enough English in the city to support a host of commercial enterprises devoted to their needs. English pastry cooks could be found on both the Right and Left Banks; on the Champs Elysées the Reverend Doctor Hale established a boarding school for English boys while nearby on the same street, a Mrs. Brunson ran one for English girls. Two English-language newspapers were published: the daily *Galignani's Messenger* and the weekly *London and Paris Observer*. The city also boasted seven "English eating houses" as well as an English dairy and provisions warehouse for the supply of "ale, port, cheese, hams etc."[8]

To the horror of the French Academy, English began to crop up all over the city, not only in hotels and shops, but also in conversations at the best salons, where the crème de la crème of society was popularly known as "the happy few."

5.6 Lindsay Sloper, one of Chopin's English pupils who helped make arrangements for his teacher's final public performance at London's Guild-hall in 1848.

Ordinary French *gentilhommes* called themselves "gentlemen," while the more fashionable ones prided themselves on being "sportsmen" or "clubmen." They were always attended by a young groom (generally called a "tiger"), smoked "Maryland" (tobacco), wore a "mackintosh," and bored their wives, sisters, fiancées, and hostesses by prattling on forever about "le boxing" and "le turf," "les steeplechases" and "les handicaps." Eventually a form of "Franglais" evolved in which French and English were hybridized to form neologisms like "dogue" and "bifteck." The vogue for English words extended to proper names as well. Dandies were known to dub their dogs O'Connell and their horses Frank. Baron de Rothschild preferred to be called James instead of Jacob, and George Sand chose the English George (over the French Georges). Similarly Dumas's collaborator, Auguste Maquet, took to signing his works "Mackeat."

For the dedicated Anglophile, it was not enough to talk or even dress like an Englishman. The *ne plus ultra* was to act like one—which was not always an easy task for those with a volatile Gallic temperament. By the Frenchman's standards,

Anglo-Saxon reserve seemed cold to the point of rudeness. To imitate it, he felt constrained to suppress his natural joie de vivre and behave in a chilly, disdainful manner. Politeness was avoided at all costs. It simply wasn't English. As Lady Blessington herself admitted, anyone in London who became too friendly was immediately suspected of having designs on the hearts of the ladies or the purses of the men. You could always spot a rich Englishman, she claimed, by his bluntness and stinginess. One of the most typical things about the English gentleman was his tendency to collect in small groups called "clubs." As early as 1824, the first of these was formed in Paris at No. 28 rue de Gramont. Initially called Le Cercle Français, it soon changed its name to Le Cercle de l'Union and remained for years the "gravest," most exclusive, and aristocratic of Parisian clubs. No gambling was allowed, and according to the English Colonel Raikes, the cost and quality of its meals could best be described as ordinary. Among its members were Prince Talleyrand, Baron James de Rothschild, and such noted dandies as the comte d'Orsay and his brother-in-law, the duc de Guiche. Because high-ranking members of the diplomatic corps were automatically admitted, about half of the club consisted of foreigners. Although the membership was divided almost equally between Frenchmen and foreigners, the latter were more frequently seen there. In such a heterogeneous organization, business meetings often became so noisy and disorderly that rational discussion was all but impossible.

Although the prestige of the Cercle de l'Union remained undisputed, some felt that it had become too political, and a rival club called the Jockey (modeled after the Jockey Club of New Market, London) was organized in 1834 (fig. 5.7). It came into existence as an offshoot of La Société pour l'Amélioration des Races de Chevaux en France (the society to improve the species of horses bred in France), founded the year before to assist the nation's horsebreeders, who had never fully recovered from the loss of their finest animals to Napoléon's armies. Among the twelve founders of the club were both aristocrats and commoners, including two of the royal princes (the duc d'Orléans and the duc de Nemours), Marshal Ney's son (the Prince de la Moskowa), count Demidoff, and Lord Henry Seymour. Despite the social cachet of the new club, it remained primarily a haven for sportsmen rather than dandies. When, for example, Alfred de Musset's name came up for membership, he was blackballed. "What would you expect?" Major Frazer sniffed. "He doesn't even know how to ride."[9]

Not only were social status and athletic prowess requisites for membership in the Jockey, money was an absolute sine qua non. Villemessant in his *Mémoires*

(Jockey-Club.)

5.7 Paris's famed Jockey Club was located at the northeast corner of today's rue Drouot and the boulevard Montmartre. It occupied the floors directly above a salesroom for Pleyel's pianos. Probably apocryphal is the legend that some members once rode their steeds up the stairs for a game of billiards on horseback in the club's quarters.

claims that no one with an income of less than 2.5 million francs a year could afford it. Actually the entrance fee and yearly dues were modest enough; it was the expense of maintaining a thoroughbred stable and gambling at the club's backgammon, whist, and piquet tables (not to mention simply keeping up the elegant lifestyle expected of a member) that excluded all but the most affluent from its roster. As expensive as it was, the Jockey Club flourished, and by 1835 its membership had grown to 150 (although only about fifty showed up regularly). At that time, it was still housed in its original quarters on the rue du Helder at the corner of the boulevard des Italiens. With the exception of Eugène Sue, no one from the literary, artistic, or musical world belonged to it. In 1836, the club moved to larger quarters at the corner of the boulevards and the rue Drouot. In 1838, after the city's public gaming houses were closed, the Parisian clubs flourished as never before. The Jockey alone took in nearly one hundred new members and was lit up until 5:00 in the morning as fortunes were made and lost in its exclusive sanctum.

The leading spirit of the Jockey Club's early years was its founder and first president, Lord Henry Seymour, who was then perhaps the most avid sportsman in all Paris. Although his parentage is ambiguous, Seymour seems to have been the illegitimate son of the English marchioness of Hertford and the comte de Montrond, once described by a contemporary as a "veteran of debauchery." The marquis of Hertford's undisguised dislike of young Henry seems to support this theory. In his will, Lord Hertford left his wife's son a mere shilling. Luckily the boy inherited a large fortune from a friend of his maternal grandmother, which enabled him to enjoy the extravagant pursuits of a Parisian man-about-town for the rest of his life.[10] In his appearance and behavior, the young lord came to represent everything that Eugène Sue felt the English gentleman should be. He was a superb example of "robust health... having for pleasure and relaxation the manly exercises of the chase, pugilism, hunting and shooting."[11] A great athlete, Lord Seymour exercised daily in his gym over the Café de Paris. His physical prowess was as legendary as Paul Bunyan's. According to rumor, his biceps measured nearly twenty-one inches in diameter, and it was said that he could lift 100 kilos (220 lbs.) with his little finger.

Horses, however, seem to have been Lord Seymour's greatest love, and his stables contained sixty or more, which he raced frequently in and around Paris. The Champs de Mars, Longchamps, and Chantilly were three of the most popular sites for such events (fig. 5.8). The racing colors of the aristocracy, however, were seldom seen at the Champs de Mars, which catered to a motley crowd. In spite of the increasing popularity of this new fad, not all Parisians could appreciate it. In the comte de Castellane's opinion, "If you've seen one race, you've seen them all."[12]

Another of Lord Seymour's favorite sports was pigeon shooting, which he enjoyed with other members of the "yellow-gloved brigade." The two main locations for this pastime in Paris were the English-styled gardens of the Parc Monceau, and the Jardin de Tivoli on the rue Clichy, where quail and parrots, as well as pigeons, were considered fair game. It was Lord Seymour's love of sports that eventually led to his resignation from the Jockey Club when he felt that gambling had taken precedence over the founders' original emphasis on the equestrian arts and other athletic pursuits.

Besides his reputation as a sportsman, Lord Seymour had the dandy's special fondness for cigars, which he smoked incessantly. At times he laced them with gunpowder and passed them out to friends who were seldom amused when they exploded in their faces. He also enjoyed putting itching powder in people's clothes and serving them hot chocolate fortified with potent laxatives.

Some of his acquaintances may well have deserved such treatment. Many took

5.8 The sport of horse racing was another English fad that took hold in Orleanist France. Proper enthusiasts practiced the sport at Chantilly or the nearby Longchamps racetrack in the Bois de Boulogne. True aficionados, however, considered it déclassé to be seen on the makeshift track set up in the Champs de Mars, shown here.

advantage of his wealth and generosity to borrow—or worse yet—to trick him out of large sums of money. In his study, hidden behind thick velvet curtains, Lord Seymour kept a painting of himself as Saint Stephen suffering martyrdom at the hands of his fellowmen. Eventually this sense of being perpetually abused reached paranoid proportions, causing him to sell his stables and withdraw from society completely. During his last years, he became a bitter recluse and misanthrope.

Although the Cercle de l'Union and the Jockey were the most select of the Parisian men's clubs, there were others for those of different tastes, such as Le Cercle des Amis de l'Art, which sponsored art exhibits and concerts, the Tir aux Pigeons for those devoted to bird-shooting, Le Grand Cercle (known as Les Ganaches, or "Kooks"), which was scorned by the fast set, and Le Cercle Agricole (often called les Pommes de Terre, or "Potatoes"), for those anxious to emulate the English country squire.

No discussion of the clubby scene would be complete without mentioning the Petit Cercle, which assembled regularly in the boulevard des Italien's Café de

Paris, below Lord Seymour's gymnasium. It was more loosely organized than the city's other clubs. In its heyday, however, it could rival the Jockey in exclusivity and probably exceeded it in the number of dandies on its roster. Among its founders were Lord Henry Seymour, the English Colonel Rees Howell Gronow, Roger de Beauvoir, Alfred de Musset, and the Italian Prince Belgiojoso. For the sake of privacy, they rented rooms in the café's annex. Rules and regulations were minimal: membership was limited to one hundred, political discussions were not allowed, and no one could remain in the club rooms after 2:00 A.M. The chef for the club was one of the best in Paris, and the cuisine always French— which even the most Anglophilic of dandies secretly preferred to English fare. After dinner, the evenings were taken up with smoking, billiards, and whist. Sometimes the perfumed and pomaded Colonel Gronow recited Byron, the only time his impassive Anglo-Saxon features ever revealed any emotion. During the revolution of 1848, when the Petit Cercle was forced to move, it lost its spirit of camaraderie and was never the same again.

All of this male bonding led to the social phenomenon known as *les femmes incomprises*, or "the unappreciated women." As fewer and fewer men showed up in the salons, women found themselves forced to rely on each other for diversion. According to Mme de Girardin, the establishment of English-style men's clubs was the ruin of all good society in Paris.

Contrary to the belief that imitation is the highest form of flattery, many of the English were not at all pleased by the French people's attempt to mimic their ways. Some, like Mrs. Trollope, were appalled at how misunderstood their customs were across the Channel. For instance, at a dinner party in Paris one night she was amazed to hear that everyone thought table napkins were never used in England, nor soup ever eaten there. As much as she admired the French language and relished the low cost of living in Paris, she devoutly wished that the French could be more like the English in their morals and their plumbing.

Thackeray, who had a far greater familiarity with the French than Mrs. Trollope, considered her a mere tourist whose views weren't worth a sixpence. All she knew of France, he claimed, had been learned at tea parties. Basically, though, he agreed with much of what she said. He himself realized that it was precisely in their tea parties that the French showed their basic ignorance of English values. The British, he noted, were most concerned (and rightly so) with the quality and preparation of the tea, while the French worried more about such trifles as the lighting of the room and the dresses of the ladies. He spoke highly of the Frenchman's sense of honor, but, like Mrs. Trollope, he found private morality in France of a lower order than in England. All in all he was much less tolerant of the French than was his compatriot, concluding from his observations that France as a nation was "all rant, tinsel and stage-play."[13] Even the gracious Lady Granville often found it difficult to put up with the Parisians. Beneath their elegant and engaging facades, she encountered in many a core of "ill breeding, insolence, conceit and pretention."[14]

Few Parisians exemplified these distressing traits more conspicuously than the smugly grandiloquent marquis de Custine, who once wrote disdainfully, "There is nothing natural or artistic in England. Manufacturing is the sole concern there. The whole country is simply a giant department store tended by a bunch of ill-tempered clerks."[15]

Chopin, who was not especially fond of Custine, nevertheless shared his Anglophobic attitudes. Although Lord and Lady Granville at the British embassy provided the young musician with many of his first pupils and an entrée into some of the city's most prestigious salons, his subsequent contacts with the English were less auspicious. His London publisher, Christian Rudolph Wessel, had the irritating habit of changing the names of his compositions from "Mazurkas," "Polonaises," "Valses," "Ballades," and so forth to cloying titles like "Souvenirs of Poland," "Gentle Breezes," "Sighs," and "Murmurs of the Seine." In England, music seemed to be merely a commodity to be bought and sold for money rather than an art with aesthetic value. The English, Chopin complained, calculated "everything in terms of pounds sterling and only cared for art because it was considered a luxury."[16] For them it was a ritual to listen to music night and day, be it at "a flower show, a dinner or a charity bazaar." "It doesn't matter what it's like," Chopin remarked, "nobody cares."[17] Unfortunately he did care and dreaded those evening musicales in the drawing rooms of the English and Scottish aristocracy where ladies whistled while they strummed a guitar or sang sentimental ballads to the accompaniment of an accordion. Even the London Philharmonic gave such mediocre performances that he refused an invitation to play with it.

Apart from its musical life, England irritated Chopin in many other ways. The sunless, soot-filled air of London made everything seem gray, from the sky to the buildings to the mud, while the damp mists of the countryside (particularly in Scotland) aggravated his cough. Still worse was the cigar smoking of the men around the dinner table at the end of a meal. Most of the English, he discovered, were obsessed with their pedigrees and devoted whole evenings to the recitation of their family trees. All this bored him to death. In fact, anything that wasn't boring, he declared, couldn't possibly be English.

At least Chopin was more tolerant (or merely more polite) than his friend, Heinrich Heine, who branded the English, "the most repulsive people that God in His wrath has created."[18] More amused than incensed by the English, George Sand satirized their insularity in one of her *Lettres d'un Voyageur.* "The islanders of Albion," she wrote, "carry with them a particular kind of fluid...in the middle of which they travel, as insulated from the atmosphere of the places they pass through as a mouse in a bell jar. Their constant impassivity...is because the air around us does not reach them; it is because they eat, walk, drink and sleep within their fluid, exactly as if they were inside a glass cloche twenty feet thick through which they gaze pityingly at [the rest of the world]."[19]

Such sporadic outbursts of Anglophobia didn't faze the majority of the French, who had been living under a British-style constitutional monarchy since 1814 and had slowly allowed their natural xenophobia to crumble before the onslaught of Anglo-Saxon customs after Waterloo. No sooner had Wellington taken Napoléon prisoner than all of France seemed to become captive to the influence of its neighbors across the Channel. What the nation's few Anglophobes failed to notice was that the French, in their fever of Anglomania, had absorbed much of great cultural value from England. The belated flowering of Romanticism in France, for example, was heavily indebted to the influence of English art and literature. The exhibition of works by English painters like Richard Parkes Bonington, John Constable, and Sir Thomas Lawrence received extravagant praise in the Paris Salon of 1824. A year later Eugène Delacroix visited England, where his infatuation with Shakespeare's plays led to the production of a series of lithographs on "Hamlet." Another French painter, Paul Delaroche, portrayed many scenes from English history, among them the "Execution of Lady Jane Gray" and "Cromwell discovering the Body of Charles." In literature Chateaubriand (who had lived in England as an emigré) published a French version of Milton's *Paradise Lost,* as well as French translations of other English authors including Shakespeare, Byron, the lake poets and Sir Walter Scott, which were printed in innumerable editions in both Paris and the provinces. Hugo, in the preface to his English-inspired drama *Cromwell,* issued a manifesto of freedom for the French theater. At the same time spectators throughout France were enjoying stage presentations based on English life, such as Dumas's *Catherine Howard,* Jacques Arsène and Marguerite-Louise-Virginie

5.9 Daumier's depiction of the mixed reaction of Frenchmen watching a production of Shakespeare's *Richard III*. Clearly not all Parisians were in tune with the Anglophilic tastes of the times. Except for his addiction to English fashions in menswear, Chopin, for one, was heartily Anglophobic.

Ancelot's *Lord Byron à Venise,* and de Vigny's *Chatterton* (fig. 5.9). When Charles Kemble's Shakespearean troupe came to Paris, Harriet Smithson's performances in *Hamlet, Othello,* and *Romeo and Juliet* mesmerized Berlioz, who not only married her but also took numerous Shakespearean subjects as the themes of his compositions.

Clearly Anglomania was more than a frothy social fad. Beneath the superficial mimicry of manners and fashions, there was a deeper cultural current that carried English ideas across the Channel and helped to nourish the Romantic movement in France. Taking a broad—and somewhat irreverant—view of history, one might describe the great plague of Anglomania that overran France in the early nineteenth century as England's revenge for the Norman conquest nearly eight hundred years earlier. Actually it was less a matter of revenge than the return of a favor, since the influence of one society on another creates a cross-fertilization that enriches the generations to follow.

CHAPTER 6

Musical Currents along the Seine

From Concert Halls to Dance Halls

*P*ARIS IS A CITY "DROWNED IN ... MUSIC," Heine exclaimed in
1841.[1] Word of this musical inundation had already reached another German, Richard Wagner, who arrived there in 1839, partly to escape his creditors
and partly to gain entrée to the city's opera houses, which he hoped would open
doors for him all over Europe. At that time he found the city so engulfed in music
that he scoffed, "there is a project on foot to introduce a huge orchestra into the
Chamber of Deputies, where it will be employed to provide recitative accompaniments for speeches ... and during the intermission, to impart delicacy and
grace to the hubbub raised by the deputies."[2] Although he was disappointed at
the results (or rather, lack of results) of his first visit to this musical Mecca-on-the-Seine, Wagner later acknowledged that Paris was the "culminating point" of
musical life, all other cities being "simply stations along the way.... There I was
at the source, and there I was able to grasp at once things which ... would perhaps
have taken me half a lifetime to learn."[3] Paris under the July monarchy had
indeed become the musical hub of the western world. As Chopin wrote his family in 1847, "I have to stop now to give a lesson to the Rothschilds' daughter and
after that, to a girl from Marseille. Then I have an English lady and later a
Swedish one. To finish off the day I have [to audition] some family from New
Orleans that Pleyel has sent me" (fig. 6.1).[4]

For Heine, Paris in the 1830s and 1840s was "a kind of bulletin board" where
artists could come and post their credentials for the rest of the world.[5] Those who
made a name for themselves in Paris could succeed anywhere. Few, however,
wanted to leave the city once they had a taste of it. As Berlioz put it, after two
years in Italy, life outside Paris was like being forced to unlearn music.[6]

To remain in the city, though, had its disadvantages. The great influx of foreign artists produced a highly competitive situation. "Paris, being in a continual
state of fermentation, throws up so many musicians of all sorts ... that they

6.1 A portrait of the youthful Frédéric Chopin as he must have appeared on his arrival in Paris.

either have to devour one another...or emigrate," Berlioz concluded.[7] Naturally, the international allure of Paris flattered its inhabitants, but the plethora of foreign geniuses like Chopin, Liszt, and Paganini couldn't help but offend their innate chauvinism. Such an abundance of talent put even the finest of artists under constant pressure to prove themselves. "People [in Paris] are no longer satisfied by *relative* perfection, since we have too much of that," Chopin observed. "What is needed for success is something *perfect*."[8]

Unfortunately those who came closest to achieving this perfection were often not appreciated by the city's bourgeois public, whose taste was less than perfect itself. With little cultural background, many of the middle class found themselves out of their depth in a vast sea of musical variety. The inability of the Parisians to discriminate between good and bad provoked a contemporary critic to comment that "they tap their foot to a Beethoven scherzo or an overture by Weber or Meyerbeer as they would to one of Musard's quadrilles."[9] In fact, he added, they usually preferred the quadrilles because they had a livelier beat.

In their struggle for success, many musicians turned their art into a business by exploiting its commercial aspects. The pianist Henri Herz, for example, became a major entrepreneur, manufacturing pianos, opening up a concert hall, financing a musical journal, and inventing mechanical devices to improve the performer's technique. Liszt reaped a fortune by shamelessly catering to the lowest levels of public taste and by utilizing every known trick in the showman's bag.

Only the "pop" conductors Philippe Musard and Louis Jullien could outdo the gimmickry of his performances by smashing chairs and shooting off pistols at their own concerts. Even Berlioz was not above stooping to politics for the sake of a government commission and knew how to stage incredible extravaganzas (including one at Franconi's circus) that drew crowds more for the spectacle than the music. In short, "art for art's sake" was a myth for many musicians of the period. Mammon, not music, was their god.

It would be unfair, however, to fault the early-nineteenth-century musician for commercializing his art; he really had little choice. His very survival depended on it since the eighteenth-century practice of aristocratic patronage was virtually dead in France by the time of the July monarchy. No longer were there wealthy potentates or petty princes to provide the artist with a sinecure. After 1830 the royal family continued to dispense a modicum of patronage, with the king retaining Ferdinand Paër as his court director of music, and his son, the duc d'Orléans, employing Jacques Halévy in a similar role for his private household. Apart from these few posts, the only other patronage offered by the July monarchy came in the form of government subsidies to the city's opera houses and theaters or an occasional government grant for some official ceremony. In such cases one had to deal with a host of petty bureaucrats, whom Berlioz decried as combining the worst features of "snob and mob."[10]

More and more, musicians found themselves having to rely on the public as their principal patron and demure to its tastes. Gone were the aristocratic standards of simplicity, gracefulness, and elegance in the arts. Instead spectacle, grandeur, and excitement were now favored by the newly affluent middle class, whose growing numbers demanded bigger concert halls and opera houses. It followed naturally that the larger the hall the louder the music needed to fill it, a change that would one day prove to be a serious problem for "the vaporous nuances of Monsieur Chopin's microscopic mode of playing."[11] In keeping with these trends, it was no wonder that most composers and performers soon concluded that bigger, brassier, and bourgeois added up to the same thing: more money. For the new public of bankers, financiers, and industrialists, music wasn't merely a pleasure to be cultivated and enjoyed; it was also a commodity to be bought and displayed for its social prestige. This meant that the aspiring musician had to focus more on the marketability of his art than on its merits.

Nowhere perhaps was the musician pressed into a commercial role so much as in his attempts to organize a concert. The burden of such an enterprise discouraged all but the most hearty virtuosi and was one of the major reasons why Chopin acquired such an aversion to the concert stage. Because impresarios were virtually nonexistent at that time, musicians had to fend for themselves in all business matters related to their professional careers. Finding a place to perform was one of the artist's first problems, and as Berlioz observed, a truly major one. "We do not possess a single good public concert hall," he complained, adding, "It would never occur to any of our Midases to build one."[12] According to the *Gazette Musicale,* the only decent auditorium in Paris was the Conservatory's at No. 2 rue Bergère. Although it was "dark and smoky," the hall had the best acoustics in the city and could accommodate over a thousand people.[13] Furthermore its location, just north of the boulevard Montmartre, placed it within acceptable reach of all the best residential areas of the city. Unfortunately it couldn't be rented out from January through May (when the Conservatory orchestra gave its annual series of concerts), and due to professional intrigues, it often remained closed to such outstanding artists as Chopin and Berlioz for long periods of time. Eventually, though, both men were to achieve triumphs there before audiences considered to be the most discerning in Paris.

The second largest hall in the city was probably the Hôtel de Ville's Salle Saint-Jean. Despite its size—the auditorium could easily accommodate orchestras large enough to perform a Beethoven symphony—its facilities were considered primitive and its location too far east to suit the fashionable crowd. The next best halls were generally much smaller and belonged to piano manufacturers. Among the most desirable were those owned by Pleyel, Erard, Herz, and Pape.[14] All were located on the Right Bank (the main center of cultural life then) and designed for the comfort of an affluent clientele who were potential buyers of their pianos. Many less prestigious piano manufacturers also maintained their own concert halls, as did some musical organizations like the Chantereine Hall Society (to which Chopin belonged for a while) and the Gymnase Musicale. A number of enterprising music teachers also gave concerts in their private "salons de concert" (that is, their living rooms), while popular dance palaces and "pleasure gardens" often dignified their premises with the title of "concert halls."

Unfortunately for the performing artist, a large portion of the receipts from his or her concert went toward the rental of the hall (light and heat were extra), as well as for a substantial poor tax that the city of Paris levied on all public performances. In addition, the artist was burdened with the chores of advertising his concert and selling tickets for it. Box offices weren't a standard fixture in concert halls then, so the performer had to find other sales outlets. For many this proved to be the local music store. In Chopin's case his publisher, Maurice Schlesinger, sold tickets for his concerts and gave them advance publicity in his journal, the *Revue et Gazette Musicale*. From a purely business point of view this made good sense for Schlesinger since the pianist's performances always increased the sales of his compositions.

Until the 1840s, another task of the performing artist was finding other musicians to "assist" him on the program. The day of the solo recital hadn't yet arrived, and it was still considered essential to have an assortment of singers and instrumentalists to hold the public's attention. In cases where the program required an orchestra or chorus, the recruiting problem was even greater. To meet these demands, a certain reciprocity developed among members of the musical community, based on the philosophy "if you help me, I'll help you."

Whether we blame the materialistic orientation of the new social order or the loss of integrity of the artist, the fact remains that music under the Orleanist regime was riding the flood tide of commercialism. And as often happens with any severe inundation, an outbreak of pestilence followed. In Paris this took the form of what Heine called a "veritable plague of piano-playing," the chief symptom of which was an excess of empty virtuosity.[15] Soon this malaise reached epidemic proportions. "Everyday the piano becomes more and more of a disaster," the journalist Mirecourt wrote. "No wonder men flee to their clubs and coffee houses."[16] Some Parisians even took to calling their city "Pianopolis." By 1847 there were at least 180 piano manufacturers in Paris. The four most outstanding, Camille Pleyel, Pierre Erard, Henri Herz, and Johann Pape, all won medals in the international industrial expositions held regularly in Paris.

The majority of pianos turned out in the Parisian factories were intended not for the concert hall but for the home, where they rivaled the harp and guitar as the most popular instruments on which young ladies accompanied themselves while singing the poignant romances of the period.[17] Because the harp and guitar cost less, they were found more frequently in the homes of the poorer classes. The piano, on the other hand, "was expensive enough to be socially desirable" and hence a symbol of affluence.[18]

The piano was also a versatile instrument on which one could reproduce (with varying degrees of success) music written for the voice or orchestra, including complex scores of operas and symphonies. Whatever one's need, there was some manufacturer somewhere who had just the piano to meet it. Besides conventional "grands" and "uprights," there were pianinos (or spinets); square, round, oval, or hexagonal pianos; fold-up pianos; pianos with keyboards that could be pulled out or pushed in like a drawer (to serve as tables when not in use); and double pianos, built back-to-back like a partners' desk. In addition, there were pianos with concave keyboards, pianos with white keys only, pianos with shifting keyboards that could transpose automatically, and pianos with foot pedals, page turners, and attachments to imitate drums, cymbals, and triangles. Other pianos could imitate the sound of two pianos or produce echo effects. One manufacturer, feeling that such innovations had gone far enough, decided to return to the past and invented a piano that sounded like a harpsichord. Most, however, continued to experiment, producing pianos with strings made of platinum (rustproof but expensive), strings in the shape of mattress springs, and strings that were made to vibrate by gusts of air rather than hammers. At the industrial exposition of 1844, M. Pape presented a stenographic piano that recorded music on rolls of paper, much like later "player pianos." This ingenious manufacturer also designed a piano-oven that could cook a meal while the owner relaxed at the keyboard. His eight-octave piano achieved special popularity due to its increased width, which allowed two ladies in their voluminous skirts to sit side by side as they performed the prized four-hand duets of the era.

In this piano-crazed society, Hector Berlioz stood out by virtue of his marked aversion to the instrument. "When I think of the appalling quantity of platitudes for which the piano is daily responsible," he wrote in his *Mémoires,* "I can only offer up my gratitude to chance which taught me perforce to compose freely and in silence, and thus saved me from the tyranny of keyboard habits."[19] He especially disliked the upright piano, which he called a "dull and indecent thing... that offends all good company."[20] To possess one was no less than "a crime of *lèse-art.*"[21] In light of Berlioz's outspoken scorn for the piano, it is no wonder that he and Chopin seldom saw eye to eye on musical matters.

Because Berlioz's main interest was the orchestra, it is understandable that he had little concern for the piano, an instrument that he never really came to master. He was, however, highly knowledgeable about most other instruments and even wrote a lengthy treatise, "On Instrumentation," for the *Gazette Musicale.* To cover such a subject was no easy task in an era when inventive minds were creating and patenting new musical instruments at breakneck speed. Many of these innovations were operated by keyboards and therefore didn't particularly attract Berlioz's attention. Some, nevertheless, are worth mentioning, such as the panorgue-piano, "a happy and fruitful idea" that sounded like a piano with orchestral accompaniment, the claviharpe with silk-covered strings that were plucked to mimic a harp, and the phonomine that could imitate the human voice (male voices only).²² Of all these new keyboard inventions only a small pump organ, called a harmonium or melodeon, piqued Berlioz's curiosity enough for him to write some compositions for it.

Given his penchant for the grandiose, it is amazing that Berlioz failed to compose anything for the mammoth steam organ invented by M. Sax *fils*, who claimed it could be heard throughout an entire province. "This monster organ," the *Gazette Musicale* prophesied, "will be destined for popular solemnities and for railroad inaugurations."²³ It might well have enhanced Berlioz's "Song of the Railroad," written for a ball in Lille to celebrate the opening of the new Northern Railroad line. Perhaps, though, the composer feared that the colossal organ, which could "drown out...thunder" would drown out the soloists as well.²⁴

If Berlioz neglected Sax's organ, he was quite impressed by the saxhorn and the saxophone, two instruments invented by the young man's father (fig. 6.2).²⁵ The first public performance of the saxophone was given at Paris's Salle Herz in February 1844, where its inventor played a work written for it by Berlioz.²⁶ Although its debut was not particularly successful, M. Sax *père* was invited the following year to demonstrate his new instruments before the royal family. In some of his later works Berlioz included the bugle-like saxhorns alongside his beloved ophicleides (other members of the brass family replaced by today's tuba).

In 1835 a M. Samson demonstrated his new harmonica, which "completely overwhelmed" one of the editors of the *Gazette Musicale* but left most serious composers unmoved. Other remarkable but unappreciated inventions of the period were M. Lauren's crystal flute, M. Isoard's "violon aeolique" (with a single string vibrated by air currents), and M. Glon's mechanical improvisers exhibited at the Paris Exposition of Industrial Products in 1834. The same exposition also included an ordinary-looking rain hat that could play musical pieces like a bagpipe. If most inventors of new musical instruments failed to share in the profits of France's belated industrial age, so did the composers and performers for whom their products were created. While Paris was drowning in music, many of its musicians were also drowning in debts. Often they had to neglect their chosen profession to search for other ways of feeding themselves and their families. In Berlioz's case, the economic alternative to writing music was to write criticism for the Parisian journals, a task to which he grudgingly devoted forty years of his life.

Although literate people of all eras had jotted down their thoughts about

6.2 Adolph Sax *père*, inventor of the saxhorn and the saxophone (perfected in 1845 and 1846, respectively). He came to Paris in 1842, where he manufactured musical instruments, many of which he attempted to modify. Unfortunately these unlicensed changes led to a number of lawsuits that bankrupted him.

music, it was not until the nineteenth century that the rise of journalism created a new variant of this literary species known today as music critics. Unlike their predecessors, who were often aristocratic and wrote mostly for their own diversion, professional music critics wrote mainly for money. Many of them, as Berlioz lamented, lacked any musical background, although this seldom deterred them from issuing dogmatic pronouncements that were readily accepted as gospel by an unsuspecting public. One of the first musical journals in Paris with a qualified music critic was the *Revue Musicale*, founded in 1827 by François Joseph Fétis, who single-handedly assumed virtually all its duties, including that of critic.

Prior to the *Revue Musicale*, a number of other Parisian journals with a broader scope featured articles on music from time to time. It was with one of these, *Le Corsaire*, in 1823, that Berlioz began his lifelong career of journalism, which was to earn him far more money than his compositions. As much as he disliked writing musical criticism, he did it well, in an observant, often witty style, and contributed greatly to this nascent art. Berlioz's candid remarks and crusading spirit, however, often made him feared by his colleagues. Inevitably he made enemies, many of whom would throw obstacles in the path of his musical career later on. Although he wrote for a host of publications with divergent political and artistic viewpoints (the *Journal des Débats*, *Le Rénovateur*, *Le Monde Dramatique*, and others) it was not until Chopin's publisher, Maurice Schlesinger, created the *Gazette Musicale* in November 1834 that Berlioz found an adequate outlet for his views on the Parisian musical scene. From its beginning, the journal was

6.3 George Sand, who grew up in a musical environment, learned to play the piano, harp, and guitar. By the time she met Chopin, Sand had joined the staff of the *Revue et Gazette Musicale,* which was a literary as well as a musical journal.

largely produced by him and became a vehicle for his ideas. Unlike the *Revue Musicale,* the *Gazette Musicale* extended its scope into the field of literature as well as music. This gave Berlioz the chance to express his reflections on writers like Goethe, Byron, Walter Scott, and Shakespeare, who were the inspiration for many of his musical compositions. Among the Parisian literati on the *Gazette*'s staff were writers like George Sand, Honoré Balzac, and Alexandre Dumas *père* (fig. 6.3). In time Berlioz would bring the young, unknown, and penniless Richard Wagner onto its staff where he, too, would endure many agonizing hours writing prose rather than music.

The man at the helm of the *Gazette Musicale,* Moritz-Adolf Schlesinger (known as Maurice in Paris) was the oldest son of a German-Jewish family who owned a book and music shop in Berlin. After fighting with Napoléon's troops in his early youth, Schlesinger came to Paris in 1819, where he opened a bookstore that was later closed by the police because of his liberal political views. By 1824 he had established himself at No. 97 rue Richelieu as a music publisher of both instrumental works and opera. Among his clients were Mendelssohn, Liszt, Chopin, Berlioz, Johann Strauss, César Franck, Meyerbeer, and Halévy. In 1840 he married Elise Foucault, with whom Flaubert was once in love. Under her influence, he embraced Christianity. For Chopin this was purely a cosmetic conversion, and he continued to deride the publisher as "that Jew [who is] forever trying to make a big impression on people."[27] Although he complained that "Schlesinger has always played tricks on me," he had to admit that the man never broke his word once he'd given it—which was more than he could say about some of his other publishers, like Pleyel.[28]

All in all Chopin sold about forty of his works to Schlesinger. The publisher's volatile temperament, however, often strained their relationship. In 1834 he drew Chopin into a lawsuit against one of Henri Herz's pupils. Later his clashes with another publisher, Eugène Théodore Troupenas, and a rival journal, *La France Musicale,* also caused Chopin considerable discomfort. Still he continued his collaboration with Schlesinger until the latter sold his business in 1846 and retired to Baden-Baden. After that, Chopin remained with Schlesinger's successor, the firm of Brandus et Dufour, who published most of the composer's final works.

Despite Schlesinger's personal shortcomings, his influence on the musical world of his time was widely appreciated. The czarina of Russia (consort of the Francophobic Czar Nicholas I) once presented him with "a magnificent diamond ring," and Queen Victoria later awarded him a medal engraved with her portrait for his contributions to the progress of music in 1841.[29] Besides his publication of the many important composers already mentioned, Schlesinger's influence on the course of musical events in the early nineteenth century was due to the ideas and information disseminated through his *Gazette Musicale.* A weekly journal at first, it was originally designed to promote the sale of works put out by his publishing firm. Before long, however, it had absorbed Fétis's *Revue Musicale* (to become the *Revue et Gazette Musicale*) and doubled its output with two editions a week. (Despite this merger, the combined journals continued to be called *The Gazette Musicale,* which is how I will refer to it.) Many issues included lithographic portraits of famous musicians and copies of new songs or piano vignettes. A further bonus offered by the journal was an annual concert series, which took place in various halls around the city. With its large staff of journalists, music critics, teachers, composers, concert artists, chapel masters, poets, novelists, playwrights, and foreign correspondents, Schlesinger's journal, like a multiheaded Hydra, was able to see and hear all that went on throughout the width and breadth of musical Europe (fig. 6.4).

The Gazette Musicale did more, though, than merely mirror the musical events of the continent. Under Schlesinger's direction, members of the journal's staff were encouraged to become crusaders, advocating reforms where needed and promoting the development of tastes and techniques that would advance the musical and literary arts. Berlioz, for example, protested the practice of hiring unqualified music critics with no formal musical education, while Liszt expressed

8ᵉ Année. — 1841.

N° 31.

REVUE

ET

GAZETTE MUSICALE

DE PARIS.

Journal des Artistes, des Amateurs et des Théâtres.

RÉDIGÉE

PAR M. G.-E. ANDERS, G. BENEDIT, F. BENOIST (professeur de composition au Conservatoire), BERTON (de l'Institut), BERLIOZ, HENRI BLANCHARD, MAURICE BOURGES, CASTIL-BLAZE, F. DANJOU, DUESBERG, ELWART, FÉTIS père (maître de chapelle du roi des Belges), ÉDOUARD FÉTIS, AD. GUÉROULT, STEPHEN HELLER, EDME SAINT-HUGUÉ, JULES JANIN, KASTNER. LISZT ADRIEN DE LAFAGE, J. MARTIN, MARX, CHARLES MERRUAU, ÉDOUARD MONNAIS, AUGUSTE MOREL, D'ORTIGUE, PANOFKA, HIPPOLYTE PREVOST, L. RELLSTAB, GEORGES SAND, ROBERT SCHUMANN, PAUL SMITH, SPAZIER, A. SPECHT, RICHARD WAGNER, etc.

PRIX DE L'ABONNEMENT
A LA
REVUE
ET
GAZETTE MUSICALE.

Paris.	Départ.	Étrang.
3 m. 8	9 »	10 »
6 m. 15	17 »	19 »
1 an. 50	54 »	58 »

ANNONCES :
50 c. la ligne de 28 lettres.

La Revue et Gazette musicale paraît
le Dimanche.

On s'abonne au bureau de la *Revue et Gazette Musicale de Paris*, rue Richelieu, 97 ; chez MM. les directeurs des Postes , aux bureaux des Messageries; et chez tous les libraires et marchands de musique de la France et de l'étranger.

Paris, Dimanche 2 mai 1841.

Il sera donné à MM. les Abonnés, outre les deux feuilles par semaine pendant les mois d'hiver et une feuille pendant les mois de l'été :
1. Douze Mélodies composées par MM. HALEVY, MEYERBEER, PROCH, SCHUBERT, Mlle PUGET, etc.
2. Des Morceaux de piano composés par MM. CHOPIN, DOEHLER, STEPHEN HELLER, F. HUNTEN, KALKBRENNER, LISZT, MENDELSSOHN, MOSCHELES, ROSENHAIN, THALBERG, E. WOLFF, etc.
3. Plusieurs recueils des Archives curieuses de la musique ;
4. Des Portraits d'artistes célèbres ;
5. Des Fac simile de l'écriture d'auteurs célèbres.
6. PLUSIEURS CONCERTS.

SOMMAIRE. Concert de Chopin; par F. LISZT. — Académie royale de musique : représentation au bénéfice de Duprez, et reprise de *Don Juan.* — Concert de F. Liszt. — Concerts ; par H. BLANCHARD. — Soirée musicale de l'institution Gasc. — Nouvelles. — Annonces.

Bientôt nous donnerons à MM. les Abonnés les Portraits de nos célèbres violonistes Baillot, Artôt, de Bériot, Ernst, Haumann et Panofka, avec leurs biographies.

MM. les Abonnés recevront successivement morceaux suivants expressément composés pour la *Gazette musicale*, savoir :

1. *Mazurka*, par Edouard Wolff.
2. Un morceau par F. Liszt.
3. Un morceau par Th. Doehler.
4. Un morceau par Osborne.
5. Un morceau par Kalkbrenner.
6. Un morceau par Chopin.

Pour le Chant.

1. Trois Mélodies par J. Dessauer.
2. Deux romances, paroles françaises et italiennes, par Th. Doehler.

CONCERT DE CHOPIN.

Lundi dernier, à huit heures du soir , les salons de M. Pleyel étaient splendidement éclairés; de nombreux équipages amenaient incessamment au bas d'un escalier couvert de tapis et parfumé de fleurs les femmes les plus élégantes , les jeunes gens les plus à la mode , les artistes les plus célèbres , les financiers les plus riches, les grands seigneurs les plus illustres , toute une élite de société , toute une aristocratie de naissance, de fortune, de talent et de beauté.

Un grand piano à queue était ouvert sur une estrade ; on se pressait autour ; on ambitionnait les places les plus voisines; à l'avance on prêtait l'oreille , on se recueillait , on se disait qu'il ne fallait pas perdre un accord, une note, une intention, une pensée de celui qui allait venir s'asseoir là. Et l'on avait raison d'être ainsi avide, attentif, religieusement ému, car celui que l'on attendait, que l'on voulait voir, entendre, admirer, applaudir, ce n'était pas seulement un virtuose habile , un pianiste expert dans l'art de faire des notes ; ce n'était pas seulement un artiste de grand renom , c'était tout cela et plus que tout cela , c'était Chopin.

Venu en France il y a dix ans environ , Chopin , dans la foule des pianistes qui à cette époque surgissait de toutes parts, ne combattit point pour obtenir la première ni la seconde place. Il se fit très peu entendre en public ; la nature éminemment poétique de son talent ne l'y portait pas. Semblable à ces fleurs qui n'ouvrent qu'au soir leurs odorants calices , il lui fallait une atmosphère de

---

6.4 The front page of the *Revue et Gazette Musicale*, Sunday, May 2, 1841. On it is a review of a Chopin concert written by Franz Liszt and his mistress, the comtesse d'Agoult. The condescending tone of their remarks irritated the Polish pianist immensely. Later, Liszt and his subsequent mistress, the princess Carolyne von Sayn-Wittgenstein, wrote one of the first biographies of Chopin. Its florid fantasies wander far from the facts of his life and no doubt would have angered Chopin even more than the review shown above.

concern about the state of sacred music under the July monarchy. At that time, sacred music was a relatively neglected genre, shackled with numerous archaic restrictions. Women, for instance, weren't allowed to sing in churches, and the use of a piano at religious services was considered little short of sacrilege. When Liszt and Chrétien Urhan once performed Beethoven's grand duo for piano and violin in the sanctuary of Saint-Vincent-de-Paul, church officials were scandalized. On the other hand, a secularized nuptial mass composed of operatic fragments from Meyerbeer's *Robert le Diable,* given at Saint-Eustache the same year, met with approval because it was accompanied by an organ.

For all his pose as a reformer, Liszt continued to write and play florid transcriptions of current operatic arias, which he whipped up into the glistening musical confections demanded by a public that couldn't get its fill of "themes and variations." His *Grand Fantasy* on Meyerbeer's *Robert le Diable* sold five hundred copies on the day it came out and was praised by the *Gazette Musicale* as "the most brilliant and difficult piano piece written to date."[30] Even Chopin fell victim to this musical fad of operatic pastiches and contributed his own variations on Meyerbeer's *Robert le Diable,* Rossini's *La Cenerentola,* Hérold and Halévy's *Ludovic,* Bellini's *I Puritani,* and Mozart's *Don Giovanni.* The two high priests of this popular art form were the raffish pianist Henri Herz and the *Gazette Musicale*'s opera critic F. H. J. Castil-Blaze. Naturally the *Gazette* favored the latter and wrote rather harshly that his competitor's compositions were full of "atrocious passages which should have been omitted out of pity for our ears."[31]

Such criticism would have been equally appropriate for many of the so-called salon pieces published by Schlesinger's firm. For the superficial music lover with a short attention span, there were frothy little compositions with fanciful titles like "Fantaisies," "Bagatelles," or "Plaisanteries," as well as kaleidoscopic pastiches labeled "Pot-Pourris," "Mélange pour piano," and "Mosaïques." Bolder Sturm und Drang addicts could glory in the tumultuous "Grands Marches," "Galops," and "Galopades" (or just about anything labelled *brillante*), while the tender-hearted fluttered over syrupy *morceaux* with names like "Pensées," "Souvenirs," or "Les Regrets." Naturally everyone reveled in his or her particular *Air Favori,* among which were many with flowery titles like "Les Fleurs Mélodiques des Alpes" or "Les Fleurs des Salons." By 1838 flower titles had become such a vogue that the music journal *Le Ménestrel* published an article called "Musique Végétale" in which it ridiculed the plethora of compositions with horticultural allusions like "Lilacs," "Violettes," "Orangers," "Roses"—even "Roses Artificielles." Any waltz, it claimed, was assured of success merely by undergoing a "floral baptism."[32] Most of these works were aimed at the amateur with assurances that they were well within the range of his or her competence.

In an age that tended to equate sensitivity with sentimentality, melancholy became the most prized of all emotions, and the ability to weep freely emerged as the hallmark of a true Romantic. One night at the apartment of Chopin's friend, the music critic Legouvé, the lamp was turned out while Berlioz and others lay on the floor, listening in tears as Liszt played a Beethoven sonata. This rage to appear melancholic reached such heights that some complained Paris had become "a suburb of Père Lachaise. On the streets one strolls beside the half-living while passing by the half-dead."[33] Berlioz was among those who fell victim to this fashionable malaise at an early age. "My youthful essays in composition were of a melancholy cast," he admitted, "almost all my melodies were in the minor mode. I was aware of the defect but struggled against it in vain."[34] If he portrayed this aspect of his character as a weakness, others praised it as a virtue. The *Gazette Musicale*, writing about a piece by the Saint-Simonian composer Félicien David, stated that it was "suffused with a solemn and monotonous melancholy which indicated in the composer ideas of an elevated nature."[35]

Nowhere was the mania for melancholy more evident than in the popular romances of the time. These came in sheet music with covers depicting pensive young ladies, weeping muses, and dying poets, most of whom cradled a lyre in their arms. One such work was simply called "Mélancholie," whereas others had more imaginative titles like "The Storms of the Heart," "Don't Comfort Me," "Oh, How I Despise My Passion!" and "No More Happiness without You." Some, like "Memories of Edinburgh Prison," "I Am Dying of Hunger," and the ultimate "Dead from Love" reached even greater depths of gloom and despair. The last of these, about a young girl who drowned herself in the Seine as the result of an unhappy love affair, was composed by Loïsa Puget, the period's acknowledged queen of romance writers. Although she specialized in the sorrows of the lovelorn, Puget was also an expert in marital discord and family strife, the latter being the subject of another of her romances, "The Request in Marriage," subtitled "The Savage Brothers, or Family Hatreds Infinitely Too Prolonged."

Despite the banality of these romances, they appealed to sophisticated audiences and were standard fare in the salons of such distinguished social and literary figures as the comtesse Merlin, baron Gérard, Charles Nodier, and Delphine de Girardin. In fact the very simplicity of the romances made them particularly adapted to the intimacy of a salon. It also meant that the performer didn't need an exceptional voice to master them. One actually wonders if any vocal apparatus was necessary at all since devotees claimed that in a romance "it is the heart which sings."[36]

The ability to pronounce clearly was by far the most important skill required in performing these romances, where the principal effect came from the words rather than the music. Even with that in mind, it is hard to feel any great rush of emotion in the following lines of a "typical" romance stripped of its melody:

> "I know it now, I am betrayed
> Another's won your heart away.
> But even though your love can fade,
> Mine will be true to you for aye."
> Refrain:
> "Just summon me, I will return,
> Just summon me, I will return."[37]

Although such verses may seem vapid to the present-day reader, they had a wrenching effect on sensitive Parisians in the 1830s. As Bouteron assures us, the manufacturers of handkerchiefs then "made a fast fortune...in an effort to stanch the tears, the sighs, the sobs and desperate cries which constituted the obligatory repertoire of society singers."[38]

One reason for the mediocrity of so much music during the Louis-Philippe era was that composers no longer strove to gratify the tastes of a cultivated aristocracy. Most now geared their musical efforts toward a less tutored middle class, while some even sought out the working classes as the public of the future. Chopin's friend Adolphe Nourrit, for example, trained choirs of workers to sing cantatas, while Maurice Bourges, an editor of the *Gazette Musicale,* cited two popular piano numbers called "The Daisies" and "The First Flowers" (more examples of musical flora) as useful "to the needs of the working class in our social order."[39] The growing tendency of the arts to focus more and more on the proletariat during the July monarchy was consistent with Romanticism's emphasis on the emotional aspect of human nature. Feelings alone were held to be the common denominator that unified all mankind and reduced to insignificance such accidental factors as birth, intelligence, and education. The result was a cult that glorified the simple, artless individual, untainted by the hypocritical morality of a materialistic society. For proto-Romantics like Rousseau, this guileless individual had been the "noble savage," whereas the aristocrat, at the opposite end of the social spectrum, represented corruption and decadence. From 1830 on, however, the bourgeois capitalist was to become the new perpetrator of false values and the arch-enemy of the Romantic artist, while the noble savage, now evicted from the idyllic garden of Eden, adopted the role of a militant rebel. In a short story for the *Gazette Musicale* entitled "Le Contrebandier" (The smuggler), Mme Sand presented the protagonist as a Romantic hero whose disregard for the repressive rules of bourgeois society symbolized the new ideal of artistic liberty.

The popular use of folk melodies (in the Polish mazurkas of Chopin and the Hungarian rhapsodies of Liszt) was a further reflection of the trend to extol the commoner. In the *Gazette Musicale*, articles abounded on the folk music of Germany, France, Poland, Bohemia, and even such remote outposts as China, India, and Africa. Program music was another method employed by the Romantics to reach the masses, who were not considered sophisticated enough to grasp art in an abstract form. Opera, of course, had always relied on drama to heighten the effect of music, but it wasn't until Berlioz came along with his dramatic symphonies that the narrative element began to assume a similar importance in concert music. This attempt to "verbalize" through music was spoofed in a skit at the Opéra ball of 1835, which caricatured Berlioz conducting a musical work that "described" the intricacies of tying a bow tie.

Such musicological sparring was of little concern to most readers of the *Gazette Musicale*, who accepted the early-nineteenth-century concert for what it was, a variety show not unlike those on television today. Until 1839 when Liszt introduced the solo piano recital in Rome, concerts were a potpourri of vocalists and instrumentalists, along with an occasional thespian thrown in for dramatic effect. Because vocal music was preferred by Parisian audiences over instrumental works, no one dared plan a concert without at least one singer. Unfortunately the city's prefect of police felt compelled from time to time to ban singing at evening concerts to protect the state-run opera houses from competition.

To satisfy the pleasure-loving Parisians, concerts were given year-round. Those in the summer consisted mostly of light dance music, often performed outdoors, while more serious programs usually took place in winter and spring—especially during Lent, when balls were forbidden. A casual atmosphere (which wouldn't be tolerated except in rock performances today) prevailed during concerts then. Few ever started on time, and the delay was often so great that the *Gazette Musicale*'s critic, Henri Blanchard, made a practice of arriving late to

avoid waiting for an hour or more while the piano was being tuned. Often performers didn't show up, and a harpist might fill in at the last moment for an absent
prima donna. In addition, unannounced rearrangements of the program were
common. This naturally confused many in the audience, who would burst into
wild applause at some banal work by Kalkbrenner, thinking they had just heard a
masterpiece by Mozart. According to Berlioz, the orchestra members generally
followed the score in a haphazard fashion. Only when inspired by some chef
d'oeuvre, or called upon to play a solo passage, did they ever give a performance
their full attention. Audiences often behaved with equal indifference. Most concerts were excruciatingly long, often including an orchestral overture or symphony interspersed with "a mass of Italian cavatinas, fantasias for piano, excerpts
from masses, flute concertos, lieder with solo trombone obbligato, bassoon duets
and the like."⁴⁰ Small wonder the concertgoer often became restless and took to
milling around, talking, laughing, and even eating during a performance.

   To jolt the blasé music-lover out of his apathy, drastic measures were often
required. Favorite techniques were the use of novelty, noise, and numbers—indi-
vidually or in combination. Although the piano was no longer new enough to be a
novelty, it could at least make a lot of noise, especially if used in numbers. Furthermore, it is one of the few instruments on which two people can play simultaneously. Years earlier the young Mozart and his sister demonstrated the wonders
to be had from simply doubling the output of a single piano. By 1830 four-hand
piano music had become enormously popular both in the home and on the concert
stage. Inevitably someone concluded that eight hands at two pianos could create
even more of an effect. In time, Kalkbrenner pushed this logic still further by producing a spectacular *Grande Polonaise* for six pianos and twelve hands. Chopin,
still young and impressionable at the time, was persuaded to add this mammoth
dazzler to his Paris debut in 1832. Not to be outdone, Henri Herz scored an operatic transcription for sixteen hands at eight pianos and later (to awe his American
public) he composed a *Grande Marche Triomphale* for no fewer than forty pianos.
At the California premiere of the piece, however, only eight instruments could be
rounded up. As a result the world record in the multi-piano marathon seems to
have fallen to Franz Stoepel, a friend and concert companion of Chopin's who
gave a program at Paris's Hôtel de Ville in 1838 with twenty young ladies performing "several *grands morceaux* for four hands on ten pianos all at once."⁴¹

   For those obsessed with making a novelty out of numbers, it was clear that
Berlioz stood head and shoulders above the crowd (fig. 6.5). In August 1844, this

6.5 Hector Berlioz, with whom Chopin performed in public on several occasions. The two men, however, were poles apart in their musical conceptions. While Berlioz explored the complex and grandiose realms of orchestral and operatic composition, Chopin excelled in the intimate sonorities of the newly perfected piano.

great orchestrator staged a concert with 1,022 musicians in the Hall of the Exhibition of Industrial Products. To help him, he had two assistant conductors and five chorus masters, aided by seven additional time-beaters. Their "eyes never left me for an instant," he reported, "and despite the distance between us, our arms rose and fell with incredible precision.... I do not think anything like this can often have been experienced."[42] The strain of it all, however, forced the maestro to take a lengthy break midway through the performance. "A miniature dressing-room was constructed out of a dozen harps, with their covers replaced," which allowed him to rest and change clothes without being seen.[43] Berlioz's power to regiment such vast armies of musicians caused Wagner to dub him the "Napoléon of music."[44]

Because few musicians had the means (or the magic) to match the grand musical conceptions of a Berlioz, they had to find other ways of attracting an audience. Wojciech Sowiński (a Polish emigré and former classmate of Chopin's from Warsaw), for example, included a "piquant morceau" for trombones and harps in one of his concerts. Another of their compatriots, Michael Joseph Gusikow, donned a traditional Polish-Jewish costume to perform at the Opéra Comique and the Salle Pleyel on a homemade xylophone of wood and straw. Elsewhere in the city, a Hungarian family named Zingaris offered a potpourri of zither works interspersed with cymbal solos. Family groups could usually count on a good reception in

Paris, especially if they included one or more child prodigies like the Grassll family from Bavaria. The father, a farmer, butcher, and distillery worker, had seven children aged two to twelve who were, to say the least, versatile. With the exception of the two youngest, all were "virtuosos" on the violin, flute, clarinet, horns, trumpet, and trombone, which they traded back and forth on stage. As for the two little ones, they imitated cuckoos by blowing into wooden cones. Although the *Gazette Musicale* found their performance monotonous, the audience applauded heartily, and Louis-Philippe invited them to play at court.

Quite astonishing for the time was the dapper pianist Sigismond Thalberg (a "fop" in Chopin's opinion), who stunned a Conservatory audience in 1836 by playing from memory. His rippling arpeggios made Berlioz exclaim that he seemed to have "three hands instead of two."[45] Even such virtuosos as Paganini and Liszt, who had no need to rely on gimmickry, liked to whip up their audiences with programs that were a "mixture of the concert hall and the circus."[46] Paganini, for example, always tuned his violin a half-tone higher than the orchestra to make it stand out. Like most virtuosos of his day, he preferred to play his own compositions, which were written expressly as vehicles for his technical prowess. When he performed the works of others, he often embellished them beyond recognition. A young lady, referring to this, once remarked, "M. de Paganini's playing is admirable but all things considered, I prefer music."[47] In spite of his disregard for others' works, Paganini commissioned Berlioz to write the *Harold in Italy* symphony with a special viola part for himself. Although he was deeply moved on hearing the finished composition, he refused to play it in public because it didn't provide an adequate showcase for his skills.

Equal in virtuosity to the Italian violinist, Liszt was often called the "Paganini of the piano." So incredible was his agility at the keyboard that the sculptor Jean-Pierre Dantan portrayed him with four hands instead of two. Although Liszt's technique was universally admired, his style was not. He belonged to the Parisian school of virtuosos, who were often criticized as "specious, dashing [and] sentimental" in contrast to the "pure, graceful [and] formal" style of German pianists like Mendelssohn and Clara Wieck Schumann.[48] Not only did Liszt's playing possess all the fire of Paganini's; his youth and health gave him more stamina than the older Italian to endure the exhausting gymnastics of his performances. In 1844 the music journal *Le Ménestrel* described the Hungarian's antics on stage: "Franz-Listz [*sic*] plays alternately on two pianos back to back, first of all, so the ladies can admire both profiles of his inspired face and poetic forehead, and secondly to let the instruments have a rest. Franz-Listz changes pianos like other people change horses so as not to tire the poor beasts out."[49] According to Heinrich Heine, he seemed to make the very piano keys bleed. Both the intensity of Liszt's playing and the charismatic nature of his personality roused audiences to a frenzy. Ladies rose from their seats, screamed hysterically, and tossed perfumed handkerchiefs onto the stage before passing away in a dead faint. One excited lady even threw her tiara at him, but it fell short (so Berlioz tells us) and landed on the head of a German who was too busy applauding to notice it. Some ladies carried around small vials into which they poured the pianist's leftover coffee; another kept an old cigar butt of his pinned to her underclothes for years.

Those who knew Liszt well were aware that beneath his brash and showy facade was a fragile, insecure person whose precocious talents had outstripped his emotional development (fig. 6.6). Adult in years, he remained, for Heine, "a childish child...a gigantic dwarf."[50] Certainly his tinsel-laden operatic transcriptions and whirlwind renditions of galops and polkas display a sophomoric mentality. It is perhaps more in his writing than in his music that Liszt reveals his inner self during the early years of his career. For example, in his *Artist's Journey* (a significant part of which appeared in the *Gazette Musicale*), we see him agonizing over the dilemma of musicians (such as himself) whose mission is to reveal the True, the Beautiful, and the Good to a shallow, materialistic society that they disdain. To communicate with the public, they are forced to lower themselves to its level or be condemned to remain apart from the world in a state of lonely isolation. Like any hot-blooded youth in his twenties, it was virtually impossible for Liszt to rise above the flesh. On the other hand, how could the artist within him ignore the deeper values that governed his innermost self? It would be many years before Liszt's troubled mind could resolve this dilemma and reconcile the life he was leading with the ideals to which he aspired.

Meanwhile, the Hungarian virtuoso continued to prostitute his talents to the demands of the public. Once, for example, he interrupted an all-Beethoven concert to insert his electrifying piano arrangement of Rossini's *William Tell* overture. His extravagant posturing on stage seemed to enhance rather than distract from his music, although some of his most legendary performances were said to have taken place in the dark, where his listeners were forced to rely on their ears rather than their eyes. Apparently his pupils learned as much about the art of body language as the art of music in their lessons with him. In 1840 the *Gazette Musicale* complained that one of them, Mlle Rosario de los Hierros, had her

6.6 Franz Liszt at around age twenty, when Chopin first met him. Their initial friendship was eventually marred by a disparity in their personalities and their musical tastes, as well as by an overt animosity between their mistresses, George Sand and the comtesse Marie d'Agoult.

teacher's habit of constantly rolling her head about while she played. These and other Lisztian affectations, adopted by many pianists of the time, exasperated the *Gazette*'s critic, who wrote that "All those contrived poses, that swaying back and forth, those movements of the head, those eyes lifted heavenward which certain artists tend to exploit don't deceive the public as to their real value."[51]

Another musical vogue attributable to Liszt was the attempt to generate an orchestral sound out of the piano's limited resources. His Herculean keyboard arrangements of symphonies and operas were often written for four hands to simulate the fullness of the original scores. Although Parisians may have appreciated them simply as technical tours de force, outside the capital they were often the only form in which opera, symphonies, and other complex musical works ever reached a provincial audience.

Beside the incomparably dynamic Liszt and the exquisitely delicate Chopin, Heine regarded most other pianists of the period as mummies. Among these he singled out the pompous and egotistical Friedrich Kalkbrenner, with his embalmed smile and "candied sugar-cake exterior."[52] As much an entrepreneur as a musician, Kalkbrenner (who was a partner in Pleyel's publishing firm) approached everything with a methodical business-like manner. When he once offered Chopin a three-year course of piano lessons, the wise young Pole refused. Another of Heine's mummies was the irascible opportunist Henri Herz. "He is only distinguished by his beautiful music hall," the poet wrote, adding "he has long been dead and was recently married" (fig. 6.7).[53]

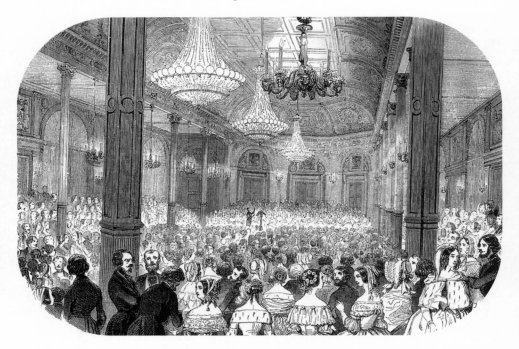

6.7 A prominent concert hall in Paris, the Salle Herz on the rue de la Victoire. Although Chopin performed in public with the owner, Henri Herz, on several occasions, he was never in tune with his flashy showmanship and mercenary orientation. No doubt Chopin often attended performances in the Salle Herz (he and George Sand lived less than three blocks away from the hall for many years). There is no record, though, that he ever appeared on its stage.

In contrast to Liszt and the "thunder gods" of the "Donner und Blitzen" school of virtuosity, Chopin saw no need to transmogrify the piano into something it was never intended to be. For him the instrument had its own particular beauty, one more akin to the intimate quality of the voice than the vast tonal range of an orchestra. Over and over he admonished his pupils to make the piano "sing." It was, in his view, a vehicle for personal expression rather than mass emotions, an instrument more suited to private gatherings than public exhibitions. Because of his delicate and ephemeral style, Chopin was often called "the sylph of the piano" and his playing described as a gentle shower of pearls.

If Liszt were to be judged solely on the flamboyant brilliance of his early virtuoso career, he would not merit his present-day place in history as a respected composer, teacher, patron, and musical visionary. He did, however, make at least one major contribution to the history of music during those glittering years of his youth. On March 27, 1841, at the Salle Erard, he introduced Parisians to his recent innovation, the solo piano "recital." His first performance of this sort, which he called a "musical soliloquy," had been given in Rome two years earlier. Shortly afterward he gave several such soliloquies in London, where the weekly journal *John Bull* described them as "recitals," an expression that was subsequently adopted in Paris as well. The *Gazette Musicale*, knowing the restless temperament of Parisian audiences, tried to discourage Liszt from giving solo recitals there, but the instant success of his performances drew quick praise from the journal's critic, who opened his review with a quote from Pierre Corneille, "Moi! moi, dis-je, et c'est assez" (Me! me, I say, and that's enough). Here "we have an original concert ... the complete opposite of the Monster-concert. The very idea is so ambitious ... who would dare to imitate him? Twenty-five years ago such an attempt would have been impossible ... [but] the artist emerged victorious."[54] Between numbers, Liszt often gave his listeners a rest by stepping down from the stage and strolling about to chat with them. Among those present was his future son-in-law, Richard Wagner, who seems to have been more impressed with Liszt's profits than with his performance (fig. 6.8). "He appeared alone," the young German wrote, "nobody else played or sang. The tickets cost 20 francs each, and he earned a total of 10,000 francs with no expenses ... what assurance! What infallibility. ... Unfortunately I have no understanding for matters of this kind. ... On this particular day I developed such a violent headache, such violent twitchings of the nerves that I had to go home early and lay myself to bed."[55]

Wagner, who had an "inborn gift for debt-making," naturally envied Liszt's success and the money he reaped from it.[56] As for himself, Wagner had only one significant triumph during the two and a half years he lived in Paris. In February 1841, François-Antoine Habeneck, conductor of the Conservatory orchestra, performed his *Columbus Overture* at the school's concert hall.

Outside of the city's opera houses, which drew audiences often more concerned with social prestige than artistic appreciation, the Conservatory was the main focus of musical life in Paris. At the time of the July monarchy, it was a relatively new institution, having only been founded in 1784 just before the great Revolution. Its concert hall, however, had been reconstructed under Napoléon in 1811, with a handsome red and gold interior typical of the elegant Empire style. The seats were notoriously uncomfortable, but if the derrière suffered, the soul gloried in the magnificent sounds that Habeneck elicited from the institution's superb orchestra. His

6.8 Richard Wagner, who in the 1840s lived briefly in Paris with his first wife, Minna, received little recognition of his music there. In lieu of composing, he wrote copy for the *Revue et Gazette Musicale* in the company of other staff members, including George Sand, Hector Berlioz, and Franz Liszt.

favorite composer was Beethoven, whose symphonies he performed to the point of excess, according to an 1835 article in Fétis's *Revue Musicale*.

As late as 1841, fourteen years after Beethoven's death, Parisian audiences remained perplexed by the German giant, whose compositions had a weightiness foreign to the French élan. A performance of Beethoven's *Eroica* symphony at the Conservatory on Sunday, January 26, 1841, was described by Berlioz as taking place "in a small dirty humid room where the oil lamps of several chandeliers illuminated the shadows to reveal some pale ladies with eyes raised toward heaven in carefully studied poses, and red-faced men doing their best not to fall asleep, nodding their heads out of rhythm to the music and smiling whenever an orchestra member got lost and let out a cry of desperation.... From time to time the puzzled audience would turn to each other and ask why the symphony was called 'heroic.'"[57]

Although Chopin acknowledged that "the conservatory sets the fashion in serious music," he felt it had become a complacent institution that "lives on old symphonies which the orchestra knows by heart."[58] New works were seldom performed because the faculty shunned innovation. Earlier masters like Handel and Bach were also generally neglected as being too outdated for contemporary tastes. Certain professors at the Conservatory, however, were noted for their efforts to bring the the best of music to their audiences. The violinist Pierre Baillot, for instance, organized a string quartet that gave chamber music programs with works

6.9 Maria Luigi Cherubini was one of the last contemporaries of Mozart still living in Chopin's time. For many years until his death in 1842, he was director of the Paris Conservatory. Although he and Chopin were never particularly close in life, they now rest only a stone's throw apart in the cemetery of Père Lachaise.

by Bach, Mozart, Haydn, and Beethoven. At Chopin's Paris debut, Baillot added an extra viola to his ensemble for a performance of Beethoven's *Quintet* in C, opus 29. Another faculty member, Pierre-Joseph-Guillaume Zimmerman, director of the Conservatory's piano department, gave weekly soirées with exceptional performances at his apartment in the square d'Orléans. Besides Cherubini (who was Zimmerman's teacher and head of the Conservatory until 1842), others present at these musicals often included Chopin and the pianist Kalkbrenner, both of whom lived in the square d'Orléans. Zimmerman's pupils Ambroise Thomas and César Franck also attended many of these performances (fig. 6.9).

Along with the Conservatory, a number of privately organized societies devoted themselves to the performance of music purely for its artistic merit rather than its technical bravado. One of these, the Chantereine Hall Society, included the pianists Chopin, Liszt, and Henri Herz among its founders in 1834. Its performances were given in a "humid, obscure and smoky" hall that was so small it could not even accommodate a full orchestra.[59] A similar society, the Gymnase Musicale on the boulevard Bonnes Nouvelles, opened in May 1835 with Liszt performing a work by Weber before an audience that included Rossini and Meyerbeer. A month later, Berlioz gave one of his "grand concerts" there. Beethoven and Mozart figured frequently on the Gymnase's programs, while

Beethoven's works were often featured at the Athénée Musicale's concerts in the Hôtel de Ville's Salle Saint-Jean. In addition, so-called serious music could be heard in the "Concerts Historiques" organized by François-Joseph Fétis, the former editor of the *Revue Musicale*, who exposed Parisians to sixteenth- and seventeenth-century composers from the Elizabethans to the Scarlattis.

Since the early part of the nineteenth century, a subtle distinction between "light" and "serious" music had been creeping into the musical vocabulary of Europe. Only a few decades earlier, prior to the Revolution of 1789, most musicians owed their living to some aristocratic patron and were obliged to compose or perform whatever music fitted his mood: devotional music for religious observances; light-hearted divertimenti for a banquet; minuets, gigues, and contredances for a ball; as well as a variety of instrumental and vocal music for the many other social events that filled the lives of a leisured class. A musician's social status might then be considered on a par with a skilled craftsman, whose function was to produce something primarily useful in as beautiful a style as possible. By the early nineteenth century, however, the Romantics' transformation of music from a social amenity into a metaphysical abstraction to be revered like some Platonic ideal challenged this pragmatic view of art. George Sand, in her novel *Spiridion* (much of which was written in Majorca, where she was under the spell of Chopin's Preludes), epitomizes the new cult-like veneration of music and the musician. "Music," she wrote, "ought to be the true poetic expression of man, ... capable of conveying the most elevated ideas which are too sublime to be expressed in any other language."[60] This sort of quasi-religious attitude toward art was largely responsible for bringing about the nineteenth-century distinction between "serious" (transcendental) and "light" (mundane) music that remains prevalent today.

In Louis-Philippe's Paris, "serious" music was usually confined to opera houses, concert halls, and the private salons of musical artists, amateurs, or connoisseurs. "Light" music, on the other hand, was generally heard in cafés, casinos, dance halls, or pleasure gardens. Philippe Musard, whose orchestra was one of the most popular in Paris, even rented out the vast arena of Franconi's circus for some of his performances, while Isaac Strauss (the so-called Parisian Strauss, unrelated to the more famous Viennese Strausses) played his engaging waltzes, polkas, galops, and quadrilles in many of the city's well-heeled salons, as well as in its various commercial establishments.

Musard began his musical career as a Conservatory-trained violinist and orchestra conductor who wrote string quartets. At the Opéra he directed such "serious" productions as *La Sylphide* with the ethereal ballerina Marie Taglioni. His real success, though, came when he began conducting the carnival balls at the Théâtre des Variétés, where he popularized the new can-can. One night a young woman dashed onto the dance floor wrapped in a cashmere shawl, which she promptly shed to dance the can-can dressed only in a feather boa and arm-length black gloves. The scandal that followed undoubtedly cost the bold lady her reputation, at the same time that it firmly established Musard's. Shortly afterward he was asked to conduct the Opéra balls. Soon he began giving concerts in the Salle Valentino, a former riding school on the rue Saint-Honoré where a huge orchestra occupied the center of the room, surrounded by a dance floor large enough to accommodate a swirling crowd of 1,200 couples. Later he moved to quarters in the rue Vivienne that included an adjacent café and garden. In Galignani's guidebook, it was recommended as an establishment in which one could find "good music...and respectable company."[61] The programs, according to Mrs. Trollope, began at 7:30 and lasted for two hours. Ladies, clad simply in their daytime *toilette* of shawl and bonnet, often came together in small groups without an escort. The concerts, which consisted almost exclusively of dance music, were loud and brassy with many solo passages for cornets and ophicleides. Among the endless waltzes, contredances, and polkas that Musard liked to play, one might hear a quadrille taken from the *Dies Irae* of some mass or a galop based on a theme from Mozart's *Requiem*. During a typical concert, the music would gradually rise in an impassioned crescendo to end in a finale where the orchestra members smashed chairs and fired off pistols, driving the audience into a frenzy. At times the police had to intervene when Musard's diabolical quadrilles and cancans became too tempestuous—all of which leads one to suspect that the company present on these occasions was not as respectable as the Galignanis claimed. During the summers from 1837 on, Musard took to staging his explosive antics under a tent on the Champs Elysées, where he was able to shoot off muskets and cannons as well as pistols.

Johann Strauss, who visited Paris in the fall of 1837, conducted several programs with Musard and added the Parisian quadrille to his repertory of Viennese waltzes. His six-month stay in the French capital created quite a stir. Among those who attended his opening concert on November 1 were Meyerbeer, Cherubini, Adam, Halévy, Auber, and Berlioz. At the end of the performance, Auber tossed him a bouquet of violets, the French dubbed him "the German Musard," and Berlioz wrote a flattering article comparing him to such musical titans as Beethoven, Gluck, and Weber. To cap his success, the royal family invited him to play at the Tuileries, where his orchestra was allowed to mingle with the court after the concert.

Nineteen years younger than Musard was his brief rival, Louis Jullien, who also trained at the Paris Conservatory but left in 1826 after a falling out with Cherubini. He then took up conducting at the Jardin Turc, the Salon d'Apollon, and other popular dance halls (fig. 6.10). As a showman Jullien employed all of Musard's tricks and more, adding fireworks, barking dogs, and the clanging of fire alarm bells to his concerts. He, along with Berlioz, was one of the first to popularize the use of the baton in orchestral conducting. An American once described his baton as the "wand of an enchanter," while the *New York Herald* referred to it as his "scepter."[62] On stage Jullien dressed foppishly with an abundance of gold chains across his chest. At the beginning of a performance, he would seat himself on stage in a large gilt armchair covered in red velvet while a liveried servant brought out a pair of kid gloves. After donning them he would leap onto the podium, where his athletic prowess often overpowered the audience more than did his musical skills. From time to time he laid down his baton, picked up his favorite instrument, the piccolo, and played along with the orchestra. The works on his programs were typically embellished with the sound of sleigh bells, train whistles, and cracking whips. Often he added visual effects like colored lights and waving flags. At the height of his popularity, Jullien opened his own casino, where the din of his late-night performances caused the police to charge him with disturbing the peace. To avoid arrest, he fled to London and later America. Before long his extravagant habits led him into debt, and in 1859 he returned to Paris, a broken man who eventually went mad.

Toward the middle of the century, Jacques Offenbach began to emerge as the leading figure of "light" music in Paris. He first arrived there from Germany in 1833 at age fourteen and sang in the city's synagogues to pay for cello lessons at the Conservatory.[63] After a year, however, he left the Conservatory to study privately and play in various orchestras, including that of the Opéra Comique. Through Friedrich von Flotow, the German opera composer who lived in Paris then, Offenbach was introduced into the salon circuit, where he proved to be an adept musical comic who could make his cello imitate other instruments—sometimes even animals. In 1836 the flamboyant Jullien performed one of his compositions in public, and five years later Offenbach made his own concert debut, playing a

6.10 The Jardin Turc (Turkish Garden), a popular dance hall on the boulevard du Temple where the foppish conductor, Louis Jullien, created pandemonium with his frenzied orchestral arrangements of the latest waltzes, polkas, mazurkas, and can-cans. These performances were enlivened by the noise of smashing chairs, barking dogs, pistol shots, and fire alarm bells. As a finale, a dazzling display of fireworks often left the café shrouded in smoke.

Beethoven sonata with the young Russian pianist Anton Rubinstein. It wasn't until the advent of Louis-Napoléon's regime, however, that Offenbach became the prolific composer of those sparkling operettas we remember him for today.

By 1850 Paris, still recovering from the disastrous effects of the revolution of 1848, found itself in a musical ebb tide. The great wave of composers and virtuosi that had swept over it during the 1830s and 1840s had crested, leaving the city in an artistic trough. Many of those who once brought lustre to the concert and operatic stages of Paris had now returned to that great empyrean from which they had temporarily descended. Among those whom death had taken away were virtuosos and composers like Chopin, Paganini, Kalkbrenner, and Paër. At the Conservatory a void had been left by the death of its long-time director, Cherubini. The operatic world also suffered its losses, including composers like Bellini and Donizetti, as well as the tenor Adolphe Nourrit and many of the singers to be mentioned in Chapter 7. Of the survivors, Henri Herz had left the city for the

United States to make money and escape his mistress, while Liszt had taken up with a new mistress and moved to Weimar. Rossini had married his mistress and retired, while Fétis, whose fickle mistress had left him for Pleyel, was now living in Brussels as head of the Conservatory there. Berlioz, who had fled to England during the revolution of 1848, soon came back with his mistress, whom he couldn't marry because his wife was still alive. As before, however, he found it difficult to make a living in Paris and tarried there only briefly before leaving for Russia and the German states—where he would find the musical and monetary rewards he deserved. Richard Wagner, who received little recognition from Paris while living there, had also moved on to greener pastures in Germany, where his operas were beginning to be produced.

To other young hopefuls on the musical scene, Paris was kinder than it had been to Wagner. Among the geniuses germinating in the fertile soil of Paris during Chopin's last years were Charles Gounod, César Franck, Anton Rubinstein, Camille Saint-Saëns, and Georges Bizet. As this new generation of talent matured, Parisian musical life was soon destined to rise above the low-water mark it had reached at the midpoint of the century.

CHAPTER 7

Opera

A Vocal Art and Social Spectacle

*F*OR MOST PARISIANS throughout the nineteenth century, opera was "the central point of civilization."[1] Those with any claim to cultivation could not have imagined life without it. The realization that certain parts of the world actually suffered such a deprivation appalled the novelist Stendhal (Marie-Henri Beyle). It was bad enough, he wrote, that in America "one is forced to bore oneself the whole day long by paying serious court to the shopkeepers in the street, and become as dull and stupid as they are." Worse yet, he gasped, "over there one has no Opéra."[2]

If these observations seem to imply that opera and a bourgeois society were incompatible, Stendhal can perhaps be excused on the grounds that he had been living abroad and didn't realize how bourgeois the Paris Opéra itself had become since Dr. Louis-Désiré Véron had taken it over in 1831. Even the "dull and stupid" middle class had succumbed to the magnificence of opera, that sublime blend of musical, literary, and visual arts. If some didn't fully appreciate the spiritual elevation it offered, they were quick enough to recognize its social advantages. As Véron himself put it, the Paris Opéra had become the Versailles of the new reigning social order. King Louis-Philippe himself, the supreme personification of bourgeois taste in all Paris, saw clearly that opera was a lustrous jewel in anyone's crown, but appreciated it chiefly for its decorative value. "The Comédie Française," he stated, "is the pride of our nation; the Opéra is but the vanity of it."[3]

The Opéra that Louis-Philippe referred to was the Académie Royale de Musique, located on the narrow rue Le Péletier since 1821 (fig. 7.1). Although it remained there until destroyed by fire fifty-two years later, it was meant to be a temporary structure after the Archbishop of Paris condemned the former opera house on the rue Richelieu because it had been desecrated in 1820 by the murder of the duc de Berry, heir to the French throne. Because the city couldn't afford an expensive project then, the Opéra's interim quarters were built mostly out of materials salvaged from the old house, on a lot already owned by the municipality just north of the boulevard des Italiens. Despite a limited budget, the new structure was equipped with a deep stage, excellent acoustics, gas lighting, and a host of mechanical devices to create the latest stage effects. These innovations required the maintenance of a vast artistic, business, and housekeeping staff as well as machinists, lamplighters, and firemen. The main facade (facing west onto the rue Le Péletier), was said to have been copied from a Palladian basilica in Vicenza, although Heinrich Heine claimed it looked like a flat-roofed stable. Above its facade were eight of the nine muses, which aroused endless speculation as to which of the cultural maidens had been omitted. Some suggested that the muse of architecture had been left out, but Heine insisted it was the muse of music, who had leaped from her pedestal in despair at the dreadful singing coming from below.

The interior proved more luxurious, with a vast 180-by-25-foot foyer where newspapers, opera glasses, musical journals, and scores were sold. At either end a café opened onto a terrace. The construction of the boxes and stage were identical to those of the old house, having simply been transferred intact to the new location. The lower levels (including the royal box at the right of the stage) were decorated in white and gold, and the upper levels in blue and gold. The effect was pleasing to the eye, but the Galignanis found the seats "hard and inconvenient."[4]

Because of the narrow streets around the Opéra, there was an incredible congestion of carriages before and after each performance. It was not uncommon to wait forty-five minutes to an hour for one's coachman at the end of the evening. Those who came by foot usually entered through two parallel passages that ran from the boulevard to the opera house. They were connected by a transverse passage and lined with music shops, reading rooms, and a plethora of flower girls and candy sellers. Singers and dancers from both the Opéra and the nearby Théâtre des Italiens often congregated here at intermission.

As might be expected in a city like Paris, which was the musical center of Europe throughout the 1830s and 1840s, the civilizing force of opera was not restricted to a single proscenium. Besides the Académie Royale, the muses from Parnassus also found refuge on the migratory stages of the city's Théâtre des Italiens and the Opéra-Comique.[5] Between them they provided discriminating Parisians with every nuance of operatic art from opera seria to opera buffa, classical to Romantic, and French, German, or Italian in style.

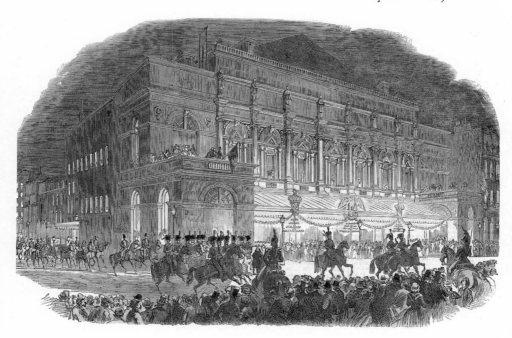

7.1 In Chopin's time, the Académie Royale de Musique in Paris, better known as the Paris Opéra, was located on the narrow rue Le Péletier just north of the boulevard des Italiens. Carriages arrived and departed at the rue Le Péletier entrance (shown here), while pedestrians found it more convenient to come and go through two enclosed passages that connected the house with the nearby boulevard.

Throughout most of the Restoration, all three opera houses were operated year-round, although winter was always considered the fashionable season. In 1828, however, the Italian theater began limiting itself to a six-month season (from October through March), which gave its singers a six-month break to tour the provinces and nearby foreign capitals. Later, to avoid competing with each other, the Théâtre-Italiens (often called "Les Bouffes") and the Académie Royale de Musique (known simply as the Opéra) agreed to alternate the nights of their performances, with the Opéra playing Mondays, Wednesdays, and Fridays and the Italians, Tuesdays, Thursdays, and Saturdays. The maverick Comique, however, went its own way, putting on a show every night of the week. This didn't bother either the Opéra or the Italian theater, which spurned the less affluent and less discriminating audiences attracted to the Comique.

Of the Opéra's three weekly performances, Friday evening always drew the most elegant crowds. That was traditionally the night men brought their mistresses; wives were relegated to the less glamorous Monday nights. As a rule the boxes at the Opéra didn't fill up until the beginning of the second act, when the director customarily inserted a ballet into the performance—whether the composer had planned it or not. The ballet invariably attracted the dandies from the boulevards, who found few opportunities (outside the boudoir) to ogle a bare feminine calf. The most dashing of these young men gathered together in the box of the marquis du Hallay-Coëtquen, which became known as the *loge infernale*. The free-wheeling marquis belonged to the Café de Paris set and had a passion for duels, ballerinas, and pornography. In his box were many members of the Jockey Club, who wore white camellias (the accepted badge of lionhood) and applauded discreetly by bringing their yellow-gloved hands together in an elegant gesture that could be seen but not heard. Such men-about-town as comte Alexandre Wałewski, Prosper Mérimée, and Honoré Balzac alighted there regularly in their nightly peregrinations between dinner and some favorite salon. Typically Balzac (forever absorbed in the real life, out of which he crafted his *Comédie Humaine*) sat with his back to the stage watching the audience instead. Unfortunately his view was no longer as dazzling as it had once been. The Opéra's new director, Dr. Véron, anxious for a fast franc, had increased the number of boxes by reducing their size and adding two huge ones at the sides of the orchestra that became known as the omnibus boxes because of the middle-class crowds who filled them. The more people Véron packed into the house, the more the elite patronized the Théâtre Italiens to avoid the raucous crush of the nouveaux riches. Inside the Théâtre Italiens, according to Heine, society found an oasis of bon ton and the best of bel canto. For him the Théâtre des Italiens was "the very threshold of heaven" where "the sacred nightingales sighed" and "the most fashionable of tears flowed."[6] (figs. 7.2, 7.3) Outside its walls, Paris seemed nothing more than a vast musical Sahara.

In the novels of Stendhal and Balzac, a box at the Italiens is repeatedly portrayed as the ultimate of worldly goals. Most were inherited by aristocratic families along with their chateaux and *hôtels privés*. Rich bankers and businessmen went to great lengths—some even fought duels—to obtain one. As at the Opéra, boxes in the Italiens often provided a spectacle more intriguing than that on stage. Sophie Gay, for instance, noted the great care that a fashionable lady took to create a commotion on entering her loge. The more richly dressed and bejewelled she was, the greater

7.2 An audience departing from the Théâtre-Italien (Salle Ventadour) after an operatic performance in the mid-1840s. According to a Polish friend of Chopin's, the lobby of the Italian theater
was always filled with the most refined and fashionable society in all Paris.

7.3 The Salle Ventadour on the rue Marsollier, which became home to the Théâtre-Italien in 1841.
Of the three opera houses in Paris during Chopin's time, the Salle Ventadour is the only structure
surviving today.

the hubbub she provoked. Those most skilled at making a grand entrance timed it to coincide with a high point of the opera to maximize the distraction.

At the Italiens, according to Mme Gay, one had the feeling of being in a salon rather than a public theater. There, "a lot of words are spoken but little said. They talk about Lablache, the cut of a coat, Malibran, the Bois de Boulogne, Rossini, a fashionable raout, the Apponyi's balls . . . and when they tire of all these empty words they let their eyes wander about discreetly in search of some new interest to satisfy their heart or their vanity."[7]

At the Opéra-Comique, the pleasures enjoyed in the boxes were not always so tame. In the new Salle Favart, where the troupe moved in the spring of 1840, half of the boxes were equipped with a private salon hidden from public view. These cozy little nooks were carpeted and furnished with a mirror, table, and sofa. The opportunities they offered for seduction may have caused more raised eyebrows than skirts, but whatever the case Charles de Boigne, an aristocratic boulevardier of the period, seems to have been right when he claimed, "What people love most about the Opéra is not the music."[8]

As the contemporary historian Bailbé points out, opera in Chopin's time served three purposes: first and foremost it helped to solidify one's social position; second, it provided a refuge from boredom; and third, it happened to be a place where one could also enjoy music. Having touched briefly on the first two of these points, I now come to the business of music—and it was a business, unfortunately a ruinous one for many. Until Dr. Véron's arrival in 1831, the Paris Opéra had not made a profit since the seventeenth century, when the composer Lulli directed it. At the outbreak of the 1830 revolution, the famous house was under the management of the vicomte Sosthène de la Rochefoucault, who had no artistic or business qualifications for the job to which his father had appointed him. His main concerns were that audiences behaved in a respectable manner, that ballerinas wore respectably long tutus, and that nude statues had their private parts hidden with respectably placed fig leaves. Due to these trivial pursuits, the Opéra suffered a respectably large deficit.

Once Louis-Philippe came to power, he placed the Opéra under the jurisdiction of his minister of the interior, Charles-Camille Bachasson de Montalivet, a man with a capitalistic turn of mind. To reverse the Opéra's long history of financial disasters, Montalivet sought an entrepreneurial director willing to risk his own capital in the hazardous business of running the insolvent institution. The government, he proposed, should continue to provide a subsidy for the house, which was to diminish yearly as the new director assumed more and more responsibility for the fiscal success of its operation.

The man for the job turned out to be an unsuccessful physician named Louis-Désiré Véron. Although the poor man could never attract enough patients to make a living, he managed to feather his nest by promoting a chest balm that he touted as a remedy for ailing singers and consumptives. Thanks to the profits of this patent medicine, Véron was able to abandon his medical career. He then took to writing assorted literary and political articles and eventually founded his own highly esteemed *Revue de Paris* in 1829. Even with the revenues from these new sources, Véron had to borrow an additional 200,000 francs to secure his post as director of the Opéra. As time proved, it was money well spent. By the end of his second season, the house had taken in 2.5 million francs, an amount far greater than any previous year. But success always breeds envy, and Véron soon found himself subject to criticism, ridicule, and outright abuse. "The sentiment which dominates M. Véron's life," de Boigne complained, "is the love of money. He adores the sound, the sight and the feel of it."[9] Heinrich Heine, seldom temperate in his judgments, called the erstwhile doctor a "God of materialism" who had found the perfect prescription for eradicating music.[10] Daumier poked fun at him in a number of caricatures, and the historian Viel-Castel derided his amorous adventures as the clownish escapades of a pompous old roué. His corpulent figure, "round like an egg and as pot-bellied as Sancho Panza," hardly seemed the type to inspire passion.[11] One of the doctor's contemporaries claimed that he actually knew nothing about women. Worse yet, the *Gazette Musicale* asserted that he "didn't even possess the most elementary notion of music."[12] None of these affronts, however, ruffled the glib doctor—none, that is, until the government decided in 1834 to reduce his subsidy because he was making too much money. Struck in the pocket, where it hurt most, Véron immediately gave up his post and returned to private life, some 900,000 francs richer than he had been three years earlier.

Through all his tribulations, Véron clung steadfastly to the belief that living well is the best revenge and proved it by working as hard at playing the bon vivant as being an opera director. In all the best districts of Paris, his splendid English brougham became a familiar sight, drawn by two fine horses with scarlet ribbons on their ears. His face was always half-hidden in the large white cravat that billowed up around his cheeks to hide the unsightly scars on his neck left by childhood scrofula. Because he had all the pretentions and ostentatiousness of the middle class, Arsène Houssaye, director of the Comédie Française, called him the "bourgeois gentilhomme," an epithet that Véron took with good grace. Later, when he wrote his autobiography, he called it quite candidly *The Memoirs of a Bourgeois*. His father, after all, had been the owner of a small bookstore and stationery shop.

From the prima ballerina Fanny Elssler, Véron obtained an excellent cook named Sophie and entertained with a lavishness that bordered on vulgarity. At his celebrated late-night suppers, he hired naked girls to assume provocative *poses plastiques* and often sent his guests home with pralines wrapped in thousand-franc notes. Because of his extravagant *gaucheries*, Véron was seldom invited into the homes of *le beau monde* and passed most of his time in the world of so-called café society. He belonged to the Petit Cercle at the Café de Paris, which was one of his favorite restaurants because its service was so slow he had time to digest his food leisurely.

How then did this brash and boorish middle-class doctor, a fat, pushy show-off with no musical credentials, manage to achieve such unparalleled success at a job that had proven the nemesis of his predecessors? First of all he had the astuteness to cultivate the goodwill of a rich Spanish banker named Aguado who enabled him to buy the concession for running the Opéra. Second, he had the high-pressured tactics of a salesman who could market anything from patent medicines to prima donnas. When, for example, an unknown eighteen-year-old soprano Cornélie Falcon was about to make her debut, he placed glowing ads in the papers touting her "prodigious" talents. Following her debut, he announced a "second debut" with similar tantalizing phrases and relentlessly plugged the "continuation of her debuts" for some time afterward.[13] On Sundays and other nights when there were no performances at the Opéra, Véron rented out the house to artists like Liszt or Paganini, whose performances invariably filled both the house and its coffers.

In addition, Véron knew how to practice the art of public relations long before it became a recognized profession. He saw to it that his subscribers received special privileges like being allowed backstage to mingle with the singers and dancers. He even gave some the opportunity of appearing on stage as extras in walk-on parts that didn't require any talent. On the occasions when he himself received a favor, he never failed to reciprocate it in some effusive fashion. He seemed, in fact, to be forever handing out money to anyone for anything—although gossip had it that what he gave out by day (at least to the fair

7.4 The interior of the Paris Opéra house on the rue Le Péletier was so vast, a friend of Chopin's once commented that you couldn't tell if a lady seated on the opposite side was beautiful or ugly, young or old. This illustration shows the house as it appeared during one of the Opéra's masked balls, when the floor was raised to the level of the stage to accommodate the dancers who flocked to the rowdy events every Mardi Gras.

sex), he took back at night. In addition, he sponsored gala performances with parties afterward and revived the tradition of giving Opéra balls from Christmas to Mardi Gras (fig. 7.4). At first these were glittering affairs with the parterre raised up to stage level for dancing. One year even Louis-Philippe and Marie-Amélie attended, along with the king and queen of the Belgians. Eventually, though, the balls acquired a tawdry aspect, becoming "part nightclub and part house of assignation," filled with a rowdy, thrill-seeking crowd.[14] By 1835 Berlioz claimed that "nothing is more tiresome than an Opéra ball."[15]

Finally and most importantly, Véron instinctively sensed the musical tastes of the Parisian public. Because of its passionate love of ballet (called "visual music" by Théophile Gautier), he made sure that no production in his house lacked such a performance. Many evenings were devoted entirely to the dance, which featured the finest ballerinas to be found in Europe. The fees he had to pay for them were high, but the revenues they brought were even higher. As for the public's taste in opera, Véron quickly discovered the magic recipe that Parisians relished: equal parts spectacle and sentimentality, with a dash of the supernatural. By calling on the aid of such experienced "chefs" as Giacomo Meyerbeer and Augustin Eugène Scribe, he was able to serve up the musical fare they craved. All this he accomplished within the limitations imposed on him by the government, that is, he had to give three performances a week, mount six new productions a year, maintain a troupe of a certain size, and perform only works in the genre assigned him ("grand" opéra, "petit" opéra, and ballet). These and a host of other lesser stipulations remained the working contract for directors of the Paris Opéra until 1936.

In the days prior to Wagner's music dramas, opera remained primarily a vocal art, with the orchestra providing little more than an accompaniment. In most cases the libretti were of even less importance. Fortunately the banality of their content was usually obscured by the music. As Mrs. Trollope put it, "That which is not worth saying they sing."[16] Once after hearing *La Juive* at the Paris Opéra, she concluded that the lines certainly hadn't cost the poet many sleepless nights.[17] As it happened the poet was Eugène Scribe, the major librettist of the period and a highly prolific playwright as well.

During much of the early nineteenth century, opera in Paris was actually two vocal arts rather than one: besides the French school there was an equally important Italian school. The former represented the old bombastic declamatory style, which had been popular on the French stage for well over a century. It was particularly adapted to what Mrs. Trollope called "the dry heavy recitative."[18] The French themselves called it *hurlement,* which can be translated (depending on the dictionary one uses) as roaring, yelling, bawling, bellowing, screaming, wailing, or howling like a wounded animal. It certainly didn't appeal to everyone's taste, and Mrs. Trollope was not alone in finding it abrasive. Worse yet, most French singers by 1831 complained that it placed a great strain on their vocal cords. Rather than give up such a venerable tradition, though, the French modified it by adapting features of the new Italian method, with its softer, more natural, lyrical style called bel canto, or "beautiful singing." This Italian-styled opera was written primarily for the voice, with the orchestra assuming a secondary (sometimes almost insignificant) role. Its highly ornamented vocal line possessed both a brilliance and grace that could be at once thrilling and soothing. Chopin was captivated by it and strove to translate its liquid beauty to the piano. Repeatedly he urged his pupils to visit the Italian opera and learn to play as Grisi, Pasta, and Rubini sang in the glorious operas of Bellini and Donizetti.

From a technical point of view, both the French and Italian vocal styles of singing required arduous training. To succeed, one had to start at a very young age. Although the great tenors Adolphe Nourrit and Mario di Candia proved that such early training was not always essential, most singers had already perfected their art enough to debut during their teens. Unfortunately for many, such intense preparation overtaxed their voices and brought their careers to a premature end. For some like the singer Cornélie Falcon, whose voice gave out suddenly on stage at the age of twenty-six, the experience was heartbreaking (she threw herself onto the floor in front of the audience and sobbed bitterly as the curtain fell). For others the cult of the diva, which came to full flower around 1830, brought fanatical adulation and soaring salaries that made the agonizing struggle worthwhile. But despite their successes on stage, few were welcome in the city's salons except for the purpose of entertaining guests. This was partly due to the modest backgrounds of many and partly to the social taint that still afflicted anyone in the theatrical world. The great tenor Giovanni Matteo, cavalière di Candia, for example, came from an aristocratic family that forbade him to tarnish their name by using it on stage. He therefore performed in public simply as "Mario." Among the limited number of operatic singers who found social acceptance were two close friends of Chopin, Adolphe Nourrit and Pauline Viardot, whose intelligence and cultivation placed them well above the average performer of their time.

In the musical education of an early-nineteenth-century singer, the emphasis was always on the vocal techniques in vogue, with little or no attention to dramatic coaching. Nourrit and Falcon at the Opéra were among the few who understood the value of a well-timed gesture or an appropriate facial expression (fig. 7.5). At the Italian theater hardly anyone ever gave a thought to acting. Only at the Comique, where productions had long stretches of spoken dialogue without any music to divert the audience, were performers forced to exploit whatever dramatic ability they had. Because the plot of an average opéra comique was seldom profound, however, it didn't require a lot of in-depth acting (fig. 7.6). At the same time, it should be remembered that members of the Comique not only had to sing and act, but dance as well. Versatility, with some competency in all three skills, was therefore more useful than an outstanding ability in any one. The result of these multi-disciplined requirements was that singers at the Comique were generally second-rate in all respects. They sang badly, Théophile Gautier claimed, on the pretext that they were actors, and acted badly on the pretext that they were singers.

7.5 The tenor Adolphe Nourrit (shown here in the role of Orpheus) was a close friend of Chopin, who admired the great depth of feeling in the artist's singing. When a new tenor, Duprez, began to supplant him at the Opéra, Nourrit grew despondent and committed suicide on a trip to Italy. As his body was being returned to France, Chopin performed at a memorial service for him in Marseille—on an organ rather than a piano.

7.6 The Théâtre des Nouveautés, which housed the Opéra-Comique until 1840, when it moved into the reconstructed Salle Favart. Afterward the Vaudeville theater took over the Nouveautés.

Although certain traits characterized the singers of each of the three opera houses, it would be a mistake to overemphasize them. The distinctions were not so great as to be insurmountable, and a number of singers passed from one house to another with relative ease. For instance, Mme Cinti-Damoreau and the tenor Roger sang at both the Opéra and the Opéra-Comique, just as Pauline Viardot and Mario moved back and forth with equal facility between the Théâtre des Italiens and the Opéra.

Government restrictions on the type of work given by each house, however, made it difficult for all singers to be so flexible. Napoléon, who had a penchant for regimentation, decided early in the century which genre (or genres) should be

7.7 In 1842, Daniel François Auber
succeeded Cherubini as director of
the Paris Conservatory. For the
most part, Chopin was not particularly impressed with Auber's
music. In 1830, however, the Polish
pianist improvised on a theme
from Auber's opera, *La Muette de
Portici,* in a concert at Breslau.

performed by which company. In accordance with these regulations, the
Académie Royale de Musique couldn't stage any work with spoken words, or use
libretti in any language but French. Because of this it was necessary for the spoken parts of Weber's *Der Freischütz* to be converted into musical recitatives, and
Mozart's *Don Giovanni* to be sung in French. Actually, most works at the Opéra
had to be translated due to the fact that almost everything given there was by a
foreign composer such as "Gluck, Piccini, Salieri, Sacchini, Spontini, Rossini,
Mozart, Weber [or] Meyerbeer."[19]

The Comique also produced only French-speaking compositions, but found
enough native composers like Hérold, Auber, Adam, and Halévy to fill its needs
(fig. 7.7). Even so, it was not averse to presenting foreign works (like Donizetti's *La
Fille du Régiment*) so long as the libretto was in French. No matter how successful
any production was, it rarely stayed in the company's repertory for more than three
or four years, which the *Gazette Musicale* attributed to the fact that the talents of the
cast rather than the merits of the score determined a production's success.

Only at the Théâtre des Italiens could foreign language opera be heard in
Paris. In a way this was fortunate for the bel canto works performed there would
not have been so beautiful had they been sung in any other language than the
original Italian. Despite the innate chauvinism of many Frenchmen, Parisian
parents preferred the Italian theater, where their young daughters could enjoy
the music without comprehending the explicit declamations of the love scenes.

7.8 Vincenzo Bellini, the master of bel canto opera, was greatly admired by Chopin, who often tried to adapt the fluid lyricism of his vocal line to the piano.

Apart from the language, the *fioriture*, or flowery style, of Italian singing made the words of most libretti so unintelligible that some critics regarded bel canto singing like so much bird chirping. Obviously posterity didn't agree, as the works of Rossini, Bellini and Donizetti have retained their popularity to the present time (fig. 7.8). By contrast, little of what was given at the Opéra or the Opéra Comique from 1830 to 1850 is still performed today.

One of the great advantages that Italian composers had over their French colleagues was the freedom to pursue their artistic goals without being hemmed in by bureaucratic regulations and an ossified operatic tradition. At the Paris Opéra, for example, only works of four specific genres could be performed under the July monarchy: serious and light (*grands* and *petits*) operas and ballets. A further restriction—and one of great significance—was that all opera libretti had to be submitted to government authorities for approval.

Of the four genres available to it, the Paris Opéra took most pride in its productions of grand operas. These were staged with spectacular extravagance, including brilliant costumes, elaborate scenery, large choruses, and dramatic technical effects produced by complex mechanical devices and the recent introduction of gas lighting. Many were interminable, lasting from five to six hours. That such works were certainly grand no one could deny, but whether they deserved to be called opera was questioned by some devotees of the Italian school, who didn't regard the French style of *hurlement* as true singing. Paradoxically the one aspect of French grand opera most open to debate was its "Frenchness." Although opera in France was already established and flourishing in the time of Louis XIV, the type specifically referred to as "French grand opera" did-n't appear until the early nineteenth century. One of its first exponents was the German composer Gasparo Spontini, who presented his opera *La Vestale* in 1807. Rossini later shifted from the Italian to the French school with his *William Tell* in 1829, but it was the cosmopolitan Giacomo Meyerbeer who represented the apogee of this form with his three great triumphs, *Robert le Diable* (one of the first operas that Chopin saw in Paris, in 1831), *Les Huguenots* (1836), and *Le Prophète* in 1849 (the last opera Chopin attended in Paris). Strangely enough, only two outstanding works in this genre were actually written by Frenchmen: Auber's *La Muette de Portici* (1828) and Halévy's *La Juive* (1835).

Characteristic of French grand opera during these years was a modified type of *hurlement* (barking) style of singing, which was less lyrical than bel canto although technically just as difficult and demanding even greater vocal strength. Also typical was the increased importance given to the orchestra, which gradu-ally emerged from its secondary role of accompanying the singers to become a partner with them, albeit a limited one. Choruses, too, began to step out of the background and take a more significant part in the narrative. As for the drama, it conformed to the Romantic tastes of the time by having plots highly charged with action and emotion.

What typified French grand opera more than its musical or dramatic charac-teristics was its visual effect. With a multitude of acts and scenes, it was an ever-changing kaleidoscope of color and movement that delighted the public. Such overdone staging, however, made Delacroix (whose sensitive eye was certainly not immune to the beauties of color and movement) lament that music and poetry weren't allowed to stand alone. Berlioz agreed, commenting that "good music" had come to mean "music which doesn't interfere with the rest of the opera."[20] Of a similar opinion was another composer-critic, Castil-Blaze, who found all the scenic hoopla of French grand opera fit only for "the young, the deaf and the ignorant."[21] Although Chopin had a decided preference for the bel canto operas performed at the Italian theater, he was overwhelmed by Meyer-beer's productions at the Opéra. Writing to a childhood friend in Poland during his first months in Paris, Chopin could barely contain his enthusiasm. "I doubt that anyone has ever achieved such magnificence as was seen in *Robert le Diable*, the latest opera in five acts by Meyerbeer.... It is a masterpiece of the modern school. In it enormous choruses of devils sing through megaphones and spirits arise from their graves...as many as fifty or sixty at a time....What is most impressive, though, is the sound of the organ on stage which thrills and amazes you as it all but drowns out the orchestra in the pit below. Meyerbeer has raised himself to the ranks of the immortals."[22] In the midst of the feverish reaction to this spectacle, Chopin's publisher, Maurice Schlesinger, commissioned him to compose something based on the opera's themes. The result was one of the young musician's least memorable works, a *Grand Duo Concertante* for piano and cello, undoubtedly popular at the time but almost unknown today.

The two men responsible for the extravagant staging of the Opéra during this period were the artists Pierre-Luc-Charles Ciceri and Henri Duponchel. Until their arrival, little attempt was made to create historically accurate scenic design. Anachronisms abounded that would strike one as ludicrous today. It was Duponchel, a fellow art student of Delacroix's, and Véron's successor at the Opera, who first strove to keep the visual part of a production in harmony with its historical setting. To do this he employed so much scaffolding, painted canvases, and other props that the time involved in scene changes required him to drop the curtain between acts for the first time in operatic history. Prior to that the curtain had remained up from the beginning to the end of an opera.

The composer whose works became the epitome of the colossal spectacles at the Opéra was Giacomo Meyerbeer (fig. 7.9). Born in Berlin as Jacob Liebman Beer in 1794, he came from a rich Jewish banking family and set out early on an eclectic musical career, composing first German-style operas, then Italian ones, and finally the French grand operas for which he is most famed. His great wealth and fantastic musical success inevitably gained him enemies. One of these, a rival composer Gasparo Spontini, was supposedly seen in the Louvre bending over the mummy of an ancient Egyptian pharaoh and cursing him for letting the children of Israel go. Rossini, who withdrew from the musical scene at the time of Meyerbeer's arrival in Paris, shared Spontini's sentiments and vowed not to attempt a comeback until "the Jews have finished their Sabbath."[23]

In the face of such hostility, Meyerbeer maintained his equanimity, although he was acutely sensitive to it. According to a contemporary, Anaïs Bassanville, the slightest criticism wounded him to the core, and any pleasantry of which he was the butt drove him to despair. He was particularly vulnerable to anti-Semitic slurs like those of Spontini and Rossini, and once remarked that Jews who didn't hemorrhage to death the day after circumcision were obliged to bleed from it for the rest of their lives.

7.9 Giacomo Meyerbeer's first "French" opera, *Robert le Diable,* produced a profound impression on Chopin when he saw it shortly after his arrival in Paris. "It is all the rage!" he exclaimed. No doubt Chopin's enthusiasm was based more on the scenic extravaganza of the production than the quality of the score. Whatever the case, he attended Meyerbeer's subsequent operas, *Les Huguenots* and *Le Prophète,* which offered equally dazzling stage effects.

   A prime example of one who suffered from this chronic exsanguination was the petulant and self-pitying Heine, who once tried to become a sort of press agent for Meyerbeer. When his offer was rebuffed, Heine avenged himself by calling the composer's music "colicky and hemorrhoidal."[24] The vast majority of the Parisian public, however, thought otherwise. George Sand, who wrote for the *Revue et Gazette Musicale* and considered herself something of a musical connoisseur, called Meyerbeer "a great dramatic poet." Chopin, as already noted, was completely awed by the composer's *Robert le Diable,* although his enthusiasm was directed more toward the theatrical effect of the production than the music itself. The opera's visual tour de force was later equalled, if not surpassed, by the composer's subsequent works. In *Les Huguenots,* he introduced a titillating bathing scene (at least by early-nineteenth-century standards), while in *Le Prophète,* he inserted a roller-skating ballet (roller skating having become the rage in Paris then). Chopin was particularly eager to see the latter work, which premiered at the Paris Opéra on April 16, 1849. Although he was near death at the time, he managed to drag himself to its opening night primarily for the sake of hearing his dear friend, Pauline Viardot-Garcia, who sang the role of Fides, mother of "the prophet" (fig. 7.10). He was also eager to witness the composer's latest scenic extravaganza. "They are preparing a sunrise for *Le Prophète* which is supposed to be more magnificent than any in the tropics. You only see the sun come up and it doesn't last long; but it is so brilliant that it puts everything but the music in the shade. It is all done with electricity."[25]

7.10 Pauline Viardot-Garcia, despite her rather homely appearance, not only thrilled the ears but also won the hearts of all who came to know her. George Sand regarded her as a daughter and modeled the heroine of her novel, *Consuelo,* after her. Chopin was equally fond of her, and the two performed in concerts together both in Paris and London. On the composer's death, Mme Viardot paid him a final tribute by singing at his funeral.

Perhaps the most overwhelming of the opera's scenic splendors was the "marvelous fire scene," which took place at the end of the opera when a palace explodes on stage.[26] This pyrotechnical finale was to be Chopin's last glimpse of the operatic world he loved so much. When he died six months later, Meyerbeer, along with Prince Adam Czartoryski, led the funeral procession on foot from the church of the Madeleine to the cemetery of Père Lachaise.

The production of such trompe l'oeil effects as those in *Le Prophète* was a complex procedure requiring crews of machinists and artists. Under Véron, the Opéra employed six scenic designers, each with his own particular specialty, such as architecture, clouds, curtains, or landscape. The machinery needed for these illusory effects (such as hoisting ballerinas in midair) was primitive, noisy, and dangerous. During the premiere of *Robert le Diable,* three accidents occurred when heavy props and lighting equipment fell onto the stage and the leading tenor accidentally fell through a trap door.

Although Schumann put Meyerbeer's operas on a par with Franconi's circus, there is no doubt that they delighted Parisian audiences at the time. When the composer returned to Paris in 1835 with the score to *Les Huguenots,* Mirecourt reported that "the capital rioted, the Opéra shrieked with joy, the salons applauded and the stock market soared!"²⁷ So popular was Meyerbeer's brand of French grand opera that the works of other foreign composers like Mozart, Weber, Rossini, Donizetti, and Verdi were stretched, squeezed, and twisted to fit into the same mold. Mozart's *Don Giovanni,* for example, was rewritten for a tenor lead, while Rossini's *La Donna del Lago* got chopped and blended with earlier scores to concoct a musical stew called *Robert Bruce.* In the case of Verdi's *I Lombardi,* the composer was forced to change the title to *Jerusalem* and add a ballet as well as a special scene for the tenor Duprez. Even a Frenchman like Berlioz couldn't expect the approbation of his fellow Parisians as long as he insisted on pursuing his own course rather than the official path of French grand opera. In 1836 his *Benvenuto Cellini* flopped so badly that the satirical journal *Le Charivari* claimed the audience went to sleep and woke up hissing.

Most composers who followed the path of popular taste usually did so in the company of French grand opera's official librettist, Eugène Scribe. He (or one of his myriad collaborators) wrote the libretti for Meyerbeer's Parisian operas as well as many for the operas of Rossini, Cherubini, Donizetti, and Halévy. Scribe and his colleagues were also responsible for the text of numerous opéras comiques and petits opéras by Auber, Adam, Boïeldieu, Hérold, and Thomas. His subject matter, however, was often mundane and his poetry generally mediocre, weaknesses that were conveniently camouflaged by the melodrama and pageantry of the operatic stage. Like other librettists of his day, Scribe wasted little time on the finer details of character portrayal, the art of a polished phrase, or the subtleties of satire and innuendo. He knew after all that singers usually distorted his words beyond recognition and that it was easy enough for audiences to follow the plot by merely watching the action. The Romantic taste for medieval and supernatural subjects is reflected in many of Scribe's operatic plots. Their illogicality once prompted Wagner to claim that the Frenchman's libretti were "a series of effects without causes" even though their influence is suspiciously evident in the medieval and supernatural themes of Wagner's own music dramas.²⁸ If the public seldom noticed the haphazard quality of Scribe's libretti, critics often did. "No one could write as bad lines as those of Scribe," Théophile Gautier once observed.²⁹ Many present-day critics concur. Jacques Barzun refers to him as a mere "tradesman,"³⁰ while Patrick Smith calls his verse "at best hopelessly banal and at worst atrocious."³¹

Because Scribe was not a profound thinker, he avoided subjects of any substantive nature. The theater of his time, however, was beginning to reflect the public's growing social consciousness. Inevitably Scribe became attuned to this, and themes of political freedom and religious tolerance appear in his libretti for *William Tell, La Muette de Portici, La Juive,* and *Les Huguenots.* The introduction of such themes, in all probability, was not due to the author's concern for such issues so much as his recognition of their timeliness to the people who made up his audiences. Through his sensitivity to these trends, he was able to bring "popular drama to the opera," which more than anything else seems to have been the secret of his enormous success.[32]

Of the many elements involved in the splashy staging of French grand opera, ballet was probably the most popular. From an economic point of view, it became the Opéra's "financial legs"; any performance without a ballet was simply a bore. Cherubini's opera *Ali Baba,* for example, played to a near-empty house until Véron added a ballet for the leading ballerinas Marie Taglioni and Pauline Leroux. Such dancers rivaled and often outshone the best of prima donnas.

Two schools of ballet flourished at this time, led by the famous ballet masters Auguste Vestris and Filippo Taglioni. The former emphasized sensuality, which sometimes shocked even the lusty Dr. Véron. Even so, he willingly paid an exorbitant price to bring its leading exponent, Fanny Elssler, to the Opéra (fig. 7.11). Although her provocative dancing often drew criticism, it also drew crowds. By contrast, Taglioni's school stressed a gossamer lightness and delicacy of movement. Ironically his homely daughter (a neighbor of Chopin's in the square d'Orléans) suffered from a childhood spinal deformity. Despite this handicap, she became the symbol of this pure and limpid style of dancing. The ethereal quality that Marie Taglioni achieved in her most noted ballet, *La Sylphide,* was due partly to her adoption of the new technique of toe-dancing, as well as the use of a delicate white gauze-like gown (a longer version of today's tutu) and a series of air-borne feats accomplished by means of a harness that carried her aloft. Because of the dangers involved in such technical feats, she and the other ballerinas who took similar risks were paid extra by Véron. The fragile and flammable tutus were also a source of danger. On a number of occasions, they caught fire in the gas or oil footlights, leading to serious injuries and even the death of some dancers.

Taglioni's angelic gracefulness contrasted with Fanny Elssler's pagan voluptuousness (fig. 7.12). As the ardent ballet lover Charles de Boigne described them, "Fanny Elssler is the most ravishing, the most perfect expression of worldly and sensual dancing as Taglione [by then retired] had been the incarnation of the modest and ethereal elements of the dance.... How could the earth be

7.11 The fiery Fanny Elssler represented the sensuous school of ballet dancing in the Romantic period. Chopin first encountered her as early as 1829, when the two of them performed on the same program at the Kärtnerthor Theater in Vienna. The following year they again appeared on the same bill at a concert in the Austrian capital's Redoutensaal.

7.12 The ballerina Marie Taglioni, one of Chopin's neighbors in Paris's square d'Orléans, epitomized the spiritual qualities of the dance, aptly embodied by the diaphanous tutus she popularized.

jealous of the air?"[33] At the latter's farewell on April 25, 1837, two young ladies, intoxicated by her dancing, jumped from one of the balconies onto the stage. The audience watched in horror as Taglioni flew to help them. A moment later she stepped up to the footlights and spoke the only words she ever uttered on stage: "Personne n'est blessé" (No one is hurt).[34]

As popular as ballet was at this time, only Adolphe Adam's *Giselle* is still performed with any frequency. Its scenario, written by Théophile Gautier, was based on a Slavic legend recounted by Heine in his essay "Elemental Spirits." The prima ballerina who first danced it in 1841 was Carlotta Grisi, a sister of Gautier's mistress at the time (fig. 7.13).[35] Oddly enough, Heine didn't care much for ballet, which he

7.13 The ballerina Carlotta Grisi, a cousin of the Théâtre-Italien's prima donnas Giulia and Giuditta Grisi, is shown here in Adolphe Adam's ballet *Giselle*. Its plot was adapted by Théophile Gautier from a story by Heinrich Heine.

considered "too disciplined and ascetic" for Romantic tastes.[36] The popular Parisian can-can appealed to him much more because of its lusty sensuality.

Véron's decision to allow the public backstage drew great crowds to the *foyer de danse,* where the young ballerinas assembled before a performance to stretch their legs and rehearse their steps. On such evenings the low-ceilinged room at the back of the Opéra was always crowded with amorous males of the "best society," including ambassadors, deputies, peers, and ministers all anxious to make a conquest of some prima ballerina or one of the younger novices, called *figurants.* By contrast, the nearby singers' *foyer du chant,* a spacious white and gold room with a piano in the center and banquettes along the sides, was staid and quiet with few visitors.

Success being the elusive quality that it is, the Paris Opéra didn't rely entirely on its artistic merits to attract a fickle public. Like many other Parisian theaters, it employed the services of an organization known officially as *La Société d'Assurance des Succès Dramatiques,* more commonly known as the claque. This was not today's informal band of enthusiastic opera buffs who applaud loudly and scream "Bravos" at the end of their favorite singer's arias. They were a strictly regimented group of forty to sixty professionals whose function, so they claimed, was to heighten the emotional impact of a performance. This could be accomplished in a negative way by hissing, booing, whispering out loud, stomping one's feet, or creating other forms of distraction. More often, though, the claque performed in a positive way by cheering, clapping, throwing bouquets (which were later collected and returned to them for the following act), weeping audibly throughout the heroine's death scene, or shrieking uproariously at the comic basso's clumsy pranks. During intermission they carried on their trade in the lobby or a nearby café, where they made loud remarks about the faults or merits of the performance. These members of the Opéra's claque were considered masters of their art, each having his own particular specialty such as the well-timed faint or the ear-splitting whistle. The "weepers" were especially adept at their calling since many served as professional mourners during the day. Although the claqueurs' behavior was often boorish, the Parisian ones never went so far as their London colleagues, who sometimes urinated from the balconies onto the audience below.[37]

Quite the contrary, the claqueurs at the Paris Opéra were said to be "the most civilized... in the world."[38] The man responsible for their model deportment was Auguste Levasseur, the city's ranking *chef de claque*. Considering the cultural and social status of the Opéra, Auguste insisted that his claqueurs dress and behave in a suitable manner. Those who didn't conform were dismissed and forced to proffer their services to lesser institutions like the Comique or the Vaudeville. Auguste himself purposely wore gaudy outfits so he could be spotted easily by his crew, who took their cues from him during a performance. Gloves were the one item strictly forbidden in a claqueur's dress code because they muted applause. Rumor had it, though, that Auguste's real reason for prohibiting gloves was the impossibility of finding a pair large enough to fit his enormous hands.

The efficiency of the Opéra's claque was due to its excellent organization, which Auguste structured along the lines of a Roman legion with its hierarchy of generals, brigadiers, lieutenants, sergeants, and so forth. Auguste, in fact, referred to his men as "Romans." On the day of a new performance, he met with them at a wine merchant's shop near the Opéra to provide last-minute instructions on the timing and extent of their demonstrations—for example, moderate applause for a first act entrance, a standing ovation with wild cries of delight at the end of the last act finale, noisy cheers to cover up Mme **** 's shaky high C and frigid silence throughout Mlle ****'s performance (because she was behind in her payments to the claque). These instructions represented weeks of preparation by Auguste, who attended rehearsals and conferred with the composer, the librettist, the director of the house, and all the major artists. Although largely self-taught, Auguste had gleaned enough knowledge of opera for Véron and Meyerbeer to alter a production at his suggestion.

Members of the claque, after being coached in their duties, would enter the theater around 5:00 in the afternoon and take up their positions before the audience arrived. The seats they occupied were made available through tickets given to Auguste by the management—and often by the performers as well. Most of Auguste's income (estimated at 20,000 to 40,000 francs a year—more than many opera singers earned) came from these tickets, some of which he distributed to his claqueurs before selling the rest for his own profit. In addition he received further "gifts" of money from singers as well as composers, especially on the night of a debut or a premiere. One prima donna paid him 50 francs a performance for the fifteen years she sang at the Opéra. Others were reported to have bestowed lifetime pensions on him. Once Fanny Elssler, put off by his "fees," hired Santon, the chief claqueur of the Gymnase theater, with such disastrous results that she quickly returned to Auguste's protection.

As his power grew, Auguste exploited it to the point of trying to banish the public completely from certain performances on the grounds that its spontaneous reactions could destroy the "successes" he had programmed. At the Comique the chief claqueur, Albert, was even more stringent in his demands, insisting that the public be kept out of *all* first-night productions.

Although some people considered the claque a corrupting influence on the opera and theater of its time, Théophile Gautier rose to its defense. "If the claqueurs were suppressed," he claimed, "the public would be shouting for their return within a week."[39] Why? Because of the many benefits offered by the claque. For one thing, it gave encouragement to deserving new works that an uninformed audience might not appreciate at first. Furthermore, by delaying the failure of an expensive production, the claque protected jobs and allowed the work to gross some money before it closed. Finally, the stimulation of the claque often whipped up the artists to perform better than they might have otherwise. Although its virtues were dubious, the claque persisted in an organized form until the last quarter of the nineteenth century.

Only one important theater in Paris failed to utilize a claque: the Théâtre des Italiens, where an intense band of bel canto enthusiasts formed its own spontaneous claque. In general, audiences at the Italian theater were more attentive than at the Opéra, where only certain scenes or arias (and above all the ballet) commanded silence. Even during the height of the Paris Opéra's popularity under

Véron, Mrs. Trollope noted that it was fashionable to feign boredom and act "ennuyé à la mort" (bored to death) with the music. The Turkish ambassador even brought a prayer rug along to fulfill his religious obligations during performances. The Opéra, of course, had serious devotees of music as well, although their numbers were fewer. Occasionally, though, some were fanatical enough to take their grievances to court if the management made cuts or substituted singers that displeased them.

At the Italiens, everything was subordinated to the star singers, whose pampered lives, according to Wagner, were all "laurels and banknotes."[40] Its orchestra was half the size of the Opéra's, and its small chorus of indifferent quality. In some people's estimation, this concentration on the soloist made the Théâtre des Italiens seem more of a concert hall than an opera house. There the great tenor Rubini was said to have sung the same as he did in a salon—with total indifference to the art of acting. His sole dramatic talent appears to have been one common to Italian tenors then and now: the art of vocal sobbing. As the critic Legouvé put it, "No artist knew how to shed tears to music like Rubini."[41] In general artists at the Théâtre des Italiens went by the philosophy, "You sing well, you get applause; you sing badly you get silence."[42] Singing well for them invariably meant transposing and embroidering arias at will to show off their talents. Many even inserted works from other operas that particularly suited their voices, the so-called trunk or baggage numbers that singers often hauled around with them from stage to stage.

Although it was to be expected that most of the artists at the Italian theater would be Italian, there were a few exceptions such as Mme Damoreau (née Montalant), Mlle Heinefetter and the Garcia sisters, la Malibran and Pauline Viardot. Nor were the operas performed there always Italian ones. From time to time Italian translations of Gluck, Mozart, or Beethoven appeared on its boards. The vast majority of its vocalists, however, did come from Italy, the most famous being the so-called Puritani quartet, consisting of Giulia Grisi, Luigi Lablache, Antonio Tamburini, and Giovanni Rubini (later replaced by Mario di Candia from the Opéra) (figs. 7.14, 7.15).[43]

If Véron's Académie de Musique was noted for spectacle and the Théâtre des Italiens for singing, the Opéra-Comique was something of a compromise, combining (though seldom equalling) the features of its rival houses. The very fact that the Comique produced nearly a hundred works a season limited the amount of attention it could give to artistic details. Nevertheless it was considered by

7.14 Luigi Lablache was the unsurpassed basso of his time. "You can't imagine what Lablache is like," Chopin exclaimed after hearing him for the first time in Paris. At the composer's funeral, Lablache sang the bass part in Mozart's *Requiem*, a work that was later performed at the singer's own funeral.

7.15 Antonio Tamburini (portrayed in this *Charivari* cartoon) was unique in being one of the least flamboyant and most self-effacing of the Romantic era's operatic stars. Twice he and Chopin performed on the same program: once at a benefit given by Berlioz for his future wife in the Salle Favart (1833), and later at the home of the duke and duchess of Sutherland in London (1848).

Schlesinger's *Gazette Musicale* to be "the most national" of the city's theaters. Its success from 1830 to 1850 was largely due to its director, François-Louis Crosnier, a vaudeville writer and former manager of the porte Saint-Martin theater. Among his assets were an innate dramatic flair, first-hand experience with public taste, and Dr. Véron's bourgeois acquisitiveness.

The genre of opéra-comique had its origins in the eighteenth century with composers like Pierre Alexandre Monsigny, Nicolas Dalayrac, and André Ernest Modeste Grétry. Louis-Philippe was particularly fond of their works, which Crosnier shrewdly revived to attract the patronage of the royal family. By then

7.16 Louis-Joseph-Ferdinand Hérold, a composer of operas and operas-comiques, was well known to Chopin before he ever came to Paris. While still in Warsaw, the Polish musician composed variations on a theme from his opera *Ludovic*. Later in Paris he performed a duo on another of his themes (from *Le Pré aux Clercs*) with a colleague, Jean-Amedée le Froid de Méreaux.

the composers most in vogue at the Comique were Auber, Adam, Hérold, Halévy, and Boïeldieu (fig. 7.16). Both Wagner and Rossini had high praise for Auber, while Chopin found Hérold's *Pré aux Clercs* and Boïeldieu's *La Dame Blanche* delightful.[44] Few of these men's works, however, are heard today. The reason the Comique could present so many productions a year was that opéras-comiques had relatively few musical numbers, far fewer, in fact, than today's Broadway musicals. A composer could therefore write them quickly while Scribe tossed off the lyrics to most with equal haste.

Ironically the production of greatest significance at the Opéra Comique from 1830 to 1850 was Berlioz's *Damnation of Faust*, which the composer staged on his own without any assistance from the house. Although a critical success, it received only two performances, which tempts one to blame the lowbrow tastes of Comique audiences. As Berlioz once remarked, the Comique was, after all, "a theatre which the smart world is not given to frequenting."[45]

In 1847 the Comique presented a small work by one of the cellists in its orchestra, a young German-Jewish immigrant named Jacques Offenbach. For some time he had been trudging around the streets of Paris with his cello case full of groceries, which he was too proud to carry in a bag. Until then he had written mostly "serious" music but was gaining popularity as a hired salon performer, noted for his lighthearted musical antics. The word "operetta" had already been coined as early as 1842, but Offenbach's unique version of the genre was not to flower until the glittering years of France's Second Empire.

Even though the Comique never achieved the social prestige or artistic esteem of its competitors, it managed to survive throughout most of the twentieth century, long after the Théâtre des Italiens had closed its doors. Today the Opéra alone continues as an active institution, although no longer in the rue Le Péletier house, which burned in 1873. Shortly afterward, the Comique's Salle Favart met a similar fate, leaving the Salle Ventadour the only remaining opera house from Chopin's time. The interior of the Salle Ventadour, however, has been gutted and replaced by business offices more appropriate to the capitalistic concerns of a bourgeois society than the bel canto arias of a bygone age.

CHAPTER 8

Bohemia and the Demimonde

Two Operas in the Making

*H*ENRI MURGER'S *Scènes de la Vie de Bohème* and Alexandre Dumas *fils*'s *La Dame aux Camélias* have been called the swan songs of French Romanticism. They appeared just before the midpoint of the nineteenth century (at a time when most of Romanticism's "great men were dead or had become politicians") and marked the end of an artistic movement that had begun in England and Germany late in the previous century.[1] Although Rousseau's antirationalistic cult of nature provided a foretaste of Romantic values, Chateaubriand's *Génie du Christianisme* (1802) is generally regarded as the official advent of Romanticism in France. Mme de Staël, writing from Germany during the Napoleonic era, further acquainted the French with the new movement, as did the aristocratic emigrés who returned to Restoration France from abroad. By 1822 the word *romantisme* had come into popular use, and later in the decade Théodore Géricault and Eugène Delacroix brought French art into the Romantic fold. Shortly afterward, Alfred de Vigny with his adaptation of Shakespeare's *Othello* and Alexandre Dumas with his *Henri III et sa Cour* were challenging the hegemony of Classicism on the French stage. In February of 1830 the so-called battle of *Hernani* at the Théâtre Français in February 1830 was to establish France securely under the banner of Romanticism for the next two decades.

Strangely enough, while Chopin the musician represented the supreme embodiment of Romanticism, Chopin the man was to become the antithesis of everything it represented. He was, as Jeremy Siepman aptly observed, a "reluctant Romantic," with an inborn reserve quite at odds with the clear-cut Romanticism of his compositions. In his adult years, the charming exuberance that once filled his boyhood correspondence in Poland was transformed into the polished elegance and impeccable savoir-faire of a Parisian socialite. Almost from the beginning of his life in France, Chopin settled into a restricted sphere of society and rarely strayed outside its boundaries. Because Bohemia and the demimonde lay beyond that pampered world, he took little notice of them. Although friends like Delacroix dabbled in the Bohemian drug scene, and other acquaintances like the Orleanist princes enjoyed the company of of an occasional demimondaine, Chopin himself remained fastidiously aloof from these worlds. Since our personalities are often defined as much by what we dislike as what we like, I have included in this chapter two aspects of Parisian life that Chopin conspicuously shunned. Ironically both the nether worlds of Bohemia and the demimonde were to be immortalized in opera, one of the most sacred domains of music in Chopin's estimation. Although he never knew the real-life prototypes of Puccini's *La Bohème* or Verdi's *La Traviata*, he shared a memorable time and place in history with them.

Early in the fifteenth century the word "Bohemian" had been introduced into France as a synonym for gypsy, that is, one who belonged to a vagabond race from the land of Bohemia. Living on the fringes of society, they refused to obey its laws and conventions. By the 1830s, the term "Bohemian" was being applied to artists who, like gypsies, lived a footloose existence with no fixed niche in the established social order. Exuberant and carefree, these young Bohemians cavorted about the city, readily recognized by their long hair, beards, pointed hats, red waistcoats, and velvet jackets. At that time, George Sand (minus the beard) shared the masculine camaraderie of this Bohemian world, when she lived along the quais of the Left Bank. Unlike many of her companions, though, she escaped the pitfalls of this society where industry and productivity gave way to indolence and pleasure. Those who lacked her self-control eventually drifted into the stagnant backwaters of Bohemia with little hope of returning to the mainstream of life.

From its birth, Bohemia carried within itself the seeds of its own destruction. It was a society born of rebellion and imbued with negativism, a fact often obscured by the facile idealism of its youthful adherents. Whereas the early nineteenth century French Romantics rebelled against the burnt-out forms of Classicism and forged a viable artistic movement in its place, most latter-day Bohemians never progressed from protest to creativity. Many were simply poseurs who affected a Bohemian lifestyle to mask their basic lack of talent, while others were affluent young dandies merely out for a lark. By the 1840s the romance of Bohemia had begun to fade, and those still in its thrall took a more realistic view of their lives. For them the Bohemian world had become a sad place, "bordered on the North by deprivation, on the South by misfortune, on the East by illusion and on the West by the hospital."[2]

What went by the name of "Bohemia" then was not a single counterculture but a conglomeration of subcultures, each with its own distinctive personality and value system. One of the first of these anti-establishment cults, the *petit cénacle* (little circle), arose out of opposition to the increasing bourgeois influence on French culture. Its leader, Petrus Borel, was a rabid iconoclast, prone to express his views through exhibitionistic displays rather than rational dialogue. Most of his followers were artists and writers, including the reclusive Gérard de Nerval and the ebullient Théophile Gautier, once described as "the most perfect incarnation of Romanticism."[3]

Because contentment was considered a bourgeois vice, discontent became a virtue to members of the *petit cénacle*. During the July revolution of 1830, they took the opportunity of posing as radical Republicans to express their dissatisfaction with earlier Romantics like Chateaubriand and Hugo, who had been royalists. A year later, having become equally dissatisfied with the Orleanist regime, they settled into a large, sparsely furnished room at the foot of Montmartre, which they used as a base to fight the philistinism of the new regime. There Petrus Borel worked on his *Rhapsodies,* a volume of poetry full of rancor and revolt, while his followers gave vent to their social outrage by lounging around the garden naked. Soon their irate neighbors (presumably bourgeois), gave vent to their own outrage and had the police evict them.

At this point Borel moved his little clan to the rue d'Enfer on the Left Bank, where they assumed the new title of "Bousingots."[4] Although they had abandoned nudity as a tool of protest, Balzac claimed that their long beards, dirty fingernails, and greasy coats made them almost as offensive dressed as naked. Soon these restless dissidents exchanged the title of Bousingots for the more heroic-sounding Les Jeunes France (Young France). After reconciling themselves to Victor Hugo, whom they briefly respected as the leading spirit of Romanticism, they soon turned against him. The fact that he was making money from his art proved that he had gone over to the camp of bourgeois materialism. At this point, Les Jeunes France vowed to take up the battle where Hugo had left off and bring about a major revolution in the arts. Their first step was to create a journal called *La Liberté,* which fired off salvos in all directions—at Hugo and his followers, the adherents of Classicism, the government, the Academy, the university, and any other institution or individual identified with the social establishment of the July monarchy.

Such extremism inevitably led to reaction, which was to come from one of their own ranks, Théophile Gautier. An unusually level-headed Romantic, Gautier began to see Borel as more of an agitator than an artist. In his 1833 volume of short stories entitled *Les Jeune France*, he satirized the futility of Borel's plans to revolutionize the arts. Revolutions in general, he observed, consist of nothing but "people who fire bullets into the street and break a lot of windows. Hardly anyone but the glaziers find it profitable." [5]

What ultimately caused the disintegration of *Les Jeunes France* was less Gautier's barbs than Borel's negativism. Driven by anger, bitterness, and defiance, Borel knew how to attack and destroy but lacked the ability to reconstruct what he had laid waste. From an artistic point of view, his revolutionary zeal far outstripped his creative talent. For awhile his literary formula of sadism, shock, and satanism was effective in drawing public attention. It appealed especially to the Parisian dandies, who raised it briefly to the level of a fashionable affectation. For Borel, however, it was the serious expression of a paranoid personality that eventually drove away his disciples and extinguished the fanatical flame of *Les Jeunes France*.

When Gautier left Borel's encampment on the rue d'Enfer, he moved with Gérard de Nerval into an apartment on the impasse du Doyenné, a blind alley in the cramped slum that lay between the Tuileries and the Louvre. Several of their literary and artistic friends had already settled there. Together they formed a gregarious lot whose boisterous parties drew the likes of Eugène Delacroix, Théodore Rousseau, Alexandre Dumas *père*, Théodore Chasseriau, and a young man named Sulpice-Guillaume Chevalier (better known as Gavarni), an artist famous for his fashion sketches, costume designs, and book illustrations. For those familiar with the area today, dominated by the Louvre's glass pyramid and surrounded by the eclectic elegance of baroque and Beaux-Arts facades, it is difficult to imagine the slum that existed there in Chopin's time. Then it was an area of narrow medieval streets, in the midst of which lay the shattered dome of Saint-Thomas du Louvre strewn among weed-infested lots. Nothing had been done for decades to repair the neighborhood's dilapidated buildings, which were scheduled for demolition in a long-delayed program to renovate the Louvre. Giant blocks of stone assembled for the project merely added to the clutter. This "outrageous eyesore," Balzac wrote, had "existed for thirty-six years in the heart of Paris facing the Tuileries palace where ... three dynasties ... received the elite of France and Europe."[6] The impasse du Doyenné and the other alleyways that criss-crossed this "sombre and deserted" stretch seemed to be inhabited "by ghosts."7 "Passing in a cab through this dead area...a chill strikes one's heart, one wonders who can possibly live here and what may happen here at night." Wedged as it was between the Louvre and the Tuileries, it represented for Balzac "that intimate alliance of squalor and splendour which is characteristic of [Paris], the queen of capital cities."8

For the convivial coterie that settled there in 1834, though, the area was far from gloomy. Because many were from affluent backgrounds (for which they came to be known as La Bohème Galante), they could afford to furnish their small apartments with such luxuries as fine tapestries, Renaissance beds, Florentine marquetry tables, and Ribera paintings. This new breed of Bohemians, most of whom were well educated and cultivated, purposely withdrew into this depressed section of the city to escape their families and the restrictions of their social class. They did it not out of anger or any sense of alienation from society, but simply to find the freedom to express themselves as they wished. As a result they didn't exhaust their energy in dissent like Borel and his followers, but diverted it, instead, into channels of artistic productivity.

These enterprising individuals had a touch of the capitalistic spirit and enjoyed earning money. Poverty, as Gautier observed, was not an essential prerequisite of talent. If the members of La Bohème Galante didn't scorn money like the Bousingots, neither did they make a religion of it like the bourgeoisie. In place of Borel's satanic cult, they substituted Gautier's credo of art for art's sake, expounded in the preface to *Mademoiselle de Maupin*, his controversial novel about a bisexual (fig. 8.1). There, Gautier summarized his philosophy in the following words: "All my moral notions can be reduced to this: whatever is physically beautiful is good; whatever is ugly is bad."9 The sole purpose of art, he claimed, was to give pleasure. "There is nothing truly beautiful except that which serves no purpose." Given this premise, it would seem to follow that woman, whom Gautier extolled as "Nature's finest work," must therefore be its most useless creation, an implication unforeseen and surely unintended by the "galant Bohemian." "Everything useful," he went on to say, "is ugly because it is merely the expression of a need and man's needs are crude and disgusting."10 The most useful place in a house, he pointed out, is the toilet, which certainly doesn't create much of an aesthetic impact on the average user.

By making pleasure the ultimate criterion of artistic validity, Gautier was preaching a gospel of hedonism that put him at odds with the teachings of the Christian church and the bourgeoisie. He felt, for example, that an exquisitely

8.1 A *Charivari* cartoon of the often outrageous, iconoclastic Théophile Gautier in his heady Bohemian years, Around this time, he was living in the impasse du Doyenné.

proportioned human body was as much a work of art as any inanimate creation by man, and he considered sexual gratification an aesthetic experience equal to hearing a great opera or viewing a fine painting.

In his emphasis on physical beauty, Gautier identified himself more with the spiritual values of ancient Greece than with those of the Christian world. He refused to believe that the flesh was evil and that it was necessary to subjugate it. Because he appreciated the human body and the magic of its movement, ballet became one of Gautier's favorite art forms, and the love of his life was to be the great Romantic ballerina Carlotta Grisi. Circumstances, however, forced him to settle for her less attractive sister, Ernesta, who became his mistress and the mother of his daughters.

If the sensualism of Gautier's philosophy wasn't disturbing enough to his bourgeois compatriots, his acceptance of bisexuality in *Mademoiselle de Maupin* left them totally aghast. Why, he asked, shouldn't a beautiful body be equally appreciated by both sexes? After all, he added, "It sometimes happens, that the sex of the spirit doesn't correspond at all to that of the body."[11] Although the outward pattern of his life was that of a heterosexual, he was certainly not insensitive to the beauty of the male form. "Since the time of Christ," he noted, "no one has ever made a single statue of a man in which his adolescent beauty was idealized and rendered with the care of the ancient sculptors." It perplexed him that Christianity accepted woman as "the symbol of spiritual and physical beauty," while man, he lamented, "truly fell from grace on the day the child of Bethlehem was born."[12]

For the sybaritic Bohemians of the impasse du Doyenné, frolicking was as essential to life as philosophizing. Like the Bousingots, their high jinks were often aimed at shocking the middle class, but more as an outlet for their exuberant spirits than a manifestation of contempt. In the shabby gentility of their modest quarters, they held late-night suppers, dances, and costume parties. By day, though, most of them worked, either at some creative project or at some paying job that would support their aesthetic pursuits. If La Bohème Galante lived on the fringes of society, it didn't burn its bridges to the world it left behind. Unlike Borel's group, its eventual disintegration was not due to ostracism and failure but to the financial rewards of artistic productivity, which drew many back into the more conventional spheres of social life

By that time Gautier had become well established in a journalistic career. He would have preferred to devote himself to poetry, but after becoming a father in 1836 he had to face up to economic realities. During the early 1840s, he wrote the book for two successful ballets, *Giselle* and *La Péri*. Like many of the Romantics, he had a passion for traveling to exotic places, among them Algeria, from which he returned sporting a bernouse (an Arab robe with a hood) and coddling a baby lioness. In time, though, he settled down to a less frenetic lifestyle, having gotten "bored to death by the vehement."[13] Although he could never bring himself to admire the middle class or their values, he no longer flailed against them as before. What was the use? After all, the bourgeoisie, by then, "included pretty nearly everybody."[14]

Despite these changes in his life, Gautier maintained contact with his former Bohemian comrades, some of whom had moved into an elegant but run-down mansion on the île Saint-Louis's quai d'Anjou. It had been built in the seventeenth century and is known today as the Hôtel Lauzan (for the duc de Lauzan, one of its early owners). In the 1840s, however, it was called either the Hôtel des Teinturiers (because of the dye works located on the ground floor) or the Hôtel Pimodan. Directly above the dye works, on the *piano nobile*, was a splendid Louis XIV suite occupied by the elegant Roger de Beauvoir, whom Gautier had first met at the housewarming party in the impasse du Doyenné. Beauvoir was a writer of gothic novels, full of those medieval horrors so dear to both English and French Romantics. He was better known, though, as a fashionable man-about-town who changed his gloves three times an afternoon, a compulsion some of his contemporaries described as "chronic elegantiasis."[15] According to Gautier, he possessed great wit—especially after three glasses of champagne—and attracted many of the era's celebrated dandies like Delacroix, Dumas *père*, Balzac, and Musset to his dinner parties.

It was probably in Beauvoir's apartment that Gautier first met Charles Baudelaire, who had two rooms and a bath in the attic of the same building. Only the year before, Baudelaire had come into a sizable inheritance and was spending it at a reckless rate. His apartment, although small, was luxuriously furnished. In the center of the salon was a large oval seventeenth-century table, around which Baudelaire had placed oversized chairs and divans to give the impression that a race of Titans lived there. Heavy damask curtains covered the windows, and on the glazed red and black flowered wallpaper he hung Delacroix's lithographs of Hamlet under glass without frames. More than most young Romantics, Baudelaire loved to shock the public. At times he walked down the street in a workman's smock with pink gloves, talking nonchalantly of having just assassinated his father or eaten the brains of a newborn infant. He also liked to stroll into an apothecary's shop and stun the clerk by asking to be given an enema. Like Borel, his love of the macabre was coupled with a sadistic streak that led him to string up cats by their tails from his windows.

A year after Gautier first met Baudelaire, the latter's family took court action to place his dwindling fortune under the control of a legal guardian. This put an end to the young man's lavish living and forced him to earn money by writing reviews of the annual salons at the Louvre and making French translations of the works of Edgar Allen Poe (who shared his love of the macabre). Still Baudelaire continued to spend far more than he made.

Around this time Beauvoir moved out of the Hôtel Pimodan and turned over his grand second-floor apartment to an upstairs neighbor, Fernand Boissard de Boisgenier, who has been described as a "man of letters, musician, painter and art-collector."[16] The new occupant's favorite pastime seems to have been the consumption of hashish, and he soon formed a club of hashish eaters that included Gautier, Balzac, Baudelaire, and, occasionally, Daumier. Women were welcome, and George Sand's daughter, Solange, was among those who made a sporadic appearance there. Upon arriving, each guest was given a thumb-sized piece of greenish paste (a mixture of honey and hashish called "green jam"), which was washed down with a thick, bitter Arab coffee. By the time they assembled for dinner, most of the guests were beginning to feel euphoric. Some, in fact, were already hallucinating and fell to the floor with screams of ecstasy. To prevent anyone from jumping out a window or harming themselves in other ways, there was always an abstinent member who stood guard over the crowd. At the end of the evening, he would sit down at the piano and strike a loud chord to break the guests' trance and bring them back to reality.

In a broader sense, the Bohemian world of Paris in the mid-1840s was facing a return to reality that would cause it far greater trauma than the momentary withdrawal from a hashish high. Times were changing, and in the realm of the arts, Romanticism was on the wane. Its idealistic band of youths, who had rebelled against the "gerontocracy" of the Restoration, were now succumbing to age themselves. Many of the dilettantish Bohemians of the Hôtel Pimodan and the impasse du Doyenné eventually caved in and rejoined the ranks of bourgeois society, while those who resisted often tempered their views and learned to coexist without sacrificing their values. By no means, however, did the defection of these family-subsidized "Bohemians in ruffles" spell the end of "Bohemia." [17]

The growing industrialization of France was creating new socioeconomic conditions that converted a number of Romantics into Realists. As Paris became a magnet for the unemployed in search of jobs, the unsanitary districts where they congregated became breeding grounds of vice, squalor, and disease. The widespread existence of such conditions could hardly escape the notice of even the most indifferent members of society. More and more it was impossible to view life through the rose-colored glasses of Romanticism. Truth, once a beautiful but distant ideal, had become a harsh presence, too hideous to face but too ubiquitous to ignore. If the calloused tried to turn their heads, the more sensitive looked on with compassion and outrage. Thanks to the expansion of primary education in France, the lower classes were becoming more articulate in voicing the misery of their plight. These social changes were soon reflected in Bohemia, whose numbers swelled with an influx of less privileged, more practical-minded individuals from the ranks of what we now call the proletariat. They did not, like their predecessors, populate Bohemia by choice but out of necessity. From a financial and social point of view, no other world was open to them.

This new Bohemia, which sprang mostly from deprived elements of society, was a shabby lot compared to the brash sophisticates of La Bohème Galante and the dashing dandies of the Hôtel Pimodan. They couldn't boast of any social background, economic resources, or educational accomplishments. They had no parental allowance and no hope of inheriting a fortune. Most grew up in families with little awareness (and even less appreciation) of the arts. Their parents couldn't understand why anyone wanted to indulge in such futile pursuits as writing or painting. For these youths, with neither financial backing nor emotional support, Bohemia wasn't a make-believe world they could walk away from whenever they got bored. On the contrary, they were like indentured servants who had to earn their freedom through their work. This made them more cynical and materialistic than their earlier counterparts. They couldn't afford to waste time on art for art's sake, but had to struggle daily for whatever fame and fortune their talents could bring them. Some still believed in a transcendental world of Truth and Beauty, but most would gladly have cashed in their artistic integrity for a one-way ticket out of poverty.

Perhaps the most successful member of this new order of Bohemians—or at least the most articulate one—was Henri Murger, a native Parisian born in 1822 and baptized in the quarter of today's Notre-Dame de Lorette (fig. 8.2). His father was a concierge who had a small tailoring business on the side. Although the young boy's education was skimpy, he had an early introduction to the arts through his father's tenants, who included the singers Lablache, La Malibran, and Pauline Viardot-Garcia, as well as the writer Joseph-Etienne de Jouy. Murger's early ambition was to be a painter, but having little aptitude for this, he took up poetry instead. Among his first mentors was the worker-poet and early socialist Eugène Pottier, remembered today chiefly for having written the "Internationale." In order to support his literary career, young Murger took a part-time job as secretary to count Jacques Tolstoy, a Russian diplomat-cum-spy, stationed in Paris. When not at work, the would-be poet spent much of his time with a group of artists, sculptors, and poets who congregated in an old farmhouse on the southern edge of the city near the Barrière d'Enfer. They called themselves Les Buveurs d'Eau (Water Drinkers) because they couldn't afford the cost of wine. To provide themselves the bare essentials of existence, they took odd jobs in lawyers' offices, gave drawing lessons, painted signboards, ran errands for publishers, and wrote "pot-boilers" for second-rate journals. Although few of their number possessed great talent, all were fanatically devoted to their art and frowned on any member who took a full-time job to the neglect of his true calling. They banded together not only for mutual encouragement and the exchange of ideas, but also to pool what little money they had in order to survive. Because of their poverty, many were malnourished and chronically ill. Whenever one of them dropped out of sight, it was tacitly assumed

8.2 Henri Murger, portrayed on the frontispiece of his novel *Le Pays Latin*. Although it is a moving story, the novel lacks the flavor of reality that captivated readers of his earlier *Scènes de la Vie de Bohème*.

he had taken refuge in a hospital. Many never returned, having died there, usually from tuberculosis or malnutrition.

It is difficult to determine exactly when the Water Drinkers came into existence—probably a little before or after 1840. Within less than a decade those who still survived had either worked their way out of Bohemia or abandoned it to seek financial security as government clerks or shopkeepers. Adrien Lelioux, a poet who shared an apartment with Murger in the rue Monsigny ("furnished principally with air"),[18] first brought his roommate to the Water Drinkers' semi-rural quarters. Once a month on Sunday, the group made an excursion into "real" country for the sake of artistic inspiration as well as amusement. At other times they lounged around in hammocks or perched between the chimneys of their barn's roof to enjoy the view. Often they talked throughout the night, sharing their ideas, their projects, and their hopes. According to the group's rules, each member had to produce one serious work a year. Few of these "masterpieces," though, ever saw the light of day. To make ends meet, the Water Drinkers walked instead of taking omnibuses, pawned their clothes, sold their books, and used their furniture as firewood. For food some were reduced to eating stewed cat, a dish they euphemistically called "hare of the short-eared, long-tailed variety."

It was at the Water Drinkers' that Murger first met Jules Champfleury, a young novelist and journalist a year older than himself. In 1843 the two men shared an apartment for several months on the rue Vaugirard near the Luxembourg. Often they collected with the Water Drinkers in the Right Bank's Café Momus, which the group had adopted as their home away from home. It was located on the rue des Prêtres-Saint-Germain-l'Auxerrois, just east of the Louvre. There Murger discovered that for the bargain price of 25 centimes one could have a cup of coffee (usually shared by several other persons), smoke, read a newspaper, and play backgammon. Already it had become a favorite rendezvous for local literati, particularly the staff of the *Journal des Débats*, which had offices next door. M. Louvet, the owner, reserved the upstairs room specifically for artists and writers. Soon the Water Drinkers' raucous bonhomie drove all other patrons away, leaving the premises entirely to themselves.

Two former inhabitants of the impasse du Doyenné, Théophile Gautier and Gérard de Nerval, also frequented the upper room at the Café Momus. In addition, Baudelaire, who had by then left the Hôtel Pimodan for Neuilly, often joined the revelers there. Lack of money had curtailed his dandyism, but his eccentricities, if anything, had multiplied.

Significant at that time was the fact that a newcomer in their circle, Gustave Courbet, had begun to experiment with a new form of art called Realism. He was a handsome young man of peasant stock with a rugged physique and radical convictions. Those who visited his Paris studio found it full of livestock, which he insisted on painting from life to achieve maximum authenticity. The intensity that Courbet brought to his artistic career was equally evident in his social and political life. A friend and follower of the radical reformer Pierre-Joseph Proudhon, he advocated the abolition of private property and the establishment of a Marxist-like economy. During the revolution of 1848, he and other companions from the Café Momus (including Champfleury and Baudelaire) became ardent Republicans.

In their migrations among the "clouds" (as the Bohemians liked to refer to their garret rooms), five of the regulars from the Café Momus's upper story alighted in a run-down tenement called the Hôtel Merciol located on the rue des Canettes just north of the church of Saint-Sulpice. Murger took a room on the sixth floor because, as he explained, there was no seventh floor. Champfleury, Baudelaire, and Courbet took rooms elsewhere in the building. For these young artists and writers, the Hôtel Merciol rivaled the Cafe Momus as the focal point of their existence. Here they gathered for dinner (whenever there was anything in the larder); here they brought their mistresses, and here they worked—or, more often, idled away their time. On nights when their cupboards were bare, Champfleury would open up a cookbook, read aloud the recipe of some succulent dish to his fellow sufferers, "and all their stomachs would be instantly appeased."[19] Sometimes when he had nothing to eat, Murger would take a little opium to sleep. Among Bohemians there was a saying that "He who sleeps, dines."[20]

It was while living in the Hôtel Merciol that Murger began writing his famous *Scènes de la Bohème,* a bittersweet chronicle of the hopes and hardships of a band of young Bohemian artists and their mistresses. These journalistic vignettes, covering a four-year period from 1845 to 1849, appeared in the satirical journal *Corsaire-Satan.* The work evolved in a haphazard fashion with no coherent plot, each episode being based on events that had occurred only a few days before. For the author, they were merely "pot boilers" to allow him time for more serious poetic works.

Many of the scenes portray hospital life, known only too well to Murger who was first hospitalized at age eighteen for a chronic bleeding disorder. When he himself wasn't in the hospital, his friends and mistresses often were. At times one followed the other in the same bed on the same ward. Early deaths were common in their circle. As he wrote in the preface to the book form of his *Scènes de la Bohème* (entitled *Scènes de la Vie de Bohème*), "Bohemia is a stage in the artistic life; it is the preface to the Academy, the Hôtel-Dieu or the Morgue."[21]

In his original sketches the hero, Rodolphe, presents himself to Mimi as a poet, much as Murger liked to think of himself. At the time of the series' first installment, Murger was only twenty-three, but looked much older. He had already become quite bald and according to a contemporary was "very small and dirty," "very *gauche*," and "very ugly."[22] Due to a problem with a tear duct, one eye always watered, while a chronic runny nose made him sniffle loudly and left his moustache constantly wet. His personality was equally unheroic. Champfleury describes him as a passive individual who didn't choose his mistresses but simply accepted those whom chance happened to cast in his path. Perhaps, Champfleury speculated, he never really loved them. Whatever the case, he often treated them in a cold, detached way. "I calculate," he once wrote, "that this new mistress of mine will provide me enough copy for six issues."[23]

Murger was only seventeen when he met Marie Fontblanc, who may have served as the inspiration for his earliest sketches of Rodolphe's fictional mistress, Mimi. Earlier Marie had been arrested for having assisted her husband in a series of robberies. Her subsequent affair with Murger was brief, and she soon left him for a debauched life in the public dance halls of Paris. Long after their separation,

Murger continued to treasure the mementos of their short liaison: a velvet cloak with a mask, a pair of gloves, and a bouquet of withered flowers.

Later, at a picnic in the summer of 1845, Murger met a pale, blond, blue-eyed shop girl named Lucile Louvet. The Mimi of his subsequent *Scènes de la Bohème* seems to bear more resemblance to her than to Marie. Lucile was a delicate, melancholy girl whose life had been blighted by poverty, illness, and marital problems. Her sweet, docile manner must have touched Murger profoundly, for she appeared to have few other assets. Virtually illiterate and lacking in wit, she remained silent during the lively philosophical discussions of her lover and his Bohemian friends. Besides her conversational ineptitude, she was physically awkward and had a complexion "as pock-marked as a honey cake."[24]

When Lucile moved into the Hôtel Merciol with Murger, she brought the sum of her household possessions—three green plaster figurines (of Homer and two rabbits). They were placed on the mantel, where she felt they gave the room a warm look. Whether Murger really loved Lucile or simply used her as literary fodder for his articles, their affair survived for two years despite repeated fights and reconciliations. Like Rodolphe's and Mimi's life together, it was a "hellish existence for both of them."[25] Finally in 1847, when Lucile was maliciously told that Murger still loved Marie Fontblanc, she left him. To survive she resorted to the life of a grisette, which she supplemented by making artificial flowers and modeling for artists. By December of that year, she had become too sick to support herself and was evicted from her room in the rue Faubourg Saint-Denis. Desperate, she thought of returning to Murger, now living at 78 rue Mazarine, but feared that he had taken a new mistress. For hours she wandered around the muddy streets before getting up the courage to knock at his door. When he saw her shivering in the hallway, looking so ill and wasted, he couldn't turn her away. The next day he tried to get her admitted to a hospital, where she might at least have some food and warmth. Not until three months later, though, could he find her a bed in La Pitié hospital. On the way there, Lucile stopped the carriage several times to look at clothes in the shop windows. By the time they reached the hospital she was in a bouyant mood and teased Murger for weeping as he left her. The next Sunday—the only day visitors were admitted to the wards—she sat waiting for him all day with her hair combed, her nightgown smoothed, and the sheets neatly folded across her bed. He never arrived, his excuse being that he couldn't afford the bouquet of violets he had promised her and was too embarrassed to return without them. He saw her only once afterward.

8.3 An early photograph of Marie-Christine Roux (*right*) and her sister. Marie-Christine was the prototype of Musette in Murger's *Scènes de la Bohème* and Puccini's later opera, *La Bohème*. Jules Champfleury, who was Murger's model for the fictional artist Marcel, has left us with a more detailed and factual account of the life of Marie-Christine in his novel, *Les Aventures de Mademoiselle Mariette.*

Early in April, when Murger happened to be in the Palais Royal's Café de la Rotonde, a medical student from La Pitié brought him news of Lucile's death. Too overcome to speak, he walked over to a window, wept silently for a moment, then left. Shortly afterward he learned that the student had been mistaken and that Lucile was still alive. Ironically she was to die on the next visiting day, April 9, 1848, just moments before Murger came to see her. As he rushed down the corridor to the ward, her body was wheeled past him on its way to be autopsied. When he tried to stop the procedure, he was told that charity cases like her were property of the state and there was nothing he could do. That afternoon the faculty of medicine, after witnessing the autopsy, pronounced her death as due to consumption. The next day her remains were buried in a pauper's grave.

It was Marie-Christine Roux, an artists' model and former mistress of Champfleury, who had introduced Lucile to Murger in 1845 (fig. 8.3). Later Mlle Roux was to become the inspiration for Musette in Murger's *Scènes de la Bohème*. A volatile, quixotic person, Marie-Christine lived purely for the day. "Tomorrow is a piece of nonsense devised by the calendar," she once said.[26] Because of her beautiful singing voice, Murger nicknamed her Musette. She knew all the popular street songs and regularly entertained her Bohemian friends with them. Unfortunately the fickle Marie-Christine had one unquench-able passion in life: money. Because of this she eventually abandoned Champfleury for a rich cabinet minister. Alas, Marie-Christine's heady life of pleasure ended tragically when she drowned in a shipwreck off the coast of Algeria in 1864.

The character of Marcel, Musette's fictional paramour, was appropriately based on Marie-Christine's real-life lover, Champfleury. Although he dabbled in painting, Champfleury was primarily an author of realistic novels and secondarily an art critic.

Among the other principal characters of Murger's *Scènes de la Bohème* who appear in Puccini's opera was the musician Schaunard, based on a contemporary painter, Alexandre Schanne. He once studied art with Léon Cogniet, a popular salon artist of the period whose *Lions in the Desert* hung in Chopin's Paris apart-ment. Schanne's real love, however, was music. He aspired to be a composer, but his major work, a *Symphony on the Influence of Blue upon the Arts*, has long since vanished and we can only guess at its merits.

The opera's philosopher, Colline, was drawn from two of the Café Momus's habitués: a theological student, Jean Wallon (who translated Hegel and published scholarly socio-religious tracts) and a philosophy professor, Marc Trapadoux, who authored *Lives of the Saints*.

Shortly after the last installment of *Scènes de la Bohème* in *Le Corsaire*, Théodore Barrière, a clerk in the ministry of war and author of a moderately successful string of vaudevilles, suggested that Murger turn his journalistic sketches into a play. His proposal was greeted with enthusiasm, and the resulting drama premiered at the Théâtre des Variétés on November 9, 1849, with the pres-ident of the new republic, Prince Louis-Napoléon Bonaparte, present in one of the boxes. Nearby in another box was Marie-Christine Roux, blazing with jew-elry from her new lover, a political advisor to the prince-president. Many other Bohemians were present, squirming uncomfortably in the black suits and yellow gloves they had bought or borrowed for the occasion. Among them were Champfleury, Wallon, Trapadoux, and Schanne, as well as Baudelaire, Gautier, Nerval, and Courbet.

The great success of the play led Murger to rework his *Corsaire* sketches into a book entitled *Scènes de la Vie de Bohème*, published two years later, in 1851. Rich now, he abandoned Bohemia for an apartment on the Right Bank's rue Nôtre Dame de Lorette, where he adopted the lifestyle of a proper bourgeois. Here in the company of the district's famed "lorettes," he discovered for the first time in his life that there were women in the world who actually smelled good. Although Murger continued to produce novels, short stories, and a volume of poetry, he never achieved another success to rival his *Scènes de la Bohème*.

On February 1, 1896, thirty-five years after Murger's death, Puccini's opera *La Bohème* premiered at Turin's Teatro Reggio, with Toscanini conducting.[27]

As a pendant to the struggling Bohemian who sought to rise above poverty by virtue of his artistic talents was the ambitious beauty who sought to better her lot through the time-honored art of seduction. Among these were the humble grisettes of the Latin Quarter, the sophisticated "lorettes" of the Right Bank, and their gilded sisters, the "grand horizontals" of the demimonde, a world Théophile Gautier referred to as "the Bohemia of pleasure."[28]

The term "demimonde" was popularized by Alexandre Dumas *fils* in his 1853 play, *Le Demimonde*.[29] He never intended, though, for the word to convey the sense of back-street morality that it has acquired today. For him the demimonde didn't imply a murky realm of ambiguous virtue populated by courtesans, adventuresses, and the proverbial "other woman." It was simply a rung on the social ladder halfway between the unwashed masses at the bottom and the crème de la crème at the top. Because the French traditionally referred to the latter as *le monde*, "the world," Dumas chose the word demimonde to designate those individuals who, being neither fully "in" nor fully "out," existed in a sort of social limbo.

The inferior status of the demimonde, in Dumas's view, resulted from its failure to meet the standards of decorum demanded by *le monde* rather than any failure to live up to its moral expectations. After all, covert affairs and illicit liaisons had always flourished in the best of circles, from royal bedchambers to aristocratic boudoirs. Some were conducted in private, others quite openly. What distinguished the two worlds was not their sexual habits but the grace and elegance with which they comported themselves in or out of bed. Promiscuity could always be forgiven, but vulgarity was seldom condoned.

The crudely disguised ambition and aggressiveness characteristic of the demimonde were qualities often accepted in men but condemned in women. For example, fictional heros like Julien Sorel, Eugène de Rastignac, and Lucien de Rubempré, who schemed their way up the social ladder, were fawned over if they succeeded or forgotten if they failed. Rarely were they reproached. For women such behavior invariably brought social ostracism at the least and civil or criminal penalties at the worst.

The demimonde, like any social entity, possessed its own internal hierarchy. The artist Gavarni has given us touching sketches of the humblest of its members, the lowly grisette of the Left Bank, a simple shop girl attached to her student lover, naively confident that he would one day become a successful doctor or lawyer and lift her above the dreary workaday world in which she lived. The very fact that such girls were called grisettes (from the cheap, dull-gray material of their dresses) is symbolic of the drabness of their lives. In his description of Mimi, Murger conveys the harsh reality of their existence: "Those pretty girls, half bee and half cicada, who sing at their work all week, ask nothing of God but a bit of sunlight on Sundays, make love in a dreary but heartfelt fashion and sometimes throw themselves out a window as a result of it."[30] Although the grisettes of the Latin Quarter received the most notoriety, others lived in the working-class districts of the Right Bank, where their lovers were mostly laborers, artisans, or tradesmen. Even those who settled into a stable relationship with a faithful lover could seldom hope for the respectability of marriage. In many cases, a grisette and her lover simply couldn't afford the cost of a wedding license. "A large number of well-meaning couples," Balzac observed, "live together without marriage, for want of thirty francs, which is the least sum for which the legal profession, the Registrar, the Mayor and the Church are able to unite two Parisians."[31] Rich lovers who could afford the obligatory 30 francs were usually older and already married.

Restricted by ignorance and poverty, the poor grisette lived on a plane far below the worldly demimondaines described by Dumas, those "lorettes" clustered around the church of Notre-Dame de Lorette, near Chopin's and George Sand's quarters in the square d'Orléans (fig. 8.4). "She [the lorette] is a special product of our busy ways," Gautier noted, "the free-and-easy mistress of an age which has not time to fall in love and which is greatly bored at home."[32] Most, he claimed, were music teachers, actresses, or supernumeraries on one of the city's stages—at least these were reputed to be their official "professions." According to Balzac, however, they were primarily practitioners of the art of being "every kind of woman to a man."[33] Undoubtedly it was this art that accounted for the major portions of their incomes. Murger, who moved into the lorette district following the success of his play, found its denizens "impertinent ... second-rate beauties with a complexion somewhere between paste and flesh." "Most of these empty headed creatures," he complained, "lack the intelligence of the birds whose feathers they wear in their hats."[34] Those whom

Gautier knew, however, were a more substantial breed with some grace and talent to augment their sexual charms. Many could speak "the slang of sport, of
the studio, of the stage, . . . dance splendidly, play a waltz, sing a little bit and roll
a cigarette like a Spanish smuggler."[35]

Gautier's description suggests that he may well have had in mind one of the most
notorious ladies of the demimonde, the "Spanish" dancer Lola Montez, who first
rattled her castanets on the stage of the Paris Opéra on March 30, 1844. At that
time few Parisians suspected that the fiery Flamencan was, in fact, Eliza Gilbert,
born in Limerick, Ireland, in 1818. The few dance lessons Lola had taken in the
rue Le Péletier hardly prepared her for the discriminating tastes of Parisian audiences. At her debut on the Opéra's stage, her graceless gyrations triggered loud
boos and hisses. In response she ripped off her garters (along with other unspeci-
fied apparel) and flung them at her detractors. The next day's reviews of her talents ranged from harsh to scathing.

    Less pretentious but equally colorful was another dancer of the demimonde:
"La Reine Pomaré" or "Queen Pomaré." Like Lola Montez, her background
remains a bit blurred. The few facts available tell us she was named Héloise-
Marie Sergent and came from a poor family in Normandy. Although she lacked
Montez's beauty, she had an intuitive grace of movement. Brought to Paris by a
lover who soon left her, she took to frequenting the city's dance palaces—from
the Left Bank's La Chaumière, full of students and grisettes, to the faubourg
Saint-Honoré's Salle Valentino, where the city's elite enjoyed the spirited
rhythms of the new mazurkas, polkas, and can-cans. Almost invariably, she
appeared in a severe black and white outfit, to which she added a flamboyant
array of jangling bracelets. At the height of her fame in 1844, a wharf worker
nicknamed her "La Reine Pomaré" because of her supposed resemblance to
Queen Pomaré of Tahiti, whose lithographic image he had seen in the Paris journals of the time. Like most "queens" of the demimonde, Pomaré's triumphs were
fleeting, and she ended her days in poverty and obscurity.

    Juliette Drouet, although not a dancer, belonged to that coterie of "music
teachers, actresses and supernumeraries" who comprised a large segment of the
demimonde as described by Gautier (fig. 8.5). The daughter of a provincial tailor, Juliette was born in 1806. Later, while attending a convent school, she was on
the verge of becoming a nun. Providence, however, had another calling for her,
and in 1825 she became an artists' model. Once when posing nude for the sculptor

8.4 The church of Notre-Dame de Lorette was completed in 1836 and gave its name to the district in which Chopin and George Sand lived for many years (on the rue Pigalle and in the square d'Orléans). Some called this recently developed *quartier* "The New Athens" because it was inhabited by many devotees of the arts. To most Parisians, however, it was best known for the courtesans who gravitated there.

James Pradier, she succumbed to his attentions and gave birth to a daughter by him. After enduring the abuse of several later lovers, the poor girl sought financial independence in a stage career. With no dramatic training and little talent, her prospects were limited. In 1832, however, she was given a bit role as Princesse Negroni in Hugo's *Lucrèce Borgia*. From then until her death in 1883, she and Hugo remained inseparable. A decade after the beginning of her liaison with the author, Chopin wrote his family about "this actress...who has been kept by Hugo for a long time in spite of Mme Hugo, his children and his poems on family morality."[36]

Juliette's gentle self-effacement and fidelity were unusual among her colleagues in the demimonde. Most were social climbers who would use any means, sexual or otherwise, to get ahead. Their lives were a tissue of false names, false talents, and false titles. "Alice Ozy," for example, was a false name for a young actress christened Julie-Justine Pillory. Addicted to aristocrats and artists, Pillory's conquests included Louis-Philippe's son, the duc d'Aumale, the comte de Perregaux (who later abandoned her for the lady of the camellias), the Spanish duke of Alba, and the artists Théodore Chasseriau and Gustave Doré. In the course of her amorous transitions, Alice came to know Théophile Gautier. During one of their hashish evenings together, Gautier asked her to take off her clothes. "I've always wanted to see a nude woman with a green ass, straddling the highest branch of a tree and howling at the sky," he said.[37] Probably neither remembered what happened after that.

Among those courtesans accomplished enough to grace a salon as well as a boudoir was the ravishing Olympe Pélissier. Like many a lorette, she had enough native intelligence and taste to make up for an indifferent education. It would be stretching a point, of course, to pretend that all guests confined their calls to her salon. Certain ones like Balzac, the duc de Fitz-James, Rossini, Eugène Sue, and the artist Horace Vernet also penetrated her boudoir. Subsequently Balzac and Sue portrayed her viciously in their novels. Rossini, on the other hand, expressed his gratitude by marrying her.[38] Afterward the newlyweds maintained a musical salon at their suburban home in Passy, where they enjoyed a "domestic bliss . . . so unclouded as to be positively uninteresting."[39]

The idyllic union that Olympe found in her later years was rare among ladies of the demimonde. Most preferred the variety and excitement of their restless lives and would have been bored by the restraints of marriage. Such was Appolonie Sabatier, whom Gautier dubbed "La Présidente." As her nickname suggests, Sabatier was a strong-willed woman more inclined to rule than to submit. Blessed with beauty and that full-blown figure so admired by the Romantics, she became an artists' model. On one occasion, she posed for George Sand's son-in-law, the sculptor Clésinger, who used her as the subject for his *Woman Bitten by a Serpent*. When it was exhibited at the Salon of 1847, its graphic eroticism aroused a storm of controversy. Chopin called it "worse than indecent," but was hardly surprised.[40] Someday, he predicted, the irascible sculptor would probably carve his own wife's breasts and "little derrière" in white marble for all the world to see. "He's just the type who would have the nerve to do it."[41] As to the artistic value of Clésinger's work, the critics were divided. George Sand's good friend Gustave Planche denounced it as vulgar, while Gautier considered it delightfully realistic—so realistic that Delacroix called it a daguerreotype in stone. It was, in fact, so true to life that Planche insisted it was a literal copy from a plaster cast until Dumas squelched his theory by pointing out that the sculpture was well over seven feet long. Although the Goncourts described Apollonie as a "biggish woman," she was hardly that big.[42]

Fond of the Bohemian life, Apollonie frequented the Hôtel Pimodan on the île Saint-Louis, where Baudelaire became infatuated with her. A number of the poems in his *Les Fleurs du Mal* were inspired by her. The poet's obsession with Appolonie, however, was purely a fantasy, and when she surrendered to him (for one night only), he became disillusioned. Her subsequent affairs with the rich Belgian banker Alfred Mosselman and the famous English art collector Sir Richard Wallace, led Chopin to refer to her as that "very well-known kept woman in Paris."[43] Although the city at that time abounded in libidinous older men resigned to paying for feminine favors ("At 52 love costs 30,000 francs per annum," M. Crevel complained bitterly in Balzac's *Cousine Bette*), few demimondaines were as successful in finding them as Mme Sabatier.[44]

Among those successful few was Rose-Alphonsine Plessis, born in Normandy, January 16, 1824, to a drunken peddler and his consumptive wife (fig. 8.6). Little is known of the child's family background other than the fact that her paternal grandparents were a country priest and a prostitute. After the death of her mother (when Alphonsine was eight or nine), her father hired her out as a housekeeper to an elderly bachelor who probably became her first lover. By 1839 she had found her way to Paris, where Nestor Roqueplan ran into her on the Pont Neuf one cold January morning. What he saw was a thin, foul-mouthed, vermin-infested waif, dressed in rags and heavy wooden clogs. Out of pity he bought her a bag of fried potatoes and went on, little suspecting that he would later run into her under very different circumstances. For awhile Alphonsine worked in a vegetable stall, then a laundry, before becoming a typical grisette in a draper's shop near the Palais Royal. There she met the owner of one of the palace's restaurants, who took her as his mistress and set her up in a small apartment on the rue de l'Arcade. Later, at an Opéra ball, Alphonsine caught the eye of the young duc de Guiche, a member of Saint-Germain society, who lured her away from her bourgeois restauranteur and installed her in finer quarters on the rue Mont-Thabor. There he became her Pygmalion, hiring tutors to instruct her in grammar, music, art, and the social graces. Eventually de Guiche's father broke up the affair. But by then Alphonsine had acquired enough polish to attract another aristocratic lover, Edouard de Perregaux. Together they spent an idyllic

8.5 Juliette Drouet, Victor Hugo's long-standing mistress, began her career as an actress with a minor part in one of his plays. George Sand found her exceptionally beautiful. Although Hugo remained devoted to Juliette throughout her life, his insatiable libido was such that Mme Sand estimated he had no fewer than two hundred mistresses between 1848 and 1850.

summer in a country house west of Paris, with trips to Chantilly for the races and Baden-Baden for the waters. Shortly afterward, Perregaux's father threatened to cut off his son's income if he didn't give up the girl. Within a matter of days, the country house was sold and Alphonsine returned to an apartment in Paris on the rue d'Antin.

The next summer, Alphonsine met the elderly count Stackelberg (a retired Russian diplomat), who seduced her with his paternalistic attentions and settled her into lavish quarters on the boulevard de la Madeleine. A languorous idleness now filled her days. Each morning, she lounged in bed until late. When she finally got up, she would play for awhile with her English spaniels before trying out some of the latest romances or operatic airs on her piano. Later, like most fashionable ladies of the period, she called her carriage and drove out to the Bois de Boulogne for a stroll before returning to write letters, read a bit, and receive guests. At night she could usually be seen in one of the city's theaters, preferring those given to vaudevilles rather than serious dramas. A late-night supper and a bit of gambling ended her day. By then champagne had loosened her tongue, and her conversation took on a ribald tone, revealing the lower-class origins of the suave and sophisticated "Marie Duplessis," as she now called herself.

It was at this time, in 1844, that Alexandre Dumas *fils* first caught a glimpse of her in a box at the Théâtre des Variétés (fig. 8.7). Both were just twenty. He was a handsome, swarthy octoroon; she, a pale and delicate creature with jet black hair.

8.6 Perhaps the most famous of all Parisian courtesans in Chopin's time was Rose-Alphonsine Plessis (a.k.a. Marie Duplessis and the comtesse de Perregaux, as well as her fictional personae, Marguerite Gautier ["the lady of the camellias"] and Violetta Valery ["La Traviata" or "the lost one"]).

Dumas already knew of her reputation, but wasn't prepared for her exquisite beauty and elegant bearing. "She was very slight," the actress Judith recalled, "almost too thin; but oh, so refined looking, so marvelously graceful."[45] Marie carried herself like a duchess, Gautier said, and according to Dr. Véron she was the best dressed woman in Paris. Whether she always wore camellias as Dumas would have us believe, however, is open to question. Judith, who knew her well, insisted that Marie's supposed passion for camellias was purely an invention of Dumas.

By coincidence Dumas's companion at the theater one night happened to be a friend of Marie's, a plump, gossipy woman named Clémence Prat. Once a successful procuress, Mme Prat had gone into the millinery business after serving a jail term for corruption of minors. Thanks to Mme Prat, Dumas was invited to Marie's apartment for a midnight supper ordered from the Maison Dorée, one of Chopin's favorite restaurants. In the course of the evening, Marie played the piano and got a little tipsy before having to leave the room due to a severe coughing spell. When she failed to return, Dumas took the liberty of entering her bedroom, where he urged her to give up the life she was living. She refused, however, claiming such a sacrifice would surely kill her.

Although Marie dismissed Dumas's advice, she accepted his affection and the two became lovers—with one stipulation: that Marie be allowed to continue her liaisons with Stackelberg and any other rich lovers she might attract. Dumas acquiesced and, as she had done with de Perregaux, the couple took a house in the

8.7 Alexandre Dumas *fils*, one of Rose-Alphonsine Plessis's many lovers, who offered her not only love but also immortality through his novel *La Dame aux Camélias*.

country, where they enjoyed the simple pleasures of rural life. This time, however, Marie's bliss was not to be cut short by the angry demands of her lover's father. On the contrary, the lecherous Alexandre Dumas *père* lusted for her as much as his son did.

Gradually the younger Dumas came to realize that Marie was a selfish, sybaritic creature who saw nothing wrong in deceiving her lovers in order to exploit them. "Lies whiten the teeth," she liked to say. Still he adored her, even though the cost of her love was ruining him. When he found it impossible to pay for the luxuries she demanded, she simply obtained them from other men, a situation that soon drove him mad with jealousy. Finally on August 30, 1845, a little over a year after they first met, he wrote her, "My dear Marie, I am neither rich enough to love you as I should like, nor poor enough to be loved as you would like. There is nothing for us to do but forget."[46] What may have seemed to Marie like the casual end of another affair was, in fact, the beginning of her immortality, for it is largely through Dumas's *La Dame aux Camélias* (and Verdi's subsequent operatic adaptation of it, *La Traviata*) that she is remembered today.

In 1845 Marie encountered Franz Liszt in the green room of a boulevard theater. In the weeks that followed, the two saw each other frequently. At one point Marie offered herself to him, and in an emotional moment, Liszt promised to carry her off to Constantinople. As it turned out he never kept his promise, but the intensity of their brief affair was such that Liszt later told his former mistress,

Marie d'Agoult, he had never really loved anyone in his life as completely as he did Marie Duplessis.

The following year, Marie and her earlier lover, the comte de Perregaux, eloped to England where they were married in a civil ceremony before the registrar of Middlesex County. The reason for their marriage is somewhat uncertain considering that the two never lived together afterward. In all probability, it was an act of generosity on the part of Perregaux to give Marie a facade of respectability and the use of an aristocratic title. At the same time it left Perregaux legally unfettered since their English nuptials were not recognized in France. Although Marie put the Perregaux coat of arms on her carriage, her china, and her violet-colored stationery, she still went by the name of Duplessis and continued to designate herself as "single" on legal documents.

Strangely enough, this marriage that Marie undoubtedly wanted was the harbinger of doom rather than the beginning of a new life. She now entered a period of physical and emotional decline. Stackelberg had understandably withdrawn his support after her wedding, and Marie now found herself in financial straits. To pay her bills, she began to pawn many of her precious possessions. The fewer jewels she wore at the theater, the more people noticed her increasing pallor. In the Bois de Boulogne, she now remained in her carriage while the coachman walked her dogs.

During the summer of 1846 Marie was heavily in debt and could ill afford the expensive spas where she went to restore her health. Her physician Dr. Koreff could do nothing for her, and friends gradually drifted away in search of more vivacious company. The last time that Marie was seen in public, at a vaudeville in the Palais Royal theater, she had to be carried to and from her box by two footmen. Touched by her plight, both Stackelberg and Perregaux came to visit her. "I know well that I shall die young," Marie told the actress Judith. "If I could find happiness I should live."[47] Time, though, had taught her that there was no happiness without love, yet the life she had chosen denied her the very love she desired. On February 3, 1847, shortly after her twenty-third birthday, the frail lady of the camellias died. Perregaux, some claimed, was at her bedside.

At the time of Marie's death, Dumas *fils* was in Marseille on his way back from a tour of Spain and Algeria with his father. The funeral, which took place on February 5 in the Church of the Madeleine (patron saint of fallen women), was attended by a large crowd. Théophile Gautier reported that the best and the worst of Paris had turned out for the occasion, including the era's social "lions,"

8.8 The tomb of Alphonsine Plessis in the cemetery of Montmartre. To this day Parisians and others, touched by her tragic fate, come daily to the grave of the lady of the camellias with offerings of her beloved flower.

Jews, prostitutes, and even some of the city's grandes dames. Perregaux was present, but not Stackelberg. Following the service, Marie was buried in a temporary grave in the Montmartre cemetery, her body shrouded in lace and her coffin covered with camellias. Eleven days later she was reburied in a permanent plot bought for her by her husband. Here he erected a monument to the memory of "Alphonsine Plessis"—rather than the "comtesse de Perregaux" (fig. 8.8).

After her death, Marie's apartment and its contents were put up for auction. Although she was forced to sell a number of her possessions before she died, many valuable items still remained. The viewing of her estate before the sale drew curious crowds to her quarters, including many ladies of impeccable social standing who would never have dreamed of setting foot in the courtesan's salon if she were still alive. Among the items auctioned off were Marie's clothing, silver, pet bird, and even her love letters. Eugène Sue bought her prayer book (to the applause of those present), while Dumas *fils* bought a gold chain. All in all the three-day sale realized between 80,000 and 90,000 francs. This and the rest of Marie's estate were bequeathed to her younger sister in Normandy, Delphine, on the condition that she never set foot in Paris, a city that had corrupted and destroyed so many young girls like herself.

Across the Channel, Charles Dickens deplored the stir created by Marie's death. From his Victorian point of view, so much adulation paid to a courtesan was highly deleterious to public morals. "Paris is corrupt to the core," he inveighed. "For...days, every question: political, artistic and commercial has been neglected by the newspapers. Everything is wiped out before an event of the highest importance, the romantic death of one of those glories of the demimonde, the celebrated Marie Duplessis. You would have thought it was a question of the death of a hero or a Joan of Arc."[48]

The following May, Dumas *fils* was stranded in Saint-Germain-en-Laye one night after missing the last train back to Paris. There he was haunted by memories of Marie for the two had often gone horseback riding in the nearby countryside. Under the spell of her memory, he began the first chapters of *La Dame aux Camélias*. Within a month he had finished the novel, which was published in 1848, a year and a half after Marie's death. Its instant popularity required three successive editions to satisfy the public. Later, he made a stage adaptation of the book that caused his father to break down in tears when he read it. Although the elder Dumas predicted that the play would be a great success, three boulevard theaters rejected the script before it was finally accepted by the Vaudeville. At that point the government banned it on the grounds of immorality. Eventually the minister of the interior (Louis-Napoléon's half-brother, the duc de Morny) lifted the ban and allowed the play to open on February 2, 1852. After some initial reservations about the subject matter, the audience left emotionally devastated by the end of the performance. In the theater that night was the actress Rachel, who had expressed a passing interest in the lead role. As she watched the drama unfold, she grew so distraught that she collapsed in tears and had to leave before the final curtain. Night after night, the place de la Bourse filled up with the carriages of those coming to witness the touching history of the city's most renowned courtesan. As a contemporary recounted in his *Souvenirs*, it seemed as if "all Paris went to see her die."[49] Giuseppe Verdi, who happened to be in Paris then preparing for a production of his *Les Vêpres Siciliennes* at the Opéra, went to see *La Dame aux Camélias* one night. It moved him so much that he borrowed the plot for his next opera, *La Traviata*, which premiered in Venice's Gran Teatro La Fenice on Sunday, March 6, 1853. Unfortunately the use of contemporary costumes disturbed the audience, while the choice of an obese soprano to portray the dying consumptive provoked gales of laughter in the final death scene. Today, however, the opera's popularity has easily outstripped that of the play on which it was based.

Murger's *Scènes de la Vie de Bohème* and Dumas's *La Dame aux Camélias* were indeed the swan songs of Romanticism. It was the unique gift of the Romantics to idealize the world around them and to enhance the direst of life's misfortunes with a touch of the sublime. Chopin shared this gift and was able to make his music conjure up the image of a proud and powerful Poland in one of the bleakest moments of its history. If Romanticism couldn't alter the harshness of reality, it at least offered mankind a glimmer of beauty in some of the darkest avenues of its earthly journey.

CHAPTER 9

Penning a Profit

Literature Becomes Lucrative

"*ANY NOVEL CAN BE SOLD, good or bad*—you just need determination," Baudelaire wrote his mother in 1847.[1] There was little exaggeration in what he said. Even a cursory survey of the literary scene during the years of the Orleanist monarchy reveals a depressing lack of quality in vast amounts of the material published then. Sensationalism and sentimentality, those bastard off-spring of Romanticism, had glutted the market with such morbid works as *To Love, To Weep, To Die* and *Woman's Role: To Pardon All*, pseudo-moralistic tales like *Louisa; or, the Sorrows of a Love Child, Passion and Duty*, or just plain spicy fare like *The Prima Donna and the Butcherboy*. During his first weeks in Paris, Chopin was wide-eyed to see vendors along the boulevards hawking such lurid volumes as *The Love Affairs of Priests, The Archbishop of Paris and the Duchess of Berry*, and *The Art of Making Love and Keeping It Alive*. These were hardly the works that Chateaubriand had in mind when he spoke of literature as responsible for the preservation of history and the glory of the world.

A cut above the bawdy level of such literary grist were the popular novels of Paul de Kock, a one-time banker lured into the writing business by the riches it offered. Frequently called "the chambermaids' novelist," he possessed a mildly titillating style that delighted the *petite bourgeoisie*, who reveled in his platitudi-nous generalizations, improbable coincidences, and Pollyanna-like endings. Even the pope was said to have enjoyed his stories, and the dour Chateaubriand found them "uplifting" because they never portrayed "humanity in a way that saddens you."[2] Although critics usually denounced de Kock for the thinness of his plots and the weakness of his characters, Théophile Gautier detected a cer-tain charm in his nostalgic portrayal of Paris and Parisians before they became "invaded and submerged by American civilization."[3]

Comparable to de Kock in his output of best-sellers was the indefatigable Frédéric Soulié, whose ghoulish novels (such as *The Two Cadavers* and *The*

Mémoires of the Devil) often came off the presses at the rate of one a month. Some earned him as much as 50,000 francs apiece at a time when George Sand considered herself lucky to make 5,000 francs for her masterpiece, *Lélia*. Balzac, whose output exceeded Sand's, frequently earned less per novel than she did because of the printer's fines he incurred for his incessant revisions. Sometimes he demanded ten proofs before allowing a novel to go to press. As a result, his immensely popular *Wild Ass's Skin* brought him only 1,135 francs after settling with the printers. No individual author, of course, could begin to rival the assembly-line production of Dumas's famous novel factory. Clearly, Parisian publishers during the July monarchy were enjoying an unprecedented boom in business.

Unlike the youthful Baudelaire, established writers who had already made a name for themselves worried less about selling their novels than about the price they could get for them. As the ever-acquisitive Balzac was fond of saying, "A profit is not without honor."[4] Even Victor Hugo, whose candor occasionally shone forth between clouds of pomposity, once admitted, "My wish is to ennoble literature, yet I work in order to make money."[5] George Sand, more straightforward than Hugo, didn't try to gloss over the fact that she had chosen a literary career purely for mercenary reasons. Without access to her inherited income, which was controlled by her husband, she resorted to writing only after attempts at sewing, embroidering, and painting ornamental boxes failed to provide her the wherewithal to survive in Paris. Equally money-minded was Heinrich Heine, who also found Paris shockingly expensive when he settled there a few months before Chopin's arrival in 1831 (fig. 9.1). Despite his vociferous attacks on the commercialization of art, Heine was willing to write anything, be it poetry, travelogues, criticism, or political editorials, to put a few extra francs in his coffers. On the theory that an independent income was the best stimulus to literary productivity, he shamelessly milked an allowance out of a rich uncle and finagled an annual stipend of 4,800 francs from the Orleanist government that he professed to despise. In spite of his own mercenary orientation, Heine condemned the monetary morality and philistine tastes of the era. "Money is the god of our time and Rothschild is its prophet," he lamented.[6] Typical of the veneration inspired by this prophet was a scene Heine witnessed on a visit to the famous banker's office. "A liveried servant," he recalled, "carried his [Rothschild's] chamber pot across the corridor and a spectator who happened to pass by took off his hat reverently to the mighty pot."[7] In Balzac's *La Maison Nucingen*, Rothschild's fictional counterpart, the Jewish financier, baron Nucingen, announces that all

9.1 A portrait of Heinrich Heine in his youth. Heine came to Paris in 1831, the same year that Chopin arrived and George Sand settled there with her lover Jules Sandeau. By the following year, both Sand and Chopin had become acquainted with Heine and saw him frequently during the 1830s and 1840s.
Although Heine considered Chopin a genius comparable to Mozart, Raphael, and Goethe, the musician had difficulty appreciating the acid wit and cynical philosophy of the German-Jewish poet.

material happiness comes down to numbers. In another of his novels, *Cousine Bette,* the same author speaks of "Her Holiness the Bank" and says that Louis-Philippe "knows as we all do, that above the Charter, there stands the holy, venerable, solid, the adored, gracious, beautiful, noble, ever young, almighty franc!"[8] Summing up his thoughts on Balzac's *Comédie Humaine,* Henry James was to comment years later that the chief protagonist of the Frenchman's magnum opus was the five-franc piece.

Although most Romantics extolled high-minded feelings over high-powered finance, few felt any qualms about soliciting favors from the materialistic, bourgeois government that they publicly disparaged. At a time when royal patronage had slowed down to a trickle, there was a frantic demand for the few juicy sinecures still to be found in the cultural desert of middle-class mediocrity. The novelist Charles Nodier, for example, clung tenaciously to his government post as librarian of the Arsenal, even though his stipend now came from a bourgeois legislature rather than Charles X's royal purse—and the literary critic Charles-Augustin Sainte-Beuve gratefully accepted the state's offer to make him librarian of the Mazarine library at the Institut. The best plum of all, though, fell to the poet-playwright Alfred de Musset, when his childhood schoolmate, the duc d'Orléans, appointed him librarian for the ministry of the interior, which had no library. At that time, the versatile author de Vigny urged the government to go beyond the sporadic sinecure and provide subsidies for all writers of talent. Per-

9.2 Honoré Balzac. This paradoxical genius is perhaps the crown jewel of nineteenth-century French literature. Readers today appreciate his brilliance as much as or more than did his contemporaries. His amalgam of naivete and cynicism, generosity and greed, industry and sloth, fantasy and practicality offers something for everyone.

haps, though, it was just as well that his suggestion got rejected; all too often money poisoned the muse it was meant to nourish.

Nowhere was this danger more evident than in the explosive growth of French journalism during the 1830s and 1840s, when Murger, Champfleury, and a host of their Bohemian cohorts concluded that a pocketful of change was worth more than a headful of ideals. Many such writers began their careers like the visionary young poet Lucien de Rubempré, in Balzac's novel *Lost Illusions*, only to be corrupted by the cynical, mercenary world of journalism. In the end they, too, would come to hear the "insistent tickings of the great money pendulum"[9] and cry out like Lucien, "Great God! Gold at all costs."[10]

With the possible exception of the elder Dumas, it would be hard to find anyone to rival Balzac's insatiable lust for the almighty franc. Among the latter's endless money-making ventures were such non-literary enterprises as growing pineapples in Passy, reactivating old silver mines in Sardinia, buying up shares of Rothschild's Northern Railways, and making railroad ties out of Ukrainian oak. On one occasion he even speculated on how much he could get from the sale of his love letters. Even though Balzac shared Lucien's obsessive adulation of wealth and the power it could buy, he never let greed and ambition affect the quality of his work. Unlike the opportunistic Lucien, who readily prostituted his pen for the sake of financial gain, Balzac refused to compromise his aesthetic standards even when printers fined him for his extra proofs and editors rejected his novels as unsuitable for serialization in the newspapers (fig. 9.2).

Despite Balzac's chronic addiction to moneygrubbing, his basic literary integrity stands in marked contrast to the widespread concern of early-nineteenth-century writers with financial reward. Such undisguised materialism seems strangely at odds with the professed idealism of Romanticism. In general, Romantic heroes and heroines were great-hearted and high-principled, devoting their lives to the pursuit of such laudable ideals as Love, Marriage, Family, Chastity, Charity, Beauty, Justice—and of course in France, Liberty, Equality, and Fraternity. Typical of the lofty sentiments of Romantic heroines was Adrienne de Cardoville in Eugène Sue's *The Wandering Jew*: "Adrienne loved physical beauty, and admired it passionately; but she had too superior a mind, too noble a soul, too sensitive a heart, not to know how to appreciate moral beauty, even when it beamed from a humble and suffering countenance."[11] Such elevation of character, all too often lacking in the social order of the times, had to be searched for in exotic settings, preferably the Middle Ages and the Middle East. Both represented societies deemed more primitive, hence purer than those of Western Europe, which was then in the throes of industrialization with all its inherent evils.

It would seem, though, that what Romanticism actually rebelled against—at least in its early phase—was not so much a materialistic, over-mechanized society that lacked spiritual vision as an intellectual and artistic tradition that imposed arbitrary standards on the creative mind. Throughout the eighteenth century, music, poetry, and drama were governed by rules almost as inflexible as scientific laws. No poem, play, or musical composition could be called a work of art if it didn't conform to certain conventions. With such strict regimentation, originality was limited, emotion restrained, and spontaneity often lost. As Chateaubriand observed, "The reasoning spirit, by destroying the imagination, undermines the bases of the fine arts."[12] For an enthusiastic Berlioz, this brief statement contained the very essence of Romanticism. Imagination as he (and other Romantics) saw it was the key to creativity that freed the Arts from the clone-like uniformity fostered by classical restrictions.

What started as a pursuit of freedom in the arts eventually became a dedication to "Freedom" in the abstract. Just as Hugo had flaunted the classical unities of time and space on stage, subsequent Romantics sought to free themselves (through the exercise of their imaginations) from the spatial and temporal limitations of everyday life. In their mental time machines, the Romantics traveled into bygone eras or soared into the realm of eternal verities, where they communed with such transcendental entities as Truth, Beauty, and the human Soul. Spatially they envisioned themselves in the exotic civilizations of the East or the savage wilds of America. Some actually visited these remote areas; others saw them only through the mind's eye as havens from civilization, populated by a pure and noble race. In their imaginations (stimulated by the reading of Rousseau's *Emile* and Chateaubriand's *Atala*) they fancied these beings as "children of Nature," vestiges of Eden whose innocence had somehow survived the fall of Adam. Nature to the Romantics represented the manifestation of universal order and as such, the source of basic values. Some even deified nature as the embodiment of God and evolved a pantheistic form of religion. Heinrich Heine was one who drifted in this direction after failing to find fulfillment and repose in the Judeo-Christian tradition. George Sand, in her lifelong philosophical quest, also experienced an attraction toward pantheism, which she attempted to expound in her novel *Spiridion*. Her publisher, however, refused to print the book on the grounds that it was long-winded, pompous, and boring. Thackeray concurred, calling it "wretched nonsense."[13]

In real life, few Romantics ever returned to nature to live the life of Rousseau's noble savage. Who, after all, could erase the indelible stains of civilization and revert to a life of Neanderthal simplicity? As an alternative, many Romantics strove to "liberate" themselves from the material world in a metaphorical way, convinced that the artistic spirit, unlike the scientific mind, could soar beyond the finite. Whether or not this was possible didn't really matter so long as they *felt* it was. Eventually the struggle for artistic liberation, which spurred Romantics to free themselves from anything that hampered their self-fulfillment, took on a broader, more altruistic aspect. The second-generation Romantics (who from 1830 on had been subjected to the bourgeois regime of the July monarchy) viewed themselves as apostles of freedom, concerned not just with their own personal liberty but with that of humanity at large.

This moral mission of the new socially conscious Romantic was especially evident in the novels of such authors as George Sand and Eugène Sue. In his *Paris Sketch Book*, Thackeray ridicules the pretentious preachings of "Saint Sand" and others who set themselves up as prophets (fig. 9.3). In England, he claimed, writers were not so presumptuous. "Mrs. Trollope has never declared that her novels are inspired by heaven. Even Sir Edward Bulwer...never ventured to say that he had received a divine mission and was uttering five-act revelations."[14] Heine also found a priggish quality in the smug utterances of Mme Sand's socio-philosophic

9.3 William Makepeace Thackeray, who later became one of Victorian England's major novelists, spent much of his youth in Paris studying to become an artist. While there, he wrote his *Paris Sketch Book*, which revealed his keen observation of human nature and his budding skills as an author.

9.4 Victor Hugo, poet, novelist, playwright, and egotist par excellence, once claimed to have "exerted a permanent influence on literature . . . well beyond the borders of France." In Chopin's words, "He pretends to be very high-minded . . . and carries on as if he were superior to the rest of humanity."

novels. In them, he claimed, she wrote like a true democrat straight from the ranks of the people, that is, "sincerely, simply and badly."[15] Another of the Romantics quick to don the moral mantle and speak out against the evils of society was Victor Hugo (fig. 9.4). As early as 1831, in his novel *Notre-Dame de Paris*, he portrayed a priest and a nobleman as villains to draw attention to corruption in the church and the aristocracy, two institutions he had once revered. But even Hugo (and other writers who went about their moral missions with a religious fervor) often expected suitable monetary rewards for contributing to the welfare of humanity. Hugo, in fact, considered it his due. As he once claimed, "People . . . know that my work entitles me to compensations beyond the ordinary."[16]

Romanticism in the 1830s had become (to borrow a modern phrase) a "liberation movement" concerned primarily with freedom of expression. Although such freedom germinated in the arts, it gradually came to influence virtually every aspect of society. At times the Romantics' stress on individuality tended to breed eccentricity and above all, egocentricity. Chateaubriand, it was said, had three main subjects on which he expounded: Religion, Nature, and Self.[17] All became prominent themes of Romanticism, but the concentration on "self" is particularly characteristic of most Romantics, who, like Chateaubriand, were obsessed with their own uniqueness. In their self-oriented worlds, many, like Baudelaire and Hugo, fell prey to megalomania and saw themselves as Byronic supermen above and beyond the laws that governed others. Chopin was but one of many who were put off by the latter's egotism: Hugo, he once complained, "pretends to be very high-minded every chance he gets and carries on as if he were superior to the rest of humanity."[18]

Typical of Hugo's conceit was his claim that he instinctively thought in poetry and had to force himself to speak prose. Unfortunately age failed to mellow him. On the eve of his eightieth birthday, he proclaimed (speaking of himself in the third person), "Hugo's poetry will live as long as the French tongue is written and spoken, and novelists will be indebted to him for centuries to come."[19]

Along with egocentricity, Romanticism's emphasis on individuality encouraged diversity—a trait that had both beneficial and detrimental effects on the artistic world and society in general. The fecundity of Romanticism's ideas certainly enriched the lives of all those affected by it. At the same time, it led to a chaotic plethora of subjective impressions and dictums that became a divisive factor in the cultural life of the period. In addition the Romantic artists' conviction of their unique status made many struggle to set themselves apart from society (especially "the masses," whom they scorned). In doing so they found themselves alone and alienated from the bulk of humanity. In this lay the origins of the era's famous *mal de siècle:* melancholy. The sadness and suffering brought on by the "sweet melancholy" of their isolation was exploited by many Romantics to prove their artistic genius. As the poet de Musset once told the actress Judith, "Never is the muse of poetry more beautiful than when her eyes are full of tears."[20]

Other forms of psychological malaise (ennui in particular) and even physical suffering also served as lesser proofs of divine inspiration. For example "a diseased liver, a heart complaint, a hectic cough or chronic dyspepsia" sometimes passed for an infallible mark of genius.[21] Pain for the Romantics was the raw material of ecstasy. It provided a psychological purge that ennobled the soul by ridding it of emotional imperfections. Tranquility, on the other hand, symbolized the complacency of the bourgeoisie, who never experienced the purifying effects of pain. During his liaison with George Sand, de Musset once told her that he loved his suffering more than life. This, Sainte-Beuve assured the young authoress, was the highest of compliments, for "Love means tears. If you weep you love."[22] Firm in the conviction that the suffering they inflicted on each other was a sign of true love, Sand and de Musset continued to torture each other for years just to prove their devotion.

Although some degree of social alienation was to be expected among those Romantics who rejected conventional, middle-class values, not all of them reveled in the loneliness and melancholy it entailed. Many gathered together in small cliques (or *cénacles*) like those organized by Charles Nodier, Victor Hugo, Petrus Borel, and the Water Drinkers. At their meetings, members read each other their latest works, hoping for praise, reassurance, or at the very least, some constructive criticism. Although today's psychologists would probably consider them "support groups," a late-nineteenth-century critic called them mutual admiration societies, where each individual claimed to have "a masterpiece in preparation . . . and all of them together *a monopoly on French Genius.*"[23] In spite of the spiritual encouragement and camaraderie derived from these literary associations, some like Henri Murger and Jules Champfleury eventually fled back into the fold of bourgeois society. Still others like Chopin and Delacroix, who remained intensely Romantic in their work, divorced their personal lives from everything Romantic and found an escape from loneliness in the crowded salons of the fashionable faubourgs. For the more conscience-stricken "moral missionaries" of Romanticism like George Sand, Eugène Sue, and Victor Hugo, social activism provided the means by which they coped with the problem of artistic isolation and reconnected to their fellow men and women.

Unfortunately this sense of isolation created a disturbing fad among certain Romantic youth of the period. Suicides during Louis-Philippe's reign reached epidemic proportions, causing concerned debate in the nation's legislative chambers. This wave of suicides, which became "the devouring plague of the times,"[24] was attributed by the pontifical Mrs. Trollope to "an excess of literary excitement"—no doubt with some truth.[25] For many a disillusioned Romantic, suicide was the supreme opportunity for artistic expression. To die at the Opéra by ingesting a hallucinatory opiate while listening to glorious music was the ideal of sentimental Romantics like Raphael in Balzac's *Wild Ass's Skin*. In 1846 a Suicide Club was actually formed in Paris for individuals between the ages of eighteen and thirty. (After thirty it was feared that death might be interpreted as a physiologic event rather than a philosophic statement.) The aim of the club was to extol the nobility of self-destruction as an alternative to the degradation of social or artistic compromise. Because the act was meant to be a form of aesthetic expression, any method of suicide that created physical disfigurement was prohibited. Fortunately only one member of the club, a student at the Sorbonne, actually killed himself.

The burden of personal freedom imposed on the Romantics by their cult of individuality was clearly enormous. Those who were able to shoulder it, though, experienced not only intellectual and aesthetic rewards but often economic compensation as well. If some scorned financial gain (as a compromise with bourgeois materialism), many like Hugo, George Sand, Balzac, and Dumas were not the least bit squeamish about driving a hard bargain with their publishers. Others in the fields of music, painting, and sculpture could be equally aggressive when it came to money. Chopin, usually a model of gentility and decorum, often lashed out at his publishers in vituperative, even vulgar language. Liszt, Paganini, the actress Rachel, and a host of temperamental prima donnas shamelessly sold their talents, while painters and sculptors could be conniving and cutthroat in their scramble for government commissions. Such a crass concern for money, which seems so inappropriate among artists dedicated to the pursuit of spiritual values, was, in fact, a simple extension of the Romantic demand for individual liberty in the financial sphere as elsewhere. Viewed in this light, authors of the period saw no conflict between the desire to write well and to earn well at the same time. Of the many fortunes made by this new species of literary entrepreneurs, the largest went to men like the elder Dumas who could combine economic ingenuity with artistic productivity.

It was primarily these self-appointed high priests or "moral missionaries" of Romanticism that decried the gulf between the idealism of the artist and the materialism of the capitalist. Such writers professed a dedication to social reform and freely criticized the profit-motivated orientation of the Orleanist regime. Ironically many of these literary moralists were themselves financial opportunists, skilled at transforming the intangible wealth of their talents into the hard cash of economic profits that enabled them to lead comfortable, even luxurious lives. By regarding these profits as purified by their pious pretentions, they were able to banish any clouds of conscience that might dim their enjoyment of them. Certainly one has to admire writers like George Sand, Victor Hugo, and Eugène Sue, who gave freely of their time and money to better the lot of the poor. At the same time these social benefactors had few qualms about reserving much of what they earned for the betterment of their own lives. Mme Sand, who liked to boast of being a communist, never saw fit to give up her country estate at Nohant, while Victor Hugo, a Royalist-turned-democrat, considered the expenses of maintaining separate establishments for his wife and mistresses a noble example of his innate generosity. Ironically, Eugène Sue's conversion from a foppish spendthrift to a dedicated socialist brought him riches well beyond the expectations of most capitalists.

In the eyes of some, the financial success of these writers aroused envy and suspicion. Thackeray, for instance, tended to view them as hypocrites, comparable to the "limousine liberals" of today. He doubted the sincerity of their beliefs and suspected that their ostentatious concern for the underprivileged was merely a ruse to justify their economic exploitation of the literary marketplace. Furthermore, he accused them of violating the Romantic's sacred creed of individual freedom by trying to impose their own sociopolitical standards on others.

Considering the times, it would certainly have been difficult for any French author to resist the temptation of succumbing to the *enrichessez-vous* philosophy of the July monarchy's bourgeois regime. Indeed, in an era of vanishing patronage, it was virtually imperative that they do so to survive. Even aristocratic authors like Chateaubriand and de Vigny, whose family fortunes perished with their ancestors in the great revolution, were reduced to making a profit from their pens. Along with the younger generation that followed, they learned to bend with the supply-and-demand vagaries of a literary Bourse. Fortunately in the early 1830s two factors worked to their advantage: first, the bourgeoisie's desire to improve their cultural credentials now that they had risen to power, and second, the July monarchy's campaign to improve the nation's literacy rate. Both led to a rising interest among the public in literature as well as the other arts. Although many of the nouveaux riches middle class merely aped the tastes of their social betters, others developed distinct aesthetic preferences of their own and demanded a literary, musical, and artistic fare they could appreciate. Because they had the money, they were able to get what they wanted. By the end of the July monarchy, the bourgeoisie had become the major consumers of art. Most writers, painters, and musicians of the era were compelled to satisfy their tastes or suffer the economic consequences.

Unlike novels, which Baudelaire claimed could always be sold regardless of their merits, poetry, at its best, was never a very marketable item, especially in Orleanist France. This hardly surprised Heinrich Heine, who described French poetry as "rhymed burping" and "perfumed curds."[26] Even under the Restoration, when poetry was more popular, it didn't bring a very high price. Strangely enough, many of the foremost writers of the era like Chateaubriand, Balzac, Sand, Mérimée, Stendhal, and Dumas lacked any poetic skills. In Balzac's opinion, poetry was nothing but the self-indulgence of passive egotistical people. Whenever he felt the need to insert poetry into a novel, he pressed his poet friends into writing it for him.

By the late 1830s, when newspapers had begun to publish novels in weekly installments, Balzac was among the first to exploit this lucrative opportunity. Soon the *roman-feuilleton*, or serialized novel, was to become the source of sumptuous incomes to several of the period's top-flight novelists.[27] Eugène Sue, for example, received 100,000 francs for his *Wandering Jew* from Dr. Véron at *Le Constitutionnel*. This fee, which was over three times what Balzac usually got for a novel, upset the latter so much that he refused to read the book. Sue, however, lacked the fertility of Balzac's imagination and could never match his prolific output. At his peak Balzac wrote up to two thousand pages a year, producing one hundred novels over a thirty-year period. If it weren't for his incredible extravagance (he "wore sparkling jewels on a dirty shirt front, and diamond rings on unwashed fingers") and his far-fetched financial schemes, Balzac could easily have become the millionaire that he always dreamed of being.[28] By 1840 he was already 262,000 francs in the red, and his debts continued to mount steadily until the time of his death.

George Sand, who averaged two novels a year for over four decades, rivaled Balzac in output. But because her long-time publisher, François Buloz, paid women authors less than their male counterparts, she couldn't match Balzac's income. Far less of a spendthrift than Balzac, she still found that the cost of maintaining her children, her lovers, and her socialist causes often left her in serious economic straits.

Victor Hugo was another author who made a handsome fortune during the Louis-Philippe years. (This Heine attributed to the fact that the French mistook his lack of taste as originality.) Even though Hugo went for ten years without publishing anything after the accidental drowning of his daughter and son-in-law in 1843, his royalties continued to bring him an income of 60,000 to 70,000 francs a year.

The king of literary breadwinners under the July monarchy was undoubtedly the elder Dumas (fig. 9.5). Because of his chronic braggadocio, however, it is difficult to verify his financial claims. In later years he boasted that he had made over

9.5 Alexandre Dumas *père* made a fortune through the serialization of his novels on the front page of the era's first daily newspapers, a literary form known as the feuilleton novel. The money he was to reap from such works merely increased the enormous profits that he was already making from the conventional marketing of his other works.

18,000,000 francs during his lifetime. Lest people think him rapacious, he let it be known that his career was responsible for bringing great economic benefits to France. By his calculations, it had given employment to 2,150 persons, including printers, stage hands, actors, and publishers, not to mention the host of "collaborators" who labored in his "factory of novels." According to one of his contemporaries, Dumas often solicited manuscripts from aspiring writers, stole ideas from them, and then returned them as "unpublishable works." At other times he would buy a manuscript for a few thousand francs, touch it up, and sell it to a publisher as his own work for three or four times that amount. Among the great number of writers on his assembly line were two of George Sand's ex-lovers, Félicien Mallefille and the actor Pierre Bocage (both "pre-Chopin"). At its peak, Dumas's "factory" could turn out as many as sixty novels a year. According to Mirecourt's mathematics, no one person could possibly have copied out that many volumes even if he spent twenty-four hours a day at it. When accused of plagiarism, Dumas glibly replied that he didn't steal, he conquered, and compared himself to Napoléon who achieved his victories by delegating power to his marshals.

Although there was substantial truth in Mirecourt's accusations, Dumas sued for libel, won his case, and had the pleasure of seeing his accuser sentenced to two weeks in jail. His triumph, however, didn't deceive the public, among whom the following jest became popular: when Dumas once asked his son, "Have you seen my latest work?" the latter replied, "No, father, have you?"

Estimates of just how much the prolific novelist actually earned at his peak vary from 200,000 to 500,000 francs a year. In order to protect his profits, he joined with Hugo, Balzac, and Frédéric Soulié in 1839 to form the Société des

Gens de Lettres, which was to regulate authors' publishing rights. France at that time was lax in enforcing its copyright laws and had no control over literary works published outside the country. Foreign publications were a problem primarily with the continental countries since English and American publishers generally shunned French novelists as too risqué for their tastes. George Sand in particular raised the Anglo-Saxon eyebrow. "She is a woman of superior talent," the British Colonel Raikes observed. "[She] writes with great ease and elegance... though not much regulated by the principles of morality."[29] The colonel was equally critical of Balzac. "There are few of his works," he claimed, "that can be submitted to the perusal of a well-disposed young woman, [and] many that are too gross for the eyes of any female."[30] In regard to Victor Hugo, Mrs. Trollope found that despite the "meretricious glitter" of his works, they lacked moral virtue.[31] George Sand likewise struck her as morally "stained and bruised."[32] The French themselves had mixed feelings about Mme Sand. Baudelaire, for instance, referred to her as a latrine. On the other hand, Chateaubriand hailed her as the Byron of France, and Hugo considered her works deathless.

For French writers, Belgium proved to be the most flagrant copyright violator. Publishers there continually pirated their neighbors' works, reprinted them and then exported them back to France for sale without royalties. During the early years of the Société des Gens de Lettres, the quixotic Balzac served as its chairman with a questionable degree of effectiveness. From its beginning, the critic Sainte-Beuve compared the society to a trade union and deplored it as one step further in the "industrialization" of literature.

Ironically Sainte-Beuve, as a newspaper critic, contributed to this commercialization of literature, since journalism was the major force transforming literature from a profession into a trade. More and more unskilled writers with no professional training appeared on the scene. "Musicians were presumed to read music and carpenters to handle a plane, but men of letters simply announced themselves."[33] When, for example, George Sand "announced" herself in 1831, an older author bluntly told her that she was better off making babies than novels. At that point she, like many other aspiring writers, turned to journalism. Not only did this give such novices a chance to try out their writing skills, it let them earn a few francs while gaining valuable experience.

During the first years of the July monarchy, journalism was still in its adolescence with few daily publications. Most newspapers contained only four to eight pages and were not sold by the individual copy but through subscriptions that generally cost 80 francs a year, a sum beyond the reach of many people. For those who couldn't afford such prices, there were *cabinets de lecture* (reading rooms) where for a small fee one could come and read an assortment of books and newspapers. So long as the nation's literacy rate remained low, there was limited demand for books and newspapers. Even during the late 1830s an edition of 2,000-3,000 copies of a novel was considered profitable, and best-sellers rarely went beyond 10,000 copies.

By 1840 the commercial aspect of journalism was fast fulfilling Sainte-Beuve's worst fears. As Balzac wrote in his *Lost Illusions,* "Instead of being a priestly function [as many Romantics were prone to regard their art] the newspaper has become... merely a trade.... A journal is no longer concerned to enlighten, but to flatter public opinion."[34] To a great extent this shift was the result of revolutionary changes in the newspaper business introduced by Emile de Girardin's *La Presse,* founded in 1836 (fig. 9.6). Its subscription rate was only 40 francs a year, half that of other daily papers then. This low price attracted even the petite bourgeoisie and caused a tremendous boost in circulation. Within three months *La Presse* had 10,000 subscribers, twice the number of its closest competitors. Two years later that number had risen to 40,000. Before long *Le Siècle, Le Journal des Débats,* and other Paris dailies began to follow Girardin's example. Their success led to a rapid proliferation of journals throughout the city.

Besides Girardin's reforms, technologic advances in printing and paper-making gave further impetus to this journalistic surge. The increasing utilization of lithography (developed earlier in the century) dramatically enhanced the appeal of newspapers, which now carried scattered illustrations, including popular cartoons of political and social interest. All of these factors served to increase the influence of journalism on daily life. "Everybody reads the papers these days," Balzac commented.[35] By 1848 it was estimated that there were six hundred journals in Paris alone, twenty-six of which were dailies. Editorial offices tended to concentrate in the area around the place des Victoires, while most printers and their presses were located farther north, in the vicinity of the porte Saint-Denis.

Prior to the establishment of *La Presse,* journals usually originated to espouse some cause, such as a political party, an artistic movement, or some scientific endeavor. Their editors were more concerned with promoting intellectual goals than with making money. It was the arrival of Girardin and *La Presse* that converted journalism into a capitalistic venture where money was the overriding concern.

Once Girardin had proved that literature in the hands of a skillful manipulator

9.6 Emile de Girardin. The new literary form known as the feuilleton novel was introduced by the Parisian journal *Le Siècle*. Its subsequent success, however, was largely due to the journalistic revolution created by the publisher Emile de Girardin, who founded *La Presse*, the first popular daily newspaper. In order to put out seven issues a week at half the price charged by the current weekly or semi-weekly journals, Girardin sold advertising space in his paper, which yielded profits that more than covered the reduced price of a subscription.

could be a lucrative operation, the temptation to start new journals became so irresistible that a glut of periodicals soon choked the Parisian market. Besides political, scientific, literary, and artistic publications, dozens of small specialty journals appeared. Among the professional ones were *Le Journal des Ponts et Chaussées* for highway engineers, *La Revue Asiatique* for Orientalists, and *Le Commerce* for the bourgeois businessman. Patrons of the city's bathing establishments perused *La Naïade*'s india rubber pages printed with indelible ink that was readable even under water. With so many new journals looking for subscribers, competition among them became intense. To attract new readers some offered free watches, clocks, or books. One paper, *Le Bien-Etre*, promised a retirement pension with a thirty-year subscription along with burial expenses (second class) and a hundred-franc indemnity for the widow and heirs.

This sudden plethora of newspapers and periodicals enticed many advertisers anxious to reach buyers. *La Presse* was able to generate 50,000 francs a month from advertising alone. Although Girardin was among the first to exploit the field of advertising, he certainly didn't invent it. Advertisements could be found in newspapers as early as 1798. Many of these first advertisements, known as *réclames* and "puffs," utilized subtle techniques. *Réclames* appeared to be news items when, in fact, they were paid inserts to publicize some person, product, or event. Today one would hire a public relations agent or firm to accomplish the same end. Often the *réclame* was disguised as an article on some topic like Parisian restaurants, where the remarks on any given establishment were determined by the amount of the client's contribution to the journalist rather than the quality of his cuisine. Others reported various "events of interest" that were actually calculated attempts to promote the client's goals. For example, "Our ravishing prima donna, Mlle Clarisse who exhibited such spirit and sensitivity in her latest role was held up last night as she returned home and robbed of all her jewels."[36] What Mlle Clarisse really wanted from her advertisement was to attract the sympathy of some rich benefactor. Today she would probably have placed a forthright statement in the "Personals" column of some newspaper or magazine. Utilizing a more direct approach, another *réclame* stated: "It has been estimated that Zephyr, M ****'s magnificent horse has earned his owner more than 100,000 francs in his last few races."[37] Although not specifically expressed, Zephyr was up for sale and M. So-and-So would gladly consider suitable offers. Today such a statement would be found among the "For Sale" ads.

"Puffs" were a more indirect means of obtaining publicity without having to pay for it. For example, "feuds" might be purposely staged between rival prima donnas or competing manufacturers for the sake of getting attention in the press. Similarly a doctor might circulate rumors of some fantastic new cure he had discovered in the hope that a journalist might consider it worth mentioning. Others would submit some "invention" to the Academy, knowing that the institution's proceedings were automatically recorded in the newspapers.

Although early *réclames* were usually written by a staff member of the newspaper, it later became common for independent entrepreneurs to rent a certain number of lines or columns from an editor for the same purpose. The journalist Villemessant mentions in his *Mémoires* how he paid Girardin 100 francs a week for space in *La Presse* and reaped a handsome profit from the publicity he gave to jewelers, clothing stores, and so forth. Earlier the same journalist had started his own fashion journal called *La Sylphide*, in which he sold advertising space. For his first issue he sprayed the pages with a Guerlain perfume that he had been paid to promote. Unfortunately a number of subscribers returned their copies, complaining that the odor made them sick. However much Sainte-Beuve might rail against the "industrialization" of literature, it did create two new and lucrative fields for early nineteenth-century writers: advertising and public relations.

A further boon that journalism offered the literary profession was the field of criticism. This proved to be a source of income for many individuals who were not, in fact, professional writers at all. The composer Berlioz, who hated writing, was forced for financial reasons to submit to the "horrible humiliation"[38] of becoming a music critic for the *Journal des Débats*, the *Gazette Musicale*, and *Le Rénovateur* (where he wrote "a delicate and penetrating study of Chopin as pianist and composer").[39] Richard Wagner, on the other hand, felt himself lucky while in Paris to be able to earn a little money writing for the *Gazette Musicale* at a time when he couldn't get any of his operas produced there. Liszt (who was certainly not strapped for money) also wrote for the *Gazette Musicale*, often in an attempt to improve the status of music and musicians—and once to take a stab at his rival, Chopin.[40] Like Berlioz, Liszt had a certain literary flair that made his writing "good copy."

As a lot, critics often drew more criticism than they dispensed. Even those who were intelligent and well educated often knew little about the fields they attempted to appraise. This was especially true in the realm of art criticism, where poets and novelists like Baudelaire, Heine, and Stendhal or politicians like Thiers and Guizot had, at most, an amateur's familiarity with their subject.

There were, of course, full-time professional critics like Charles-Augustin Sainte-Beuve, Jules Janin, and George Sand's confidante, Gustave Planche. Both Sainte-Beuve and Janin tried their hands at creative writing, without much success. The literal-minded Sainte-Beuve lacked sufficient imagination to stimulate his readers. By contrast, Janin's unbridled fantasies overtaxed the credulity of his public in such florid concoctions as *The End of the World* and *The Dead Ass and the Beheaded Woman*. A similar creative deficiency on the part of most critics led Gautier to remark, "You don't become a critic until it has become abundantly clear to you that you cannot be a poet."[41] The more caustic Mirecourt dismissed critics in general as literary eunuchs. In a similar vein, Lamartine spoke of literary criticism as "the power of the impotent."[42] Poor Sainte-Beuve unfortunately had a eunuchoid anatomy that raised doubts about his masculinity. In one of the more vitriolic passages of their journal, the Goncourt brothers wrote that "all the femininity of his [Sainte-Beuve's] talent" could be explained by his difficulty in performing the gymnastics of love... [because of] the imperfections of his genital organs."[43] Victor Hugo, however, had reason to think otherwise, having once accused Sainte-Beuve of seducing his wife.

Despite these assaults on their persons and their profession, critics were widely feared in the artistic world. Being feared, though, had its advantages as Janin, the self-styled "prince of critics," discovered (fig. 9.7). He and his colleagues, who reviewed such diverse subjects as opera, theater, and literature, could extract sizable sums of money from authors, actresses, and singers anxious for a good write-up.

9.7 Jules Janin, the "prince of critics." The transformation of the journalistic critic from an amateur to professional status culminated in France during the second quarter of the nineteenth century. At that time the field was less specialized than today. Although a few critics focused on one particular area (Baudelaire on art, Berlioz on music, and Sainte-Beuve on literature), most, like Janin, covered a wide range of subjects.

Much of the public, however, especially the culture-hungry bourgeoisie, had great respect for critics and relied heavily on their opinion to shape their own untutored tastes. "The crowd which fills the [art] galleries of France rarely judges by itself," Planche observed. "It relies voluntarily on several skillful commentators."[44] Unfortunately not all skilled critics were honest ones. Planche, for instance, had such an intense vendetta with Victor Hugo that he blindly attacked anything Romantic just to spite him. Hugo, in return, denounced literary criticism as the lowest depths to which an author could sink.

Balzac further disparaged critics—even honest ones—simply because they were the products of journalism, which he considered a slipshod form of writing. "When you decide to write a great and fine work... you can put your ideas and your whole soul into it, stand up for it, defend it; but articles written today and forgotten tomorrow are only, in my view, worth what we get paid for them." In short, "Art is long but articles are fleeting."[45] Nevertheless Balzac himself turned critic on occasion—generally for the sake of writing a glowing review of his latest novel.

As much as he was tempted by the easy money to be made from journalism, Balzac deplored the sleaziness and lack of principle rife among the journalists of his day. His novel, *Lost Illusions,* is an extended exposé of the journalists' world. In it he states, "Journalism is an inferno, a bottomless pit of iniquity, falsehood and treachery."[46] Anyone who enters the "mental brothel" of journalism finds himself forced to "barter away his soul, his intellect and his thought."[47] According to his fictional critic, Lousteau (modeled on Jules Janin), "Every man bribes or is bribed."[48] To buy a good review, theater managers and publishers offered Lousteau free tickets and newly published books, which he then resold for his own profit. In addition authors, composers, singers, actors, and other performers regularly supplemented his income with cash, gifts, and lavish hospitality to safeguard their artistic reputations. The high cost of fame in the arts, Balzac estimated, was "twelve thousand francs in reviews and three thousand francs in dinners."[49]

Plagiarism and the use of ghostwriters were two other forms of chicanery commonly practiced in the early days of journalism. The elder Dumas was repeatedly guilty of both in the innumerable novels he serialized for such journals as *La Revue des Deux Mondes, Le Journal des Débats,* and *La Presse.* In a comment from *Lost Illusions,* aimed at Dumas, Balzac states, "The key to success in literature is not to work oneself, but to exploit others' work."[50] In those days the definition of plagiarism was somewhat elastic, and people viewed the matter far more tolerantly than we do today. Although Sainte-Beuve excoriated Dumas's behavior, he was less upset with what he had done than the fact that he did it for money.

Blackmail, libel, and the abuse of power were still other sins that corrupted the infant world of journalism in the 1830s and 1840s. Most often these practices had to do with politics. "The newspaper," Balzac noted, "has become a political party weapon."[51] No other form of communication could rival the press in those days. Its ability to reach an increasingly literate population made it the medium of choice among aspiring politicians like Adolphe Thiers and François Guizot. For both of them journalism had been a stepping stone into the political arena, confirming Balzac's conviction that "political power has been transferred ... from the Tuileries Palace to the newspaper offices.[52]

Although journalism may have had a particular appeal for political and financial opportunists, it attracted serious writers as well. In fact, virtually all French writers by the 1840s had dabbled in journalism at one point or another in their careers. For some like George Sand, Henri Murger, and many a struggling Bohemian, journalism provided an entree into more serious literary careers. Not all writers, though, were as fortunate. Théophile Gautier, for example, longed to devote his life to writing poetry, but was forced to remain a newspaper critic for most of his sixty-one years. Perhaps this was just as well in light of de Vigny's claim that no one "ever lived absolutely on poetry save those who died of it."[53]

Novels, on the other hand, as Baudelaire noted, were readily marketed. Their popularity—and profitability—received a sudden boost in August 1836 when *Le Siècle* first serialized *Lazarile de Torme,* based on a mid-sixteenth-century Spanish romance. Girardin's *La Presse* immediately countered with Balzac's *La Vieille Fille* in October 1836. This innovation was an instant success and brought such an increase in the number of subscribers to these papers that other journals like *Le Journal des Débats, Le Corsaire,* and *Le Constitutionnel* quickly adopted the practice. The boon to author and publisher alike was immense. The popularity of these serialized novels, or *romans-feuilletons,* was so great that crowds lined up at every public reading room in Paris and the provinces to enjoy the latest installments. Many boulevard cafés and working-class estaminets took out subscriptions to attract customers. Even the illiterate found someone to read the episodes to them. The ready availability of these *romans-feuilletons* at much less than the cost of a printed book was an important factor in their widespread popularity.

Among the most successful feuilleton novelists were Eugène Sue and Alexandre Dumas *père*. Both received up to 100,000 francs per novel and wrote with a flair that mesmerized their public. Sue's *Mysteries of Paris* was begun by its dandified author as a lark to shock Parisians with the wretched poverty and rampant crime in the city's slums (fig. 9.8). Its publication in *Le Journal des Débats* from 1842 to 1843 created such a sensation that people waited three to four hours in a lending library for the latest chapter. According to Théophile Gautier, the sick and dying struggled to stay alive until the last episode appeared. Marshal Soult, then prime minister of France, even had Sue released from prison (for evading his National Guard duty) to prevent any interruption of the installments. In the deluge of mail received by the author, many individuals recounted their own personal misfortunes, hoping they would appear in future chapters. Working-class readers praised Sue's sympathy for the underprivileged and offered him endless advice on improving the lot of the poor. Often he took their suggestions and incorporated them into the novel, which gradually changed from a racy thriller meant solely as entertainment to a sobering social protest.

At this stage of the book, Sue decided to see how the people he had described from his imagination really lived. Disguising himself as a worker, he wandered through the impoverished quarters of Paris, observing the misery, vice, and degradation to be found there. His subsequent account of the squalid conditions and shocking depravity he encountered became a scorching indictment of French society. The Catholic Church accused him of preaching communism and—as a matter of fact—his work did attract the attention of Karl Marx, who

9.8 Eugène Sue was another writer who, like Dumas, made immense profits from the feuilleton novel. He is shown here surrounded by many of the characters from his works. A doctor-turned-dandy, Sue evolved into a socialist while researching his novel, *The Mysteries of Paris,* which dealt with the plight of the poor.

was living in Paris then. Together with Friedrich Engels, Marx analyzed Sue's novel in a work called *Die Heilige Familie,* published in 1845. Although the two were impressed with Sue's observations, they disagreed with his view that the socioeconomic ills of the times could be solved by class cooperation rather than class conflict. Other readers of Sue's work responded with a surge of charitable actions. Some wrote asking for addresses of people needing financial aid or the names of orphans to adopt. Sue himself took to giving a portion of his earnings each month to the poor. Of all the tributes garnered by the author for his work, the most bizarre was undoubtedly that of a poor soul who sneaked into his apartment and hanged himself, inspired by the thought of dying in the home of someone who loved and defended the poor.

Overnight Sue became lionized. Fellow authors like Sand, Hugo, Sainte-Beuve, Balzac, and Lamartine put aside their professional rivalries to praise him. At the Porte Saint-Martin theater, a play based on his novel starred one of the era's most popular matinee idols, Frederick Lemaître, and ran for seven hours every evening. Years later Hugo was to pay the author that highest of all compliments, imitation, when he wrote *Les Misérables,* his own paean to the People.

From outside the literary world came other accolades. A *grand morceau de piano* by a M. Latour bore the name of the novel, and the son of the flamboyant dance conductor, Musard, composed a new galop entitled "Les Petits Mystères de Paris." At the Jardin des Plantes, several new species of roses were named for characters in Sue's book.

Envious of the profits reaped by the *Journal des Débats,* Dr. Véron at *Le Constitutionnel* sought to lure the popular author to his own paper. In many respects Véron and Sue were kindred spirits. Both had been practicing doctors who eventually abandoned their medical pursuits for more lucrative careers in literature. Both were consummate hedonists, addicted to lavish spending and amorous adventures. The success of Véron's negotiations with Sue was to yield the author 100,000 francs for the serialization of his later novel, *The Wandering Jew,* while the wily publisher emerged with an even greater profit of 500,000 francs for himself. The tremendous appeal of the book led to nearly a sixfold increase in the number of subscribers to *Le Constitutionnel.* As the novel neared its last installment, Véron was so reluctant to see his good fortune end that he induced Sue to extend the narrative even though the plot had already reached its denouement. Artistically this proved to be a mistake, but financially it was a *succès fou.*

Sue's close rival in the production of feuilleton novels was Alexandre Dumas *père,* whose *Count of Monte Cristo* in the *Journal des Débats* and *The Three Musketeers* in *Le Siècle* brought him comparable revenues. George Sand didn't begin serializing her novels until 1844 (with *Jeanne* in *Le Constitutionnel*). Despite her late start, she had considerable success as a feuilleton novelist, although she never commanded the high fees of Sue or Dumas.[54] Even more of a socialist than Sue, she preached her doctrines with the didactic authority of a school marm, which alienated many publishers. When, for example, she offered *Le Constitutionnel* her *Meunier d'Angibault* (a work described as packed with "social dynamite"), Véron turned it down. Eventually she sold it to the more radical *La Réforme.*[55]

Strangely enough, one of the era's greatest and most prolific novelists, Honoré Balzac, had difficulty adapting to the newspaper novel. Part of the problem was that his works often contained long psychological analyses of characters and minutely detailed descriptions of their environment, which interfered with the movement of the plot. This didn't sit well with the expanded readership of the new dailies, which preferred action and suspense to literary merit in their serialized novels. Sue and Dumas understood this and catered to the public's tastes, while Balzac refused to alter his style. As prolific as he was, Balzac remained a slow, meticulous writer who couldn't adapt to the fast-paced schedule of professional journalists always racing from deadline to deadline. According to Gautier,

Balzac "didn't believe that a work done quickly could be good."[56] In a business that paid by the line, this attitude put the author at a disadvantage. In the long run, though, the tortoise-like Balzac ultimately overtook the journalistic hares. When he died at age fifty, he left one of the world's most valuable (and voluminous) literary legacies. Once when asked what Balzac died of, his colleague Léon Gozlan replied, "of forty volumes."[57]

Besides the ability to write speedily, successful authors of *romans-feuilletons* depended on many other "tricks of the trade," enough, we are told, "to make even an American stare."[58] A favorite ploy of journalists who were paid by the line was to reduce each line to one or two words. No one became more adept at this literary padding than the elder Dumas. A contemporary of his has left us the following parody of his sparse, staccato dialogue:

> "Have you seen him?"
> "Whom?"
> "Him."
> "Whom?"
> "Dumas."
> "Father?"
> "Yes."
> "What a man!"
> "To be sure!"
> "I agree."
> "And how prolific!"
> "Yes, indeed!"[59]

The use of sensationalism, whether in news bulletins, editorials, or fiction, was as common to journalists then as now. Balzac once wrote, "Every suicide is a poem sublime in its melancholy. Where will you find...a book that can vie in genius with a news-item such as: 'Yesterday, at four o'clock a woman threw herself into the Seine from the Pont des Arts.'"[60] The shocking revelations of Sue's *Mysteries of Paris,* the spine-tingling thrill of the supernatural in Soulié's *Mémoires of the Devil,* and the hair-raising escapades of Dumas's *Three Musketeers* all tantalized the reading public. Even Lamartine's *History of the Girondins* had enough blood and guts to captivate the readers of *La Presse* and earn him 250,000 francs. Such an achievement, Dumas exclaimed, raised history to the level of the novel.

One of the most popular devices of feuilleton writers was the cliff-hanging chapter ending that held readers in suspense until the next installment. An early example of this technique appears in George Sand's 1834 novella, *Leone Leoni*, which she serialized in Buloz's *Revue des Deux Mondes*. There a typical chapter ends with the frazzled heroine describing her turbulent emotional state: "Surprise, dismay and fear had frozen my blood. I thought that I was going mad; I put my handkerchief in my mouth to stifle my shrieks, and then, succumbing to fatigue, fell back upon the bed in a stupor of utter prostration."[61] What next? Ever resilient, the heroine revives in the following chapter only to collapse again on its last page. "I thought that he was going to kill me; I threw myself out of bed, crying: 'Mercy! mercy! I won't tell!' and I fainted just as he seized me."[62] Only after days of nail biting did the public learn that their heroine had not been murdered. Indeed, by the last installment, the long-suffering maiden had eloped once more with the very man who caused all her suffering, forcing the reader to conclude that she was either hopelessly obtuse or incurably masochistic. With such dramatic maneuvers, Sand could have prolonged her saga of feminine perils ad infinitum. Apparently, though, she felt that her publisher had received as much as he paid for and spared her heroine any further tribulations.

Later Eugène Sue, in his *Mysteries of Paris*, was to carry Sand's technique even further, with added touches of the macabre. At the end of one chapter, Sue writes: "Pursued by the avenging punishment of his vice, chance had carried him [Jacques Ferrand] to the grave of his child.... Having exhausted his savage energy, he was seized with a weakness and sudden alarm. His face was covered with an icy sweat, his trembling knees shook under him, and he fell senseless across the open tomb."[63] Merely senseless or dead? The reader was left to wonder. In a later chapter, the same villain, still very much alive, "fell backward, stiff and inanimate; horrible convulsions stamped his features with unearthly contortions like those forced from dead bodies by a galvanic battery...'my flesh smokes—spectre—bloody—no, no, Cecily!' Such were the last words of Jacques Ferrand."[64] But with more installments to follow, was the evil that Ferrand committed to live after him, and how?

The authors of feuilleton novels were not alone in using suspense to gain the reader's attention; their publishers were also adept at the game. From time to time, they would suspend a novel at a critical juncture of the plot without explanation. The speculation this aroused among readers brought the paper welcome attention and often increased its circulation once the serialization was resumed.

Occasionally, of course, the interruption of a novel was not a publicity stunt but the result of circumstances beyond the publisher's control. Balzac, for instance, had the exasperating habit of submitting the chapters of his novels in a random fashion. The first two or three were usually on schedule, but after he had received his initial advance, he often went on a spending spree and forgot about subsequent chapters. When and if he resumed the installments of his book, he was apt to turn in the ending without ever having supplied the middle.

More than once a novel was interrupted because its author had been imprisoned for some violation of the censorship code. Theoretically censorship had been abolished after the July revolution. Fieschi's attempted assassination of Louis-Philippe in 1835, however, led to renewed policing of the press. Fines and prison terms now became routine for anyone who insulted the royal family or encouraged revolution. Far from being an onus, these penalties were often a welcome step toward fame and fortune for the ambitious journalist. Early in her career as a writer at *Le Figaro,* for example, George Sand was elated over the prospect of being arrested. "If particular articles are incriminated, mine will *certainly* be included," she wrote a friend. "I shall declare myself its author and shall get myself jailed. Great Heaven! What a scandal.... But my reputation will also be made and I shall find a publisher to buy my platitudes and fools to read them."[65]

Despite legal attempts to curb the press, journalism continued to flourish throughout the July monarchy and was experiencing an unprecedented boom when revolution broke out in 1848. Unfortunately this convulsive "year of the people" left the masses little time for reading fiction and heralded the end of the *roman-feuilleton.* By 1850 the genre had all but disappeared. In its day it had served as a great political organ, disseminating liberal ideas throughout the lower-middle and working classes who weren't "highbrow" enough to read books but enjoyed their daily newspaper. Although Louis-Philippe had been slow to recognize the threat of such novels to his authority, Louis-Napoléon sensed it quickly and placed a tax on all journals publishing *romans-feuilletons.* In 1850 the prince-president's government officially outlawed the serialization of novels because of the "subtle poison" they exerted on the public. Even though most authors of the genre (including Mme Sand) survived the edict, it spelled financial ruin and artistic extinction for the last purveyors of Romanticism's swashbuckling action and vapid sentimentality.

CHAPTER 10

Stage by Stage

The Evolution of Theatrical Taste
from the Battle of "Hernani" to the Reign of Rachel

"*T*HIS EVENING INSTEAD OF GETTING ALL DRESSED UP and going to the faubourg Saint-Germain," Chopin wrote his family in the spring of 1847, "I went with Alkan to the Vaudeville [theater] to see [Etienne] Arnal in a new comedy by M. Duvert: *What a Woman Wants.*[1] Arnal, as usual, is very funny. In it he tells the audience how he was desperate to pee-pee on a train but couldn't get to a toilet until they stopped at Orléans. There wasn't a single vulgar word in what he said but everyone understood and split their sides laughing."[2]

Next to opera and the concert hall, the theater was probably Chopin's favorite artistic haunt in Paris. His expatriate friend, Heinrich Heine, was also an enthusiastic theatergoer who felt that France was the true home of the dramatic muse. "French players," he asserted, "surpass their colleagues in all other countries for the very natural reason that all Frenchmen are born actors."[3] Certainly, Orleanist Paris in the 1830s and 1840s was a thespian's paradise. There, two dozen or more government-licensed theaters vied daily to cater to—and sometimes cultivate—public taste. Such competition naturally kept the dramatic arts in a continuous state of flux. If there was one constant on the Parisian stage throughout this bourgeois-dominated era it was the simplistic, earthy vaudeville, which attracted both the lower and middle classes of the city along with a mix of aristocratic society and such fastidious artists as Chopin and Alkan.

At that time Hugo and Dumas *père* were pelting the Goliath of French Classical tragedy with the slingshots of Romantic drama, determined to inflict a mortal blow on him. Eventually a series of triumphs on the boulevards convinced the disciples of Romantic drama that they had finally delivered the coup de grâce to the hateful ogre. In the midst of victory, however, they found their turf invaded by the Vaudeville theater, which had moved from the northern suburbs of Paris to more accessible quarters in a department store on the boulevards. Shortly afterward it would settle into the place de la Bourse, the very nerve center of middle-class avarice so despised by the Romantics.

Far more distressing to the Romantics, though, was the unexpected rejuvenation of their old enemy, French Classical tragedy. To their chagrin, this hoary survivor from the courts of Louis XIII and Louis XIV, baptized by Cardinal Richelieu and catechized by his successor, Cardinal Mazarin, had refused to die. Instead, nursed by a scruffy child of the streets named Rachel, he revived and infused new life into the sanctuary of his ancestors, the hallowed Théâtre-Français. Soon after his resuscitation, Romantic drama met an inglorious demise. Its brief lifespan can be measured roughly from the 1829 debut of Dumas's *Henri III et sa Cour* to the disastrous appearance of Hugo's *Les Burgraves* in 1843. The miraculous renaissance of French Classical tragedy was also short-lived, beginning with Rachel's debut in Corneille's *Horace* in 1838 and ending with her death in 1858.

Throughout the course of these events, no other theatrical genre could equal the popularity of vaudeville, which Gérard de Nerval called "the bastard comedy of bourgeois society."[4] It had little in common with later stage reviews popular in the music halls of England and America during the late nineteenth and early twentieth centuries. What the French called vaudeville was a completely different genre that originated around the fifteenth century on the fairgrounds of Normandy in the region of the river Vire. At first they were spontaneous affairs, relying heavily on improvisation like the sixteenth-century *commedia dell'arte*. By the early nineteenth century, though, vaudevilles were composed of written dialogue, interspersed with a few vocal selections. They differed from *opéras-comiques* in their brevity, the preponderance of spoken to sung lines, and their reliance on popular street tunes or current operatic melodies (rather than original compositions) as a source of music for their vocal numbers.

The most popular vaudevilles of the Louis-Philippe era were undoubtedly those written by Eugène Scribe (fig. 10.1). Like all vaudevilles, they revolved around a farcical situation. Their humor relied on the clever manipulation of a plot into which wooden characters were introduced like puppets programmed to perform the author's will. The orderliness of these scenarios and the inevitable happy ending appealed to the middle class, who felt reassured by the portrayal of a world as regimented and morally correct as their own. Because the artless bourgeoisie could assimilate the serious aspects of life only when diluted by the palliative syrup of humor, tragedy was generally an unwelcome guest on the boards of a vaudeville theater. Although Charles Merruau of the *Revue et Gazette Musicale* praised

10.1 Eugène Scribe became famous among his contemporaries as a playwright and librettist. Outside of France, today he is probably best remembered for his operatic libretti. Although some of his plays still crop up in the repertoire of the French theater, the vaudevilles that were the mainstay of his popularity in Chopin's day seem naive and outdated now.

Scribe's vaudevilles as the finest of the day, others considered their emotional blandness and their concentration on social trivialities a sign of intellectual vacuity. To the vast majority of the public who adored him, though, it didn't matter what the critics said. They weren't interested in being preached to; they simply wanted to be entertained. And as the late-nineteenth-century critic Brander Matthews pointed out, Scribe "could talk on stage better than anyone else." Unfortunately, "he had absolutely nothing to say."[5] For Théophile Gautier, however, it was precisely this charming banality that was the secret of Scribe's success. Only a mediocre author, he added, could appeal to the audiences of the time, made up as they were of "women and social types with no interest in art or literature."[6]

Gautier seems to have been right. For decades the Parisians' loyalty to Scribe remained unshakable. Not only in Paris but throughout France, "everywhere and always, it was M. Scribe."[7] In fact, Gautier feared that the whole world was on the verge of succumbing to Scribemania. "You can be sure," he wrote, "that right now in Timbuctu [*sic*] there are some actors in the process of learning a vaudeville by M. Scribe.... Even the Chinese in their bamboo theaters... translate and perform M. Scribe's vaudevilles which sinologists then translate back into French and pass off as works from the Hong [*sic*] or Hing [*sic*] dynasties."[8]

For today's theatergoers, it is hard to understand the Orleanist public's craze for vaudevilles; most, when read now, seem uninspired and often naive. When seen on stage, though, their effect may have been very different. Certainly the costumes, scenery, and music would have enhanced these simple dramas, but it was probably the performers of the time who did the most to bring them to life. Even those actors and actresses who considered vaudeville a superficial genre recognized it as a valuable way station on their ascent to that pinnacle of French theatrical success, the Comédie Française. Some, like the Comédie's tragedian, Samson, and its perennial ingenue, Mlle Mars, continued to perform in vaude-villes even at the peak of their careers. Both, for example, appeared in vaudeville roles at an 1833 benefit for the actress Harriet Smithson, arranged by her lover, Hector Berlioz. As it happened, Chopin played a piano duo with Liszt at the same benefit and may well have watched from the wings as Samson took part in a one-act vaudeville, *Rabelais,* while Mlle Mars and other members of the Comédie Française performed Mazères's *Chacun de son Côté.*

In general, audiences at most of the city's vaudeville theaters weren't treated to artists of this caliber. In fact, it wasn't even necessary to be an actor to get on the stage, as long as you had sufficient notoriety to attract a crowd. Such was the case with the midget Tom Thumb (Charles Sherwood Stratton), who appeared at the Vaudeville theater in 1845 as the star of a production entitled *Le Petit Poucet* (fig. 10.2). In this rather whimsical production, the diminutive actor played the part of commander-in-chief of a fictional army.

Compared to Samson and Mlle Mars, most professional vaudevillians of the era were lesser talents, seldom remembered in this century—at least not for their acting. Among these was the ebullient Virginie Déjazet, whose notoriety often had more to do with her actions off stage than on (fig. 10.3). In the theater she was best known for her transvestite roles, where she impersonated such men as Napoléon and Voltaire. In the words of Victor Hugo's brother-in-law, Paul Foucher, she was the theater's "last gentleman"[9] because she knew how to "raise the coarse joke to the level of art."[10] Despite her penchant for male roles, there was nothing masculine about Mme Déjazet. On the contrary (to quote Foucher again), she was "champagne in skirts."[11] Many an admirer, however, preferred her without the skirts. According to a contemporary bon vivant, Arsène Hous-saye, she was once served up at a midnight supper dressed only in a little thyme and parsley. Not the least bit inhibited, she readily admitted to being free with her favors. "Love," she insisted, "is like [a lady's] personal linen. . . . You have to keep changing it if you want it to last."[12]

As for the host of other vaudeville actors who fell into oblivion, Louis Huart, in his *Galerie de la Presse,* has a ready explanation: most, he claims, were frus-trated doctors or lawyers who took to acting as a second career after having failed

10.2 In 1845, P. T. Barnum brought the seven-year-old "General Tom Thumb" to Paris, where he performed in a vaudeville production and was presented to the king. In May of that year the midget came to visit George Sand in the square d'Orléans. She invited Delacroix over to see him, and it is very likely that Chopin walked across the square to join them.

10.3 Virginie Déjazet was a popular vaudeville actress in Chopin's time, especially known for the transvestite roles she played from early youth to old age. Offstage she was a wily femme fatale whom few men could resist.

in their chosen calling.[13] Perhaps these would-be doctors and lawyers might have fared better had they opted for the melodrama stage, which was littered nightly with victims of violence in dire need of both medical and legal aid. So excessive were the villainous deeds and shocking horrors that took place behind the foot-lights of these performances that the boulevard du Temple where most took place was dubbed the "boulevard du Crime." During a single season at the height of melodrama's popularity, a contemporary journal estimated that in two of the boulevard theaters alone there were "195 assassinations, 300 poisonings... 400 arson attempts, 780 robberies—150 of them armed, 200 by ladder and 300 with skeleton keys."[14] All this may have been thrilling to the audiences, but for the actors and actresses it was a highly stressful business. Over a twenty-year period one actor named Tautin got stabbed 16,302 times, another named Morty succumbed to poison 11,000 times, while a poor creature named Fresnay met his death (by a variety of means) 27,000 times. Women were equally victimized; the long-suffering Adèle Dupuis, for example, was "seduced, abducted or drowned" 75,000 times in her career.[15]

In 1836 the boulevard du Temple had six theaters. Scattered between them and across the street were a number of restaurants and cafés, some of which provided entertainment as well as food and drink. Actually the entire boulevard was an amusement district that catered to the petite bourgeoisie and the working classes. Here was the capital of melodrama, although its domain extended to outposts on the Left Bank and the *banlieue,* or suburban, theaters around the city's fringes. Besides melodrama, the boulevard du Temple was home to an assortment of miscellaneous diversions, both inside and outside the theaters. Amid its carnival-like atmosphere, one could find jugglers and trained fleas, dwarfs and giants, fat ladies and living skeletons, acrobats hanging from chandeliers, daredevils walking on burning coals, children who drank boiling oil, men who swallowed snakes, and dogs who could count.

At the southernmost end of the boulevard was the tiny Lazzari, "the most vulgar of all the boulevard theaters," an oppressive smoke-filled den that reeked of sweat.[16] Bordering it on the north was Mme Saqui's theater, which according to Heine featured wretched dramas and miserable music hall pieces. The owner was a celebrated tight-rope walker who called herself the foremost acrobat in France. At age seventy-five she crossed the Paris Hippodrome on a tight rope forty feet above the ground, a rouged-up, scrawny-legged, toothless creature in a loose-fitting leotard, whom Paul Foucher described as the epitome of "tinselled senility."[17]

Beyond Mme Saqui's was the unpretentious but popular Funambules theater, which the government allowed to produce vaudevilles, dramas, pantomime, and acrobatic performances. Despite this variety, the Funambules didn't enjoy much popularity until an incredibly expressive actor named Debureau appeared on stage as Pierrot, the white-faced mute of the ancient *commedia dell'arte*. By Gautier's account, he was "a creature pale as the moon, mysterious as silence [and] supple...as a serpent."[18] His appeal was instantaneous and drew the best of the beau monde away from the boulevard des Italiens to the oppressive confines of the fetid little Funambules. Here the famous mime "reigned in silence" until the fateful day when he struck and accidentally killed an overzealous fan who had harassed him on a Sunday stroll.[19] Although he was never convicted, the public

10.4 Franconi's Cirque Olympique presented dramas and tableaux with a combined cast of horses and humans. There Chopin witnessed an 1831 production purporting to depict "the last decades of Polish history." It had so many blatant inaccuracies that the young musician was "amazed the French could be so stupid!" (Chopin, *Correspondance,* 2:60).

deserted him, and an unrelenting sense of guilt eventually destroyed both his career and his life.

Proceeding up the boulevard from the Funambules were the Gaîté and the Folies Dramatiques theaters, two of the grandes dames of Parisian melodrama. Beyond them, the enormous Cirque Olympique with its moorish-styled interior boasted a seating capacity of six thousand, which made it the largest theater in Paris (fig. 10.4).

In 1823 one of the most memorable of Parisian melodramas premiered in the Ambigu theater, which at that time still stood on the boulevard du Temple. The work, entitled *L'Auberge des Adrets,* was a mélange written by three authors who incorporated "every cliché known to melodrama."[20] It starred a young actor named Frédérick Lemaître in the role of the irrepressible Robert Macaire, a brash and blustery con artist. The intention of the play's authors was to produce a stock-in-trade tearjerker where the weak and innocent are victimized by the unscrupulous Macaire and his toadying companion, the slow-witted Bertrand.

Lemaître, however, perceived the play as a social satire, and through his comic ad libs he subtly revised the play each night until he had transformed the sticky little melodrama into a sparkling burlesque of bourgeois greed and opportunism.

Today such a theatrical success would inevitably entail a long run, possibly of several years. In the small world of early-nineteenth-century Paris, however, not even the wildest success could hope to sustain itself for more than a few months. Revivals, though, were common, and in 1832 *L'Auberge des Adrets* reopened to even greater crowds in the larger porte Saint-Martin theater. By then the artist Honoré Daumier had begun using the figure of Robert Macaire in his satirical cartoons as a symbol of the Orleanist regime trying to conceal its corrupt and deceitful conduct beneath a facade of pompous piety. Through both the newspapers and the stage, astute Parisians now came to recognize in the wily Macaire and his bumbling sidekick, Bertrand, a stinging indictment of the nation's government and society.

The great popularity of Macaire in his second incarnation prompted Lemaître to revive him once more in a theatrical sequel entitled *Robert Macaire*. Although audiences found it hilarious, the government considered it far from a laughing matter and banned the play after a short run.

Robert Macaire, although it had its origins in the melodrama *L'Auberge des Adrets*, reached a level of sophistication rarely found in that genre. The first melodramas appeared in the last years of the eighteenth century and owed much to English literary and theatrical influences. Shakespeare, for example, was the inspiration for J. B. A. Hapde's *Les Visions de Macbeth* and Cuvelier's *Le More de Venise*, which exploited themes of the supernatural and exhibitions of violent passions. Plots were also borrowed freely from such Walter Scott novels as *Kenilworth*, *The Bride of Lammermoor*, and *Woodstock*. These English sources provided sensational, horror-filled plots, sufficient to hold an audience that had little interest in character development, emotional subtlety, or the exploration of arcane philosophical questions. The message of melodrama, which appealed primarily to the petite bourgeoisie and lower classes, was a straightforward visual one, meant purely to excite the emotions without straining the intellect. As Pixerécourt, the most popular and prolific of French melodramatists, once said, "I write for people who can't read."[21] To enhance the play's visual effect, music was added—the word "melodrama" itself being derived from the Greek "melos" and Latin "drama," that is, a "song-drama." In contrast to vaudeville, however, there was seldom any singing in melodrama. Instead, instrumental music was used as a background to enhance the dramatic effect of the action, comparable to the use of florid piano or organ accompaniments in early silent films.

Because French melodrama became such a popular form of theater in the early nineteenth century, it attracted many writers eager for the money it could bring. Foremost among these was the undisputed king of the genre, René-Charles Guilbert de Pixerécourt. Not only did he create a successful formula for fast-paced, action-packed entertainment, he also contributed to a significant reenergizing of the French stage of his time. For roughly two hundred years, the nation's theatrical life had suffered from a terminal geriatric condition known as the French Classical Drama Syndrome. Strangely enough it was Pixerécourt and the lowly melodrama (often said to thrive on everything but art) that began the healing process and restored French theater to its former vitality. Long before de Vigny, Hugo, and Dumas *père* started verbalizing their objections to the archaic regulations of the past, Pixerécourt and his colleagues set out to achieve similar ends through actions rather than words. With a casual disregard for past conventions, they proceeded to allow actors and actresses to shout, scream, slug, stab, and even kill each other on stage. Such gross displays of uncivilized behavior before an audience had been banned for centuries by the Academy, which decreed that any unpleasantness requiring a violent resolution had to be conducted offstage. This mandate, of course, severely narrowed the dramatic scope of the playwright and deprived him of those two perennial crowd pleasers: violence and sensationalism.

In two other aspects melodrama also proved itself an artistic pioneer. First, it ignored the Academy's unities of time, place, and action. Second, it abandoned the austere scenic decor prescribed by tradition. Instead it cluttered up the stage with eye-catching sets, colorful costumes, and an assortment of mechanical devices that created startling effects. Strangely enough, hardly anyone took notice of these deviations from the path of dramatic propriety. Melodrama, after all, was too menial an art to merit serious attention. Only later, when proponents of Romantic drama like Hugo and Dumas *père* incorporated these innovations into their plays, did they acquire the halo of sanctity.

If there seemed to be a touch of the preposterous in both melodrama and Romantic drama, the explanation was simple enough, according to Thackeray: all French drama was absurd. Oddly enough, he felt that melodrama redeemed itself in part by having some sense of morality. Its happy endings proved, at least, that its authors were "good and right-hearted," while he considered "Victor

Hugo, Dumas and the enlightened classes...profoundly immoral and absurd."[22] Not everyone agreed. Both then and now, most critics regarded melodrama's facile morality as one of its greatest weaknesses. First of all the audience's foreknowledge that the play would always have a virtuous ending impaired any suspense the author may have hoped to create. Furthermore, it saddled him with the virtually impossible task of weaving all the dark threads of villainy into a shining cloak of virtue by the end of the last act. To accomplish this feat, he was forced to utilize such trite stage conventions as the improbable "coincidence," the loud stage whisper (audible to all but those whom it concerned), and the last-minute revelation about someone's past. In brief, the demand for a happy ending placed the melodramatist in the awkward position of having to create a logical resolution of his plot through illogical means.

Although melodrama appealed mainly to the simpler, less educated classes of society, it also attracted such budding geniuses as the adolescent Victor Hugo and Alexandre Dumas *père*. With maturity, their tastes became more sophisticated, but the melodramas of their youth were to exert a significant influence over the type of theater they created as adults. It is almost exclusively to those two men (with some assistance from Alfred de Vigny and Casimir Delavigne) that we owe the development of so-called Romantic drama, which first emerged at the end of the Restoration and flourished throughout much of the Orleanist era. Romantic drama was a new but not entirely original genre. Hugo, as its chief theorist, felt the need to revitalize the French stage, which had become either entrenched in traditional forms (playing to an empty house at the Théâtre-Français) or trivialized by the boulevard theaters, which offered frivolous fare to a shallow-minded audience. His goal was to create a new type of drama, one more elevated than the existing boulevard fare yet less constrained than the classical dramas of the seventeenth and eighteenth centuries. "For a new people, a new art," he proclaimed.[23] As Hugo searched for a recipe that would appeal to this new audience, he helped himself freely to the ingredients that had sustained melodrama's popularity for so many years. To these he added a pinch of poetry, a dash of exoticism, and a sprinkle of realism. All this he then subjected to a period of intellectual incubation at highly emotional temperatures—and voilà!—a raw dish of melodrama became a culinary pièce de résistance called "Romantic drama."

Like the melodramatists, Hugo had also been influenced by English literary and theatrical sources. In 1826 he used Shakespeare as a model for a play of unwieldy length entitled *Cromwell*. With no prospect of getting his leviathan-like drama produced, he sat down and wrote a lengthy preface explaining the artistic concepts embodied in it. All this proved was that Hugo could preach the gospel of Romanticism better than he could practice it. Clearly *Cromwell* had bombed, and no amount of words could alter the fact. As the elder Dumas once put it, "Prefaces are for failures."[24]

Paradoxically, failure often serves as the fertilizer that enriches the soil of creativity. Out of the debris of *Cromwell* sprang the rich flowering of Romantic drama. Among the genre's salient features was a "harmony of contraries," by which Hugo meant a juxtaposing of comedy with tragedy as in Shakespeare's plays. Furthermore, Hugo insisted that the action of a drama be portrayed and not merely narrated on stage. In ancient Greece, the heavy masks and buskins worn by actors had impaired their mobility and prevented them from performing any rapid or violent movements. It was for this practical reason rather than any artistic consideration that action had been driven offstage. By the nineteenth century this outdated convention, largely discarded in the boulevard theaters, was still being observed in French Classical drama for the sake of maintaining the actors' "dignity." "Instead of scenes we have narrative," Hugo complained, "instead of tableaux, descriptions. Solemn-faced characters...tell us what is going on in the temple, in the palace, on the public square, until we are tempted many a time to call out to them: 'Indeed! then take us there! It must be very entertaining!'"[25]

In his tirade against the artistic tyranny of the past, Hugo went on to attack the unities of time and place. To limit all plays to twenty-four hours and to one geographic location seemed to him as impractical as a cobbler who tried to fit every foot to the same shoe. On the other hand, he had no objection to the unity of action (which kept an author from introducing ancillary characters, subplots, and other dramatic diversions). The truth was, by the 1820s adherence to the unities was seldom being observed except at the state-run theaters—that is, the Théâtre Français and the intermittently operated Odéon, where traditions were so entrenched that "originality was regarded as a mark of bad taste and insufficient culture."[26] By Hugo's time the aim of playwrights who wrote for the Comédie was to copy Voltaire, who copied Racine, who copied Corneille, who copied the Greeks.

Actually *Cromwell* didn't depart as radically from classical models as one might expect from Hugo's inflamed rhetoric. If it didn't adhere entirely to the unities, it approximated them. Furthermore it was written in poetry, a feature of classical drama for which its author readily admitted great admiration. Poetry, he claimed, kept a play above the level of the "insignificant and trivial."[27] Hugo did lash out, however, at the restricted vocabulary allowed on the classical stage. There only certain words were considered "elevated" enough for its flowery declamations, which routinely clothed the simplest idea in yards of ornamental verbiage. Hugo's goal was to incorporate modern words of everyday usage into the theater so that its actors and actresses could speak in a direct, "natural" manner, devoid of pomposity and artificiality. "The French tongue is not *fixed* and never will be," he wrote. "Languages and the sun do not stand still."[28] The fact that this "innovation" (like his rejection of the classical unities) was already an accepted practice in most boulevard theaters doesn't lessen the impact of his idea on the insulated sphere of "official" French drama.

Shakespeare, whom Hugo often extolled in his youth, was little known then in France except through some late-eighteenth-century verse adaptations of his plays by Jean-François Ducis. In 1827, after the failure of earlier English actors to popularize Shakespeare's plays in Paris, a troupe of Shakespeareans (including Charles Kemble, Edmund Kean, and Harriet Smithson) received a warm welcome. Encouraged by their reception, Alfred de Vigny—no doubt with the help of his English wife—made a French adaptation of Shakespeare's *Othello*, which was a great success at the Comédie Française in 1829.

The acclaim given to de Vigny disgruntled Hugo, who was even more upset by the fact that the first great triumph of Romantic drama on the Paris stage, *Henri III et sa Cour* at the Théâtre-Français, was written by a relatively unknown clerk to the duc d'Orléans named Alexandre Dumas. For the tradition-bound Comédie-Française to gamble on a Romantic drama—especially one by a novice—indicated that the state-sponsored theater was not as reactionary an institution as Hugo had portrayed it. On the contrary, the actors and actresses who governed it were a surprisingly egalitarian lot. Most theaters in Paris then were run by a director who hired actors on salary to perform in plays he himself had selected. The Comédie-Française, by contrast, was a share-holding company of actors and actresses, known as *sociétaires*, who selected plays by majority vote and divided the theater's profits among themselves at the end of each year. Like most repertory companies, the Comédie rotated plays each night, except for new productions, which were allowed to run as long as possible.

Even though the Comédie was still generally conservative in its tastes, its directors' willingness to produce de Vigny and Dumas gave Hugo hope, and in 1830 the company accepted his newest play, *Hernani*, which made its raucous debut in the rue Richelieu on February 25 of that year. By confronting the polished formality of Classicism with the florid emotionalism of Romanticism, the play divided *le tout Paris* into opposing camps, pitting young against old, aristocrat against bourgeois, past against future. In preparing for its premiere, Hugo armed himself for an all-out offensive. Fearing the bias of the theater's claque, he assembled his own, composed of young admirers and disciples who clustered around him in his *cénacle* (literary circle) on the Left Bank's rue Notre-Dame des Champs. Among this energetic lot of aspiring poets and playwrights were Théophile Gautier, Gérard de Nerval, and Petrus Borel, who considered themselves part of an artistic avant-garde. To prove it they affected leonine masses of hair, grew voluminous beards, and "dressed in every fashion but the reigning one."[29] Swirling capes, Spanish sombreros, Renaissance doublets, and medieval tunics set them apart from the English fashions of the "philistines" on the boulevards and in the salons. To swell their numbers, Petrus Borel rounded up additional students from the Latin Quarter. The task of coaching this untrained claque took Hugo longer than the three weeks he had spent writing the play.

Rehearsals were conducted on a frigid stage in one of the worst winters Paris had ever known. The Seine remained frozen from December through February. As in Dumas's *Henri III,* Mlle Mars departed from her saucy ingenue roles to take the lead in a serious Romantic drama. It was a challenge that strained her talents and Hugo's patience. At one point the playwright threatened to replace her, but backed down when the cast flocked to her defense.

Finally the day of the premiere arrived. Hugo's militant claque (led by Théophile Gautier in green trousers and a bright crimson waistcoat) arrived at one o'clock in the afternoon and was forced to mill about the theater's entrance until two o'clock when the doors opened. Their bizarre appearance soon attracted the attention of hostile crowds, which pelted them with garbage, stones, and whatever else they could find. Only the fear of being arrested and missing the performance kept the claque from retaliating. At two o'clock they finally took shelter inside the darkened theater, where the atmosphere, in Gautier's words, was as shadowy and somber as a Piranesi print. There, until eight o'clock when the curtain went up, they passed the time singing, playing games, imitating barnyard animals, and memorizing the cues for their applause during the performance. They also consumed liberal amounts of wine and garlic-laced sausages, which left the theater smelling like a tavern by the time the well-to-do habitués of the Comédie began to enter their boxes.

The first line of the play immediately elicited cries of indignation that continued throughout the performance. Although the dialogue was in verse, there was an absence of the fanciful circumlocutions that theater audiences had come to expect on the Comédie's stage. This and the use of everyday words that weren't considered "poetic" gave Hugo's verse a pedestrian air. For an audience of 1830, this simply wasn't art. An abstract painting or an atonal symphony would scarcely have shocked them more. As the play progressed, hisses, whistles, and catcalls gave way to scuffles and fistfights. In the midst of it all, the playwright Eugène Scribe, that "antithesis to Romanticism," stood up and laughed loudly throughout the entire spectacle.[30]

Considering the pandemonium of the evening, one wonders how the critics were able to hear enough of the play to review it. With the exception of the reporter for the *Journal des Débats*, most reviewers were hostile. In many cases they directed their attacks more at Hugo's rowdy claque than at his play. But despite the riots and the reviews, *Hernani* survived and was given a total of thirty-six performances (which speaks well for the fortitude of its cast).

Throughout the play's run, most nights were as turbulent as the first. In the boxes the Classicists sat with their backs to the stage. Many came armed with "a formidable artillery of whistles, bird-calling devices [and] pitch pipes" to do battle with Hugo's aggressive claque.[31] Out of spite some rented boxes that they didn't use, simply to prevent others from attending. By the time of the last performance on June 22, Gautier claimed there wasn't a single word in *Hernani* that hadn't been applauded or hissed ad nauseam.

After 1832, Hugo abandoned the use of verse in his plays (except for *Ruy Blas*, first produced in 1838). Without the garnish of poetry, it was often difficult to distinguish Romantic drama from melodrama, and the Comédie Française, uncertain about the artistic value of the new genre, cast it into the limbo of the boulevards. Looking back on Hugo's dramas some decades later, the critic Brander Matthews concluded that they are, in fact, only "melodramas written by a poet."[32] Not only the absence of poetry but also the addition of background music in *Lucrèce Borgia* and the reliance on bizarre situations and grotesque character roles did indeed make Hugo's later theatrical efforts sink to the level of boulevard melodrama. As Thackeray noted, "Every piece Victor Hugo has written since *Hernani* has contained a monster.... There is Triboulet, a foolish monster (*Le Roi s'amuse*); Lucrèce Borgia, a maternal monster; Mary Tudor, a religious monster... and others."[33] Just as he created monsters in great abundance, Hugo dispensed poison in generous draughts. For example, "Hernani poisons himself, and so does his bride; Ruy Blas takes poison; Angelo thinks to poison his wife; and Lucrèce Borgia poisons a whole supper-party. In fact, to read Hugo's plays straight through is almost as good as a course in toxicology."[34]

If the Comédie-Française began to have second thoughts about the merits of Hugo's dramas, opera houses all over Europe found "their melodramatic poses, their complex plottings, and their stagily effective climaxes" a superb reservoir of potential libretti.[35] The two best-known operas derived from his plays are undoubtedly Verdi's *Ernani* (*Hernani*) and *Rigoletto* (*Le Roi s'amuse*).

Dumas *père*, Hugo's major rival in the field of Romantic drama, wrote plays even more akin to melodrama than Hugo's. Although the employment of a five-act rather than three-act format and the intermittent use of poetry represent definite departures from melodrama, most other distinctions between the two genres appear to be more a matter of degree than substance. Granted, Romantic drama fleshed out its characters better than did melodrama, relied less on trite, artificial plot devices, and often insisted on historical accuracy in scenery and costumes. As might be expected, though, not everyone was pleased with these "improvements," and there were those who missed the pat morality and happy endings of melodrama. Among these was the queen, Marie-Amélie, who condemned romantic drama as licentious. "This school ... is a perpetual insult to virtue," she lamented. It is "a school of idlers, unintelligible scribblers [and] sceptics ... Their satanical invectives arouse more pity than indignation."[36]

At least one Romantic playwright escaped the queen's wrath: the idealistic and aristocratic comte de Vigny, who was a friend of her eldest son, the duc d'Orléans. Although de Vigny was already an established poet, novelist, and dramatist, he required the assistance of the duc d'Orléans to get his masterpiece, *Chatterton*, staged by the Comédie. The fact that the author wanted his mistress, Marie Dorval, to take the lead provoked heated objections from the theater's company. Mme Dorval, after all, was a boulevard actress. Only the duke's intervention broke down their opposition. At the premiere on February 12, 1835, Marie-Amélie and her son were present in the royal box to witness de Vigny's greatest triumph. The play's plot concerned a talented young poet driven to despair and death by a calloused and materialistic society. Its spiritual theme, coupled with the devastating effect of Dorval's performance, overwhelmed the first-night audience. George Sand was there with her lover, the poet-playwright Alfred de Musset, and both were so overcome they cried like babies. "I left in tears without wanting to say a word to anyone because I simply couldn't speak."

Sand wrote Dorval afterward.[37] Although George confessed that she was not at all fond of de Vigny (he had once called her a lesbian), she begged Marie to make him happy because "such men need and deserve it."[38] Others present that night were equally affected. The critic Sainte-Beuve wept, Berlioz sobbed, and the journalist Maxime du Camp fainted.

The spiritual values that Marie-Amélie appreciated in *Chatterton* didn't threaten her like the political and social reform that Hugo injected into his dramas. Over and over, the latter's message remained the same: those who committed evil were always hubris-laden aristocrats or materialist-minded bourgeoisie.

Dumas found Hugo's moralizing tiresome and his plays dull. Hugo, in turn, deplored Dumas's ineptitude as a poet. Such criticism, however, didn't deter Dumas from using verse in his Romantic drama, *Christine*. At its premiere in the Left Bank's Odéon, the play encountered nearly as much opposition as did *Hernani* itself. A hostile audience caused so many interruptions that the play didn't finish until the wee hours of the morning. At one point in the epilogue when Christine asked her doctor how long she had to live, someone from the pit cried out, "If she's not dead by one o'clock, I'm off!"[39]

By 1831 when Chopin arrived in Paris, Romantic drama was at its zenith, with Dumas's *Antony* and Hugo's *Marion de Lorme* playing to packed houses. Their exhibitions of prostitution, adultery, and murder were followed the next year by Dumas's *Tour de Nesle* and Hugo's *Le Roi s'amuse*, both of which featured lust, seduction, and more murder. Afterward came Hugo's *Lucrèce Borgia* and *Marie Tudor*, each filled with tempestuous scenes of illicit love, bastard children, executions, and poisonings. Later Dumas's *Don Juan de Marana* abounded in "duels and deaths... suicides, seductions, elopements, murder, poisonings, ghosts, and spectral visions," while his *Richard Darlington* boasted a "first" in boulevard murders when the heroine was thrown out a window. As a Parisian of the times remarked, "People have come to believe that one only sees abandoned infants and fallen women on our streets."[40] Certainly Chopin's first impressions of Paris tended to support this notion of a decadent city full of "filth... vice... noise, chaos and pandemonium on all sides."[41]

Actually there wasn't that much more violence and immorality in Romantic drama than in French Classical tragedy or the boulevard melodramas. What made it seem so was the fact that such sordid events were presented on stage in full view of the audience—unlike traditional tragedy—and depicted with greater realism than in melodrama. These two differences not only affected the

10.5 Frédérick Lemaître was a leading boulevard actor known particularly for his portrayal of the unscrupulous Robert Macaire, who represented the worst elements of bourgeois society under the July monarchy. In later years Lemaître still managed to mesmerize his audiences, even though age and alcohol often impaired his performances.

viewers of Romantic drama but also put extraordinary demands on the actors and actresses who performed them. In the tragedies of Racine and Corneille, where audiences were told rather than shown what happened, actors generally conveyed emotion with their voices and some facial expression but a minimum of bodily movement. In melodrama such emotions were expressed mechanically through a simplistic vocabulary of stereotyped gestures. Romantic drama, however, forced actors to portray events realistically, which often involved a taxing amount of physical effort.

Frédérick Lemaître, one of the outstanding exponents of Romantic drama, learned at an early age the value of emoting effectively (fig. 10.5). In his theatrical debut as a child, he spoke no words but merely roared as the lion in *Pyramus and Thisbe*. His "roaring success" in this role may well have had less to do with talent than the fact that he was, by nature, a loud and blustery individual. Given such a personality, he could hardly fail to succeed as Robert Macaire, his best-known role in melodrama. But Lemaître was also a tremendously versatile actor. In the field of Romantic drama, he achieved his greatest triumph in Dumas's *Kean,* where he played the part of Edmund Kean, the English tragedian who, like himself, was an alcoholic. Night after night during the play's run at the Théâtre des Variétés in 1836, he drank two bottles of wine from a salad bowl on stage. Although he often forgot which play he was in and mixed up his lines, Gautier pronounced him the finest actor in France, if not the world.

10.6 Pierre-Martinien Bocage-Toussez, known simply as "Bocage," was a handsome matinee idol of his day who had a penchant for melodrama and the new Romantic dramas popular then. For a brief period prior to George Sand's liaison with Chopin, he and the author had an affair.

It wasn't Lemaître, though, but Pierre-Martinien Bocage-Toussez (known simply as Bocage) who was the great matinee idol of the time (fig. 10.6). Although he made a few forays into the Théâtre-Français and the Odéon, Bocage was primarily a boulevard actor. Born to a poor family of wool-carders, he didn't learn to read or write until the age of thirteen. Because of a broken nose in childhood, he spoke with a nasal voice that made him sound as if he had a chronic head cold. His flamboyant gestures, though, always made it clear what he was saying even when nobody understood his lines. In 1837 George Sand added the actor briefly to her list of lovers. After their short affair, the two remained good friends, largely because of their shared political convictions: both were radical Republicans. According to Paul Foucher, Bocage often interpolated his political views into a performance, making it resemble "an evening newspaper."[42] In 1849, during the second republic, when he became director of the Odéon, Bocage produced a highly successful stage adaptation of "Citizen" Sand's *François le Champi*, just a month after Chopin's death (fig. 10.7).

In spite of the popularity of Lemaître and Bocage, male actors, like male dancers, hardly ever achieved the notoriety or adulation given to their female counterparts. Although a leading man or *premier-danseur* might be admired, he

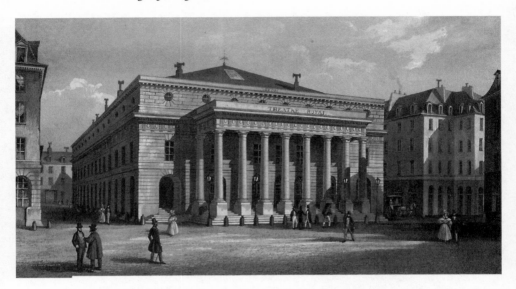

10.7 The Odéon theater was one of Paris's two official, state-run theaters, sometimes referred to as "the second Théâtre Français." Its Left Bank location, however, away from the city's major entertainment areas, posed a great inconvenience for many theatergoers. As a result, the government operated it on a sporadic basis.

was seldom worshiped. Women who expressed an excessive interest in a male actor were considered indiscreet if not immoral, while men who waxed enthusiastic over such performers became sexually suspect. It was therefore the actresses of the time who have left the greatest imprint on France's theatrical history.

Among the most talented of these actresses were Mlle Mars and Mlle George, who managed a dual career in the Comédie and on the boulevards. By 1830 when the battle of *Hernani* had secured a foothold for Romantic drama on the Parisian stage, both were well past the bloom of youth: Mlle Mars (Anne-Françoise-Hippolyte Boutet) was fifty-two, and Mlle George (Marguerite-Josephine Weimer), forty-three. Chopin had come to know Mlle Mars as early as April of 1833, when both participated in Berlioz's benefit for the actress Harriet Smithson at the Salle Favart (fig. 10.8). Earlier, in 1832, Chopin had admired her on the stage in Soulié's *Clothilde* at the Théâtre-Français. A critic who reviewed her performance then stated, "People will come in droves to see this play for three reasons— First of all? Mlle Mars—Secondly? Mlle Mars!—Thirdly? Mlle Mars!!"[43] At that time the English expatriate Captain Gronow noted that the actress had begun to

10.8 Mlle Mars was one of the most versatile and enduring members of the Comédie Française. Shortly after Chopin's arrival in Paris, he came to know and admire her. During her long career, Mlle Mars performed in both comedies and tragedies at the Théâtre Français as well as in the dramas and melodramas of the boulevards.

10.9 Mlle George, like Mlle Mars, was an actress of diverse talents who could span the gulf between the codified formalities of French Classical theater and the unrestrained emotionalism of Romantic drama. Only in her very last years did age and obesity diminish the power of her theatrical presence on the Parisian stage.

show the lines of age, but acknowledged that her voice and mannerisms remained youthful. This ability to convey the spirit of youth long after she had lost the appearance of it encouraged Mlle Mars to persist in playing pert little ingénue roles—even at an age when Gautier claimed she could only be considered seductive by decrepit army contractors from the Revolution or aging empire generals. With the advent of Romantic drama, the actress was able to escape those stereotyped girlish roles that no longer fitted her. But she found the transition a strenuous one. Highly passionate in her private life, she had difficulty portraying intense emotions on stage. In spite of the acclaim she received in *Henri III, Hernani,* and *Ruy Blas,* she preferred playing the comedies of Marivaux and Molière at the Théâtre-Français, and returned to the boulevards only sporadically in some of Dumas's later comedies. Unfortunately at the end of her career she exhibited a disregard for the one quality most essential to any comic actress: a sense of timing. She simply didn't know when to retire. At age sixty-two, after her "definitely final farewell performance," Richard Wagner, then living in Paris, commented that "indeed many were under the impression that she had already stopped acting some time ago."[44]

Mlle Mars's colleague at the Comédie, Mlle George, also had a problem with timing, one fatal to many leading ladies: she didn't know when to stop eating (fig. 10.9). Even in her youth Mlle George had a physical structure euphemistically referred to as "statuesque." "She seems to be a Titan," Gautier wrote. "Her build has something cyclopean...like a granite column."[45] Napoléon, who was obsessed with grandeur in all forms, found Mlle George seductive and took her as his mistress. Just how the Titan and the Little Corporal managed the logistics of love-making must have titillated many an imagination.

As age amplified Mlle George's proportions, her girth became a public joke. Horses could gallop around the Champs de Mars in four minutes, it was said, whereas it only took one minute more to make it around Mlle George. What was amusing offstage, though, could be awe-inspiring onstage, when the imposing actress intoned the tragedies of Corneille and Racine with commanding force. By the time of the July monarchy, Mlle George had become the mistress of a theatrical manager, Charles-Jean Harel, who urged her to take up Romantic drama. Following his advice, she achieved remarkable success in Dumas's *Tour de Nesle* and Hugo's *Lucrèce Borgia*. For Heinrich Heine, she had become "that immensely bright and shining sun of flesh who illuminates the theatrical heaven of the Boulevards."[46]

After Harel's death (from insanity), Mlle George's figure waxed as her talents waned, and she eventually found her career consigned to the banlieue and provincial theaters. Once, on a tour toward the end of her life, the obese actress sank to her knees in a dramatic scene and couldn't get up. As the audience roared with laughter, she remained helpless on the floor with tears rolling down her cheeks—a sad finale for the one-time favorite of an emperor.

While Mlles Mars and George forced themselves to adapt to Romantic drama, Marie Dorval had an inborn talent for it. An illegitimate child of "the people" with a highly emotional personality, Dorval was well attuned to the Romanticism of her time. For a while she studied acting at the Conservatory, which gave her a certain professional discipline without suppressing her native talents. To audiences steeped in the tradition of French Classical drama, her acting appeared untutored, plebeian, and melodramatic, but what was considered anathema at the Comédie was called art on the boulevards. Audiences drawn to those stages came

10.10 The actress Marie Dorval, intensely passionate both on and off the stage, became the embodiment of Romantic drama in its brief, explosive existence. The force with which she threw herself into her roles was so physically exhausting that it may well have contributed to her early death at age fifty-two.

mostly from the working classes and the petite bourgeoisie. What they sought in the theater was an emotional thrill, and the more gut-wrenching it was, the better they liked it. "They are a public who weep so wonderfully well," Nerval observed.[47] Today's pollsters would doubtless have devised a "lachrymal index" to calculate the success or failure of these boulevard productions. On a scale of one to ten, for example, the "magnificently tearful success" of the vaudeville *Grâce a Dieu* would surely have scored a ten.[48] So would Soulié's *Proscrit*, which moved George Sand to write Dorval, "You made me weep like a calf."[49]

No other actress could equal Dorval's ability to overdose an audience on emotion without sating them (fig. 10.10). The huskiness of her voice, noted in most contemporary accounts, was probably due to the strain on her vocal cords from the intensity of her performances. A review of her acting as the heroine of *L'Incendiare* in March 1831 gives us a vivid account of the dramatic energy she brought to her roles: "She arrives on stage...she throws herself down on her knees before the priest, she is choked with tears, she screams, she speaks, she sobs, she clasps her hands to her face, she tosses her hair from side to side, she flails her arms about, she loses her mind, she regains her senses...she tears her handkerchief, she weeps, she dries her tears and then weeps again."[50] When Dumas saw her, she took his breath away. He found her *magnifique* and recruited her for his *Antony* later that year. On its opening night, Dorval sent her audience into a frenzy with a performance that was more painfully realistic than intended. In the final scene, when Antony stabs her, the actor Bocage accidentally knicked her with his dagger, evoking a bloodcurdling scream that chilled the entire theater. As Théophile Gautier reported, "The audience was truly delirious; they applauded, they sobbed, they wept, they screamed."[51] In short, they responded to her with a performance that all but equaled her own.

As Dorval's career proved, the life of a Romantic actress demanded a daily workout worthy of an Olympic athlete. For example, in Victor Hugo's *Marion de Lorme,* also given in 1831, we find poor Dorval struggling to cope with the script's merciless stage directions:

"Marion (throwing herself at Laffemas's feet)"
"Marion (on her knees, clasping her hands)"
"Marion (falling upon her knees and lifting her eyes to heaven)"
"Marion (still on her knees)"
"Marion falls on her knees at the door."
"Marion lifts herself with difficulty and staggering, falls on the threshold. . . ."
"She [Marion] falls on her knees, turns towards the grating of the prison; then
    rises with a convulsive effort and disappears through the great door. . . .
    Suddenly she discovers Didier, gives a cry, runs and throws herself
    breathless at his feet."
"She falls again at Didier's feet and sobs."
"Marion (dragging herself up to the litter [of Cardinal Richelieu] on her
    knees and wringing her hands)."
"Marion (alone, lifts herself half way up, and drags herself along by her
    hands . . .)"

It must have been with a deep sigh of relief that Dorval came to her final stage cue, which instructed her to "fall senseless."[52] At that point, what else could she do?

As if all this falling and crawling weren't enough evidence of Dorval's dedication to her art, when de Vigny asked her to throw herself down a whole flight of stairs at the end of his *Chatterton,* she was willing to "go the extra step," no doubt because de Vigny happened to be her lover then. Rumor had it that George Sand was also her lover at the same time, a fact that many, including Balzac, were ready to believe. In his novel, *La Fille aux yeux d'or,* he portrayed Dorval as a lesbian and later commented that Sand had no more sex appeal for him than would a man. In 1845 Dorval achieved what some considered her greatest triumph in a drama called *Marie-Jeanne,* where she uttered such a shattering cry of grief for three hundred nights that she ruptured a lung and was gravely ill for many weeks. As a testimony to Dorval's moving performance, Chopin reported, "Everyone was in tears and all you could hear throughout the theater were the sounds of people sniffling, sobbing and blowing their noses."[53] Surely another ten on the lachrymal index.

Several times in her career Dorval performed at the Théâtre-Français in the Romantic dramas Victor Hugo produced there, for example, *Marion de Lorme, Angelo,* and several revivals of *Hernani.* Although she was welcomed by the theater's audiences, she was treated condescendingly—often rudely—by the cast. Later when she applied for the position of *sociétaire* in the company, her bid was unanimously rejected.

Undoubtedly Dorval's most disastrous undertaking at the Théâtre-Français occurred during the spring of 1840, when George Sand persuaded her to take the title role in her play, *Cosima.* The author, who had written mostly journalistic articles and novels, decided to try her hand at drama as a solution to a spate of financial problems that plagued her then. The cost of her trip to Majorca with Chopin the year before, her husband's mismanagement of her personal fortune, and huge expenditures on her house in Paris had put Mme Sand 80,000 francs in debt.[54] On the assumption that she "could make more of a profit with less effort working for the theater than the bookstores," she set out to write two plays, *Hatred in Love* and *The Mississippians.*[55] After various revisions, Hatred in Love was renamed *Cosima* and presented to François Buloz, who had just become director the the Théâtre-Français. From the very outset, things went badly. Sand, who lacked any experience in the theater, immediately antagonized Buloz by demanding the same contractual terms given to such veteran playwrights as de Vigny, Dumas, and Scribe. Later when she asked for Dorval to play the lead role, she met with opposition because the actress wasn't a member of the Comédie. Briefly she considered Mlle Mars, until Buloz warned her that the aging star "couldn't handle a long role any more."[56] When the Comédie finally withdrew its objections to Dorval, Sand faced a new setback with the departure of her male lead, the glamorous Lockroy.

Interminable delays followed. At one point, Sand threatened to publish the play in the *Revue des Deux Mondes* rather than wait until Judgment Day to have her drama produced. When rehearsals finally began, most of the actors found the play (about an unfaithful wife who is pardoned by her generous husband) so detestable they urged Sand to cancel it. In exasperation she agreed, but Buloz, having already paid her a sizable advance, insisted on going ahead with it. Subsequently several members of the cast came down with "the grippe," which led to further delays. By then all Sand wanted was to get the play over and done with. As she told Jules Janin, "It has cost me more effort, time and health to mount this platitude than to write a four-volume novel when all I may get for it is a barrage of stewed apples" (commonly thrown on the stage by agitators during a bad performance).[57]

This, as it turned out, is exactly what she got on opening night, partly because the play was mediocre (if not as "detestable" as the actors claimed), and partly because the author refused to use the theater's official claque. On opening night, April 29, 1840, George had reserved stalls for Balzac, Liszt, and his mistress, Marie d'Agoult. Among others who showed up were Mme Récamier, Dumas *père*, Mrs. Trollope, the physician to the pasha of Egypt, and a number of Chopin's aristocratic Polish friends and pupils. What they witnessed was a raucous spectacle not unlike the opening night of *Hernani*. "I was hooted and whistled at as I expected," George wrote later. "People cried from every quarter that the play was immoral.... The actors became flustered and confused by the uproar and missed their cues."[58] Typical of the reviews was one in *L'Artiste*, which described her play as deplorable, full of pompous moralizing, and boring. In spite of such criticism, the author refused to make any changes. "Let them rant and rave all they want," she wrote defiantly.[59] After the seventh catastrophic performance, though, she asked Buloz to withdraw the play, which he did. It would be nine years before she dared risk another theatrical venture.

When Dorval appeared in *Cosima* she was forty-two and had only nine more years to live. Upon her premature death at age fifty-one, she had already outlived the brief but blustery era of Romantic drama. Ironically it was Victor Hugo, the chief architect and exponent of the genre, who administered its death blow with the production of *Les Burgraves* in 1843. Unlike *Hernani*, *Les Burgraves* provoked no controversy; audiences and critics alike agreed the play was a flop. For Hugo this production marked the end of his career as a playwright.

Some years earlier, Dumas had already abandoned Romantic drama to write piquant comedies like *Mademoiselle de Belle-Isle* and *Les Demoiselles de Saint-Cyr*, while de Vigny, like a true Romantic hero, had succumbed to melancholy and gone into seclusion. The passing of Romantic drama, however, had little effect on the vitality of Parisian theatrical life. The boulevard theaters continued to draw large crowds, thanks to the ever-prolific Scribe and his collaborators.

10.11 The actress Rachel (to whom French Classical tragedy owed its temporary revival from 1838 to 1858) is pictured here as Roxanne in Racine's *Bajazet*. On September 12, 1840, George Sand took some friends to see Rachel in this role. Whether Chopin accompanied them or not is uncertain. The musician was a great admirer of the actress's talents, however, which he recounted on several occasions to his family in Warsaw.

New dramatists like Ponsard and Augier also attracted audiences with plays that tried to temper the excessive emotionality of Romanticism with a combination of Neoclassical restraint and sobering realism.

While the boulevard theaters were looking toward the future, the Comédie Française was now, more than ever, gazing into the past. When Hugo's *Les Burgraves* was running at the Comédie, a great disparity was noted between the near-empty house on nights it played and the large crowds that came for the performances of a brilliant young tragedienne, Rachel, who had debuted there in the summer of 1838 (fig. 10.11). Her amazing talent inspired an incredible resurgence of popularity in the seventeenth-century dramas of Corneille and Racine, unlike anything seen since the legendary performances of Talma and Mlle Duchenois during the golden years of the empire.

This theatrical sensation known simply as Rachel (her real name was Eliza Félix) was born in 1820 at a shabby Swiss inn to an itinerant Jewish peddler and his wife who sold used clothing. She was the second of six children (five girls and one boy), all of whom were eventually involved in the theater. In 1831 the eleven-year-old Rachel arrived in Paris, the same year that Chopin, George Sand, and Heinrich Heine started their careers there. In order to earn money for her impoverished family, she sold oranges in the street and wandered from café to coffeehouse singing and giving recitations in the poorer quarters of Paris. According to the Maréchal de Castellane, the lean and hungry child had the predatory look of a she-wolf. Contemporary descriptions and early daguerreotypes indicate that she had a swarthy complexion with eyes too close together in a head too big for her small, thin body. Even as an adult, the petite, frail-looking actress was never considered a great beauty. As Jules Janin described her, she was "a blade of gold in a sheath of clay."[60]

Despite her unprepossessing appearance, Rachel's talents were quickly recognized, and she was taken off the streets to study voice in one of the city's choral schools. Later she became a pupil of the actor Saint-Aulaire at his studio in the Latin Quarter. At age fifteen she took lessons briefly in the Conservatoire with the Comédie Française's Samson. Throughout the rest of her life he remained her advisor and confidant.

Rachel's early career on the stages of various small theaters brought her little attention until Delestre-Poirson, director of the Gymnase, took a gamble and starred her in a melodrama, *La Vendéenne*, based on Sir Walter Scott's novel, *The Heart of Midlothian*. Important critics like Jules Janin of the *Journal des Débats* now took notice of her, but their praise was faint. The following year, thanks to Samson's efforts, she obtained an audition with the director of the Théâtre-Français, who agreed to accept her as a *pensionnaire* at 4,000 francs a year.

Shortly afterward, on a warm summer evening in June 1838, Rachel made her debut on the rue Richelieu as Camille in Corneille's *Horace*. The theater was almost empty with only five people on the orchestra floor, among them Dr. Véron, now owner and director of the journal, *Le Constitutionnel,* and the critic, Jules Janin. It was the lecherous Véron (already infatuated with Rachel), who had induced Janin to accompany him, in hopes of getting a good review for this latest object of his desire. The critic, however, remained as tepid toward the young girl as he had been earlier. Only when he saw her a third time in September of the same year did he suddenly "discover" the novice tragedienne. From then on her fame mushroomed to the point where Louis-Philippe, after a three-year absence from the Comédie, returned just to see for himself this amazing new prodigy.

In all her twenty years at the Comédie, Rachel played relatively few roles. While she was a powerful actress, she wasn't a versatile one. For the most part she confined herself to the great tragedies of Corneille and Racine, which suited her limited dramatic range. In Gautier's words, Rachel was "magnificent in the intense, destructive emotions: irony, sarcasm, treachery and hate." But when it came to "the outgoing emotions such as love, pity and joy," he found they had "not yet been mastered by the young tragedienne."[61]

In Rachel's time the works of Corneille and Racine, written nearly two hundred years earlier, had become an acquired taste, appreciated only by well-educated Parisians from a cultivated background. They consisted of a standard five-act format, written in a specified style of poetry (Alexandrine iambic hexameter) and tailored to fit the classical unities of time, place, and action. Even the physical gestures of the actors were limited to a few accepted conventions, which did more to dehumanize the characters than to bring them to life. For Heinrich Heine, it seemed that the classical stage was populated solely by ghosts. In keeping with the unity of place, one sparsely furnished set (generally the palace of some noble personage) sufficed for all five acts.

Until the memorable tragedian Talma shocked the public by donning a toga and sandals on stage, actors in French Classical drama had been accustomed to dress as they pleased without regard to historical accuracy. Unfortunately Talma's example was ignored throughout the 1830s and 1840s, when actors and actresses continued to supply their own costumes. The expense was often burdensome. Mlle Judith of the Comédie complained that half of what she earned was spent on her stage wardrobe alone. Mlle Mars, on the other hand, didn't object as she relished the freedom of dressing in a manner that flattered her appearance regardless of its appropriateness to the drama. Mlle George also had no wish to change the status quo, which allowed her to show off her diamonds from Napoléon and her rubies from the czar of Russia. At her debut, Rachel, who had neither jewels nor any sense of haute couture, appeared on stage in a rose-colored robe of such bad taste that Gautier accused her of looking like some barbaric Visigoth queen. Later, in Racine's *Phèdre,* her brother, Raphael, appeared in the role of Theseus's son, "clad in an unconvincing panther skin at 10 francs a yard," while the actress who played Phèdre's nurse came onstage in an outfit pieced together from old dining room curtains.[62] Because the Comédie used department store chairs draped with antimacassars to furnish the "palace" in *Phèdre,* there really wasn't much point in bothering with suitable costumes.

Rachel's success as a tragedienne, of course, had little to to with costumes or jewelry. It was significantly influenced, though, by her physical appearance, which uniquely equipped her for the type of roles she was to play. Although never endowed with a conventional beauty, Rachel, simply by virtue of her presence on stage, "at once carried you back to the purest antiquity."[63] She was "born an antique and her pale flesh seemed made of Greek marble."[64] This aspect of a frozen figure fixed in time was enhanced by the fact that she dispensed with much of the stereotyped gesturing employed by other tragediennes. Neither did she bellow out her lines in the hollow, sing-song manner of her predecessors. Quite the opposite: "Her grave, deep, vibrating voice, so seldom rising loud or breaking into cries, well suited her self-contained, sovereignly calm acting."[65]

And yet this cold marble statue could project a burning passion. Not only in classical tragedy but also on her rare sorties into Romantic drama, "she seemed to detach herself from a bas-relief by Phidias to wend her way down to the footlights. . . . More than a great actress, she was a great artist."[66] Unlike so many of her Romantic colleagues, Rachel remained in control of her passion. Only a person with the utmost command of her faculties could undergo the dramatic metamorphoses that she achieved on the Comédie's stage. In the glow of the footlights, the thin, little street waif with the oversized head and pallid face radiated grandeur. In 1847 when Chopin saw her in Racine's *Athalie,* he found her transformed into someone truly "beautiful."[67]

Offstage, however, Rachel's demeanor was less than attractive. On many occasions it was downright ugly. Her avarice, for example, was proverbial. During the actress's first four months at the Théâtre-Français, its receipts increased six-fold, which encouraged her to extort outrageous sums of money from the theater. Later her demands for increases in salary, privileges, and vacation time caused constant friction with the Comédie's directors. Eventually her annual stipend rose from 4,000 to 100,000 francs, not including extra compensations for special performances. Furthermore she pressured the theater into hiring her siblings as members of the company's cast. (Fortunately most of them shared some of their sister's gifts, if not her genius.) Certainly Rachel's talents had brought new life to the almost-deserted house on the rue Richelieu, but the price for keeping her nearly bankrupted it.

Outside the theater, Rachel was equally rapacious. The free tickets she received for her performances were usually sold rather than given away, and the expensive gifts she wheedled out of friends and admirers were converted into cash at the first opportunity. Seldom did she ever participate in benefits for her colleagues, and when she did, she charged an inflated fee. One of the Comédie's actresses, Augustine Brohan, finally stopped inviting Rachel to her Thursday salons because she invariably demanded payment if anyone asked her to recite. When Rachel complained of being snubbed, Mlle Brohan replied, "Ah, my dear friend, ... you put such a high price on your talents!"[68]

Along with Rachel's fame came the challenge of moving in Paris's rigidly structured social world. Considering her unprepossessing background and modest education, this was a formidable hurdle. Not only was her spelling haphazard, her conversation loud, and her grammar imperfect, she had absolutely no sense of taste, according to Gautier. On the other hand, Mme Récamier, the city's doyenne of decorum, claimed that "her deportment was irreproachable.... The ease and promptitude with which this young girl, without education or knowledge of good society, sized its manners and tone was certainly the perfection of art.... Her success in society was immense."[69]

To secure her position in the Parisian beau monde, Rachel even attempted to create a salon of her own in the Lorette district's rue Trudon and saw to it that her two illegitimate sons were baptized. Although willing to accept the New Testament's sacrament of baptism, she blithely ignored the Old Testament's prohibition of adultery. Her lovers were legion. By way of explaining her promiscuity, she once commented that she liked a lot of tenants but couldn't tolerate owners. As for the tenants in her life, most had excellent social or financial references. Among them was Dr. Véron, who had made a fortune in the pharmaceutical, operatic, and literary trades. From a purely physical point of view, however, this potbellied, middle-aged man with a bloated face and a scrofulous neck clearly had few attractions. "It often seemed to me," Heinrich Heine wrote of him, "as if there crept from his eyes swarms of little sticky shining worms."[70] All things considered, heaven seemed to have devised an almost perfect match in these two vulgar, ambitious, and avaricious souls. Nothing, of course, lasts forever, and at one point in their stormy relationship, Rachel thought of killing her lover by shooting him from the stage as he watched her perform. Instead their affair ended in a less explosive fashion, leaving Véron to remark bitterly, "I have become old and Rachel has become rich."[71] For the young actress who was to die prematurely, age would never be a problem, and she had little sympathy for an old ex-lover. At that point in her life, the sunset of one romance merely provided a respite before the dawning of another.

Occasionally, when her "tenants" overlapped, Rachel found herself deprived of this respite. A number of her lovers, as might be expected, came from the literary and artistic world, such as the poet Alfred de Musset, the publisher Emile de Girardin, and the dramatist François Ponsard. But most (whether by accident or intent) were involved in one way or another with Napoléon Bonaparte—for example, the Prince de Joinville, who brought the emperor's remains back to France in 1840; count Alexandre Walewski, one of Napoléon's natural sons; two of the emperor's nephews; Prince Napoléon, known as "Plon-Plon" (son of Jerome Bonaparte, the former king of Westphalia); and the emperor Napoléon III.

As early as 1839, Rachel began to show the first signs of tuberculosis. At the beginning the disease progressed slowly, but by the late 1840s it was affecting her performances. In search of less strenuous parts, she turned to other genres, including Dumas comedies and a revival of Hugo's romantic drama, *Angelo*. In none of these did she make any remarkable impression. Her greatest triumph outside of French Classical tragedy was her role as the heroine of *Adrienne Lecouvreur* in 1849. The play, written by Scribe in collaboration with Ernest Legouvé, concerned an episode in the love life of George Sand's great grandfather, Maurice de Saxe. Under the circumstances it would have been natural for Mme Sand to have attended a performance, but there is no evidence that she ever did. Although she admired Rachel's magnificent talent, she could not stomach the latter's callous opportunism. All too often she had seen the actress "using love to further her fortunes."[72] Of course, Mme Sand was hardly one to cast stones over such matters. Still it remains to her credit that she always considered love a sacred gift and never a saleable commodity.

As Rachel's health gradually failed, she took more and more time off from the Comédie to tour the provinces and such distant sites as America. What these tours added to her purse, they subtracted from her life. After one summer circuit through the south of France, she returned to Paris, full of exhilaration. "What a journey! What exhaustion!! But what spoils!!"[73] In 1858, when she died at age thirty-eight, she left an estate valued at 2 million francs. Life had blessed her with talent, fame, love, and money. It had cheated her in only one thing: time.

For the incurable Romantic, Rachel lives on through her spiritual legacy. How, though, can we determine the value of that legacy? We have no movies, recordings, or videotapes by which to judge her. She left behind no school of acting, no pupils, no disciples. She was, in all probability, too unique to have had a successor worthy of the name. As for the vitality she infused into Corneille and Racine, that seems to have perished with her. As Thackeray had predicted, she could "only galvanize the corpse [of classical tragedy], not revive it."[74] Gautier concurred: "She alone maintained alive for eighteen years a dead form."[75] In the long run, her fate was to become merely "a funeral figure upon the tomb of tragedy."[76]

CHAPTER II

Delacroix, Daumier, and Daguerre

A "3-D" View of Art

"GREAT MEN SEE WHAT THE VULGAR NEVER SEE, that is why they are great," Eugène Delacroix once noted in his journal (fig. 11.1).[1] Certainly during the first half of the nineteenth century there was much to see, and those who had the gift to comprehend what they saw were truly fortunate. Delacroix was one of them. In his sixty-five years, he lived under seven different governments from the Directory to the Second Empire. During that time he witnessed vast changes in the political, social, and economic worlds around him, changes that were reflected in the artistic life of his time. Thanks to his quick eye and keen mind, Delacroix was able to grasp what he saw and transfer it onto canvas—sometimes directly, though often under the guise of history or allegory.

When Chopin reached Paris in 1831, Romantic art was at its zenith with Delacroix its acknowledged leader. At the Academy's Salon that year, the painter presented what is probably his best known masterpiece, *Liberty Leading the People*. Dramatic in style and concept, it adhered to the conventional medium of oil on canvas, which "serious" artists preferred to the new technique of lithography, invented by the German Aloys Senefelder shortly before the advent of the nineteenth century. One of the advantages of lithography was that it provided the artist with a reproductive ability comparable to a rabbit's. Several hundred copies could be produced from a single lithographic stone. Woodcuts and engravings, which had existed since the early part of the fifteenth century, offered a similar advantage, but required a tedious and time-consuming transfer of the artist's work to wood or metal before its final appearance on paper. By the third and fourth decades of the nineteenth century, the easy reproducibility of lithography had attracted many French artists, including Delacroix and Honoré Daumier.

Although lithography provided the artist with myriad extra hands to duplicate his work swiftly and accurately, Louis Jacques Mandé Daguerre and Joseph Nicéphore Niepce's ability to produce photographic images on a metal plate by

11.1 Eugène Delacroix was the preeminent Romantic painter of his time. In this particular portrait, he bears a strong resemblance to Prince Talleyrand, who is often reputed to have been his natural father. He was elegant and frail with a pale olive tint to his complexion, which made Gautier comment that he could easily have passed for a maharaja of India. Unfortunately in the conservative world of the Parisian salons the Romantic works of Delacroix were not always appreciated. "What a shame," some noted, "that such a charming man paints such horrible things" (Théophile Gautier, *Ecrivains et Artistes Romantiques* [Paris: Librairie Plon, 1933], 231).

the 1830s gave the artist an extra eye that could record forms, perspectives, and details with much greater accuracy than could the human eye. For Delacroix, though, this "third eye" lacked the creative potential of his own inner eye. True art, he insisted, should not simply record the external world but be an emanation of the artist's unique personal vision. Although the skeptic in him readily admitted that art might be nothing more than a "collection of harmonious lies," it became the only constant and inescapable reality in his life.[2] "I will finish by believing that there is nothing real in this world but our illusions," he concluded—and that belief remained with him until his death.[3]

Unlike many of his Romantic colleagues, Delacroix didn't try to elevate his illusions to the level of transcendental ideals. He didn't believe in such aesthetic sophistry. For him the illusions of art, like those elicited by the hashish he smoked with Charles Baudelaire, Théophile Gautier, and others on the île Saint-Louis, required no other justification than the heightened pleasure and perception they afforded. Ironically this man of illusions took a very down-to-earth view regarding the origins of artistic creativity. With the typical gusto of a Gallic gourmet, he touted the influence of food and wine on the creative process. "Great men, when they write their memoirs, never say enough about the influence of a good dinner upon their state of mind." Nor do they mention the "inspiration born of the bottle [which] takes us further than we could go without its help."[4]

If Delacroix's pragmatic philosophy wasn't entirely in line with the artistic credo of most Romantics, his works nevertheless represent one of the fullest expressions of the Romantic spirit. In his time, though, art was beginning to acquire a practical as well as an aesthetic function that many Romantics disdained. Men like Daumier—who was not only a painter, sculptor, and lithographer but also a journalistic cartoonist, political satirist, and social commentator—represented the flexibility of these new artists. He, along with his contemporaries Henry Monnier and Gavarni, had a more realistic perception of life that served as a kite string tying their incipient fantasies to the terra firma of the workaday world.

Another visionary with a practical bent in Paris then was Daguerre, a man remembered more as an inventor than an artist. In his youth, Daguerre studied architecture, art, and stage design, but despite these artistic accomplishments, he would probably have been lost in the shadows of history if it weren't for his collaboration with Niepce, one of the pioneers of photography. At first their new photographic process seemed little more than a fascinating toy until its potential value in journalism, commerce, science, education, advertising, and art became evident. Not only did it create its own aesthetic medium; it completely altered the course of art over the next 150 years. Realism and Impressionism were two of the earliest artistic movements to be influenced by photography. Later such technological by-products of the medium as movies and television added a whole new dimension to art: movement that could actually be perceived, not merely imagined.

In the middle of the twentieth century, there was a brief vogue for three-dimensional (so-called "3-D") motion pictures, where the impression of depth was created with special glasses worn by the viewer. The effect, of course, was illusory, but then, as Delacroix suspected, art is nothing more than illusion. Whatever the case, it would be impossible to view the artistic world of Chopin's Paris without exploring those dimensions added to it by such brilliant masters of illusion as Delacroix, Daumier, and Daguerre.

Throughout the early nineteenth century, the "Salon" (the French government's annual exhibition of art) served as the nation's official arbiter of artistic taste. It was called the Salon because its first exhibit in 1667 took place in one of the large salons at the Louvre, a practice that continued until the revolution of 1848, when the Tuileries and later, the Palais Royal, housed its expanding displays. The seventeenth-century Royal Academy of Painting and Sculpture sponsored these Salons and for nearly fifty years permitted only its own members to enter their works. After the death of Louis XIV in 1715, however, artists outside the Academy were allowed to exhibit at the Salon, and in 1793, foreigners could submit entries there as well. As more and more artists clamored for wall space in the Salon, the Academy established a jury to determine which entries merited acceptance.

From the time of its origin, the Salon took place biannually until 1830, when Louis-Philippe announced that it would henceforth become a yearly ritual. Generally the exhibits opened in March and ran as long as six months. In Heinrich Heine's review of the Salon of 1831, he counted around three thousand works on display. By the time of the "open" Salon of 1848 (when the jury was abolished and all entries accepted) nine thousand items had been put on view. Mrs. Trollope, who visited the Salon of 1835, was distressed to find much of the Louvre's permanent collection of old masters covered up by the cloth screens on which the Salon paintings were hung.

Although Delacroix, Théodore Géricault, and baron Antoine-Jean Gros had already exhibited highly Romantic canvases in the Restoration Salons, the Neoclassical tastes so popular in the First Empire were still favored by the conservative juries of the July monarchy. Even after they went out of fashion, Neoclassical subjects were often employed by Romantic artists as the only acceptable way of incorporating nudity into art. The genre most favored by Salon artists well into the 1830s was that of the large historical scene, which was sure to stand out on the crowded walls of the Louvre's congested galleries.

Besides paintings, there were also drawings, engravings, and sculpture in the Salons. Of these, sculpture, which Gautier proclaimed "the art of the gods and of kings," seems to have been the stepchild of the exhibits, relegated to the crypt of the Louvre.[5] Lithography fared even worse, not being allowed in the Salons until 1850. It popularity and availability to the masses in the form of newspaper illustrations was enough to make the Salon consider it beneath artistic recognition.

This tendency to snub lithography (and later, photography) as art forms typified the limited vision of the Salons, which tolerated only works that conformed to the juries' own brand of aesthetically correct taste. In 1827, for example, Sosthène de la Rochefoucault, director of the government-controlled School of Fine Arts, condemned the sensuous opulence of Delacroix's *Sardanapalus* and warned the artist that he would receive no further government commissions if he continued to paint "that way." Later, in the Salon of 1834, when Delacroix's archrival Jean-Auguste-Dominique Ingres received a similar rebuff, he decried the Salon as nothing "more than a picture shop, a bazaar in which ... business rules instead of art" (fig. 11.2)[6]

11.2 J. A. D. Ingres, whose neat, precise Neoclassically oriented painting appealed to Chopin, was Delacroix's arch-rival. Baudelaire, as an art critic, idolized Delacroix and considered Ingres "a draughtsman" whose works were "the result of an excessive attentiveness" that demanded "an equal attentiveness in order to be understood" (Baudelaire, *Art in Paris*, 84).

The restricted tastes of the Salon juries caused so many fine works to be rejected that Ary Scheffer (whose portraits of Chopin and Liszt are well known) staged his own exposition of artists excluded from the Salon. Equally resourceful was Chopin's neighbor in the square d'Orléans, the sculptor Dantan *jeune*, who established his own museum-gallery in the passage des Panoramas, where it became a highly profitable enterprise. Although he is known primarily for his caricatures of famous people, he chose to create a lifelike bust when he portrayed Chopin.

One of the most important forces that helped to liberate the early nineteenth-century artist from the Salon's domination was the new professional class of art critics, which emerged with the proliferation of daily newspapers in the mid-1830s. The few art critics of the previous century were usually aristocratic amateurs, often accomplished writers but with little technical expertise in their field. By the 1830s, however, art criticism, if not yet a rigidly honed discipline, had become more than a dilettantish pastime. Most critics came from the bourgeoisie and were more broad-minded than their aristocratic predecessors, who had been steeped, not to say pickled, in a century-old marinade of rococo and Neoclassical tastes. A few like Gautier were actually artists in their own right.

Perhaps the most impartial of these emerging critics was Jules Janin, who could assess both the artists and the public of his time with a fairly objective eye. Quite the opposite of Janin was the flamboyant Baudelaire, who didn't believe in objective art criticism. Fortunately his natural instincts were unusually perceptive, particularly in the case of Delacroix, whom he declared "the most original painter of ancient or modern times."[7] He praised his vivid colors, sinister shadows, and above all, the violent action of his paintings. "There was much of the *savage*" in his soul, he wrote.[8]

Perhaps it was the "savage" in Delacroix that attracted him to the American painter, George Catlin, and the band of Ojibwa Indians he brought to Paris in 1845. Like most Romantics, Delacroix thought of primordial societies as remnants of a pristine humanity, unsullied by modern civilization. On a visit to Catlin, arranged by George Sand, Delacroix made sketches of the Indians and even designed a poster to help publicize the American's touring show. George herself was equally intrigued by the Indians and brought their chief, White Cloud, a bolt of red cloth and some glass beads in the hope of getting him to talk about his people and their customs. Chopin, in a letter to his family that July, mentions the sad fate of one of these "poor creatures," who died of homesickness and was buried in the Montmartre cemetery near Chopin's childhood friend and Paris roommate, Dr. Jan Matuszyński.

Louis-Philippe (who had experienced first-hand contact with American Indians during his years of exile in the United States) also came to pay his respects and invited Catlin to exhibit his canvases at the Louvre. This was a rare honor for any contemporary artist, above all an American one. Except for the annual exhibits of the Salon, the city's chief museum rarely displayed the work of any living artists in its galleries. Visitors with a penchant for avant-garde art could find little to their taste in the Louvre. Its gallery of so-called modern sculpture, for example, featured works by Michelangelo.

Parisians nevertheless flocked to this artistic paradise, especially on Sundays, when the museum became a steamy inferno packed with a potpourri of shopkeepers, clerks, artisans, and laborers enjoying their one free day of the week. This sort of Sabbath diversion piqued the puritanical American artist Samuel F. B. Morse, who felt that all good Christians should devote the Lord's Day to purely moral and religious pursuits. Thackeray was equally offended by the Sunday crowds, but for less priggish reasons: "You can't see the pictures well, and are pushed and elbowed by all sorts of low-bred creatures."[9] Genteel people never visited the Louvre on Sundays.

Nor did anyone ever go there on Mondays, when the museum was closed in order to clean up the debris from the Sunday crowds. By Tuesday its doors were opened again to a smaller, more sedate coterie of visitors and art students, who

11.3 A scene in the Louvre showing artists sketching the masterpieces on its walls. During the annual "Salons," many of these paintings were hidden for months behind screens on which the year's entries were mounted. The absence of bourgeois hordes thronging the gallery indicates that this scene represents a tranquil weekday at the city's major art gallery.

came to scrutinize and copy the Old Masters (fig. 11.3). Among these, in the early days of Louis-Philippe's reign, was the above-mentioned Samuel F. B. Morse. In spite of his disdain for European morals, Morse had a passion for Old World culture. Because he became involved with the marquis de Lafayette's efforts to help the Polish exiles who flooded Paris in 1831, he may well have met Chopin around this time. It was not Morse's art, however, but his later invention of the telegraph that impressed the Polish musician. In a letter to his family during the summer of 1845, Chopin expressed his amazement that someone in Baltimore could order merchandise from Washington, D.C., by "the electro-magnetic telegraph" and have it in three hours' time![10]

The second most important museum in Paris during the July monarchy was housed in the Left Bank's Luxembourg palace. In it was the nation's collection of contemporary art, augmented annually by the state's purchase of new works from the most recent Salon. These, as Thackeray noted, were usually "figures of the proper heroical length and nakedness" and reflected the government's bizarre "passion for necrophilia."[11] Typical of the latter were the works of Paul Delaroche portraying the deaths of Charles I, Lady Jane Grey, Queen Elizabeth I, and the final hours of the young princes in the Tower—all examples of the era's Anglophilic tastes. Guérin's *Cain after the Death of Abel* and Delacroix's *Massacre of Scio* were other works that he cited for their obsession with death.

Throughout the Restoration and the July monarchy, the Luxembourg served as a refuge for the official "Salon painter." Such painters were derisively called *pompiers* because of the pomposity of their grandiose historical and religious works. Typically their large canvases had a slick, glossy sheen (which has been described as a "licked surface") or a piece of glass forming a barrier between the artist and his public. In time this ostentatious style of painting gave way to smaller, anecdotal portrayals of everyday life. These earthy, sentimental depictions became popular with the bourgeoisie and fitted more comfortably into their homes, which lacked the generous spaces of the aristocratic *hôtels-privés* in the faubourgs Saint-Germain and Saint Honoré. The ultimate fate of any painter in Chopin's time was never determined until his death. At that time his works either ascended from the Luxembourg into the empyrean of the Louvre or were relegated to an ignominious grave in some provincial museum. By 1850 the Luxembourg's acquisitions had ceased to reflect the current of the times, and twenty-five years later it had become a completely obsolete institution.

The Ecole des Beaux-Arts housed the city's third major art collection. Most of it consisted of lifeless imitations of classical sculpture, modeled, according to Thackeray, "half from ancient statues and half from a naked guardsman" (fig. 11.4).[12] If the collection was mediocre, the school at least had an attractive setting of courtyards and gardens within easy walking distance of the Louvre and the Luxembourg museums, where its students could view larger and better selections of art.

Each year the school's lucky winner of the annual Prix de Rome (established by Louis XIV in 1666) received the opportunity to spend two years in the culturally charged atmosphere of Rome's Villa Medici. Throughout the baroque, rococo, and Neoclassical eras, Italy was regarded as the aesthetic wellspring of true art, which it bottled and exported to the culturally arid regions of the world beyond. During the July monarchy, though, French artists found this Italian eau-de-vie less intoxicating than before. By Chopin's time the Prix de Rome seemed irrelevant to many young artists, who had seen the award fall repeatedly into the

11.4 The Ecole Royale des Beaux Arts was formed at the time of the 1789 revolution by combining the Académie de Peinture et Sculpture with that of Architecture. The building shown here, a mixture of Gothic and Renaissance styles, was begun in 1820 but not finished until 1839, eight years after Chopin arrived in Paris.

hands of undistinguished recipients. Delacroix, for example, was never judged worthy of it.

The constricted vision of the era's art establishment was further exemplified by Louis-Philippe's clumsy attempt to convert Louis XIV's palace at Versailles into a museum extolling the glories of French history (fig. 11.5). Through the exhibition of carefully selected historical paintings, he hoped to portray himself as the legitimate heir to the throne that he had recently usurped. In a symbolic effort to ensure the permanence of this self-created image, he had the paintings at Versailles built into the woodwork. History, though, could not be nailed down, and posterity has gone on to paint its own portrait of the Citizen King with features often at variance from the Versailles version. At least Louis-Philippe's restoration of the Sun-King's great palace saved it from becoming a state-run alms house and opened up one of the nation's greatest architectural treasures to

11.5 Louis-Philippe's museum of art at Versailles, with its over 4,000 paintings and nearly 1,000 sculptures, was one of the largest in France. Established more for political than artistic purposes, it was said to provide a "pleasant pastime for people who enjoyed bad art" (Louis-Désiré Véron, *Mémoires d'un Bourgeois de Paris* [Paris: Librairie Nouvelle, 1857], 4:117).

the public. To finance his magnificent obsession, the King of the French (repeatedly portrayed as an avaricious pinch-penny) lavished around 23 million francs of his own money.

"I simply must tell you that your *Medea* ... is something magnificent, superb, absolutely heartbreaking," George Sand wrote Delacroix about a painting he had exhibited at the Salon of 1838. "You are unquestionably a first-rate dauber."[13] No doubt the artist's portrayal of distraught motherhood evoked a sympathetic reverberation in the heartstrings of the novelist. Like Medea she had endured the infidelities of a philandering husband and suffered ambivalent feelings toward her two children, the one a pampered mama's boy and the other an uncontrollable little vixen. Apart from her maternal response to the subject of the painting, she appreciated it as a work of art. Calling Delacroix a "dauber" was merely Sand's playful expression of her great admiration for the artist.

Many a Parisian art critic, however, would have considered "dauber" an appropriate epithet for Delacroix, the young Romantic painter whose rough-textured canvases and splashy colors seemed intolerably crude and gaudy by Neoclassical standards. Delacroix's first Salon entries in the early 1820s generally received a harsh reception. One of the few critics who praised his work at that stage of his career was Adolphe Thiers.

The claim that Thiers was trying to win Talleyrand's favor by extolling Delacroix (supposedly the natural son of the old diplomat) has cast doubt on the sincerity of his praise. Though neither Delacroix nor Talleyrand ever acknowledged this relationship publicly, there is certainly enough circumstantial evidence to make it credible. Talleyrand, who had been a close friend of the artist's presumed father, Charles Delacroix, lived with the Delacroix family for a while in 1797. At that time M. Delacroix suffered from a gigantic thirty-pound testicular tumor, which had made him sexually inactive for many years. In light of this disability, it came as a surprise when Mme Delacroix became pregnant and delivered a son, Eugène, in April 1798. Needless to say considerable speculation ensued as to the child's paternity. Subsequently many friends noted a striking resemblance between the boy and his family's former houseguest, Prince Talleyrand. Both had a prominent lower jaw, high cheekbones, an olive complexion, and rather heavy eyelids that lent a disdainful air to their faces.

It was in the Salon of 1822 that the twenty-four-year-old Delacroix first gained public recognition with his *Bark of Dante*. Although he insisted throughout his career that he was a "pure Classicist," he was to become the leading spirit of French Romantic painting. Outside the studio, however, his tastes and behavior retained the precision, elegance, and formality of the eighteenth century. In this marked dichotomy of his private and professional personae, Delacroix closely resembled Chopin. Just as the Romantic composer relaxed by playing Bach and Mozart, so Delacroix derived endless inspiration from the works of the old Flemish and Italian masters. Although they represented the artistic avantgarde of their time, both men were products of a classical background that determined their habitual restraint in matters of religion, politics, and the social order. In spite of being professed Catholics, both viewed Christianity with the skepticism of an eighteenth-century rationalist. When it came to politics, they were just as skeptical, having strong reservations about the monarchical regime of

Louis-Philippe, and even more doubts about Republican forms of government. As for the social order, they saw in a classless society the annihilation of all cultural values and an invitation to anarchy. Through this dramatic duality, Delacroix and Chopin unwittingly fostered that favorite pastime of biographers, who love to cleave their subjects into those convenient literary fragments known as "the man" and "his work."

As for Delacroix the man, he was "a passionate dilettante, a polished sophisticate [and] a charming talker."[14] Imbued with the epidemic Anglomania of his countrymen, he was addicted to the latest London fashions and kept abreast of English literature and art. Always the gentleman, he discreetly noted in his journal his sexual conquests (of artists' models, housemaids, female cousins, and wives of friends), but never boasted of them publicly. At times he fled the *comme-il-faut* decorum of Parisian society to attend raucous costume parties and indulge in hashish highs with his Bohemian friends. Who could have suspected that within this frivolous dandy there burned what Baudelaire called the apocalyptic fire of genius?

Few today would dispute Baudelaire's assessment of Delacroix's genius, even though the youthful poet had little or no firsthand knowledge of the artist's inner self. For those privy to Delacroix's *Journal,* his irrepressible surges of libido reveal a man tormented by an ambiguous sex drive. His obsession with the female nudes who posed for him once prompted Chopin's friend the Polish countess Delphine Potocka to complain, "What is it that you artists...find so attractive in this?"[15] Contrary to appearances, Delacroix was actually a very timid lover. "My determination...vanishes when it comes to action," he confided in his journal. "When a girl does come my way...I'd give a great deal not to have to do anything: that is my real curse." [16] This curse to which Delacroix alludes seems to have been a problem with impotency, for which he consulted a physician when he was twenty-five. Later he was highly incensed when Balzac (that "chatterbox") portrayed him as the impotent painter Joseph Brideau in his Comédie Humaine.

Although Delacroix was able, with his cultivated charm, to disguise his true feelings, he was basically a misogynist. "Women," he once wrote, "are not remarkable for any great powers of imagination [but] are past-mistresses in the art of giving expression to trifles."[17] Coupled with his sense of inadequacy around women were his intense feelings of envy toward other men. He longed to have the muscular build of his nephew and later developed a fascination for daguerreotypes of male models. "Passionately...I study photographs of nude men...and I learn far more by looking at them than the inventions of any scribbler could teach me."[18]

Perhaps it was an attempt to control his inner emotions that made Delacroix cling to the eighteenth century concepts of logic and order instilled in him by his parents. Without the discipline of reason, he feared falling into the throes of dissipation, which would destroy his creativity. "The greatest genius," he once wrote, "is simply a superlatively rational human-being."[19] Through reason he hoped to control not only the sexual but also the "savage" aspects of his personality. His frequent forays into society often served to awaken the pent-up hostility within him. For example, he couldn't stand the ubiquitous presence of the middle class, which pervaded the bourgeois-dominated world of Orleanist France. Vandam, an English expatriate of the period, once commented that only Flaubert despised the bourgeoisie more than Delacroix did. The artist was even more appalled by the rowdy crowds of ill-bred Republicans who gathered in George Sand's smoke-filled apartment in the square d'Orléans. At least there he could retreat with Chopin to a quiet side-room for a cozy tête-à-tête.

Often those emotions that Delacroix couldn't acknowledge to himself (much less display to the world) found release in the Romanticism of his works. Characteristic of the "savage" element of his personality, many of his paintings deal with sensuous or violent themes. Repeatedly critics condemned his works for the brutality of their subject matter and the disorderliness of their composition. Later, after his "baptism of light" in Morocco, one such critic noted that while the painter now had sun in his head, he still had storms in his heart. This was particularly evident to Baudelaire, who declared that "everything in his work is only desolation, massacres, conflagrations.... Cities smoking and in flames, slaughtered victims, raped women, even children hurled under horses' hooves or cringing under the dagger of delirious mothers."[20] As one unsympathetic Classicist put it, "Delacroix is not the leader of a school; he is the leader of a riot."[21]

Strangely enough, the artist himself was one of the most outspoken critics of the excess and disorder that pervaded the Romantic movement not only in art, but in literature and music as well. Balzac, for example, he found guilty of "muddle [and] minuteness,"[22] while Dumas seemed to him disorganized with no "strong sense of unity."[23] As for George Sand, Delacroix believed that she suffered from excessive idealism and was always getting carried away by vague social theories she had neither analyzed nor assimilated. In the field of music (which he considered "higher than the other arts"), Delacroix could never tolerate the "appalling din" and "heroic hotch-potch" of Berlioz's music, declared Meyerbeer's operas "monstrous," and simply refused to sit through those of Verdi. Although he found Chopin "an enchanting talent," Delacroix's two favorite composers were Cimarosa and Mozart (oddly enough, in just that order).[24] Despite paying lip service to the role of reason in the arts, Delacroix never formally organized his thoughts on the subject. Like Chopin's rough sketches for a *Piano Method,* Delacroix's proposed *Dictionary of Art* was never completed. It is nevertheless apparent from both his work and his written observations that the use of color preoccupied him more than anything else. In his journal he dwells on the use of color continually, relegating line, perspective, and subject matter to a secondary level. Had he not been such a skilled draughtsman, Serullaz speculates that Delacroix might well have crossed the boundary into Impressionism.

As it was, his habit of constantly retouching his works prevented Delacroix from achieving the vaporous spontaneity of Impressionist canvases. Chopin, he noted, was also guilty of excessive revisions. His improvisations "were far more daring than his finished compositions," he argued.[25] Chopin, though, was well aware of this danger, and unlike Delacroix he usually returned to his original conception of a work after endless abortive efforts to "improve" it.

If at times Delacroix showed a subliminal drift toward Impressionism, he was repelled by the aesthetic values of the Realists. Although he found some redeemable qualities in Gustave Courbet, he was less sympathetic to Jean-François Millet, whose combination of peasant piety and rabid Republicanism annoyed him: "He belongs to that... crew of bearded artists who made the revolution of 1848,... thinking... it would bring equality of talent as well as equality of wealth."[26] At the time Delacroix wrote this, he was fifty-five and becoming more and more misanthropic with age. No doubt this dour tendency was aggravated by the Academy's repeated rejection of his candidacy. Not until 1857 was he finally admitted into the hallowed company of France's "immortals." Even during his youth, Delacroix had always been a very introspective person, despite his dandified exterior. Except for the solace of Jenny Le Guillou, his devoted housekeeper, lover, and companion, the artist had few real intimates. Outstanding among them was Chopin. Both men, despite an addiction to the gregarious world of the Parisian salons, shared their innermost lives with only a handful of confidants.

Although it is easy enough to comprehend Delacroix's affinity for Chopin, his longstanding friendship with the nonconformist, socialist-oriented George Sand remains a bit enigmatical. It began in November 1834 when François Buloz, editor of the *Revue des Deux Mondes*, sent the thirty-year-old authoress to the painter for a portrait to publicize her journal articles and recent novels. Unfortunately Buloz gave the portrait to an engraver who altered it and then published it as his own. Irate at first (with both Buloz and Sand), Delacroix seemed once more on amicable terms with the novelist when Chopin invited the two of them to a soirée at his Chaussée d'Antin apartment in December 1836. By the summer of 1838 Sand and Chopin had become lovers, and after their return from Majorca the next year, Delacroix frequented Mme Sand's salon in the rue Pigalle, where he often encountered Chopin. On the walls of her apartment, Sand hung many of Delacroix's paintings, which both she and her son, Maurice, admired so much that the boy later became a pupil of the artist.

One of Delacroix's greatest pleasures at Mme Sand's was the chance to chat with Chopin and hear him play. For the most part their conversations concerned their tailors and boot-makers or the scruffy appearance and coarse behavior of George's motley guests. Because Delacroix himself was a musician, he could readily appreciate Chopin's performance of his unique compositions on George's Pleyel grand. Once in April 1841, when the pianist was scheduled to give a concert at Pleyel's rooms, Delacroix left his sick bed to drive the pianist to the concert hall.

On three occasions Delacroix visited Sand and Chopin at Nohant, George's chateau south of Paris. "It is most pleasant here," he wrote, "and the hosts couldn't be more gracious in entertaining me. When we are not all together at dinner, lunch, playing billiards or walking, each of us stays in his room, reading or lounging around on a couch. Sometimes, through the window which opens on to the garden, a gust of music wafts up from Chopin at work. All this mingles with the songs of nightingales and the fragrance of roses."[27] He especially enjoyed his long conversations with Chopin: "He is a man of rare distinction, the most genuine artist I have ever met. He is one of the few whom one can admire and respect."[28]

Although Chopin was equally delighted with Delacroix's company, he could never appreciate his creative genius. As Mme Sand observed, her lover was a musician and only a musician, with little feeling for the other arts. Painting and sculpture were beyond his comprehension; even the works of such great masters as Michelangelo and Rubens perplexed him more than they pleased him. The only contemporary artist that he seemed to like was Delacroix's bête noire, Jean-Auguste-Dominique Ingres. When confronted with the vigorous color and exuberant action of Delacroix's canvases, Chopin seemed at a loss for words. One can imagine how the musician's painful silences must have hurt Delacroix when he took him to view his newly painted ceiling in the Chamber of Peers' library at the Luxembourg palace in 1847. As for Delacroix's appreciation of Chopin's compositions, it must be remembered that in music as in all other things, the painter preferred the past to the present. Once, following a performance of Mozart's "lovely symphony in C" at the home of Chopin's pupil, Princess Marcelline Czartoryska, Delacroix remarked, "Poor Chopin, you realize his weaknesses after hearing something like this."[29]

On his second visit to Nohant in 1843, Delacroix praised George Sand's idea of dedicating her novel, *La Mare au Diable,* to Chopin. For some reason, though, she changed her mind.[30] In 1846, when Delacroix returned to Nohant for the third and last time, he left abruptly out of disgust at the offensive way that George and her son were treating Chopin. By the following summer, his friends' nine-year liaison had come to an end.

When a puffy-faced Chopin returned from England in the fall of 1848, he was in the final stages of tuberculosis, gasping and hobbling along on swollen feet. To allay the boredom of his confinement, Delacroix often took him for long drives around the city. In October 1849, while the artist was visiting relatives in the provinces, he learned of Chopin's death. "Strangely enough, I had a presentiment of it before I got up this morning," he claimed. "What a loss he will be! What miserable rascals are left to clutter the earth, yet that fine soul is extinguished!"[31]

Later that month, following Chopin's funeral in the church of the Madeleine, Delacroix served as one of the pallbearers at his interment in the cemetery of Père Lachaise. Ironically the sculptor selected to create the monument for Chopin's grave was George Sand's boorish son-in-law, Jean-Baptiste Auguste Clésinger, whom neither Chopin nor Delacroix could tolerate. Yet when the latter saw Clésinger's tribute to the dead musician (a languid female bent over in a saccharine portrayal of grief), he made the astonishing remark, "I thought it entirely satisfactory; I feel that I should probably have done something of the kind myself."[32]

While still a youth, Delacroix had experimented with the recent German technique of lithography, producing a series on Goethe's *Faust* and a number of works inspired by Shakespeare's dramas. The man most responsible for raising the new innovation to the level of an art, however, did so more for political and financial ends than for aesthetic ones. This man, Honoré Daumier, had arrived in

11.6 Honoré Daumier is remembered today chiefly as a journalistic artist specializing in lithographic cartoons that lampooned almost every aspect of Parisian life in his time. Born into a modest background, he grew up with modest aspirations that perhaps kept him from exploiting his full artistic potential. His paintings especially and the few sculptures he created reveal a more profound and sensitive artist than is generally suspected.

Paris from the provinces at an early age (fig. 11.6). His initial efforts as a sign painter there offered little promise of a career in the arts. During the revolution of 1830, he fought alongside the working-class rebels, which left him with a life-long saber scar across his face and an implacable antipathy toward the new king, Louis-Philippe.

Among the most vocal of the government's opposition (to which Daumier belonged) was Charles Philipon, who, in 1830, founded one of Paris's first anti-Orleanist journals, *La Caricature*. In its quiver were two arrows of attack: the written word and the lithographic picture. By then lithography was already an established industry in Paris, the first lithographic press having begun operation there as early as 1802. *La Caricature*, which came out weekly, featured two lithographs per issue, frequently chosen more for their political message than for their aesthetic merit. In 1831 Daumier became part of its staff. There he collaborated with Balzac, illustrating the author's works, which Philipon published anonymously. The real-life drama of politics, however, interested Daumier more than did the fictional world of the novelist. A staunch opponent of the Orleanist regime, he adopted Philipon's satirical portrayal of Louis-Philippe as a pear.[33] This depiction of the king carried a special barb since the French word for pear (*poire*) also happened to mean "fool" or "dunce" in the vernacular.

These attacks on the Orleanist regime were soon intensified by the government's failure to fulfill its promises of a free press. In *La Caricature*'s brief lifespan (1830–34), its presses were seized no fewer than twenty-eight times, and its staff was repeatedly imprisoned. The July monarchy's concept of political liberty lacked the English throne's acceptance of "His Majesty's loyal opposition." The art of caricature (which thrived across the Channel with such formidable exponents as Hogarth, Rowlandson, Gillray, and Cruikshank) represented a serious threat to the timorous "Poire," who sat on an insecure throne twice snatched from under the royal derrières of his Bourbon cousins. In 1832 Daumier was sentenced to six months in the prison of Sainte-Pélagie for his representation of Louis-Philippe as a fat-bellied Gargantua greedily devouring the wealth of the nation. Because his notoriety as a caricaturist brought him a plague of visitors eager to have their portraits sketched, he complained of mental exhaustion and was allowed to pass the rest of his sentence in the peaceful surroundings of Dr. Pinel's suburban asylum at Chaillot.

On his return to *La Caricature*, Daumier again armed himself with crayon and lithographic stone to besiege the embattled "Poire." His greatest victory in these recurrent skirmishes came in 1834, when he portrayed the government's slaughter of innocent victims during a dispute with striking workers in Lyon and Paris. The lithograph, entitled "Massacre in the rue Transnonain" (a street in one of Paris's working-class neighborhoods) represented an artistic as well as political triumph for the twenty-six-year-old Daumier.

Although Daumier's prints usually spoke for themselves, most were given subcaptions by Philipon or other editors at the journal. In many cases, the topical nature of these written addenda detract from the universality of Daumier's message, which often seems as relevant today as it was to Orleanist France over a century and a half ago.

Encouraged by the early success of *La Caricature*, Philipon started a second journal, *Le Charivari*, in December 1832. Its purpose and format were similar to *La Caricature*'s, and its publication gave Philipon an additional outlet for his assaults on the government. The near-assassination of Louis-Philippe in July 1835 by the anarchist Fieschi led to the enactment of the so-called September Laws, which severely curtailed freedom of the press in France. As a result, *La Caricature* had to close down, while *Le Charivari* managed to carry on as a journal of social rather than political satire. From then until the overthrow of the Orleanist government in February 1848, Daumier produced no further political cartoons.

His art, however, remained as popular as ever, and it was at this time that he began to create his most brilliant series of lithographic commentaries on the bourgeois society of the era. Through a combination of his critical eye and sharp wit, these satirical works present the pretentious materialism of a self-serving middle class struggling for culture, social position, and above all, riches. By inflicting his barbed humor on the bourgeoisie, Daumier was indirectly able to continue his attacks on Louis-Philippe and the Orleanist regime. It was, after all, the petite bourgeoisie that constituted the bulk of the National Guard and maintained the law and order of the realm, while the haute bourgeoisie supplied virtually all of the government's administrative and diplomatic staff. Together these two components of the middle class formed the greater part of the *juste milieu* on which the July monarchy's power rested. In his portrayal of these social groups, Daumier betrayed mixed feelings. As much as he abhorred the unscrupulous tactics of the upper middle class, he couldn't help but empathize with the plight of the lower middle class, who were often victims of the very regime they supported.

Charivari's shift from political to social issues probably explains Chopin's later fascination with the periodical, which he read regularly. He even had it sent to him each summer when he was away at George Sand's country estate. No doubt its humor appealed to him. As a schoolboy, Chopin and a friend once edited an amateurish journal with a satirical bent called the *Szafarnia Courrier*. Whether or not he ever grasped the ideological message in *Charivari*'s biting wit, Chopin intuitively shared its sense of superiority over the middle class it derided.

As an observer and recorder of the bourgeoisie, Daumier has often been compared to Balzac, and his lithographic oeuvre is frequently cited as the visual equivalent of the latter's *Human Comedy*. Certainly Balzac had the highest regard for Daumier's work, claiming once that the artist had "Michelangelo in his bones."[34] Undoubtedly the most famous of the four thousand or more lithographs that Daumier completed in his lifetime is the series on the rakish Robert Macaire, with his "dandified rags and airs" and his mealymouthed pronouncements, which epitomized all the "cant, knavery, quackery, humbug," and greed of an increasingly powerful bourgeois society.[35] Bertrand, his inseparable sidekick, was portrayed as equally unprincipled, although not as bold or clever as his master. The character of Macaire (as noted in Chapter 10) had been derived from the sleazy trickster created by Frederick Lemaître on the vaudeville stage some years before.

For the most part Daumier leveled his sights at types rather than individuals, assailing his fellow Parisians with a pungent humor in such series as *Parisian Types, Parisian Emotions, Parisian Bohemians,* and one entitled simply *The Parisians.* Many critics regard his best collection of prints to be *The Good Bourgeoisie,* a subject dear to his heart and certainly one with which he was intimately acquainted. It was for the professional classes of the upper bourgeoisie, however, particularly doctors and lawyers, that Daumier reserved his harshest attacks. In his eyes, the medical field was full of charlatans, while lawyers practiced nothing but greed and deception. Only the petite bourgeoisie and the working classes, he felt, still adhered to the revolutionary goals of liberty, equality, and fraternity. If to amuse his public Daumier portrayed many of the petite bourgeoisie as smug, narrow-minded, bumbling, and naive, he still respected the values they represented.

Although Daumier was probably the most popular of the era's journalistic artists, he often found himself forced to take work wherever he could find it. Fortunately the increasing popularity of lithography spawned a number of new pictorial journals like *Le Magasin Pittoresque, L'Illustration,* and *Le Monde Illustré,* which fostered a new school of artists who were primarily illustrators. To compete with these new periodicals, book publishers began to fill their novels with lithographic pictures in place of the single copper engraving that previously served as the traditional frontispiece.

Because illustrators were obliged to conform to the wishes of both author and publisher, their freedom of expression was restricted. As a result, some of the era's best talents were discouraged from entering the field. Among the finest of these early illustrators were Tony Johannot (who supplied many of the lithographs for George Sand's novels), Henri Monnier, and Gavarni.[36] Eventually, though, Mme Sand replaced Johannot's services with those of her son, Maurice, who, though not a particularly inspired artist, proved adequate for the job. Like Sand, most of her colleagues seemed content with second-rate illustrators whose work didn't outshine their own.

One of the major drawbacks to journalistic art was the need to meet deadlines. Delacroix, for instance, could take years—almost a decade at times—to complete a project, compared to Daumier who often had to dash off a sketch only minutes before press time. Working under such pressure encouraged spontaneity and precluded the possibility of those excessive revisions that Delacroix found so detrimental to the effect of a finished work.

With the outbreak of the 1848 revolution, Daumier diverted his energies to the support of the new republic. When he wasn't promoting universal suffrage and freedom of the press, he tried his hand at painting in the hope of becoming a "serious" artist. In his early works, the influence of Delacroix, as well as members of the Barbizon School such as Corot, Rousseau, and Millet, is conspicuous. From 1849 to 1853, he submitted several of his paintings to the Salon without arousing significant notice.

Unfortunately Daumier's efforts in these more "serious" genres failed to sustain him financially, and he was forced to continue his cartoons for *Charivari*. As he grew older, his waning eyesight led to increasing loss of detail in his illustrations. The spare, stark character of his later figures gave them a symbolic, quasi-allegorical character. In his paintings the progressive lack of definition, combined with sharp contrasts of light and darkness, produced an impressionistic effect that was admired by younger artists like Degas and Renoir.

Daumier's fame, however, will always rest chiefly on his lithographs. Although a number of his contemporaries like Géricault, Delacroix, Goya, and Manet occasionally delved into the medium, it was Daumier who pioneered the use of lithography in journalism. By the end of the nineteenth century, photographs had supplanted lithographs as the principal form of newspaper illustration. Today, though, chromolithography (which adds color to the original process) still survives as an art form in itself and a commercial vehicle popular in the production of posters.

In 1839, midway through Louis-Philippe's reign, Romanticism still dominated the social and artistic tastes of Parisians. But in political and economic affairs, the new journalistic art of the daily newspapers was exerting more and more influence over the populace. Direct, simplistic, and informative, the lithograph was well suited to the hard-nosed bourgeoisie, who eyed the trends of the times to be sure they were reaping their full share of a prosperous economy. Men like Daumier who pioneered this infant art form are often acclaimed as the forerunners of Realism, although it seems a patent contradiction to call any cartoonist a realist. While the message of a cartoon may be realistic, its sketchy style, pictorial coding, and emphasis on caricature are anything but realistic. In 1839 the word "réalisme" didn't even exist in the vocabulary of the Parisian art world. Courbet, who is generally acknowledged to be the first of the French realists, had only just arrived in Paris that year, and far from generating an artistic revolution, spent his time copying old masterworks in the Louvre. Meanwhile, directly across the river from the Louvre, members of the Academy were learning of a new invention able to reproduce the external world with greater accuracy than any future Realist could ever hope to do.

At 3:00 P.M. on August 19, 1839, in the Institute's Collège Mazarin, the astronomer François Arago presented the scientific findings of Louis Jacques Mandé Daguerre and his late colleague, Joseph Nicéphore Niepce, to a joint ses-

11.7 An 1844 photograph of Daguerre taken at the height of his notoriety, just five years after the presentation of his scientific findings to the French Academy.

sion of the Academies of Science and Fine Arts (fig. 11.7). The process that these two men had been working on for over twenty years was capable of taking images captured by the centuries-old camera obscura and fixing them in a permanent form on silver-coated copper plates. The result, called a daguerreotype, bore many features similar to our present-day photographs. Over a hundred and fifty years later, the ability to produce such images (whether on metal, lithographic stones, paper, or collodion negatives) was to be hailed as "the most significant event of the nineteenth century." Indeed, "Daguerre altered the world more utterly than Marx and changed our view of man more radically than Darwin. The information provided by photography in conventional photographs, film, television and now in computer images has revolutionized the world like no social or scientific reformer might have dreamed possible!"[37]

At first glance this statement appears to be an extravagant piece of hype by some zealous photography buff, and yet it takes only a cursory look around us today to realize that its sweeping claims are, in fact, justified. The impact of computer technology (a scientific offshoot of early photography) on the social, political, scientific, industrial, commercial, and artistic life of today's world is truly unprecedented.

Little of this potential could possibly have been foreseen by Daguerre, whose place in history owes more to his bourgeois entrepreneurial instincts than any great intelligence or vision. So limited was his educational background that he couldn't bring himself to speak in front of the Academy for fear of embarrassment, and therefore delegated the presentation of his research to the Institute's permanent secretary, François Arago. Daguerre has been described as a second-rate artist, amateur scientist, and aggressive opportunist who had no qualms about cheating Niepce of the full credit due him. Not only did Daguerre benefit financially from the French government's purchase of his process, he also shrewdly invested in the work of his English competitor, William Henry Fox Talbot, which earned him handsome dividends for years to come. Such an economic genius was certainly worthy of being immortalized by Balzac, who perhaps excluded him from his *Human Comedy* out of pure envy.

Because Daguerre so skillfully manipulated the public, the Academy, and even historians, he is regarded by most people today as the "inventor" of photography. The truth is, his daguerreotypes (which, despite their name, owe more to Niepce than to him) were only popular for about twenty years. While they created a picture with much finer detail than other contemporary techniques, they were expensive and not reproducible. Furthermore the early images came out reversed, a defect that was later corrected by the addition of a mirror or a second lens in the camera. Despite Daguerre's blustery promotion of his (and Niepce's) invention, it was the techniques of Talbot and Archer in England that became the direct forerunners of today's photographs, dooming the daguerreotype to extinction.

What first interested Daguerre in his early exploration of photography were the possible artistic implications of the new technique. Since the age of thirteen, when he became an architect's assistant, he spent most of his life dabbling in various branches of the arts. By the age of seventeen, he had become bored with the tedious work of a draftsman and sought greater stimulation in painting. As early as 1814, his canvasses were being accepted by the Salon. His Romantic masterpiece, *Holyrood Chapel by Moonlight,* won such acclaim that he was rewarded with the Legion of Honor. In addition he studied stage design at the Opéra and later, through the ingenious use of gas lighting, achieved a spectacular tour de force at one of the boulevard theaters by showing Mount Etna erupting. Over the next few years his talent as a scenic designer earned him positions at the Opéra, the Opéra-Comique, and the Comédie-Française. His sets, as a rule, were intensely Romantic, replete with "misty landscapes, nocturnal effects, awesome scenes of nature and stately ruins."[38]

In 1822 Daguerre opened his first Diorama, a theater that created visual illusions by a sophisticated sleight-of-hand using paintings, gauze scrims, and lighting effects. Viewers sat on a revolving platform that added the dimension of movement to those of time and space, thereby enhancing the illusion of reality. The press gave the new phenomenon such rave reviews that an excited Delacroix wrote a friend, "I am dying to see this diorama with you. The newspapers claim it is something quite astonishing."[39] At that time Daguerre's establishment was located north of the boulevard Saint-Martin near an English-styled "pleasure garden" called the Wauxhall, where Chopin performed on two occasions. In the fall of 1831, at the time of Chopin's arrival in Paris, the Diorama was featuring a dramatic portrayal of the previous year's July revolution. Performances began at 11:00 A.M. and lasted until 4:00 P.M. They utilized direct and reflected light to simulate transitions from day to night with such realism that some of the audiences threw coins or wads of paper at the images to test their authenticity. That same year the Opéra used Daguerre's techniques in its production of Meyerbeer's *Robert le Diable*, creating what Chopin described as a "diorama in which one sees the interior of a church illuminated as at Christmas or Easter."[40] The effect overwhelmed him. Later Daguerre added sound effects such as falling water, claps of thunder, and the lowing of cattle. At times he even went so far as to place live animals on the stage, fooling the spectators into believing the beasts were merely another illusion created by his magic. In no time Daguerre's visual extravaganzas had spread to London, Liverpool, Berlin, Stockholm, New York, and other cities, where they aroused as much incredulity as in Paris.

Despite the phenomenal success of his Diorama, Daguerre's interest in it began to fade as he spent more and more time researching ways to convert the camera obscura's transient images to a permanent form. Earlier, in 1824, Niepce had already managed to do just that on a lithographic stone. Although the result was blurred and disappointing, it proved to be the world's first photograph. He called this and his later pictures on light-sensitive, asphalt-coated pewter plates "sun pictures" or heliographs. In 1829, Niepce, desperate for funds, formed a partnership with Daguerre that led to further improvements in his technique. Two years later, after Niepce's death, Daguerre accidentally found that an exposed plate discarded in a cabinet of old chemicals bore a distinct image the next day. The cause, it appeared, was mercury fumes from a broken thermometer. Thanks to this serendipitous discovery, the exposure time of a photograph was reduced from eight hours to thirty minutes. By trial and error, Daguerre

11.8 This early daguerreotype of Paris (ca. 1840) produced a reversed image that must be held up to a mirror to be corrected. For example, in this view of the place de la Concorde, the dome of Notre-Dame de l'Assomption appears in the left background rather than on the right. Later cameras corrected this defect with a mirror or a second lens that restored the proper perspective.

(who had no background in chemistry) stumbled on to a fixing solution of sodium thiosulfate, which made the image from the mercury fumes last indefinitely. On the basis of these accidental discoveries, Daguerre justified himself in calling the end product a "daguerreotype" with the implication that he was its sole inventor (fig. 11.8).

In the scientific world, the first daguerreotypes aroused great enthusiasm and prompted distinguished men like Louis-Joseph Gay-Lussac to encourage the government's support of the new process. Among artists, however, the response to the new phenomenon was mixed. Some, like the painter Paul Delaroche, felt threatened by this machine-made art and prophesied that henceforth painting was dead. Delacroix, on the other hand, regarded photography as a great boon to artists, for whom it provided detailed material to study and copy. His only regret was that this marvelous invention had arrived so late in his life. Among the first works he painted from daguerreotypes were his Odalisques. The money he saved by not paying a live model especially pleased him. Later he found photographs invaluable as a means of analyzing masterpieces that he could not view directly. Along with a vast number of fellow Parisians, Delacroix posed for his own photograph and even tried using a camera himself. At the same time he was conscious of photography's limitations. After all, the camera could only reproduce. It lacked the artist's gift of creativity to penetrate beneath the surface and distill the hidden essence of his subject matter.

In *Charivari*, Daumier satirized the time and effort it took to produce a single photograph. "Patience is the virtue of asses" one of his captions read, with a warning to the reader that every successful photograph required the assistance of at least two mechanics, three chemists, and a minimum of four scientists—plus the inventor himself. For poetic souls like Lamartine, the fact that the daguerreotype required a collaboration between the artist and the sun proved there was something divine about it. By contrast, Baudelaire called the daguerreotype a "trivial image on a scrap of metal" and pronounced photography "the refuge of failed painters with too little talent."[41]

Despite Baudelaire's denunciations, photography had circled the globe by the middle of the century. In Cairo, Damascus, Peking, and Rio de Janeiro, people flocked to their local photographer for a picture despite the discomfort it entailed. Even after improved techniques had reduced exposure times to a mere fifteen minutes, the immobility of the subject still had to be assured by placing his head in a metal brace while he stared relentlessly into a camera with the painful glare of sunlight in his eyes. The glazed look of those who survived the ordeal reflects the misery they suffered. Their funereal faces made Ralph Waldo Emerson comment that many looked as if they had been photographed in a casket.

What the poser had to endure, though, was minor compared to the price that photographers paid for their art. The earliest cameras (with their numerous accessories) weighed well over a hundred pounds. It was difficult enough just moving all this avoirdupois around Paris; to transport it across the sands of Egypt or the jungles of Brazil required enormous dedication and physical strength. Worse yet was the peril to the photographer's health from the poisonous chemicals with which he worked. To process a daguerreotype plate meant hours of confinement in small, closed rooms filled with the toxic fumes of chlorine or bromine. The mercury coating on the copper plate was also toxic, as was

11.9 A nude model poses for an *académie*, that is, an erotic picture. These products were to create a thriving business from Chopin's day to this.

the potassium cyanide used to remove oxidation marks on the plates. The earliest symptoms of such exposures, "fits of shyness and anxiety," were soon followed by "difficulties in speaking and moving." Eventually those who persisted in their careers experienced delirium, hallucinations, tremors, loss of teeth, deafness, blindness, and even death from kidney failure.[42]

Many a libidinous Parisian, though, was willing to risk the hazards of photography for the enticements it offered in the blossoming field of erotic art. The production of those "dirty pictures" that street vendors have long hawked to tourists up and down the boulevards and along the slopes of Montmartre became a thriving business in the earliest years of photography. By 1841 the female nude was a favorite subject of Parisian photographers. Most of their models were working-class grisettes, along with those *filles de joie* who "worked" the streets. The establishments engaged in this trade, as well as the pictures they produced, were euphemistically referred to as "académies" (fig. 11.9). Seductive poses, strategically placed mirrors, bordello-like backgrounds, and crude attempts at sexual symbolism (like the "phallic" wine bottle) abounded in these explicit productions. The long exposure times, however, often produced frozen faces with glum expressions that made sex look like a grueling ordeal. Still the popularity of these "académies" was so great that they became a major export to countries all over the world. Photographs of male nudes, like those that attracted Delacroix, were far

11.10 The only confirmed photograph of
Chopin, taken in 1849, the year of his death.
His puffy face and pained expression reflect
the ravages of tuberculosis in its late stages.

less common and presumably were intended to serve purely as anatomical studies.
Often they were surrounded by Greek columns and Arcadian landscapes to give
them a semblance of classical art and to avert any suspicion of salacious intent.

Although portrait studios and the production of erotica represent two of the
earliest commercial applications of photography, by far the greatest number of
early photographers were amateurs as eager then as now to record the people,
places, and events of their daily lives. In November 1840 Louis Viardot, director
of the Théâtre des Italiens, showed off his costly photographic apparatus to
friends (including Chopin and Delacroix) at a party given by George Sand.
Apparently Chopin wasn't terribly impressed as he didn't bother to sit for a photograph until nine years later, just before his death (fig. 11.10).[43]

In time photographs came to be accepted in the annual Salons as a recognized
form of art. Many early photographers who had originally been painters hoped
to develop this potential of the new camera. Daguerre and Hippolyte Bayard
were among the first to group objects into pleasing still lifes. Others quickly followed, using the camera to achieve aesthetic effects unforeseen by the early pioneers of photography.

Far from fulfilling Delaroche's dire prophecy, photography did not destroy the art of painting. On the contrary, it enriched the artists' world with a wealth of new techniques and directions. Instead of trading their brushes for cameras, the Realist painters of the period continued to paint, using photographs as a sort of data bank from which they could withdraw bits and pieces of reality as they liked. Later, as a reaction to the literal reportage of photography, Impressionist and Abstract painters began to draw on subjective perceptions as their principal source of subject matter rather than merely reproducing the external world. By the twentieth century, artists had learned to use the camera itself to create impressionistic and abstract effects. Today artists employ computer imaging to design fabric, wallpaper, and industrial products while plastic surgeons, with the same technique, program new faces for their patients that they later sculpt in the flesh with scalpels and lasers.

In photography science and art have truly merged and, contrary to Gautier's theory of Art for Art's sake, it is now possible to combine the beautiful and the useful—all because of that memorable day when the first photographer (be he Daguerre, Niepce, Talbot, or Bayard) learned how "to seize the light."

CHAPTER 12

"A Votre Santé!"

Coping with Poultices, Purges, and the Parisian Medical Profession

"*LEAVE ME ALONE. LET ME DIE,*" Chopin told Dr. Cruveilhier on the evening of October 16, 1849.[1] Among the family and friends who surrounded his deathbed was Charles Gavard, the brother of one of his pupils. Shortly after midnight, Gavard noted that the musician's breathing seemed to cease. Dr. Cruveilhier "took a candle and, holding it before Chopin's face, which had become quite black from suffocation, remarked to us that the senses had already ceased to act (fig. 12.1). But when he asked Chopin whether he suffered, we heard, still quite distinctly, the answer, 'No longer' *[Plus]*. This was the last word I heard from his lips. He died painlessly between three and four in the morning."[2]

Not only at the time of his death but throughout the eighteen years that he lived in Paris, Chopin found himself in close contact with the city's medical profession. It was, in fact, a physician to whom he owed his introduction to the Parisian musical world on his arrival there in the fall of 1831. During the previous year while in Vienna, Chopin had come to know Dr. Johann Malfatti and his Polish wife, the countess Helena Ostrowska, whose musical salon was one of the most renowned in the Austrian capital. Malfatti, who served as physician to the imperial family, had earlier attended Beethoven toward the end of his life. Among the doctor's Parisian friends was a fellow-Italian, Ferdinando Paër, director of music for the court of the French king, Louis-Philippe. As a favor to Malfatti, Paër took Chopin under his wing and helped him establish legal residence in Paris. He also introduced him to another Italian, Luigi Cherubini, head of the Paris conservatory, through whom the young man met many of the city's finest musicians. Because Paër, like Rossini, was in great demand as an accompanist in the Parisian salons, he also provided Chopin an entrée into the social whirl of the capital. On the Right Bank, the court director was a familiar figure in Lady Granville's drawing room at the English embassy and equally popular as a performer in the Left Bank musicales of the dapper Dr. Orfila, professor of chemistry at the Ecole de Médecine (fig. 12.2).[3]

12.1 A portrait of Dr. Jean Cruveilhier, whom an American doctor in Paris described as a "man of singularly mild and gentle manners...[who] possesses a countenance beaming with intelligence and kindness" (F. Campbell Stewart, *The Hospitals and Surgeons of Paris* [New York: Langley, 1843], 39).

12.2 Dr. Matheo-José-Bonaventure Orfila, professor of anatomy (shown here), and the American-born venerealogist Dr. Philippe Ricord were not only prominent physicians on the faculty of the Paris medical school but also great music lovers. Gala evenings in their salons were frequented by Rossini, Paër, and the leading singers of Paris's Théâtre des Italiens.

During Chopin's first few weeks in Paris, the twenty-one-year-old youth enjoyed unusually good health and gadded about the city with frenetic energy. The only illness that afflicted him then was one he aptly diagnosed as "consumption of the wallet."[4] Inevitably, though, he happened on one of "those miserable young girls" of the Parisian streets who "chase after the passersby." (They were, as he put it, like singers who always "want to perform duets.")[5] After an unfortunate encounter with one such *fille des rues* named Thérèse, Chopin was left with a "memory" (interpreted by some biographers as venereal disease) that discouraged him from any further attempts at "tasting forbidden fruit."[6]

Although Chopin's father repeatedly cautioned his son to look after his finances and his health, his advice generally went unheeded. The temptations of the opera, concert hall, and theater, not to mention the innumerable soirées to which the elegant newcomer was invited, kept him on an exhausting social tread-mill that soon aggravated both the consumption of his wallet and that of his lungs.[7] In June 1833, Chopin moved into an expensive apartment on the fashion-able Chaussée d'Antin, where he was forced to share the rent with a roommate, Dr. Alexander Hoffman, the physician-son of a professor at the University of Warsaw, where Chopin's father taught. Although this arrangement relieved the strain on his wallet, it did nothing to slow the fast pace of his night life. "I don't object to your seeking diversion by frequenting the salons of the best society," his father wrote him in December of that year, "I only fear that too many long evenings will deprive you of the rest you need."[8]

As it turned out, Dr. Hoffman didn't prove to be a very satisfactory compan-ion. For one thing, he smoked. Certainly this habit was not unusual in a sophisti-cated city like Paris, where cigarettes had become so popular that puffing on a "Maryland" was considered the very height of chic. For those who could afford it, separate rooms were set aside solely for smoking, while the more fastidous even kept a special wardrobe to be used when smoking. Such practices, however, were the exception, and neither Dr. Hoffman nor Chopin's later companion, George Sand, bothered to observe these social niceties. What the musician toler-ated in his mistress, though, he objected to in his roommate, whom he finally asked to move out. In all probability the real explanation for Chopin's desire to get rid of Hoffmann had to do with the doctor's prying eyes, which often noted that one of his pupils, the Polish countess Delphine Potocka, often lingered in the apartment after her lesson, sometimes until the next morning. For half a century or so this liaison between Chopin and Mme Potocka remained a well-guarded secret until it was finally disclosed by Hoffmann's widow, née Emilia Borzęcka, who was herself one of Chopin's Polish piano students.

After Dr. Hoffman's departure, Chopin's chronic insolvency forced him to take in another tenant, Jan Matuszyński, a former schoolmate from Warsaw who had studied medicine briefly in Germany before transferring to the Ecole de Médecine in Paris (fig. 12.3). "I am living with him [Chopin] at No. 5 rue de la Chaussée d'Antin," Matuszyński wrote his brother-in-law during the fall of 1834. "This street is a little far from the medical school and the hospitals but I have strong reasons for staying with him—he means everything to me."[9] Chopin's father had great respect for Matuszyński and was pleased to hear of the arrangement. He hoped that the young medical student would provide a sobering influence on his son, who had fallen into a sybaritic lifestyle—and for a time this

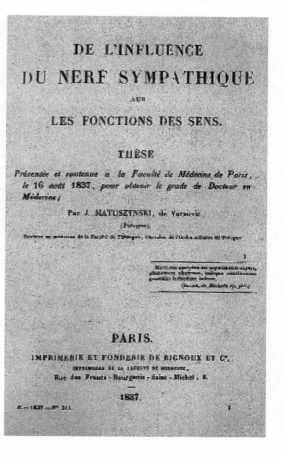

DE L'INFLUENCE
DU NERF SYMPATHIQUE
SUR
LES FONCTIONS DES SENS.

THÈSE

Présentée et soutenue à la Faculté de Médecine de Paris,
le 16 août 1837, pour obtenir le grade de Docteur en
Médecine;

Par J. MATUSZYNSKI, de Varsovie
(Pologne).

PARIS.
IMPRIMERIE ET FONDERIE DE RIGNOUX ET Cⁱᵉ,
Rue des Francs-Bourgeois-Saint-Michel, 8.

1837.

12.3 In 1837 Chopin's childhood friend and Paris roommate Jan Matuszyński completed his doctoral thesis at the Ecole de Médecine in Paris. It was entitled "On the Influence of the Sympathetic Nervous System on the Functions of the Senses." He died only five years later of tuberculosis in Chopin's and Sand's rue Pigalle quarters.

appeared to be the case. "We spend our evenings at the theater or calling on friends when we are not passing a quiet evening at home amusing ourselves," Matuszyński told his family.[10] The young doctor's early death from tuberculosis in April 1842 devastated Chopin, possibly because he foresaw in it a glimpse of his own fate. Earlier that year the musician had moved his dying friend into the little pavilions he shared with George Sand at No. 16 rue Pigalle. It was there that Sand recorded how Matuszyński "died in our arms after a slow and cruel agony which caused Chopin as much suffering as if it had been his own. He was strong, courageous and devoted, more so than one would have expected from such a frail being. But when it was over he was shattered."[11]

In the early part of the nineteenth century, the Ecole de Médecine in Paris was

12.4 The main building of the Ecole de Médecine (shown here as it appeared around 1830) was begun in 1769 and finished in 1776. Many of the physicians whom Chopin consulted during his years in Paris were on the faculty of this institution.

considered to be one of the leading medical schools, if not the foremost one, on the continent (fig. 12.4). It was located, according to the whimsical Delphine de Girardin, "on the road between this world and the next."[12] For the more practical-minded, it stood on a street called the rue des Boucheries (now known as the rue de l'Ecole de Médecine), a little north and east of the Odéon theater. Its original buildings had been erected in 1769 with some newer additions completed during the 1830s. The usual course of medical instruction then was four years. To qualify for entrance, a student had to have not only a bachelor of letters (or science) but a "certificate of morality" as well. In the final year before graduation, it was necessary to write a thesis and pass five examinations, four of which were written, while the fifth was a practical exam conducted in Latin.

By 1830 there were five thousand students enrolled in the medical school, many of whom found it necessary to spend considerably more time there than the requisite four years. After all, there was really no great rush to obtain a degree since surgeons couldn't get a hospital appointment until age thirty, and internists had to wait until age thirty-five. It was possible, of course, for a doctor to set

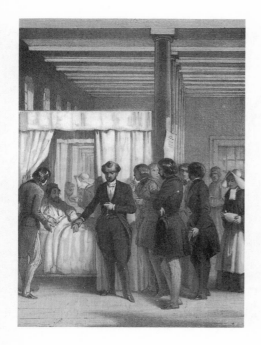

12.5 A doctor making rounds in one of the city's hospitals with students, interns, and nurses in attendance. By Chopin's time the policy of placing two or more patients in the same bed had been discontinued—except during the cholera epidemics, when the overwhelming number of victims exceeded the hospitals' accommodations.

himself up in private practice before that. But because the medical profession in Paris was so overcrowded then, only those in dire need of income did so. As an alternative, many students took paying jobs as externs or interns in the city hospitals. Because the latter had to live on the premises, they were able to enjoy free room and board during the four years of their service. In order to become an intern, a student had to spend at least one year as an extern, learning to bandage, write prescriptions, order diets, bleed patients, and apply leeches, poultices, and vesicants (mechanical or chemical agents that produced blisters on the skin). Other students, because of financial pressure or intellectual inertia, left medical school prematurely but with enough accreditation to qualify as government health officers.

The typical day of a medical student began at 7:00 A.M. with ward rounds in one of the city hospitals (fig. 12.5). These rounds were conducted by a staff physician, who always donned a silk cap and apron at the porter's gate to indicate his rank. At 9:00, immediately after rounds, clinical lectures were given in the numerous hospitals affiliated with the medical school. Under Louis-Philippe, Paris maintained at least twenty general and specialized hospitals (as well as a dozen hos-

12.6 The Hôpital Notre-Dame-de-Pitié overlooked the Jardin des Plantes and, like the Hôtel-Dieu, was one of the city's general hospitals. There in the late 1840s an obscure grisette named Lucile Louvet died of tuberculosis and was buried in a pauper's grave. Afterward her lover, Henri Murger, would preserve her memory in his *Scènes de la Bohème*; still later Giacomo Puccini made her immortal as the Mimi of his opera *La Bohème*.

pices), which were used for teaching. Most of these facilities were clustered on the Left Bank, with only a few located across the Seine (fig. 12.6). Because students had to return to the school by 10:00 A.M. for their formal courses, lectures and rounds on the distant Right Bank were generally not well attended.

The school's most popular lectures were said to be those given by Dr. Alfred Armand Louis Velpeau, the son of a blacksmith who arrived in Paris penniless and became one of its richest and most famous surgeons. Almost as well attended were the summer open-air lectures by Dr. Jean-Louis Alibert at the far-off Hôpital Saint-Louis on the Right Bank and those of Dr. Philippe Ricord in the Hôpital du Midi, located just south of the Val de Grâce. Consciously imitating Plato's discourses in the Groves of Academe, Dr. Alibert lectured in the hospital gardens, strolling to and fro as he talked. With his broad-brimmed hat cocked to one side, he often grew rhapsodic over the "beautiful" skin eruption of a patient he was presenting to the students. Although such enthusiasm may have thrilled his audience, it appalled the poor patient, who failed to see the "beauty" of his condition.

The American-born venereal disease specialist Dr. Philippe Ricord was an even more flamboyant personality than Alibert. In his youth, Ricord had been dismissed from the city's Hôtel Dieu on the grounds that he would do better in vaudeville than medicine. Time, however, proved him to be an astute clinician— even though many old-guard physicians ridiculed his iconoclastic theory that syphilis and gonorrhea were two separate diseases rather than variants of the same condition. When he published his illustrated *Atlas of Syphilis,* it was severely criticized on the grounds that visual representations of physical diseases only served to distort doctors' intellectual concepts of them. In musical circles, Ricord's wife was noted for her distinguished salon, attended by many of Chopin's favorite bel canto singers, including Rubini, Lablache, Grisi, and other members of the Théâtre-Italien. It was not surprising therefore that the Italian composer Donizetti sought her husband's help to arrest the progressive brain damage from the syphilis that afflicted him. Unfortunately, Ricord's regimens of perianal leeches, foot baths, mustard plasters, and boiled Leopard's Bane met with little success; eventually his patient returned to Italy, where he died insane.

The Hôpital du Midi, which Ricord directed, was one of the city's ten specialized hospitals. It cared exclusively for male patients with venereal diseases and was housed in a seventeenth-century Augustinian convent, next to a beautiful cloistered garden where Ricord lectured. Its lovely setting, however, was deceptive, for according to an American observer in 1843, the Midi was the dirtiest and worst managed hospital in Paris—in large part because the Sisters of Charity, who served all other hospitals in Paris, refused to care for those suffering from diseases caused by immorality. Women with venereal disease fared somewhat better because another order, the Sisters of Compassion, was willing to minister to their needs at the Hôpital Lourcine. There the majority of patients were prostitutes, whom the city required to be examined twice a week. Those found to be diseased were sent to the Lourcine, where the nuns tried to rehabilitate them spiritually as well as physically. For fear of exposing others to the deleterious influence of the prostitutes, visitors were not allowed at the Lourcine, nor were medical students permitted to attend lectures there. A few patients who were deemed "innocent" victims (of rape or wayward husbands) were sent to the Right Bank's Hôpital Saint-Lazare, where at least their souls, if not their bodies, would reap some benefit.

After years of treating venereal diseases, Ricord became such a cynic that one of his American students, Dr. Oliver Wendell Holmes, claimed that he would have automatically dosed the goddess Diana and the vestal virgins with his antisyphilitic "potions" had they walked into his office. Thanks to his use of effective agents like mercury and potassium iodide, the devastating damage to the heart and central nervous system was mitigated in some patients with advanced syphilis. Not all, however, could be saved, and many inmates at the city's mental hospitals succumbed (like poor Donizetti) to the neurological sequelae of the disease.

The government's only hospital for "lunatics" (a politically correct term in the nineteenth century) was the Maison Royale de Charenton, located in the village of Charenton four miles southeast of Paris. There only one in three patients ever recovered. Many of those needing long-term care were transferred to two of the city's hospices, Bicêtre (for men) and La Salpêtrière (for women). Through the bizarre caprices of bureaucracy, male convicts were also housed at Bicêtre, while Salpêtrière mixed sane women with demented ones. Epileptics, the mentally retarded, and the senile were also quartered in these facilities. If conditions at the Hôpital du Midi were bad, they were barbaric at the hospices of Bicêtre and La Salpêtrière until Louis-Philippe's prefect of the Seine, M. de Rambuteau, instituted reforms in the city's care of the mentally ill. Prior to his administration, many patients were kept in padded cells or underground dungeons. Even in the dormitories, no chairs or tables were allowed. Nor was glass permitted in windows, which were barred and often covered with shutters that kept the patients in perpetual darkness. At night inmates slept in wooden boxes on a bed of straw. For the purpose of discipline as well as cleanliness, it was the custom to douse patients regularly with cold water from showers ten to twelve feet above their heads.

In the case of those who could afford it, more humane care was available for patients with psychiatric disorders in the city's *maisons de santé*, or private hospitals. Among these were Dr. Blanche's asylum in Montmartre (where the poet Gérard de Nerval was housed in a "family environment"), Dr. Casimir Pinel's sanitorium in Chaillot (to which Daumier sometimes retreated), and Dr. Esquirol's establishment at Ivry, where the philosopher Auguste Comte underwent treatment for "cerebral over-excitement." Generally, under Rambuteau the quality of patient care in the city hospitals began to approach that of the *maisons de santé*. For example, convicts were removed from the hospice of Bicêtre to the prison of La Roquette, and at La Salpêtrière mentally disturbed patients were separated from the sane. The government also started paid work programs as a form of occupational therapy in many of the hospitals. By 1843, when Eugène Sue's novel *The Mysteries of Paris* appeared, conditions at Bicêtre had greatly improved. On arriving at the institution, the author wrote, "The visitor enters . . . a vast court planted with large trees and divided into grass-plots, ornamented in summer with flower borders. Nothing could be more cheerful, more peaceful, or more salubrious.... On the first floor are found spacious sleeping apartments; and on the ground floor, dining-halls, kept in admirable order, where the pensioners partake most excellent food, prepared with great care, thanks to the paternal solicitude of the directors of this establishment."[13]

Far in advance of its time, Bicêtre began using musical therapy for the management of the insane. On September 27, 1840, the *Gazette Musicale* reported how a Dr. Leuret noted "that the inmates became surprisingly calm on hearing the music of the mass on Sundays. When he began to teach them to sing hymns and patriotic songs, ... he was able to draw many out of their isolation and help them express emotion which contributed to their recovery in some cases."[14] Naturally, as with all progressive innovations, there was opposition. Dr. Esquirol, who had treated the insane for nearly fifty years, objected to Leuret's efforts on the grounds that music revived "the passions, hopes and sorrows" that had caused the patients' insanity in the first place.[15] The counsel-general of hospitals for the city, however, thought otherwise and appointed a voice professor to help Dr. Leuret with his musical therapy. On Easter Sunday, 1841, the inmates of Bicêtre performed a grand mass, reported by the *Gazette Musicale* as "truly a bizarre sight." The faces of some of the patients "bore an idiotic look of surprise while others showed evidence of a bewilderment beyond their control.... As to the medical effect of this experiment by Dr. Leuret, only the future will tell."[16] That August, Dr. Leuret received further encouragement for his musical therapy program when artists of the Paris Opéra and the Opéra Comique came to Bicêtre to perform Cherubini's grand mass for the patients.

Because both the facilities at Charenton and Bicêtre were situated well beyond the city limits, it is easy to understand the frustration of medical students who had to attend lectures and rounds in such far-flung institutions. Besides these obligations, students were required to spend many hours in the dissecting room, which (due to a city ordinance that prohibited its presence on the grounds of the medical school) added still further travel time to the students' daily schedule. The first visit to these rooms proved to be a watershed for many a would-be doctor. Berlioz, whose father insisted that he pursue a medical career, tells us of the horror he experienced on first walking into that "terrible charnel-house." He was sickened by "the fragments of limbs, the grinning faces and gaping skulls, the bloody quagmire underfoot and the atrocious smell it gave off, the swarms of sparrows wrangling over scraps of lung, [and] the rats in their corner gnawing the bleeding vertebrae. Such a feeling of revulsion possessed me that I leapt through the window ... and fled."[17] Luckily the dissecting room was on the ground floor, and the only injury Berlioz sustained was to his psyche. The damage was permanent, however, and he never went back to the school, although he continued the pretense of studying medicine in order to get an allowance from his unsuspecting father. Alfred de Musset also left medical school for similar reasons. By contrast many artists with supposedly "sensitive" natures like Eugène Delacroix and George Sand's son, Maurice, frequented the medical school's dissection rooms to study the details of human anatomy without the least bit of squeamishness.

Visits to the outpatient clinics attached to the hospitals filled the rest of a medical student's typical day. Those clinic patients who needed hospitalization for more intensive care were given a doctor's certificate and sent to the city's central admissions bureau, located on the square in front of Notre-Dame. Evening rounds at the hospitals were made by interns, leaving the students free to study. The poorer ones usually flocked to the libraries, where they could keep warm without having to pay for firewood, while the more affluent ones spent their time at "the theatre, balls or some other place of amusement."[18] In 1844 an American medical student from Kentucky was appalled to find many of his Parisian counterparts living with their grisettes or mistresses. "I would not advise that any young man be sent to Paris to improve his morals," he wrote. "Many of the citizens of Paris seem to act almost entirely from the promptings of animal passion."[19]

During the second quarter of the nineteenth century, the curriculum of the Paris medical school expanded rapidly. Although the study of human anatomy remained fundamental to any career in medicine, it was a field already well explored by 1830. Much, however, remained to be learned about the related fields of pathologic anatomy (the study of diseased rather than normal organs) and comparative anatomy. At the Jardin des Plantes, baron Georges Cuvier did extensive research in comparative anatomy and presented his findings in numerous lectures that drew not only doctors and medical students but the general public as well. Long before Darwin, Cuvier's discoveries offered substantial evidence in support of evolution. The aging baron refused to accept such a theory, however, because he considered it in conflict with Christian doctrine. As for the field of pathologic anatomy, one of its chief pioneers was Dr. Guillaume Dupuytren, surgeon-in-chief of the city's largest hospital, the Hôtel-Dieu, and a professor at the Ecole de Médecine (fig. 12.7). Highly respected for his surgical prowess and his research, he was generally disliked by his colleagues and feared by his students. According to one of his fellow professors, he was "the first of

12.7 The Hôtel-Dieu was the oldest and largest of Paris's many medical facilities under the July monarchy. Located on the south edge of the île de la Cité, it had three front doors. The central one, which served only as an exit, was flanked by two entrances, one for men and one for women. This separation of the sexes was necessary because all visitors were meticulously searched for food and beverages that might be harmful to the sick. Linking the main hospital with a group of subsidiary buildings on the Left Bank was a tunnel under the Seine as well as an enclosed, glass-roofed bridge.

surgeons and the least of men."[20] His abrasive personality, however, didn't prevent him from making millions: among his patients was Baron James de Rothschild, whose life he saved after the banker fell from a horse. With his great fortune, Dupuytren endowed a chair of pathologic anatomy at the Paris medical school, where he was succeeded by Chopin's Dr. Cruveilhier. At the time of Dupuytren's death in 1835, huge crowds attended his funeral, which Daumier recorded in one of his lithographs. Later Dr. Cruveilhier created a museum at the Ecole de Médecine in which he housed Dupuytren's extensive collection of pathologic specimens. Still to be seen there are such items as diseased bones, kidney stones, pickled cancers, hernias, and what a nineteenth-century visitor ambiguously described as various "monstrosities." For some reason, however, a "beautifully modelled" wax representation of the three stages of syphilis, once considered the exhibit's chief ornament, is no longer on view.

Two other new sciences that drew the attention of the medical profession in the early nineteenth century were physiology (the study of the mechanisms by which the body functions) and histology (the microscopic analysis of both healthy and diseased tissues). Although advances in these nascent sciences progressed slowly, important progress was made during this era, including Claude Bernard's recognition of the pancreas's role in diabetes, and his elucidation of the metabolic functions of the liver, which had once been thought responsible only for those nasty bilious humors that made people out of sorts. In 1840, Alfred Donne was reported to have taken the first photographs through a microscope. François-Vincent Raspail, remembered today chiefly as a radical Republican and political mischief-maker, was originally a chemist and biologist who contributed to the microscopic study of tissues and cells (histochemistry and cytochemistry). In keeping with his socialist zeal, Raspail established free clinics for the poor, wrote a home medical advisor, and defied the government by practicing without a license, a crime for which he was repeatedly prosecuted. Years later, in an act of atonement, the government named the Left Bank's broad boulevard Raspail in his honor.

Other notable achievements in French medicine during this period include Pierre-Fidèle Bretonneau's recognition of a contagious febrile condition to which he gave the name diphtheria, and Hérisson's contribution to the development of the sphygmomanometer for measuring blood pressure. Dr. Pierre-Charles-Alexander Louis, another of Chopin's many Paris physicians, was responsible for much of the early research on typhoid and tuberculosis. From his studies he concluded that many accepted therapies for these diseases, such as bleeding and purging, had no value, and might actually be harmful to the patient.

In several cases, technological advances in medically related fields were made by individuals other than doctors. For example the vocal coach Manuel Garcia *fils*, a friend of Chopin's and the brother of the renowned opera singers La Malibran and Pauline Viardot Garcia, invented the laryngoscope. Earlier, a blind organist named Louis Braille had devised a system of writing for the sightless. His method, which utilized raised punctate dots on paper, was adapted from the work of a soldier, Charles Barbier, whose aim had been to create a secret code for military spies.

By the early decades of the nineteenth century, empiricism had become the prevailing wind that determined the course of medicine and science both in Europe and America. In France this method was encouraged by Dr. François Magendie at the Collège de France, who stressed the importance of experimental research over theoretical speculation, and Dr. Pierre-Charles Louis, who emphasized the need to verify such research through the use of statistical analysis and controlled studies. As Claude Bernard wrote, "Systems [that is, *a priori* systems] do not exist in Nature but only in men's minds."[21] Dr. Cruveilhier agreed. Systems come and go, he observed, but facts remain. Nevertheless many early-nineteenth-century doctors continued to push, bend, and distort the self-evident into grandiose intellectual molds, whether out of innocent self-delusion or calculated self-glorification. At the Ecole de Médecine in Paris, Dr. François Broussais had the wisdom to discard the ancient humoral theory (that all disease was caused by changes in the four basic body fluids—blood, phlegm, yellow bile, and black bile), only to postulate instead that the universal cause of illness was the heat generated by engorged blood vessels in inflamed tissues. By mistaking the symptom for the cause, he had put the cart before the horse. Oblivious to his mistake, though, he persisted in driving both cart and horse down the wrong path to the even more dubious conclusion that all inflammation—hence all disease—arises in the stomach and adjacent intestinal tract. In the absence of any experimental proof, Broussais's theory was eventually dismissed as nothing but a "gut feeling." By attributing all disease to overheating of the blood, it is not surprising that he advocated frequent bleedings as the best means of combatting illness. Soon the enthusiasm of Parisian doctors for this new theory created an acute shortage of leeches in the city. By 1833 Paris was importing 41.5 million leeches a year—over sixteen times the number used by physicians nine years earlier.[22]

Mesmerism, phrenology, physiognomy, chiromancy, and homeopathy were other "scientific" systems that flourished at this time with little or no empirical foundation. Mesmerism was based on what Franz Anton Mesmer (a Viennese physician and one-time friend of Mozart's) called "animal magnetism," a sort of subconscious medium of self-revelation and communication. To tap this hidden source, Mesmer practiced what today we call hypnotism. The potentially dangerous psychological power this conferred over the "mesmerizer" was often used by early practitioners for nefarious purposes, particularly of a sexual nature. At Mesmer's prerevolutionary Magnetic Institute in Paris, nude female patients splashed about warm sulfur baths in darkened rooms. Even in the "enlightened" atmosphere of eighteenth-century France, this provoked charges of immorality. Nevertheless Mesmer's hypnotic practices seem to have alleviated the hysterical symptoms that plagued many of the young ladies attracted to his establishment. In the subsequent vogue enjoyed by mesmerism, most of the patients treated were women, and the "magnetizers" men who often pressed their knees against the ladies and massaged the "affected part" (frequently the breast). Throughout the process, the magnetizers would stare intently into the eyes of their patients, producing a hypnotic effect with a temporary loss of memory. In the eighteenth century a panel of doctors, scientists, and others (including Benjamin Franklin) pronounced mesmerism a hoax. Nevertheless it continued to be practiced well into the nineteenth century as a cure for neurologic, psychologic, infectious, traumatic, and cancerous conditions, as well as blindness and deafness.

Among Mesmer's followers was the German-Jewish Dr. David-Ferdinand Koreff, a cultivated, gregarious, and witty individual with a hooked nose, bushy eyebrows, and a pockmarked face that peered out from under a straw-colored wig. In the social and artistic circles of Paris during the early 1830s, Koreff charmed such distinguished members of *le beau monde* as Mme Récamier, countess Merlin, baron Cuvier, comtesse Apponyi, Lady Granville, Thiers, Heine, Meyerbeer, and even Talleyrand, who once commented that the devilish doctor knew everything, even a little medicine. Those who actually submitted themselves to his care included Franz Liszt; Liszt's mother and his mistress (the countess d'Agoult); Stendhal; Louis-Philippe's prime minister, Casimir Périer; and the famed lady of the camellias, Marie Duplessis. Soon laymen began to vie with the medical profession in the practice of this new "science." The Swiss poet Charles Didier, for instance, began experimenting with it on his mistress, George Sand, in 1836, the year she first met Chopin. Others took advantage of the popularity of mesmerism to pose as psychics capable of penetrating the secrets of the past, present, and future. Chopin once consulted such a person, Mme Lenormant, to learn what fate held in store for him regarding his love affair with a young Polish girl, Maria Wodzińska.

From the late eighteenth to the early nineteenth centuries, phrenology, founded by Franz Josef Gall (1758–1828), a German physician who practiced in Paris for twenty years, also aroused enormous interest among doctors and laymen in both Europe and America. It purported to reveal one's personality and mental capacity through the study of the configuration of the head. An analogous specialty called physiognomy supposedly accomplished the same ends through an examination of facial features. In the 1820s, at the hospital of Salpêtrière, one of the staff physicians, Dr. Georget, diagnosed insanity solely on the basis of physiognomy. At about the same time, the young George Sand became intrigued with physiognomy and its founder, a Swiss theologian and poet named Johann Kaspar Lavater. "I used to study the plates [of Lavater's works] with curiosity," she claimed, puzzling over the "assortment of...faces... *drunken, slothful, gluttonous, irascible, political, methodical.*[23] Finally convinced of the infallibility of his theories, she wrote Franz Liszt that those who didn't respect physiognomy fail to see the face as "the mark of the Creator's power, wisdom and mercy."[24] In the Hungarian pianist's face she detected genius, while in her own, she noted (perhaps with false modesty) the simple features of a common laborer. Lavater himself recorded that God had blessed him with a visage bearing such enviable traits as "strong imagination...spontaneous perceptiveness...immense serenity...great vigor...[and a] thoughtful nature."[25] Presumably his mirror was as unflawed as his face.

A third new "science" called chiromancy professed to determine a person's character from the shape of his hands. The chief proponent of this new vogue was a retired army captain, Stanislas d'Arpentigny, who dyed his hair green—a peculiarity that probably revealed more about the man than anything one could divine from his hands. Despite the captain's eccentricities, Chopin (who met him through George Sand) considered him an "amusing and witty" person.[26] By 1849 the pianist noted that the fifty-eight-year-old d'Arpentigny had changed the color of his hair to blond. Under Sand's tutelage, the chiromancer attempted a literary career but with little success. Writing, it would seem, just wasn't written on his palms.

For the most part, physiognomy and chiromancy remained little more than faddish pastimes. Phrenology, on the other hand, received considerable attention from both the medical profession and the public. Mothers even had the heads of their babies "read" by a phrenologist, who predicted their futures and advised them on vocations best suited to the infants' natural abilities. A great deal of effort went into "research" concerned with the locations of those parts of the skull and brain that were associated with intellectual and artistic abilities, as well as those indicative of criminal propensities. Gall and Broussais, for example, dissected the brain of comte Henri de Saint-Simon (founder of the socioreligious sect bearing his name), hoping to discover the characteristic anatomical features of the philosophical mind. Similarly the assassin Fieschi (who attempted to kill Louis-Philippe) was subjected to an autopsy immediately after being guillotined. During this procedure, special attention was given to the examination of his skull and brain for features diagnostic of criminal proclivities. Paër's great friend and devotee of music, Dr. Orfila, was obsessed with the criminal mind and studied

12.8 The skull and a wax model of the head of Joseph Fieschi, who attempted to assassinate Louis-Philippe in 1835. These remain on display today at the Ecole de Médecine in Paris, as part of a nineteenth-century phrenologic study of criminals.

dozens of decapitated heads from executed murderers at the Ecole de Médecine. His collection of wax models (made from plaster casts) of the executed men's heads and their actual skulls can still be viewed at the medical school today (fig. 12.8). At the Jardin des Plantes, the scientist Cuvier, looking for phrenologic signs of "greatness," assembled a large collection of wax models taken from the heads of famous people. The disappointing results of such studies, however, eventually led to the discreditation of phrenology. In July 1836 the Académie de Médecine officially banned the practice of it in France. This prohibition, however, didn't prevent many amateurs from continuing to dabble in the field. George Sand, for one, bought a phrenological skull that very year and delved into its meaning under the instruction of Dr. David Richard, who roomed with her lover at the time, Charles Didier. Balzac also probed the mysteries of phrenology, which led him to conclude that his literary rival, Victor Hugo, had the head of a fool.

In contrast to the passing fancy for these paramedical specialties, homeopathy still remains respected and popular in many parts of the world today. Its founder, Samuel Hahnemann (1755–1843), was the son of a porcelain painter at the Meissen factory in Germany (fig. 12.9). His initial efforts as a private practitioner and an early proponent of public health were unsuccessful, and he was eventually forced to abandon medicine and work as a translator to support his wife and their eleven children. Later, through the patronage of some of the petty German

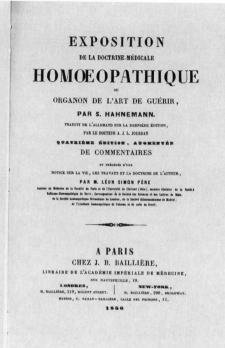

12.9 A portrait of Samuel Hahnemann, along with the frontispiece of an 1856 edition of his *Exposition of the Medical Doctrine of Homeopathy; or, Treatise on the Art of Healing.* At the beginning of the volume is an introductory essay on the life and work of the author by Dr. Léon Simon, one of Chopin's homeopathic physicians.

princes, he was able to return to the practice of medicine and engage in some research. The first observations that led him to formulate his theory of homeopathy had to do with the ability of cinchona (a precursor of quinine) to cure intermittent fevers like malaria if given in the conventionally prescribed doses. An excess quantity of the same medication, however, actually produced febrile symptoms identical to the diseases that it was meant to cure. Further experiments with digitalis, mercury, and belladonna led to similar observations. By 1805 he began writing down his findings under the name of homeopathy (from the Greek words *homoion* meaning similar, and *pathos,* meaning disease). The success of all medical therapy, he claimed, was based on "the law of similars," that is, any given illness could best be cured by those drugs that created symptoms similar to the disease itself. This was directly opposite to the ideas of most allopaths (physicians practicing the conventional medicine of the day), who chose remedies designed to oppose rather than mimic the disease under treatment. Furthermore Hahnemann emphasized that the therapeutic dose of the curative agent must be *very small,* in fact almost infinitesimal.

To some degree Hahnemann's concept is analogous to our current ideas on vaccination. In viral diseases like smallpox or influenza, for example, a similar but less virulent virus (or the same virus, which has been killed or inactivated) is injected into the patient, inducing a mild form of the disease. This then stimulates the patient's immune system to protect against future attacks by the virus. The difference, of course, is that vaccination serves as a preventive treatment, whereas Hahnemann believed homeopathy to be a curative one. How, though, could small doses of a potentially toxic drug (for example, strychnine) effect a cure? Hahnemann's explanation was that nature's "vital force," which regulated bodily functions in the healthy individual, lost its control and became a destructive force in times of illness. The purpose, therefore, of giving a patient miniscule amounts of a supposed "cure" was to immobilize this dysfunctional "vital force" temporarily and allow the body to restore itself. Although such reasoning seemed clear enough to Hahnemann, it perplexed most of the medical profession, which looked askance at his unorthodox ideas. Once again it appeared that Hahnemann might be forced to quit the practice of medicine. Certainly this would have pleased his wife, who never had much sympathy with her husband's desire to be a doctor when there were so many more profitable ways of making a living. Her death in 1827 (despite the medical benefits of homeopathy) proved to be a turning point in the beleaguered doctor's career. Less than seven years later, the still robust seventy-nine-year-old Hahnemann married one of his patients, a young French woman, Mlle Mélanie d'Hervilly, who persuaded him to move to Paris in June of 1835. There homeopathy had already become well established, and its founder received a warm reception. His new clientele, which came almost exclusively from the "higher and highest classes," flocked to his rue Milan office.[27] There they found Mme Hahnemann seated next to her husband throughout their visit. She not only took notes for him, but also advised him on therapeutic matters and prepared his medications.

Among those who converted to the new science of homeopathy were Franz Liszt and Chopin's Scottish pupil, Miss Jane Stirling. It was the latter's influence on her teacher that prompted Chopin to consult several Parisian homeopaths, although he apparently never called on Hahnemann himself. For years both he and George Sand were under the care of Dr. Molin, a homeopath who seems to have been the most trusted of all Chopin's physicians in Paris. Although the doctor's cough medicine (gum water with sugar and opium) made him sleepy, Chopin preferred it to the harsh laxatives, leeches, blood-letting, and blistering applications prescribed by most allopaths of the time. Dr. Molin, Chopin claimed, had the "secret of getting me back on my feet again."[28] During the severe winter of 1847, he even credited Molin with saving his life and refused to leave for England in 1848 without the doctor's consent. While abroad Chopin sought out two other homeopaths to attend him: the Polish Dr. Łyszczyński in Edinburgh, and Dr. Mallan in London.

Back in Paris, Chopin discovered that his trusted Dr. Molin had died, a blow from which he never fully recovered. In his stead, the ailing musician consulted two other homeopaths, Dr. Roth and Dr. Léon Simon. Apparently dissatisfied with both, he called in several physicians "of the old school," who came to see him as often as twice a day at fees the impoverished musician considered exorbitant. He was particularly annoyed with Dr. Fraenkel from Warsaw, who sometimes didn't show up for eight or ten days at a time. When he finally did come around, Chopin complained that "he didn't even bother to test my urine and talked of nothing but an English patient he had saved from the cholera."[29] Eventually he dismissed Fraenkel as a "crackpot" who didn't know how to deal with his illness.[30]

Subsequently the musician consulted four other physicians, including a Dr. Oldendorf and two noted specialists on tuberculosis: Dr. Louis (who had failed to save Marie Duplessis two years earlier) and the president of the Académie de Médecine, Dr. Jean-Gaston-Marie Blache, who attended the young Orleanist princes. At the very end, Chopin called in Dr. Jean Cruveilhier, who explained to him how fortunate he had been in seeking out homeopaths rather than allopathic physicians. "He [Dr. Cruveilhier] told me that Dr. Molin's homeopathy had helped me because it didn't overwhelm me with medicines and allowed Nature to take its own course."[31] This, as Hahnemann himself wrote in the preface to his *Organon*, was the purpose of homeopathy: to combat disease without weakening the patient. Certainly in this sense one can justifiably claim that homeopathy prolonged Chopin's life.

By coincidence it happened to be another physician, Dr. O'Meara, the father of one of Chopin's most talented pupils, Camille O'Meara Dubois, who helped him find his last apartment in Paris, at No. 12 place Vendôme.

The tuberculosis that eventually took Chopin's life was the most lethal disease in Europe at that time, with pneumonia, typhoid fever, and smallpox its deadliest competitors.[32] During the first half of the nineteenth century, 50 percent of the population in both France and England contracted tuberculosis, which ultimately killed two-thirds of its victims. Fortunately for Chopin, the medical profession in those countries considered tuberculosis a "constitutional degenerative disease" rather than an infectious one, which spared him the inconvenience of ever being placed under quarantine.[33] By contrast, other nations like Spain and Italy already recognized the infectious nature of tuberculosis. One of the main reasons for the ostracism and persecution that Chopin and George Sand suffered in Majorca during the winter of 1838–39 was the islanders' fear of contracting the musician's disease.

Although the discovery of the stethoscope by René Théophile Hyacinthe Laennec ("that man with the ear trumpet," as Dr. Broussais called him) facilitated the detection of pulmonary conditions like tuberculosis, the absence of a cure meant there was little a physician could do once he had made the diagnosis. In Chopin's case, the fact that the disease was widely disseminated throughout his body led doctors to propose multiple diagnoses for his condition, including laryngitis, pneumonia, influenza, bronchitis, neuritis, diarrhea, "swollen glands" (scrofula), dropsy, and arthritis. Because of this confusion over the exact nature of his disease, Chopin became a candidate for what is often called "shotgun therapy" today, that is, a blind attempt to barrage the patient with every existent remedy in the hope that one of them will hit the target and cure the invalid. Fortunately many of the regimens used to treat Chopin were harmless enough. Some were probably even beneficial, such as bed rest; nourishing diets of hot soups, herb teas, and caloric syrups; as well as various sedatives and the inhalation of soothing vapors.

Besides these medical recommendations, Chopin tried a number of folk remedies urged on him by well-meaning friends. Maria Wodzińska (to whom he was briefly engaged during his early years in Paris) knitted him wool socks to protect his health. This, according to the *Almanach Populaire*, was especially helpful for people with respiratory problems on the grounds that "colds" were presumed to enter through the feet. In an era when hot running water was unknown, the *Almanach* warned those who were elderly or suffered from a cough to avoid baths because of their chilling effect. Along with bathing, flowers (which Chopin loved, especially violets) were another of life's pleasures denied most invalids of the time. Plants in general, the *Almanach* cautioned, were to be kept out of the sick room because they acidified the air and had "a dangerous influence on the nervous system."[34] Opposite schools of thought, however, insisted that drinking acidified water and mild infusions of flowers like violets and mallows were highly beneficial.

Had Chopin followed the recommendations of his allopathic physicians, he would have been subjected to such debilitating measures as bleeding (either by a cut or the application of leeches), the production of painful blisters (by means of suction cups, hot irons, or irritating chemicals), the use of clystopumps (for giving enemas), strychnine-laced sialagogues to promote salivation, and foul-smelling "nauseabonds" to induce vomiting. The purpose of all these therapeutic agents was to eliminate body fluids, which presumably contained the inflammatory principles that caused disease. Instead they produced dangerous levels of dehydration that were often life-threatening. Popular diets for the consumptive featured concoctions containing sea salt, frogs, ox gall, asses' milk, and snake venom. Chopin seems to have shunned these dietary measures and, in his most debilitated moments, confined himself to the intake of bland fluids like ices and lemonade. Nor did he ever submit—so far as we know—to mesmerism, which was recommended by some Parisian doctors for their phthisic patients.

Tuberculosis, a slow but relentless killer, was a constant menace to the population (especially urban dwellers), but because of its ever-present nature the French often became inured to its threat. Cholera, on the other hand, was a disease that struck in sudden epidemics that often carried away hundreds to thousands of victims in a matter of days. No other disease created such terror among the Parisians as the great cholera epidemics of 1832 and 1849, which took the lives of 15,000 to 20,000 victims on each occasion. People who had been perfectly healthy a few hours earlier suddenly turned blue, collapsed on the spot, and died within minutes. Although death often came swiftly, it could be agonizingly painful. "I have been much disturbed in my work," Heinrich Heine wrote on April 19, 1832, "by the horrible screams of my neighbor who died of cholera."[35] So great was the panic induced by the disease that a certain countess was reported to have succumbed from pure fright without any physical evidence of infection. Although both epidemics arose in overcrowded and unsanitary working class quarters, they quickly spread throughout the city, attacking the rich and poor alike. Many shops and most public gathering places were closed. People who could afford it fled the city for their country estates. Surprisingly, the Paris Opéra remained open and even drew large crowds on such occasions as a concert by

12.10 A view of the Paris morgue on the île de la Cité. During the cholera epidemic of 1832, George Sand lived directly across from the morgue, on the Left Bank's quai Saint-Michel. From her window at that time, Sand could watch the interminable procession of carts and wagons, piled high with corpses collected from all over the stricken city.

Paganini. To disinfect the building, chlorine fumes were wafted around its auditorium and corridors by a crude ventilating system, and the front steps were scrubbed twice daily with a chlorine solution. Few people were seen on the streets except for the rag pickers, who stripped the dead of their clothes and possessions in order to sell them. In the hospitals, patients were crammed three to a bed, which only hastened the spread of the disease.

During the epidemic of 1832, George Sand and her friends met daily at a designated spot in the Luxembourg gardens to make sure they were all still alive and well. Anyone who didn't show up was immediately searched for. At that time the young authoress lived on the quai Saint-Michel across from the city morgue, where she was a daily witness to the endless procession of the dead (fig. 12.10). When the morgue ran out of coffins, bodies were stuffed in sacks for burial. Another of Heine's observations brings out the poignancy of those tragic months: "I remember that two little boys stood by me with sad faces and one asked if I could tell him in which sack his father was."[36] On the rue Faubourg Montmartre, one woman counted three hundred coffins carried past her window on a single night.

As with tuberculosis, there was no cure for cholera, notwithstanding Alexandre Dumas's boast that he recovered from the disease by swilling down a full glass of ether. Even if a cure existed, there would have been little time to administer it because of the rapidity with which cholera struck and killed its victims. The best that Parisians could hope for was to find some agent that would protect them from catching the dreaded affliction. Camphor (previously smoked in cigarette form to lose weight) soon came to be regarded as one of the principal antidotes for cholera. Women carried sachets of camphor in their purses, while men filled their vest pockets with camphor and menthol pastilles, which they inhaled periodically during the day. Tobacco was also popular as a deterrent to the disease, which no doubt encouraged Mme Sand to increase the number of cigars that she smoked daily. At the height of the epidemic, men and women alike became avid tobacco chewers. For Samuel F. B. Morse, James Fenimore Cooper, and their American friends in Paris then, two tablespoons of charcoal daily seemed to be the magic antidote that kept the plague at bay. During the cholera epidemic of 1849, the respected *Archives Générales de Médecine* went so far as to propose protecting people against the disease by inoculating them with syphilis. The Academy of Medicine, however, censured this proposal and threatened legal action against any doctor found guilty of attempting it.

Even though early-nineteenth-century medicine had arrived at the threshold of the scientific era, it was still governed as much by the folklore of the past as by the empirical insights of the time. The composer Bellini, for example, suffered the painful infliction of blisters on his skin to cure a liver abscess, while the journalist-playwright Henri Murger was treated for a bleeding disorder with still further bleeding and (as he joked) enough arsenic to supply three of the popular melodramas in the Parisian theaters. White mustard continued to be prescribed for "black humors," while Dr. Récamier insisted that eating to a drumbeat improved digestion because the "stomach loves rhythm."[37] Doctors who still practiced according to such unscientific notions, some of which dated back to the Middle Ages, found themselves in conflict with their younger, more scientifically oriented colleagues. With Hahnemann's arrival in Paris, the dissension between allopaths and homeopaths intensified. Such disputes within the medical profession naturally confused the public and provoked widespread mistrust of physicians in general.

At the time of the 1832 cholera epidemic, crowds gathered in front of the Hôtel Dieu to hurl abuse at the hospital's doctors, whom they blamed for the plague. While the lower classes accused them of malice, more educated Parisians regarded them as simply ignorant. "Doctors," count Apponyi complained, "don't understand anything about...[cholera] and it is pure luck if the patient survives."[38] Worse yet, Alexandre Dumas and Prosper Mérimée branded the National Guard's medics as the government's "death-dealing" squad. Long after the epidemic had passed, Daumier continued to denigrate the medical profession in cartoons that portrayed doctors as "pedantic, vain, avid, egoistic or hard and indifferent."[39] Worst of all, they were depicted as avaricious; one of Daumier's lithographs shows a doctor taking a patient's pulse while he calculates his bill. The debt-ridden Berlioz further reinforced this impression with his envious remark, "It is only physicians who can afford to live."[40] Certainly the millions made by doctors like Dupuytren, Koreff, and Ricord encouraged that conception. Dr. Véron, on the other hand, had to give up private practice because he couldn't earn enough to survive; his last patient walked out on him after he botched an attempt to draw her blood. Later, though, he piled up huge profits from the sale of Regnault's pectoral paste, the formula of which he obtained through dubious means from the widow of its inventor. Koreff's law suit to obtain an outrageous 400,000-franc fee for hypnotizing a patient, and Dr. Cruveilhier's ethically questionable endorsement of a mechanical device to benefit pianists (the so-called *guide-main* promoted by Chopin's friend, the pianist Kalkbrenner), further damaged the public's perception of its doctors.

Even under the rosiest of lights, the French medical profession in Chopin's time exhibited serious shortcomings, so much so that Balzac on his deathbed cried out for his fictional Dr. Bianchon (rather than any real-life Parisian physician). In order to regain the public's confidence, most doctors realized that it was necessary to establish well-defined standards for the practice of medicine, along with effective measures to enforce them. This they hoped to accomplish with the founding of the French National Medical Association in 1845 (two years before the inauguration of the American Medical Association).

The task confronting them, however, was a difficult one, extending well beyond the personal motivations and morality of the individual practitioner. Even the most conscientious doctors at that time were forced to practice an imperfect form of medicine that was grounded more in archaic traditions than in scientific precepts. Although the majority of the profession seem to have been dedicated to their calling, they were condemned to live and work in an era of limited knowledge and, worse yet, in a city with an excess of doctors and a high cost of living. All too often those who overcame these obstacles were mistrusted, while those who failed were scorned. At least most were willing to make house calls twice a day. The fact that they charged 20 francs a visit annoyed Chopin, but as Balzac pointed out, getting around a big city like Paris was an expensive business. "For a doctor, a cab is even more necessary than a knowledge of medicine," he noted with his usual perspicacity.[41]

CHAPTER 13

Visions of a Better World

Searching for Utopia from Menilmontant to the Rue Vanneau

"*A*REN'T YOU SHOCKED AND INDIGNANT, like me, at the outrageous number of redeemers and law-givers who lay claim to the throne of our moral world?" George Sand wrote Prince Talleyrand in 1835.[1] Her shock and indignation are somewhat surprising, considering that the thirty-one-year-old novelist was herself one of those moralistic reformers whom she complained about. During the previous three years, she had written nearly a dozen novels and short stories aimed at changing the sexual attitudes of a male-dominated society. Much of what she wrote came from her own bitter experiences as a victim of those very attitudes she was criticizing.

In her youth, Aurore Dupin (as George Sand had been christened) was given an unusual amount of freedom by her paternal grandmother, who raised her in the liberal tradition of the eighteenth century with an emphasis on Rousseau's belief that whatever was natural was good. As a result, the young girl grew up trusting her God-given instincts. Among the strongest of these was the instinct to love. In the rural isolation of her grandmother's estate, however, she found few people on whom to lavish her affection. To fill this void in her life, she resorted to creating her own object of adoration, a deity she called Corambé. In the woods near her grandmother's chateau, she erected an altar to this god, whom she often dressed in women's clothes but described in the masculine gender—"He was as pure and charitable as Christ, as radiant and beautiful as Gabriel."[2] Perhaps this quasi-androgynous identity that the lonely child assigned to Corambé reflected her early belief that sexual distinctions are a matter of indifference in the eyes of God. Later in adolescence, while at a convent school in Paris, Aurore's mystical instincts resurfaced in a fanatical observance of the religious rites practiced by the Mother Superior and her nuns. Even then the young girl craved a better world than the one she knew.

On the death of her grandmother, Aurore went to live with her mother, a coarse and capricious woman who had little understanding of her daughter's emotional needs. To escape her domination, the unhappy eighteen-year-old sought refuge in an impetuous marriage to a boorish alcoholic, the baron Casimir Dudevant. For nearly nine years she endured this misalliance before fleeing to Paris in the company of a lover (seven years her junior) with vague literary inclinations.

At this point, she found herself confronted with the legal exigencies of a Napoleonic code that deemed her a minor in the custody of a husband who controlled the sizable estate of her late grandmother. Although Casimir could not touch her capital, he had full discretion in the disposition of its income, and he forced Aurore to make do with a paltry allowance. By skimping on food and clothing, she was able to afford a Left Bank garret on the quai Saint-Michel. There, of an evening, she could look across the Seine as the setting sun etched out the Gothic tracery on the west front of Notre-Dame. In spite of her financial deprivations, Mme Dudevant considered herself lucky that her husband didn't prosecute her for publicly cohabiting with her new lover. He could even have murdered his adulterous wife with impunity if he were so inclined, for under the Napoleonic code's double standard such homicides were considered justifiable. Not only would the law have exonerated him; it would have rewarded him with his wife's ample fortune. On the other hand, had Mme Dudevant killed her husband for a similar offense, it would have cost her up to twenty-one months in prison. No wonder the young baroness felt she had a grievance against society and took to airing her views in the novels that she and her lover, Jules Sandeau, were beginning to write.

Soon, however, the lackadaisical Jules left the writing entirely up to his mistress. In an incredibly short time she dashed off three novels, *Indiana, Valentine,* and *Lélia,* filled with candid revelations of women's sexual feelings that left her bourgeois readers agape. She stunned them even more by insisting on a woman's right to express these feelings not only within the confines of marriage, but also outside it if need be. Furthermore she demanded that women be shown the same respect as men when exercising this right. In other words, sexual freedom was no longer to be the exclusive prerogative of the male species. Stubbornly, George Sand (as the fledgling novelist now called herself) refused to accept marriage as a master-slave relationship, even though the Napoleonic code had effectively reduced it to that. In her eyes there was a higher moral law that demanded equality between husband and wife. Where love existed, this sacred bond of equality would always be respected, but once that bond was broken, so too was the marriage. Unfortunately, because divorce then was prohibited by both church and state, there could be no way to escape the legal bonds of marriage in situations where the moral bonds had already been sundered.

Although equality of men and women in the sexual sphere was a major motif in Sand's works from the beginning of her literary career, she soon realized that it could never exist in a society where wives remained the legal wards of their husbands, without any social or economic independence.[3] The recognition of her helplessness as a minor in the eyes of the law was forcibly impressed on Mme Sand in 1835, when she embarked on a series of court battles to obtain a legal separation from the baron Dudevant and regain control over her income and property. Through this grueling and humiliating experience, she gained a broader perception of the sweeping changes needed to free all those "born in fetters," that is, not just women but oppressed people everywhere, whatever their age, sex, class, or nationality.[4]

Due to the sensational nature of her early novels, it is probably safe to say that Mme Sand gained more readers than sympathizers in the 1830s. Among the latter was a charismatic "mystagogue" named Prosper Enfantin who felt he had been called by God to transform the socioeconomic philosophy of the comte de Saint-Simon into a religious movement, over which he was to preside as its self-appointed "Pope" (fig. 13.1). Among his spiritual goals was "the rehabilitation of the flesh" and the "emancipation" of women, by which he meant the abolition of monogamous marriage in favor of temporary love relations, referred to as limited partnerships. Such unions, he naively felt, would do away with prostitution. To the bourgeoisie, however, this notion was nothing less than a license for promiscuity. Further, because most of the French saw no difference between Enfantin's views and those expressed in George Sand's novels, they were not the least bit surprised when the Saint-Simonian leader asked the young authoress to share the direction of his "New Christianity" cult as its female "Pope." "It is bandied about," Sand wrote a friend in July 1832, "that the Saint-Simonians are going to offer me the title of Popess because my book [*Indiana*] fits their way of thinking."[5]

Like the public, Enfantin had misinterpreted the message that Mme Sand intended to convey in her novel. It was her comments about the tyranny of marriage and her later remark in *Lélia* about monogamous marriage being an abnormal state that led the Saint-Simonian leader to assume she agreed with his proposal to substitute "limited partnerships" for the bonds of wedlock. The fact was, Sand regarded monogamous marriages, where workable, as the ideal condi-

13.1 Père Enfantin, the "Pope" of the
Saint-Simonians, is shown here in the
uniform that he prescribed for all his
followers. Impressed by Sand's "liber-
ated" views on women and marriage,
he offered to make her the female
"Pope" of his sect, but was refused.

tions for a fulfilling union between men and women. From her own experience,
however, she concluded that the success of such unions was so rare as to be the
exception rather than the norm. More often than not, marriage seemed to place
one of the partners (almost invariably the wife) in a permanent state of servitude
that could be remedied only by a divorce. In nations like France where this option
was not available, Sand felt that extramarital affairs were justifiable as an alternative to the bondage of an inequitable marriage.

It should be emphasized here that Sand's concept of an extramarital relationship differed considerably from Enfantin's limited partnerships. For her, the basis
of such associations had to be genuine love, not merely a libidinous attraction.
Only with the loss of that love could the relationship be broken, leaving each
partner free to seek a new companion. By these criteria, George was able to con-
done consecutive relationships while condemning concomitant ones. "So far I
have been faithful to whomever I have loved," she wrote in May 1838, on the
brink of her campaign to win Chopin's affections.[6] By "faithful," she meant "I
have never deceived anyone and...never ceased to be faithful without very

strong reasons which had killed my love through the other's fault."[7] Actually at that particular moment she was, in fact, deceiving her current lover, Félicien Mallefille, a poet-playwright who was her children's tutor.[8] Only nine years later would Chopin finally come to realize that the woman whom he had loved for nearly a decade "doesn't always tell the truth." But "that's the privilege of a novelist," he concluded philosophically.[9]

Just as Sand sought for equality between men and women in their sexual relationships, she also stressed the equal role of spirit and flesh in love. Here she agreed with Enfantin about the need to "emancipate the flesh." "To *scorn the flesh* cannot be wise or useful," she argued in her attempt to break down Chopin's resistance to the physical consummation of their affair. After all, God created the body as well as the soul, she reasoned, therefore both must be emanations of the Divine. To separate "the spirit from the flesh... [only serves to make] convents and brothels necessary."[10]

Enfantin's quest for a female "Pope" to co-govern his new communal colony in the suburb of Menilmontant, east of Paris, attracted many applicants—most of them unsatisfactory. Those accompanied by their mothers were clearly not emancipated enough, while the bizarre costumes and cryptic babbling of others indicated more interest in theatrics than theology. When Enfantin first took notice of Sand, the Menilmontant community hadn't yet been established. At that time the Saint-Simonians were operating out of several bases in the city proper, including a building at No. 6 rue Monsigny, where they published their journalistic organ, *Le Globe,* and conducted public meetings to attract new followers.[11] In addition the group maintained a "temple" on the Right Bank's rue Taitbout and a lecture hall on the Left Bank's place de la Sorbonne. By 1831, when Chopin arrived in Paris, all of these centers were busily engaged in disseminating Enfantin's "gospel," concocted out of the comte de Saint-Simon's "scientific" revision of basic Christian dogmas. As the young musician noted, these Saint-Simonians, "also called 'neo-Christians'... and devoted to the notion of equality,... are winning over an enormous number of converts."[12] In many homes of the faithful, pictures of Enfantin began to replace the crucifixes that once hung on their walls. A number of Chopin's first friends in Paris were attracted to the new movement and attended its meetings. One of these was Berlioz, who wrote an editor of *Le Globe,* "Among schemes for the political reorganization of society, I am convinced that the plan of Saint-Simon is the most effective and most thorough."[13] Heinrich Heine and the tenor Adolphe Nourrit could also be seen at their sessions, where Franz Liszt often provided the music. An evangelical atmosphere pervaded these gatherings, which featured impassioned sermons exhorting those present to love one another—not only spiritually but carnally. Sometimes the preaching lasted up to thirty hours and reached such a fever pitch that many of the devout lapsed into trances, spoke in tongues, or collapsed in convulsions.

Little of this display had anything to do with Saint-Simon's original philosophy, which concentrated on scientific and economic solutions to the problems besetting postrevolutionary France. When Enfantin (who had only met Saint-Simon once, if ever) took over the sect, he disregarded his predecessor's teachings and organized his followers into a rigidly hierarchical society of his own design. In a picturesque colony overlooking Paris from a hill to the east of the city, he assigned each of his disciples certain daily tasks. Chopin's future doctor, Léon Simon, for example, became supervisor of the kitchen, and Gustave d'Eichthal (related to one of Chopin's pupils) was relegated to washing dishes. All landed property was held in common by the sect's members, marriage was abolished, and the family structure dismantled. With Enfantin in complete control, the colony became a despotic society, run with the discipline of a military camp. Its forty members were housed barracks-style in a building that contained twenty-three beds and seventeen hammocks. The day began at five o'clock with a trumpet blast to awaken the faithful. Breakfast followed at seven, with lunch at one o'clock, dinner at seven, and lights out at half past nine. The day's work began and ended with a hymn and was interspersed with communal meals, group exercises, group singing, and lengthy indoctrination sessions billed as "discussions." Not only were the disciples' activities regimented; their dress was prescribed. Everyone wore the same symbolic uniform of white pants (representing love), a red vest (work), and blue tunic (faith). Their vests buttoned up the back (which required the help of a comrade), demonstrating each person's dependence on his fellow-man), and everyone bore his name and title across the front of his chest. On Enfantin's tunic, for example, was the title Père (father). During the community's brief existence (from May 1831 to November 1832), it became a tourist attraction, drawing as many as ten thousand spectators a day on weekends.

Initially Sand respected "the good Enfantin, despite his absurd get-up and fanciful Utopias."[14] She was even flattered by his offer to share the sect's leadership with him but declined, stating, "I never felt myself up to such a grandiose calling."[15] The truth was, she found the sect's notions disturbing. Its rigid class divisions and arbitrarily assigned occupations were the antithesis of the freedom

13.2 Félicien David, a Saint-Simonian composer who wrote music for the sect's religious rites. He also composed orchestral works and oratorios, which elicited only a lukewarm reaction from Chopin, but were praised by Berlioz for their orchestration and melody. David's two most famous works, *Le Désert* and *Christoph Colomb,* are reflected in the flora and fauna that surround him in this portrait.

she sought. Nor did she approve of the subservient role of artists, poets, and musicians in its social schemata. The function of such individuals was mainly a utilitarian one of sustaining the cult members in the performance of their duties. Félicien David, for example, wrote music for the adherents' prayers and chants, many of which were composed by worker-poets with more enthusiasm than talent (fig. 13.2). He also wrote some serious symphonic works that Chopin described as "successful," although he didn't feel they were worth listening to.[16] Furthermore, Sand, who was an heiress of moderate wealth with a comfortable chateau, a large estate, and an income-producing house in Paris, didn't take kindly to Enfantin's abolition of private property. This, she exclaimed, was pure madness.[17] As for the Père's ideas on the emancipation of women, she suspected they were simply a ruse to help men gratify their libido.

The French government took an equally skeptical view of Enfantin, finding him not only a charlatan, but a violator of the law and a menace to society. In August 1832, he and other leaders of the sect were put on trial. The verdict, in favor of the state, condemned Enfantin to one year in the prison of Sainte-Pélagie and a hundred-franc fine. By the time he was released, the colony at Menilmontant had dissolved, unable to survive without the charismatic leadership of its pope.

In his refusal to accept defeat, Enfantin set out for the "Orient" (that is, the Ottoman Empire), still searching for his "Popess" or female Messiah. Eventually he gave up his quest for this mystical embodiment of femininity and gradually became involved in more practical endeavors such as building dams along the Nile and dabbling in the economic, social, and agricultural development of Algeria. Ironically after years of pursuing his Romantic fantasies, Enfantin finally began to grasp Saint-Simon's fundamental message—that visions of a better world were mere pipe dreams until society turned its financial and material abilities to harnessing Nature's resources through the discoveries of science. Although Enfantin himself did little more than break ground for his grandiose schemes, he sowed the seeds for later projects that would lead to the emergence of credit banking, the expansion of railroads throughout Europe, and the eventual construction of the Suez and Panama canals by the Saint-Simonian engineer Ferdinand de Lesseps.

Enfantin and his cult were but one of the quasi-religious sects preaching the doctrine of so-called Romantic socialism in early nineteenth-century France. As Balzac wrote in his novel *Lost Illusions,* "The [skepticism of the] eighteenth century brought everything into question; the task of the nineteenth century is to give the answers."[18] Many like Charles Fourier, the abbé Lamennais, Pierre Leroux, Etienne Cabet, and Auguste Comte tried to provide these answers by elaborating their own versions of a perfect society. Certainly solutions to the social upheavals brought on by the industrial revolution were urgently needed. From 1831 to 1836, approximately twenty thousand people arrived in Paris annually to swell the city's working-class population. Most of these were impoverished peasants, artisans, and unskilled laborers whose jobs had become obsolete in a newly mechanized age of railroads, steam engines, and spinning looms. Such a great migration of jobless individuals overwhelmed the nation's major economic centers like Paris and Lyons. The vast size of this idle workforce allowed employers to exploit its members mercilessly. By 1840 one-third of Parisians couldn't afford the luxury of meat and were barely able to provide themselves with bread and wine. A working day in most shops and factories lasted from thirteen to sixteen hours. To make ends meet, women and children were forced to seek jobs and soon composed as much as 35 percent of the workforce. All of these pressures led to the disintegration of family life and a moral decay that encouraged prostitution and crime as alternate sources of income. The laissez-faire attitude of the Orleanist government did little to remedy these conditions. Although it did pass a law in 1841 prohibiting the hiring of children younger than eight, the government persisted in banning trade unions, which had already proved effective in coping with England's industrial problems.

As for the Romantic socialists, their attempts to remedy the social ills brought on by industrialization were conflicting and their results ephemeral. This was perhaps inherent in the very concept of "Romantic socialism," which tried to reconcile the idealism and individuality of Romanticism with the pragmatism and collectivism of socialism. Like Saint-Simon's "New Christianity," most Romantic socialists tried to adapt a Christian-based morality to an industrial economy where machines were taking the place of people and scientific laws had superseded ethical principles as determinants of personal conduct. From their observation of material progress in the sciences, Romantic socialists came to assume that people could achieve an analogous moral progress in the realm of human behavior. If the physical world was capable of perfectibility, how could man, as a child of God, not be entitled to the same privilege? Although such a notion seemed Christian enough, the idea of man's perfectibility actually ran counter to the biblical doctrine of original sin, by which Adam's fall had condemned him and his descendants to lives of moral imperfection. This gloomy view of humanity as fundamentally sinful, weak, and dependent, however, didn't conform to the optimistic mood of the early nineteenth century. The prophets of Romantic socialism, therefore, insisted that man was capable of lifting himself up by his own bootstraps through adherence to their facile "do-it-yourself" formulas.

The road to moral progress, though, was beset with many obstacles, chief among them being how to ensure the ideal of individual liberty in a collectivist society and how to preserve equality in a hierarchical organization. These unresolved dilemmas caused many of the early experimental communities to fail. For example, in the Saint-Simonian colony at Menilmontant, Enfantin's aggressive regimentation virtually obliterated both social equality and individual liberty. At the other extreme, the Fourieriste communes (known as "phalanstères," a combination of the words "phalanx" and "monastery") imposed such minimal restraints on the individual that many of the colonies fell prey to anarchy.

Despite the great gulf between their philosophies, the Fourieristes and Saint-Simonians probably had more similarities than differences. Both offered a new Romantic generation the emotional outlets of faith and love as an antidote to the arid skepticism of their eighteenth-century predecessors. To facilitate these goals on a materialistic level, each established cooperative, profit-sharing communities in which inheritance and private property were abolished, marriage rendered obsolete, and the family unit absorbed into the greater whole of the community. Although George Sand seems to have regarded the Fourieriste phalanstères as the most workable of the utopian socialist societies, her maternal instincts rebeled against their practice of raising children in common without any regard for their biological parents. She also had doubts about the sincerity of Fourier's claim that women were a civilizing force on society and superior to men (in every respect except physical strength). After all, what could a reclusive old bachelor who lived and died hunched over a clerk's desk know about the opposite sex?[19]

Unlike the youthful authoress, Fourier was more interested in the metaphysical than the physical. His complex philosophy was based on a convoluted cosmological system that can be interpreted as either metaphorical or delusional. The universe, he predicted, was to last only eighty thousand years. After an initial period of chaos, complete harmony was to reign for eight thousand years. During this beatific era, the North Pole would become warm, the seas would turn into oceans of lemonade, and the continents would teem with 37 million poets equal to Homer, 37 million scientists comparable to Newton, and 37 million dramatists as brilliant as Molière. What's more, every woman would be blessed with at least four husbands and/or lovers. Even Mme Sand, with her concern for the role of passion in women's lives, considered such eschatological fantasies "bizarre and algebraic."[20]

But Fourier was not one to be shaken by criticism. With a faith as firm as his figures, he set out to proselytize his rival, Enfantin, and solicit money from Rothschild and the czar of Russia. Success eluded him, however, and it was not until 1838 (a year after his death) that the first phalanstère was finally established at Rambouillet. Although the colony's survival was brief, Fourier's permissive philosophy soon took root in the unlikely soil of puritanical New England with the establishment in 1841 of Brook farm near Boston, Massachusetts. Its founder was George Ripley, a member of the Transcendentalist movement, which included Emerson, Thoreau, Bronson Alcott, and Margaret Fuller. Henry Ward Beecher, Nathaniel Hawthorne, and the *New York Tribune*'s Horace Greeley were among those who supported the project. In its journal, *The Harbinger*, Brook Farm's inhabitants published some of Sand's novels. Even though the author still objected to Fourierism's treatment of women, she approved of the sect's "evangelical egalitarianism" and once described the communal lifestyle she shared with Chopin, her children, and their neighbors in the square d'Orléans as a sort of phalanstère.[21]

13.3 The abbé Lamennais was one of
George Sand's most influential philosophic
mentors. Her attraction to him may have
been more than intellectual, as she once
joked about setting up house with him.
Eventually, however, Sand lost faith in the
abbé because of his sexist belief in the
superiority of men over women.

In 1835, the year before she met Chopin, Sand was introduced to the controversial abbé Lamennais, whose influence was to mold her social philosophy far more than did that of the Saint-Simonians and the Fourieristes (fig. 13.3). The abbé, born in 1782, grew up during the years of the revolution under the care of an atheist uncle and didn't receive his first communion until age twenty-two. He was to wait another twelve years before taking holy orders in 1816. By then the restored Bourbons had renewed their strong ties to Rome, an act that gratified the young priest, who believed in religion as the foundation of all social life. However, when the July revolution of 1830 brought about the fall of the Bourbons (along with their alliance of "Throne and Altar"), Lamennais found himself forced to rethink his earlier views on religion and society.

That same year, Pope Gregory XVI's failure to condemn Czar Nicholas I's suppression of the Polish rebellion against Russia convinced Lamennais that the church had abandoned its mission of protecting the weak and oppressed. With the air of a prophet destined to lead the church out of its error, he founded a journal called *l'Avenir* (The future) as a vehicle for his views. Among the controversial policies supported in the journal were universal suffrage, free education, abolition of censorship, and the separation of church and state. Both the pope and the French government opposed such notions. Faced with suspension of his journal and the threat of a trial, the abbé left for Rome in 1831 to defend his position vis-à-vis the pontiff. When the latter condemned him, the rebel priest lashed out at the church, calling its hierarchy the sons of Satan bent on destroying Christ for a second time in a modern-day crucifixion. Just as before, he claimed that there would be another resurrection, this time of the "people" who were to be the new messiah, destined to replace a decadent Rome with a purified Jerusalem.

Out of the heat of anger and the glow of faith, Lamennais published his *Paroles d'un Croyant* (Words of a believer) in 1834. Its bitterness, submerged in the beauty of its language, became an inspiration for believers and nonbelievers alike. In it Lamennais wrote that the cry of the poor reaches up to the throne of God but fails to touch the ears of men. He then announced the transfer of his faith from a deaf church to the people it oppressed.

The profoundly moving expression of Lamennais's new credo in *Paroles d'un Croyant* prompted his contemporary, Pierre Leroux, to call it the Marseillaise of Christianity. By contrast, the aging Chateaubriand was disturbed by the abbé's rejection of the church and his alliance with the common man. "What is this priest dreaming of?" he exclaimed.[22] Of course, the chief critic of Lamennais's work was the pope himself, who claimed his "book, though small in size, is immense in its perversity."[23]

When George Sand first met Lamennais, she felt an immediate attraction to him. His identification with the "people" struck a sympathetic chord in the novelist, who had always felt a greater kinship with her mother's plebeian ancestry than with her father's aristocratic forebears. In the priest's presence, she experienced an intense elation. "I am seeing the abbé de Lamennais quite often, and am crazy about him," she wrote a friend in 1836. "This has caused a lot of talk.... People are even saying that I am going to settle in Paris to keep house for him. What a superb idea!"[24] The abbé, on the other hand, strove to keep a respectable distance from his enthusiastic disciple.

Inspired by Lamennais's vision of a New Jerusalem to come, Sand didn't burden herself too much with the details of its realization. "Who cares what...banner you carry so long as your hosts are always on the march towards a Republican future!...Whether in the name of Jesus, .. or in the name of Washington and Franklin...or in the name of Saint-Simon...what matters is that right prevails."[25] Some years later she would admit that as a woman and a novelist she "didn't have a very astute head for such things."[26] This came as no surprise to Thackeray, who once commented, "Not all the big words in the world can make Mrs. Sand talk like a philosopher."[27]

In time, the novelist came to realize that Lamennais was less of a liberal than she had thought, especially in regard to women's rights. As a contributor to his

13.4 Pierre Leroux, Sand's other great philosophical icon. Like Lamennais, Leroux also preached a doctrine of "Romantic socialism." Although Sand retained her admiration for his teachings, he came to disappoint her as a person because of his laziness, which made him a financial parasite on her and his other disciples.

journal *Le Monde* she took the opportunity of developing views (already expressed in her early novels) on the equality of the sexes in love, the role of passion in women's lives, and the moral necessity of divorce. To her chagrin, the abbé showed little enthusiasm for such themes and even deleted passages from her articles without consulting her. Eventually, in 1841, when he published a pamphlet asserting the intellectual superiority of men over women, she began to look elsewhere for spiritual guidance. Although she continued to respect Lamennais as one of the "greatest intellects in our century," she now placed her faith in a man she deemed nothing less than "a new Plato, a new Christ": Pierre Leroux (fig. 13.4).[28] In this charismatic "hairy philosopher," she was to find her most sympathetic mentor, one who proved to be far warmer and more compassionate than the proud and enigmatic Lamennais.

As a youth, Leroux had been an active Saint-Simonian who briefly owned and edited the sect's journal, *Le Globe*. In 1835, one of its contributors, Sainte-Beuve, introduced him to George Sand, at about the same time that she first met Lamennais. For some years afterward, these two philosophers were often found in her salon in the rue Pigalle, where she and Chopin lived in the early 1840s. By then Leroux had abandoned the Saint-Simonians, feeling that the cult had not truly emancipated women but merely exploited them. For a while he was attracted to the Fourieristes, but refused to sacrifice his independence to the conformity demanded by their phalanstères. In 1833 he founded a journal called *La Revue Encyclopédique* in which he introduced the word "socialism" (previously coined by the London Co-operative Society's magazine in 1827). Shortly afterward he and his brother Jules joined the radical Republican society Les Droits de l'Homme, where his philosophy (despite certain overtones of Christian doctrine) became almost indistinguishable from what people were beginning to call "communism." For Heine, who considered Jesus Christ "the Divine Communist," Leroux's amalgam of the two ideologies seemed perfectly logical.[29]

It wasn't until 1840, however, that Leroux consolidated his philosophical position in a lengthy tome entitled *De l'Humanité*. In it he proclaimed that man should no longer worship some distant and intangible God but devote himself to humanity, in whose hands lay the future of the world. Mme Sand, who fervently incorporated Leroux's views into her novels for nearly half a decade, would remain one of his most avid apostles for years to come. Not everyone, however, shared her ardor. Chopin, for example, had long accepted the one time typesetter's presence in his mistress's salon, but paid little attention to his zealous pronouncements. Nevertheless, in 1844, he sent copies of Leroux's works to his family in Poland—no doubt at Sand's suggestion.

From a purely literary point of view, Sainte-Beuve complained that Leroux wrote philosophy "like a buffalo wading through a swamp." He warned Sand that she was being duped by a charlatan out to establish himself as the pope of a new brand of communism.[30] Heine also urged her to beware of the philosopher's "sterile abstractions" and "half-baked ideas."[31] No amount of advice, though, could shake George's confidence in her new mentor. Unfortunately, time was to teach her what friends couldn't: Leroux was exploiting her for money. Twice married, the man was burdened with ten children as well as several younger siblings who relied on him for support. His dreams of making a fortune from a new typesetting invention came to naught, his journalistic career at *Le Globe* had been a disaster, and his soporific philosophic works merely served to accelerate his lifelong journey down the road to penury. As much as possible, Sand tried to help him out, loaning him money when she could and providing him with access to "the right people" who might be able to further his career. "You must know," the poet Pierre-Jean de Béranger wrote, "that our metaphysician [Leroux] is surrounded by a bevy of female admirers, chief of whom is Mme Sand . . . and that it is in gilded salons under the brilliant glow of chandeliers that he makes a public exhibition of his religious principles and his muddy boots."[32]

Besides providing Leroux with money and contacts, Sand helped him to found two periodicals, *La Revue Indépendante* and *L'Eclaireur de l'Indre*, which gave him the twofold benefit of a paying job and journalistic mouthpieces for his doctrines. By then Sand had become so imbued with Leroux's belief in the inevitability of man's moral progress that she insisted not even God could stop it. Mindful of his dictum that "Art...is nothing but an aspiration toward a better world," she eagerly incorporated the philosopher's views into her novels. One of the first of these was *Spiridion,* which she finished in Majorca at the beginning of her liaison with Chopin. Strangely enough, although many of its philosophical ideas came from Leroux, they are expressed through the character of a monk named Alexis, who, according to Sainte-Beuve, was a portrait of the abbé Lamennais. In her ardor to spread Leroux's gospel, Mme Sand read Chopin and her children passages from the philosopher's works during their long evenings in Majorca, and on their return to Paris, she coerced the headmaster of her daughter's boarding school to instruct the young girl in Leroux's philosophy.

Along with Chopin, François Buloz (Sand's publisher) was not impressed by Leroux's philosophy. But because he had always made handsome profits from George's novels, he sent the manuscript of *Spiridion* on to the printers without perusing it closely. When he finally realized what a long-winded, moralistic diatribe he'd accepted, he was afraid to stop its serialization because of the author's popularity. He refused, though, to publish her subsequent Leroux-inspired works.

In 1845 Leroux founded his own journal, *La Revue Sociale,* which lasted for only a few issues due to poor management. Too much of a visionary, the philosopher lacked sufficient skill and perseverance to handle practical matters. Although Sand excused this failing as one common to great minds, Chopin saw him in a more objective light. "Leroux," he observed, "has his weak side like everybody else: he never finishes anything that he undertakes. He dreams up some great idea and then forgets it."[33] What especially annoyed Chopin was Leroux's shameless habit of bilking money out of his friends. In time Sand herself began to see her idol as more of a financial parasite than a moral guide. "Alms can't save those who won't work," she finally acknowledged. "He received much and to no avail."[34]

By the revolution of 1848, Sand's philosophical orientation had moved far to the left of Leroux's, and she began calling herself a communist. All France, she predicted, would follow her example before the end of the century. Only a few months later, the appalling carnage produced by the communists during the June Days of 1848 disgusted her, and she returned once more to her faith in Leroux's gospel of equality and nonviolence. At the philosopher's funeral in 1871 (during the rampages of the Paris Commune), she followed his casket on foot to the cemetery.

13.5 Auguste Comte attempted to establish human behavior on a scientific basis and is hailed today as founder of the social sciences. His personal life, though, was fraught with instability, and he ultimately retreated into a delusional world centered around the worship of a married woman he barely knew.

What Sand acquired from Leroux's doctrine was a deep concern for all forms of oppression. From the pleas in her early novels to improve the lot of married women, she gradually began to address a much broader variety of social issues. With this expanded perspective, Sand was able to see the problems of women as merely a single wavelength in the vast spectrum of human injustice. Because of this she often became impatient with the budding feminists of her time and disdainful of their efforts.

The word "feminism" was supposedly coined by Fourier, who, along with Saint-Simon and Auguste Comte, professed doctrines intended to "liberate" women (fig. 13.5). As admirable as their goal may have been, many people, including George Sand, thought they had gone astray in their pursuit of it. At least Fourier and the Saint-Simonians were fairly explicit in their views on the matter, while Comte, whose new philosophy of Positivism was supposed to provide a scientific basis for all social behavior, seemed strangely perplexed when it came to the opposite sex. Eventually he sought refuge in a fantasized love affair with a married woman named Clothilde de Vaux and abandoned science to organize a religious cult in which Clothilde became the patron saint of humanity. Far from emancipating women, Comte's quasi-canonization of his mistress harked back to medieval asceticism, with its dichotomous view of women as either saintly creatures or debased temptresses. Such polarized images of women left them in the equivocal position of being either superior or inferior to men but never their equals. For Sand, who felt that the fullest expression of love could be found only through a combination of its sexual and spiritual aspects, any "either-or" perception of women was unsatisfactory.

Quite the opposite of Comte's dichotomous view of women was that of a little-known utopianist named Ganneau. In 1835 he proclaimed the eventual fusion of the sexes into a single being intended to represent the universality of God. Confident that his sect (called "Evadanisme," a synthesis of "Eve" and "Adam") would soon supplant Christianity, Ganneau wrote the pope to prepare for retirement. His cult, though, seems to have found little favor with God, Man, or Woman in its time.

In November 1846 Chopin wrote George Sand (then at Nohant) of a new religious sect in Paris similar to Evadanisme in its prediction of a future unisex world. It was called Fusionisme and had been founded by Louis de Tourreil, a protégé of Sand's friend, the green-haired chiromancer Captain d'Arpentigny. Although Chopin had the opportunity to attend one of the sect's meetings, he declined, and George seems to have expressed no interest in the cult on her return to Paris. Like Ganneau, de Tourreil has been consigned to the realm of idle dreamers. Today's genetic engineering, though, may yet prove them to be prophets ahead of their time.

A glance at the psychosexual problems that afflicted many of the social reformers discussed here may cast a significant light on their programs for a gender-integrated society. Saint-Simon's only marriage lasted little more than a year. Later, after being committed to an insane asylum outside of Paris, he tried unsuccessfully to commit suicide by shooting himself. Charles Fourier, who claimed that his birth had been prophesied in the Bible, was an equally disturbed individual with a number of bizarre personality traits. Early in life he suffered such intense feelings of guilt that he confessed to having committed fornication and simony at the age of seven. For all the freedom that he granted women in his phalanstères, he was always careful to exclude them from his personal life. He never married and seems to have had no grand passion in the course of his modest existence.

Comte, who had once been Saint-Simon's secretary and "adopted son," suffered from even more severe emotional problems. In 1825 he married a prostitute with a police record, the following year he began to suffer from epilepsy, and in 1827 he attempted suicide by jumping off the Pont des Arts. Subsequently he had recurrent "nervous breakdowns" during which he raved wildly, brandished knives, and experienced fantasies of grandeur. Eventually Comte's psychiatrist, Dr. Esquirol, pronounced him incurable, and in 1842, two years before he became romantically obsessed with Clothilde de Vaux, his wife left him. Despite the instability of the man, Comte the philosopher continues to influence intellectual thought to the present day, and retains a special niche in history as the founder of the social sciences.

Even though France in the early nineteenth century was one of the most civilized and progressive societies in the world, a caveman mentality still permeated its male population. Once, when a feminist organization, the Club des Femmes, staged a public demonstration, the National Guard took its members to a remote area and whipped them. Less barbaric but far more common were the tongue lashings women often suffered from many of their masculine contemporaries. Balzac, for one, claimed in his *La Femme de Trente Ans* that to liberate a woman was to corrupt her. Both Gavarni and Daumier were of like mind and published many cartoons ridiculing bluestockings, feminists, and "socialist women." Francine Duplessis Gray, in her biography of Louise Colet, has assembled a collection of the period's most virulent male-chauvinist remarks. For example, the anarchist Proudhon once wrote, "Woman is the intermediary link between man and the animal world," while Dumas *fils* claimed that "Woman...is the only unfinished work which God left for man to complete....[She] is the last thing created by God...on Saturday night. One feels the fatigue."[35] Baudelaire, Mirecourt, the Goncourt brothers, Frédéric Soulié, and Maxime du Camp all shared similar sentiments and inveighed against any woman who violated the conventional mores of their time.

In light of this rampant male chauvinism, it is small wonder that women finally decided to determine the future for themselves. Countess Merlin was among the first to take a timid step forward, railing against the misery inflicted on society by corsets, convents, and Negro slavery. In her published *Souvenirs*, the countess's views on women's creative and intellectual potential inspired George Sand to envision a future "when women might have access to the arts and sciences, as well as philosophy."[36]

In 1832 the first feminist journal was founded by two Saint-Simonian women, Marie-Reine Guindorf and Désirée Veret. It was originally called *La Femme Libre* (The free woman), but due to the immoral implications of that title it was soon changed to *La Femme de l'Avenir* (Woman of the future). A host of similar journals soon followed, which emboldened a group of feminists to send petitions to the Chamber of Deputies proposing that Louis-Philippe change his title from *Roi des Français* to *Roi des Françaises* (king of French women).

Although Sand would eventually broaden her vista to encompass the injustices practiced by society against all downtrodden individuals, whatever their sex, this was not typical of most feminists of the period. There were some exceptions, however. Louise Colet, for example, would eventually turn her sights from purely gender-oriented goals to the struggle for Italian independence. Flora Tristan, one of the fiercest of feminists, later expanded her agenda to include the working classes and devoted herself to the organization of labor on an international level. Her perception of the proletariat and how it could most effectively battle the bourgeoisie influenced Marx and Engels, who were to incorporate many of her conclusions into their *Communist Manifesto* of 1848.

Gentler but no less intense was Pauline Roland, whose long affiliation with the Saint-Simonians led her to realize that women's rights were but a part of humanity's general struggle to free itself from all forms of enslavement—whether imposed by one's fellow man or by the forces of nature. Later, after abandoning Saint-Simonianism, Roland sought, like Flora Tristan, to organize labor into "associations" (for teachers, launderers and laundresses, cooks, and so forth) with the ultimate goal of uniting these diverse groups into an all-encompassing union of associations. Had she remained purely a feminist without these larger aspirations, her fate would have been a happier one. As it was, Louis-Napoléon's government, alarmed by her instigation of the working classes, had her arrested and deported to Algeria.

For a number of reasons, Sand distanced herself from the feminists of her time, even though she endorsed many of their goals. In particular, she resented their self-absorption, which made many oblivious to others who were equally victimized by the socioeconomic structure of their times. At an early age, Sand had become aware of the great inequities condoned and perpetuated by society. Since childhood she had been caught up in a microcosmic class warfare between her nobly descended grandmother and her gutter-bred mother. She had seen the peasants on her grandmother's estate forced to live in misery, poverty, and despair because they lacked the economic and educational advantages to better their lot. After marriage, she had suffered the legal guardianship of a husband who controlled her income as well as her property. For the free-spirited young bride, the marital state became a humiliating and degrading form of bondage. Only then did she begin to grasp the helpless state of dependency in which she and other women of her time were trapped. Later, under the spell of Lamennais and Leroux, she came to view the goal of women's independence not as an end in

13.6 Louise Colet was an assertive feminist of the period whose sincerity Mme Sand doubted. Certainly her sexual exploits confirmed her dedication to the emancipation of women. Her sycophantic attempts to bribe money from the rich for her causes, however, convinced George that she was basically a social climber and hypocrite.

itself but merely a stage in the general progress of mankind toward a better world. At that point the feminist emphasis of her early novels expanded to incorporate the larger socialist concepts she had begun to embrace. Instead of burdening her readers with social guilt like her fellow novelists Eugène Sue and Victor Hugo, she preferred to inspire them with a faith in the future. Throughout her works, she had a knack for making the harshest reality glow with the optimism of her spirit. In her pastoral novels, she paints the arduous existence of the Berrichon peasantry with the idyllic colors of a Rousseauian palette.

If Sand's alienation from most feminists of her day was due to their tunnel vision, which blocked out everything unrelated to their gender-oriented goals, why then was she equally put off by others like Colet, Tristan and Roland, who saw women's problems as part of all mankind's struggle toward the nineteenth-century goal of moral and material perfection? Perhaps it was simply due to a conflict of personalities. Sand resented the militant, egotistical, and self-righteous postures of these women, whose sincerity she often doubted. Louise Colet, perhaps more than any of the others, incited her anger (fig. 13.6). From a literary point of view, Mme Colet was undoubtedly talented, having won the French Academy's poetry prize no fewer than four times. Her skills, however, extended beyond the printed sheet to the bedsheets, where she achieved a further sort of literary fame as the successive mistresses of the young Flaubert (Mme Bovary is modeled heavily on her), an aging de Vigny, and the terminally dissipated Alfred de Musset. In Sand's opinion, Colet was a pretentious sychophant. "I understand you better than you know yourself," she once told her. "You are too much in love with fame and the literary life for me to be able to communicate with you."[37] Quite bluntly Sand accused her of trying to gain access to the salons of the rich under the guise of her charitable pretensions. "I admire your talent and am well aware of your brilliant intellect. Nevertheless it is quite clear that you belong to those elitist natures while I count myself among those with a sincere heart."[38] In spite of her self-righteous tone, Sand seems to have assessed Colet accurately. As Colet's daughter admitted after her mother's death, "Poor Maman had a character which made everyone suffer."[39]

Sand considered Flora Tristan to be yet another elitist who took up the cause of women and other disadvantaged groups after being excluded from the privileged world of her aristocratic relatives. Tristan, a year older than Sand, had been born out of wedlock to a French mother and her hidalgo lover from Peru. The circumstances of her birth were not unlike those of Mme Sand, whose mother was a Parisian plebeian but whose father had blood connections with the royal houses of Poland, Saxony, and France. In contrast to Sand, who instinctively felt a greater affinity to her maternal heritage, Tristan aggressively tried to extort recognition and money from her titled Peruvian relatives. When they rejected her, she concluded that society needed a drastic revision of its attitudes toward women and the underprivileged. With the mindset of a militant martyr, Tristan set out to revenge herself against all oppressors of the weak and defenseless. Rather than cooperate with existing feminist and socialist groups, she preferred to monopolize the moral market by posing as a solitary prophet crying out in a wilderness of her own creation. Like Colet, she had an instinctive aversion to the working classes, whom she described in her diary as vulgar, rude, brutish, vain, and disagreeable. Their ignorance shocked her and at times provoked her to call them just plain stupid. Once when she was kept waiting to address a worker's meeting, she lost her temper. "I had told them I was bringing [them] salvation," she raged.[40] Later, in a calmer moment, she vowed, "Poor worker, I shall serve you in spite of yourself."[41] And serve she did—whatever the motive—not only in her writings but also through her actions.

Some years before Engels, Tristan studied the condition of the proletariat in London, the world's largest and most industrialized city. There she concluded (ahead of Marx) that their only salvation lay in an eventual class struggle that would give them control of the means of production. During the early 1840s, Tristan held meetings in her rue du Bac apartment to discuss the formation of a workers' international union. Among those present were two radical socialists, Germain Maurer and Arnold Ruge, who were sharing a house in the Left Bank's rue Vanneau with Karl Marx and his new bride. Shortly afterward in Marx's *The Holy Family* (written during his stay in Paris), Engels contributed an article praising Tristan's advanced theories.

Although Sand respected many of Tristan's goals, she had fundamentally different ideas on how to accomplish them. Her own philosophical priority was to elevate the "people" rather than to organize them—that is, to enhance their lives morally as well as materially. Contrary to Tristan, who preached that the emancipation of women was a prerequisite for the general improvement of social conditions, Sand insisted that women would never achieve complete freedom until society itself had undergone a moral transformation. Each saw the other as putting the cart before the horse. With her penchant for hyperbole, Tristan described women as the world's last slaves and calculated the progress of feminism by the number of women who assassinated their husbands. Although Sand considered Tristan a person of far more substance than the frivolous Colet, she acknowledged a Machiavellian ruthlessness in the way Tristan sought to achieve her ends. Even the easygoing Jules Janin once said that he'd just as soon befriend a python as Flora Tristan.

Only with Pauline Roland did Sand achieve some semblance of an amicable relationship. In the mid-1830s both became disciples of Pierre Leroux. At that time Roland had formed a liaison with another of Leroux's disciples, Jean-François Aicard, by whom she had three children. When Aicard abandoned her, she moved into Leroux's communal society at Boussac, a small town near Sand's chateau in Berry. There she became one of the collaborators (along with Sand) on the *Revue Indépendante* and *L'Eclaireur de l'Indre,* dedicated to the propagation of Leroux's gospel.

When Flora Tristan died in 1844, she left a teenage daughter, Aline, alone and without means. Thanks to Roland's intervention, Aline was sent to Mme Bascan's school for girls in Paris, where George Sand's daughter, Solange, happened to be a pupil. Despite the novelist's antipathy toward Tristan, she found the daughter appealing and sought to find her a suitable husband. The man she chose was a Fourieriste named Edouard de Pompery, who worked as a political journalist. Aline, Sand assured him, was as "good and as tender as her mother was imperious and bad-tempered."[42] Fortunately for posterity, Sand's efforts came to naught. Soon afterward, Aline fell in love with a man named Clovis Gauguin and married him. Their son, Paul, one of the most outstanding painters of his time, inherited his grandmother's troubled genius. Instead of trying to reform society as she had done, he preferred to escape it and ended his life on a remote South Pacific island near Tahiti.

By the time of Tristan's death, socialism had passed beyond its infancy and was being weaned from the breast of Romantic idealism on which it had once been nourished. Although such pap may have quickened the Romantic soul, it left a void in the proletarian belly. Pragmatic goals based on economic realities were supplanting the aesthetic concepts of the Romantics. The dominant concern of this new school of reformers was to bring material comfort rather than spiritual contentment to society. Its more radical members soon took to calling themselves communists.

The year 1840 stands out as a pivotal point in the period's sociopolitical orientation. That year, Louis Blanc published his *Organisation du Travail* (Organization of labor), in which he called for state-supported workers' coops as a means of abolishing the wage system and promoting the equalization of capital. The same year Etienne Cabet, a self-educated lawyer, one-time Carbonaro, and supporter of the 1830 Polish uprising, published two brochures, "Why I Am a Communist" and "My Communist Credo." Perhaps the most inflammatory of all those who advocated social change in 1840 was the anarchist Pierre Joseph Proudhon, who published a pamphlet called "What Is Property?" In answer to his own question, the author replied that property was nothing less than theft, a form of appropriating for one's own use something that belonged to everyone. In his opinion the state, along with capitalism and the church, formed a "Satanic Trinity" that was responsible for all of society's problems. Initially Sand regarded Proudhon as "a simple worker" and "a remarkable thinker," although she would later attack him for lacking the socialist ideals of Lamennais and Leroux.[43]

In October 1843, as Eugène Sue's *Mysteries of Paris* was in its final newspaper installments, the twenty-five-year-old Karl Marx and his new bride of four months arrived in Paris. Earlier in Germany the young man had written typical Romantic prose and poetry dealing with the creative artist's isolation from an insensitive, materialistic society. Later he studied philosophy, history, and law in Bonn and Berlin, which galvanized his early idealism with the tougher metals of atheism and expediency. His purpose in coming to Paris was to study the influence of economics on social structure in a city plagued by revolutionary and industrial upheavals. On his arrival he took an immediate delight in Daumier's cartoons satirizing the selfishness, greed, and moral complacency of the bourgeoisie. He also relished Eugène Sue's vigorous attacks on their exploitation of the Parisian working classes.

Whether or not Marx was equally aware of Sand's novels, he was impressed with the socialist-oriented *Revue Indépendante* that she and Leroux published. His own ideas at that time were largely shaped by the metaphysical concepts of the German philosopher Hegel. Social progress, according to Hegel, was a recurrent cycle of conflict between opposing forces, where the victor inevitably finds himself challenged by a new opponent, leading to a renewed conflict and a further repetition of the cycle. For the youthful Marx this was a convincing theory but difficult to prove in the stagnant, semi-feudal society of early nineteenth-century Germany. Only in Paris or London could he actually visualize the dramatic unfolding of the Hegelian conflict between opposites (in this case, the proletariat versus the bourgeoisie). What he discovered in Paris was no longer some philosophical abstraction but the day-to-day struggle of a brutalized working class trying to break free from the oppression of its capitalistic masters. Ironically it was in Paris's rue Vanneau, on the fringe of the aristocratic faubourg Saint-Germain so adored by Chopin, that Marx underwent his conversion to communism.

The appearance of communism on the Parisian scene had preceded Marx's arrival in the city by several years. As early as 1841, Sainte-Beuve was already calling both Sand and Leroux "communists." At the same time, Heine claimed that most workers in the poorer quarters of Paris were communists. By 1847 it was estimated that France had at least 200,000 communists, most of whom lived in Paris. That same year Balzac, referring to conditions in the city, wrote his future wife, the countess Hanska, "You don't know how communism is gaining ground here."[44] For him communism meant "the doctrine that wants to overthrow everything and share everything."[45] Actually the word "communism" was originated in 1840 by Etienne Cabet, a provincial cooper's son who organized the world's largest working-class movement under the very nose of France's bourgeois Citizen King. The following year, Sand and Leroux's *Revue Indépendante* published an article on communism, albeit not a very favorable one (the author, Jacques Dupré, deplored the loss of individuality and the tendency toward authoritarianism inherent in a communist society). Only three years later, Sand herself adopted a definitely communistic stance in her novel *Le Meunier d'Angibault*, where she berated the rich for stealing from the poor. By then Flora Tristan was already calling for the establishment of an international workers' union. In 1845, the year Marx was expelled from France, Sand proclaimed that "the truth of communism is every bit as respectable as the truth of the Gospels since it is fundamentally the same truth."[46]

What Marx had found in Paris was an environment far more advanced in its socioeconomic views than any in Germany. In the French capital he also encountered a large German colony, which included such radicals as Arnold Ruge, Moses Hess, Georg Herwegh, and the Russian anarchist Mikhail Bakunin. For reasons that had more to do with financial needs than ideology, Marx and his wife set up a communal household with three other couples who happened to be of a similar sociopolitical orientation. Although each family had its own living quarters, all shared the kitchen, dining room, and a domestic helper. Despite being in the shadow of Paris's "noble faubourg," the group lived a frugal, almost Bohemian existence. Ruge, who was already a committed communist, had organized a party publication called the *German-French Yearbook*, which solicited articles from such potential sympathizers as Victor Hugo, Pierre Leroux, the abbé Lamennais, Lamartine, Louis Blanc, Etienne Cabet, and Pierre-Joseph Proudhon. When none responded, Ruge suggested to Marx that they contact feminists like George Sand and Flora Tristan, whom he considered "more radical than Louis Blanc and Lamartine."[47] Again the two got no response. As a result, most of the articles in the one and only issue of the yearbook (February 1844) were written by Marx himself. It was in this publication that he announced for the first time his adoption of the communist doctrine.

Only a year earlier Marx had become acquainted with Friedrich Engels, the son of a rich industrialist in England. While managing his father's factories there, Engels conceived the need for a communist alternative to the evils of capitalism. Later in 1844, on a trip to Paris, he visited Marx and pressed his views on him. Besides Engels and the German radicals with whom he shared his rue Vanneau quarters, Marx was also swayed by the writings of Adam Smith, who argued that the worker rather than the capitalist contributed most to society's welfare. Probably, though, he learned more about the Parisian proletariat from what he saw rather than what he read or heard.

Once Marx had taken his stand as a communist, he and Ruge began publishing a journal called *Vorwärts*, which was to be a mouthpiece for their political and social doctrines. Because of Sand's connection with the liberal *Revue Indépen-*

dante, Ruge wrote to her in May 1844 hoping she would contribute to their new journal. For unknown reasons, however, the novelist never replied, and as far as we know, she had no personal contact with either Ruge or Marx. Nevertheless Marx had sufficient esteem for Sand to dedicate one of his later works, *The Poverty of Philosophy,* to her. In July 1848, Sand and Marx had a brief correspondence concerning the novelist's supposed political involvement with Bakunin, one of Marx's principal opponents. After Sand's vigorous denial of any collusion with the Russian anarchist, she and Marx had no further communication. By then Sand was becoming disillusioned with the radicals, and soon afterward separated herself from them.

If Ruge failed to gain Sand's collaboration, he found a willing associate in Heinrich Heine, who was at the peak of his radicalism. As a baptized Jew, Heine berated the "Jewish poison" of capitalism, typified by rich financiers like Rothschild (whom he called "Herr von Shylock").[48] Such talk appealed to Marx (also a baptized Jew), and the two struck up a friendship. Both felt that the current socioeconomic state of Europe demanded complete restructuring. Heine, however, was appalled by Marx's vision of the working class as the basis of this new society. Not only did he find the notion of a proletarian-dominated world distasteful, he felt that society could never be regenerated on economic and political grounds without the ameliorating influence of mind and spirit. Communism, for him, heralded the end of civilization. The lower classes, in their "imbecilic egalitarian ecstasy," would surely "destroy everything beautiful and sublime on this earth."[49] As much as the two men differed ideologically, Marx claimed that Heine was the only person in Paris he regretted leaving when the French government expelled him on January 11, 1845. Although much of what Marx wrote in Paris is significant in the evolution of his thought, it had little influence on the immediate course of events in France. Engels's prophecy that Paris would be the scene of the proletariat's first revolutionary triumph was almost fulfilled with the June uprising of 1848 and again during the disastrous debacle of the Paris Commune in 1871. Not until 1917, when the Bolsheviks overthrew Russia's czarist government, did the proletariat finally achieve the victory Engels had predicted for them.

Like Heine, Sand and Sue clung to the Romantic view that economic betterment of the working classes alone would never cure the ills of society. Man had spiritual as well as physical needs, and no program of social reform could succeed without taking both into account. Sue, for example, encouraged "the lower orders" to "improve themselves, to write, to read the poets and sometimes to

13.7 A lithographic parody of George Sand's political and feminist activities. In a rather free translation, the caption below it reads, "If George Sand seems puzzling and complex, it's because true genius has no sex."

make verses."[50] As for Sand, she actively promoted proletarian poets, helping them to get into print not only for their own gratification, but for the enrichment of society as well.

With the outbreak of the February revolution in 1848, Sand felt "the people's" hour had arrived (fig. 13.7). The announcement of a republic to replace the July monarchy threw her into a fit of ecstasy. This time, the working classes would not be duped into surrendering their gains to the bourgeoisie as in 1830; this time, they were determined to retain the ground they had won. Thrilled by their spirit, Sand dedicated herself to their cause. From her son's apartment on the Left Bank's rue de Condé, she began writing for the *Bulletin de la République,* contributing articles to the left-wing *La Réforme* and her own evanescent *La Cause du Peuple.* Like Marx she remained convinced that the bourgeosie were the enemy of the people, and issued dire warnings to the rich that "the future will do away entirely with individual wealth."[51] Daily she could be seen conferring with members of the provisional government at all levels from the poet-president, Alphonse Lamartine, on down. Her activism prompted the editors of a feminist journal, *La Voix des Femmes,* to propose her as a candidate for the Constituent Assembly. Although she appreciated their esteem, she made it clear that the time had not yet come for women to play a political role in government. "What bizarre caprice drives you to engage in Parliamentary battles when you aren't even able to exert your own personal independence?" she asked them.[52] How could they ever expect a woman to hold public office as long as she remained a minor, deprived of the right to vote? Their premature—not to say illegal—attempts to thrust women into political office would only end by setting the feminist movement back years if not decades, she warned. For these reasons she remained content to advise those in power, much as the duchesse de Dino and the Princesse Lieven had formerly influenced Talleyrand and Guizot.

In April and later in May some of the more rabid revolutionaries, buoyed by their initial successes, overplayed their hand and were routed by the provisional government's forces with cries of "death to the communists!" The unspeakable atrocities and appalling death toll of the bloody June riots that followed disillusioned Sand, who blamed the communists for the debacle. Their promises had once seduced her, but their violence now revolted her. Sick at heart, she returned to Nohant, where she abandoned the role of political activist to become a simple observer of the social world around her. Without sacrificing her idealism, she came to realize that more could be accomplished through restraint than revolution. Over two decades later, the excesses of the Paris Commune left her more disenchanted than ever with the communists. By then in her late sixties, a wearied Sand wrote, "My age rebels against the tolerance of my youth."[53]

Throughout Chopin's relationship with Sand, he strove to dissociate himself from the socioeconomic and political world of his mistress—a reflection of the amazing capacity with which human beings compartmentalize their lives. Both he and Sand were lifelong Romantics, but in their artistic endeavors they took diverging paths. While Chopin's ethereal genius distilled and preserved in music the beauty of a passing era, Sand, with her more earthy genius, perceived the social ramifications of art and used her talents to bring about a better world, not only for her own generation but for all those to follow. Many of the goals she envisioned for women and the working classes have already been achieved. Her recognition of the futility of violence and the need for moderation enabled her to navigate a course between the elusive promises of communism and the inherent evils of monarchical and capitalistic regimes. At times when her judgment failed, her instincts prevailed, and she was able to pursue a life that in the end proved practical, and above all, productive.

CHAPTER 14

The Big Shadow of the Little Corporal

Napoléon Becomes a Legend

"The life of Europe centered in one man; men tried to fill their lungs with the air he had breathed. Yearly France presented that man with three hundred thousand of her youth; it was the tax to Caesar.... They well knew that they were destined to the slaughter; but ... even if one must die, what did it matter? Death itself was so beautiful, so noble, so illustrious, in its battle-scarred purple!"

"As on the approach of a tempest there passes through the forests a terrible gust of wind which makes the trees shudder ... so had Napoléon, in passing, shaken the world; ... The Pope had travelled three hundred leagues to bless him in the name of God and to crown him with the diadem; but Napoléon had taken it from his hands. Thus everything trembled in that dismal forest of old Europe; then silence succeeded."[1]

*F*OR MANY FRENCHMEN it was a reverent silence; for others it was the stillness of discontent and *ennui*. The author of these passages was the poet and playwright Alfred de Musset, who had once been George Sand's lover before Chopin. In his *Confessions of a Child of the Century,* Musset attempted to convey the physical and intellectual lassitude of the nation's youth during the post-Napoleonic era. "There is no more love, no more glory," he wrote. "What heavy darkness over all the earth! ... Man is here below to satisfy his senses.... To eat, to drink and to sleep, that is life ... the only intellectual joy is vanity."[2] Like many of the indolent and effete members of his generation, de Musset tried to evade responsibility for his own dissolute and self-destructive life by posing as a victim of the general disillusionment that permeated France then—that "fondness for despair"[3] called the *mal de siècle,* or "disease of the century."

Fate, these young men felt, had maliciously excluded them from participating in France's most heroic age and deprived them of the chance to perform those valorous deeds that would have brought honor to themselves as well as to their nation. They were barred from the incomparable drama of the Empire, filled with the thunderous clashes of titans—all played out on a stage full of imperial props gleaned from the marbled elegance of classical antiquity and the sand-swept splendor of ancient Egypt. Nothing could have been more intoxicating to the Romantic imaginations of these latecomers on the stage of history. Alas, for de Musset and the other children of his century, the curtain had fallen, the house was dark, and there were no roles left for them to play. Small wonder that in the sobering aftermath of such a dazzling performance they felt bored, idle, and sick at heart.

While these miasmic youths pined for a world they were too young to have known, those of an older generation like Stendhal—an "ambivalent Bonapartist"—were able to assess the fallen emperor and his accomplishments more realistically. In his biography *A Life of Napoléon,* the fifty-three-year-old Stendhal remarked, "My love for Napoléon is the only passion remaining to me; yet it does not prevent my seeing his faults and the petty weaknesses with which he can be reproached."[4] Few Frenchmen living under the July monarchy could make such an objective statement, for their revered emperor had, by then, become a legend, purged of all mortal imperfections in the purifying fire of a hero's apotheosis. His was the glory that Balzac once described as "the sunlight of the dead."[5]

Those who glorified the Napoleonic bee, however, tried to forget its nasty sting, which once wreaked havoc, pain, and death across vast stretches of Europe. Talleyrand, an intimate of the emperor in the days of his greatest triumphs, was one of the few who recognized this irony. "The French people are civilized," he observed, "their sovereign is not."[6] The great Napoléon was, in truth, a brutal tyrant, quite willing to sacrifice human lives, liberty, and property to the demands of his insatiable ambition. For a decade and a half, the French tolerated these flaws in the man who led them from revolutionary chaos to imperial grandeur. Even though Waterloo eventually dampened their euphoria, it didn't tarnish their nostalgia. To preserve their golden memories of the past, many of the French were willing to forget the harsh realities they had endured under the despotic emperor, whose autocratic reign had imposed a crippling censorship of the press and strict enforcement of "political correctness" in all forms of popular expression, especially the arts. Worse yet was the emperor's massive military conscription, which took a disastrous toll on the nation's youth. As Napoléon continued to drain France of its human and financial resources, he found himself unable to fulfill his great dreams for the beautification of Paris, which by the time of his departure for Elba had become an occupied city of unfinished monuments, starving people, grieving widows, destitute orphans, and maimed young men.

Hope revived briefly during the "Hundred Days," when the emperor arose, phoenix-like, out of the ashes, but this time as a bird of a different feather. No longer the flagrant autocrat of old, Napoléon flew up from Marseille to Paris, flaunting the plumage of Liberalism. He even considered (or, at least, pretended to consider) accepting Benjamin Constant's draft of a parliamentary constitution for the establishment of his new government. At Waterloo, Wellington reduced the phoenix once more to ashes. But, like the fabled bird, the tenacious Corsican was to survive and live on in the realm of legend.

After Waterloo, the Bonapartes found themselves "out," while the Bonapartists remained "in": that is to say, all the members of the emperor's family were expelled from the country, while most of his followers were allowed to resume their lives as normal French citizens. This policy evolved more for reasons of practicality than generosity since virtually everyone in France under the Empire had supported "the little corporal" (as the diminutive conqueror was affectionately known). To expel these devotees of the emperor would have literally depopulated the nation. To ignore them was equally infeasible, with the government's two legislative bodies full of "rehabilitated" Bonapartists. Despite frequent tensions with new regime, Bonapartism managed to survive by taking on the protective coloring of its environment. Cleverly these one-time devotees of the former emperor had concealed the imperial purple of their past by donning the white and gold mantle of their restored Bourbon monarchs.

From time to time during the Restoration the nouveau aristocracy of Napoleonic nobles tried to flaunt their imperial titles in public only to be disdained by those with more prestigious ancien régime patents of nobility. Actually these freshly dubbed dukes, barons, and counts comprised only a small fraction of the vast number of Bonapartists who secretly preserved the memory of the fallen hero while going about their day-to-day lives as financiers, bureaucrats, shopkeepers, clerks, and factory workers. Deep within their hearts, the flame of faith in an eventual resurrection of the empire still flickered, sustained by two slender hopes: that Napoléon might someday escape from Saint Helena and return to France, or that his son, the duc de Reichstadt, a mere four-year-old child in 1815, would eventually become king and lead France once again to triumph. The passage of time, however, soon made it clear that their young and vigorous emperor, now middle-aged and corpulent, was doomed to perpetual exile on his remote and rocky island. As for the duc de Reichstadt, he was far off in Austria, being reared by his Hapsburg relatives under the watchful eye of Prince Metternich.

After the death of the young duke (popularly known as "l'Aiglon," the eagle) in 1832, the Bonapartists' prospects dimmed, but a new hope sustained them. Because Napoléon had become their god, many Bonapartists believed that his spirit transcended the confines of the material world and remained alive. Many crusty old Napoleonic veterans, however, were baffled by such a metaphysical concept. For their comprehension, it was necessary to weave a considerable amount of fiction into the fabric of history. As early as 1800, while still a consul, "the little corporal" (who was, in fact, five foot, seven inches tall, a respectable height for Frenchmen of his time) had already begun to visualize himself as the "lawgiver, the restorer of religion, the saviour of France and of society."[7] To promote this vision of himself, he proposed political rights for Jews, ownership of land by peasants, and the legality of divorce. Later in the memoirs that he wrote on the island of Saint Helena, he strove to reinforce his image as "a democrat, a friend of liberty and peace... I am a man of the people," he declared. "I come from the people myself."[8] His empire, as he saw it, was simply an extension of the great revolution of 1789. He had in short waged war to defend and disseminate the hard-won freedoms wrested by the French nation from the Bourbons at the end of the last century. During these final years of exile, Napoléon could have had little expectation that such patent revisionism would ever alter his own fate. What it did accomplish, though, was to enhance that "sunlight of the dead" that would later cast its golden aureole over his memory.

By the time of his death in 1821, Napoléon had already entered the ranks of the world's immortals. Over the next nineteen years while his body remained on the island where he died, his spirit, duly rehabilitated and resurrected, became a pervasive influence among the French. Few observed that the regenerated "liberator" of Europe bore little resemblance to the ambition-ridden general who had ravaged Europe. Likewise few perceived that the author of the Napoleonic code was not a benevolent dispenser of justice for all, but a self-serving trickster who (as Thackeray observed) "made the law equal for every man in France but one."[9] Nor did they note the disparity between the egalitarian Napoléon of legend and the real-life elitist who dispensed aristocratic titles to his henchmen and rewarded his relatives with the confiscated thrones of Europe.[10] Finally, the typical Frenchman's *amour-propre* kept him from realizing that the cohesive spirit of fraternity that the fabled Napoléon inspired among his troops and citizenry was actually a form of mass manipulation by which he successfully duped the nation into following him mindlessly to their own destruction. Although the empire had converted the chaos of revolution into some semblance of order, it certainly didn't bring France liberty, equality, or fraternity.

Just as Napoléon extended his power throughout Europe, so the Napoleonic legend took root in many areas beyond France. In both Poland and Lithuania (as noted in the previous chapter), the concept of a Napoleonic "spirit" took on messianic overtones of spiritual redemption as well as political and social liberation. For men like Towiański and the triumverate of Polish Romantic poets, Mickiewicz, Słowacki, and Krasiński, the spirit of Napoléon assumed aspects of Christ as well as Caesar that made the legendary emperor a religious as well as secular force in mid-nineteenth-century Europe.

In the summer of 1830, when France finally lost patience with the reactionary policies of Charles X, the Bonapartists found themselves unable to seize an opportunity that seemed ripe for the picking. By then Napoléon had been out of power for fifteen years and dead for nine. During this time the nation's recollection of him had acquired an aura of enlightened liberalism that the Bonapartists sought to use to their advantage. Their plan was to dress up the emperor in new clothes designed to fit the political fashions of a leftward-moving society on the brink of a working-class revolution. Unhappily at that crucial moment, the Bonapartists discovered they had no one to wear the emperor's new clothes. Even Napoléon, were he still alive, would have preferred something of a more autocratic cut, while his heir, the duc de Reichstadt, was in the last stages of tuberculosis and had little use for anything other than a nightshirt and a dressing gown.

For lack of an alternative, the Bonapartists continued to pin their hopes on the consumptive duke, whom they acclaimed as "Napoléon II."[11] To their disappointment, l'Aiglon had become too ill to fly and was doomed to die in the maternal nest before he could ever test his wings. It didn't really matter, according to comte Apponyi, the Austrian ambassador, who claimed that Europe would never have tolerated another Bonaparte on the throne.

When revolution finally broke out in July 1830, the French steered a precarious course between the Scylla and Charybdis of Bonapartist imperialism and radical Republicanism by which they arrived in the supposedly safe harbor of a constitutional monarchy under Louis-Philippe. If the majority of Bonapartists acquiesced at the time, many had ambivalent feelings about the course taken by the ship of state. "We have made a big revolution and it has fallen into the hands of small men,"

Balzac wrote.[12] Disillusioned with the stodgy "citizen-king," the author kept a statuette of "the true King," Napoléon, in his study and swore that what this great man had failed to achieve with the sword he himself would accomplish with the pen.[13]

The dissatisfaction felt by Balzac and much of the French nation was not immediately apparent in the general exhilaration following the "three glorious days" that brought Louis-Philippe to the throne. The Bonapartists who welcomed the fall of the Bourbons developed an unlikely rapport with the *juste-milieu* of the new king. In the aftermath of the July revolution, demonstrations commemorating the dead emperor were so numerous one might almost have thought that the Bonapartists rather than the Orleanists had come to power.

"The life of Napoléon is the epic theme of our century," Delacroix once wrote, and by 1830 the truth of his observation was readily apparent.[14] In October of that year, only three months after the fall of the Bourbons, an exhibition of paintings devoted to Napoléon was held at the Luxembourg palace. The following January, the Odéon produced Dumas's bloated six-act drama in nineteen scenes called *Napoléon Bonaparte ou Trente Ans de l'Histoire de France* (Napoléon Bonaparte; or, Thirty years of French history). Its star was the equally bloated Mlle George, a former mistress of the emperor. Though no longer the svelte siren of empire days, she still had sufficient charms to lure the libidinous Dumas into a small room behind her boudoir, where she kept him under lock and key for a week until he completed this dramatic tribute to her ex-lover. According to Alfred de Vigny, it was "a bad play which he ought never to have written."[15] George Sand called it "pitiful," although she admitted being thrilled by its dazzling spectacle of Moscow in flames.[16] Despite this adverse criticism, the play became a wild success with the public.

In the months that followed, theaters all over Paris vied to present dramas about Napoléon, exhausting every aspect of the man's life from his days as a student, young lieutenant, and bridegroom to his later years as emperor, father, and political exile. At the Gaîté theatre's *Napoléon en Paradis,* he was even shown entering heaven through billowy white clouds suspended in front of a sky-blue backdrop. Floating among the clouds were veterans of the recent July revolution dispensing tricolor cockades to the angels. Undoubtedly the most grandiose of these Napoleonic dramas were *L'Empereur et les Cent-Jours* and *L'Homme du Siècle,* both staged in the mammoth arena of the Cirque Olympique. At his Diorama, Daguerre mounted a trompe-l'oeil tour de force called *The Tomb of Napoléon at Saint Helena,* which proved to be so realistic that viewers tried to break off willow branches or snip a geranium as souvenirs. Even Louis-Philippe was so impressed with this lifelike production that he had the mint issue 165 medals with memorable scenes from the First Empire. "The more the great man is portrayed before the public the more they clap; they are crazy about their emperor," a contemporary wrote. "Whenever the man of destiny is presented, the people cry: More!, more!...Don't stop! Don't stop!"[17] During one play about Napoléon's life, the actor who portrayed Hudson Lowe, Napoléon's sadistic guardian on Saint-Helena, aroused such animosity that he was dragged from the stage and thrown into a nearby fountain.

Other popular dramas extolling Napoléon featured such stars as Frederick Lemaître and Mlle Virginie Déjazet. Noted for her masculine roles, Déjazet not only played the emperor himself in *Napoléon à Brienne* but his son as well in another production, *Le Fils de l'Homme*. Lesser theatrical luminaries also impersonated the legendary emperor at the Variétés, the porte Saint-Martin, the Vaudeville, l'Ambigu, and the Palais Royal. Even the Opéra-Comique did a song-and-dance production entitled *Josephine ou le Retour de Wagram* (Josephine; or, The return from the Battle of Wagram). On the streets people who had seen these performances went around imitating Napoléon's gestures and Corsican accent. Among them was the publisher Emile de Girardin, who had the puerile tendency of striking Napoleonic poses for the sake of effect.

In other fields of the arts, Hugo wrote a poem entitled "The Return of the Emperor," while Thiers labored intermittently for years over his *History of the Consulate and the Empire*. Between Berlioz's mammoth productions, he squeezed out an ode on the death of Napoléon, and the painter Horace Vernet did an assembly-line business in Napoleonic scenes, most of which the government snapped up at 100,000 francs apiece. Among other artists of the era who lent their talents to preserving the memory of Napoléon and his empire were men like Henri Monnier, Baron Gros, Horace Vernet, David d'Angers, and above all, Eugène Delacroix, whose two brothers fought in the imperial armies. According to Le Bris, Delacroix's famous painting of Liberty leading the People was not so much a tribute to the July monarchy as a celebration of the return of the tricolor, which had last flown over France under the reign of the emperor. On a less elevated level, the rage for Napoleonic memorabilia flourished with the auction of one of the emperor's hats for 1,950 francs, nearly four times its original value.

Bonapartism, as Louis-Philippe soon learned, was more than a musty memory among aging veterans of the Grand Army. Like a spark that leaps from one tree to the next in a burning forest, the flame of the Napoleonic legend had jumped across generations to ignite the devotion of the nation's youth who never knew the man himself. As already noted, members of the *jeunesse dorée* like Alfred de Musset belonged to a host of young acolytes who tended this sacred flame of imperial glory. While branding Louis-Philippe a despot, they shut their eyes to Napoléon's far more tyrannical behavior. For these bored and idle youths, the emperor, like a modern-day "Prometheus, chained to the rocky island of Saint Helena" became a "living torch," who illuminated history with the light of freedom and justice.[18]

In this younger generation was the novelist Eugène Sue, whose father had been surgeon-in-chief to Napoléon during the Russian campaign of 1812. In his novel *The Wandering Jew,* Sue portrays Napoléon as a hero of the fictional Marshal Simon, who idolized the emperor because he "only accepted war in the hope of one day being able to dictate universal peace."[19] "Do you think that the memory of the Emperor is extinct?" his son asks. "No, no," the marshal replies, confident that the hallowed name of Bonaparte will live on in the person of his heir, the duc de Reichstadt.[20] Other contemporary novelists with Bonapartist sympathies included Dumas, Hugo (both had fathers who were Napoleonic generals), Stendhal, and Balzac. Even historians like Adolphe Thiers, who didn't particularly admire Napoléon's military exploits, praised his achievements in the field of religious freedom, education, and legal reforms.

The arrival of the Polish emigrés in the wake of the Warsaw uprising further swelled the ranks of the Napoleonic cult. The poet Adam Mickiewicz above all extolled the spirit of Napoléon, from which he claimed to draw the inspiration for his lectures at the Collège de France. He even handed out pamphlets describing his communion with the emperor's spirit as a sort of "Last Supper" with the "Holy Master." As Czesław Miłosz, the leading poet of present-day Poland, has noted, "All Polish writings of the period [that is, the Great Emigration of the 1830s and 1840s] abound in mystical appeals to the Napoleonic myth as a force which would abolish the reactionary order oppressing Europe."[21] Heinrich Heine (who took refuge in Paris to escape this oppression) became another of the cult's faithful, praising Napoléon as "the synthesis of the revolutionary and counter-revolutionary" who simultaneously tamed "the many-headed monster of anarchy" and abolished the privileges of a feudal nobility.[22] The poet's enthusiasm, however, was short-lived, and he soon came to see his erstwhile hero as a "dictator and oppressor of foreign peoples... an enemy of liberty."[23]

Heine was one of the few shrewd enough to recognize that the Napoleonic legend—whether by accident or design—had cleverly clothed the despotic wolf in the fleece of a lamb. The Christ-like role assigned to the emperor's spirit by Mickiewicz and other Polish poets went even further, implying that the little Corsican was, in fact, a reincarnation of the "lamb of God." For Louis-Philippe the greatest threat posed by these manipulations of the Napoleonic legend proved to be his own failure to recognize their danger. Faced with far more tangible threats from the Legitimists, the Republicans, and many of his fellow sovereigns, he didn't worry much about the Bonapartists, whose lack of leadership made them generally compliant to his dictates. There were exceptions, however. For example, those Bonapartists who believed Napoléon to have been a freedom fighter dedicated to the progressive goals of the revolution banded together with the Republicans. Whether from political miscalculation, overconfidence, or simple naïveté, Louis-Philippe not only tolerated the Bonapartists, he went out of his way to ingratiate himself with them. During the eighteen years of his reign, he rendered more honors to Napoléon than the latter's nephew ever did in the twenty-two years he governed France. Perhaps the Orleanist king secretly shared Adolphe Thiers's admiration of the emperor's ability to keep "both the aristocracy and the masses in their proper places, away from the seat of power."[24]

In April 1831, only eight months after he had become king, Louis-Philippe announced his intention of returning Napoléon's statue to the top of the Vendôme column in the heart of Paris. That same month, despite the ban prohibiting the presence of any members of the Bonaparte family in France, he granted an interview to Queen Hortense (wife of Napoléon's brother, Louis) who had slipped into the country illegally. What Louis-Philippe didn't know at the time was that Hortense's son, Louis-Napoléon, had also made a clandestine visit to France that year to plot with Republicans for the overthrow of the Orleanist regime. Soon the Vendôme column became a rallying point for Bonapartists, some of whom even petitioned the government to have Napoléon's body brought back to France and buried at its base. As might be expected, the request was ignored. Nevertheless, on May 5, 1831, the column was decorated with flowers and eagles for a "Manifestation Napoléonique." Although the demonstrators were dispersed with fire hoses, they continued to return, stirred by Victor Hugo's poem "Ode à la Colonne." The following year, just before his death, the emperor's son, the duc de Reichstadt, requested that his last respects be paid to this column. Shortly afterward, Heinrich Heine commented prophetically, "A thousand cannons slumber in...the column of the Place Vendôme and the Tuileries will tremble if these thousand cannons are awakened one day."[25] The new statue of Napoléon that Louis-Philippe placed on the column in 1833 wore a military uniform rather than the Roman toga of its predecessor. This, as some historians claim, was an attempt to present the former emperor in a purely human context, devoid of the mythological attributes often associated with classical drapery.

No sooner had the duc de Reichstadt died than his uncle, Joseph Bonaparte, met with General Cavaignac and others in London to plan a coup against Louis-Philippe. The following year, 1833, when the new statue on the Vendôme column was being unveiled, a coalition of Bonapartists and Republicans, anticipating the Orleanist government's imminent collapse, proposed a triumverate of Louis-Napoléon, Lafayette, and the Republican journalist Armand Carrel to govern France. Obviously the death of l'Aiglon had not delivered the coup de grâce to the Bonapartist cause. Earlier, during Napoléon's exile on Saint Helena, the emperor had had the foresight to designate an alternate line of succession in the event of his son's death. This plan stipulated that the imperial crown should descend to the offspring of his next-to-youngest brother, Louis, bypassing his own two illegitimate sons as well as the children of Louis's older brothers, Joseph and Lucien. Because Louis's eldest son, Napoléon-Louis, died in 1831 from an attack of measles, his younger brother, Louis-Napoléon, became the official Bonapartist heir on l'Aiglon's death the following year. Instantly the future Napoléon III began taking steps to ensure the realization of his imperial legacy.

Meanwhile Louis-Philippe naively rejoiced at having "domesticated" the Bonapartists, many of whom had taken refuge in the Orleanist fold. Two of Napoléon's marshals, Nicolas-Jean de Dieu Soult and Edouard-Adolphe-Casimir-Joseph Mortier, as well as another commander of the Grand Army, General Etienne-Maurice Gérard, served as prime ministers under the July monarchy. Because Chopin was in favor with the court and moved in the social circles of the *juste milieu,* he came to know many of these rehabilitated Bonapartists. For example, the duc Elie Decazes (once secretary to the emperor's mother, "Mme Mère," and later chief justice of the Orleanist Court of Peers) invited him to perform at one of his musical soirées in the Petit Luxembourg palace. Among Chopin's pupils was the comtesse de Lobau, wife of a former aide-de-camp to Napoléon, who had succeeded Lafayette as head of Louis-Philippe's National Guard. Mme de Lobau herself was a lady-in-waiting to the queen, Marie-Amélie, as was the comtesse de Hautpoul, a granddaughter of Napoléon's marshal Bertier. Mme de Hautpoul's mother, the Princesse de Wagram, was also an intimate of the Orleanist family and attended a private performance by Chopin and Moscheles in the royal palace at Saint-Cloud in 1839. Another of Chopin's pupils, Emilie de Flahaut, was the daughter of an aide-de-camp of Napoléon who later served the duc d'Orléans in the same capacity. Also prominent in *juste milieu* circles were members of Marshal Michel Ney's and Marshal Jean Lannes's families (whose musical interests were to bring them into contact with Chopin) and Marshal Andoche Junot's flamboyant widow, the duchesse d'Abrantès, noted for her literary and amorous associations with Balzac. On the surface, at least, the Bonapartists appeared to have become an integral part of the political and social fabric of the July monarchy.

This camaraderie between the Orleanists and the Bonapartists was progressing peaceably at the time Louis-Philippe prepared to celebrate the completion of Napoléon's majestic Arc de Triomphe in July 1836. His narrow escape from an assassin's bullet the month before, however, deterred him from attending its inauguration. By October, he had regained enough confidence to appear at the erection of the obelisk of Luxor, an event redolent with memories of the emperor's Egyptian campaign. Only five days later, the emperor's nephew, Louis-Napoléon, staged an abortive insurrection at Strasbourg. The dispatch with which it was put down made the whole event appear so inconsequential that the king gave no thought to imprisoning, much less executing, the hapless culprit. Instead he sent Louis-Napoléon off to America with 15,000 francs from the royal purse to ease the misery of his exile. Such foolish behavior alarmed Metternich, who cautioned Louis-Philippe that Napoléon's rambunctious nephew was not to be taken lightly and warned him against letting the Bonapartists flourish with impunity in France.

Before long, Louis-Napoléon had tired of America and recrossed the Atlantic to settle in London. There he befriended members of the Carbonari and promised to aid them in their fight for Italian independence should he eventually come to power. Among these revolutionists was Giuseppe Mazzini, whom George Sand admired greatly. Through him she engaged in a brief correspondence with the emperor's nephew, who deluded her into believing he was a man of democratic principles. In a book entitled *Idées Napoléoniennes* (Napoleonic ideas) he claimed that his uncle's spiritual legacy was "not one of war but a social, industrial, commercial and humanitarian one."[26] Such a concept was totally at odds with the militarism of the historical Napoléon. This and his later volume, *The Extinction of Pauperism*, duped many Republicans like Sand into feeling a philosophical communion with the political dogmas of this revamped Bonapartism. Not all of France, however, accepted the future emperor at face value. Even an outsider like Thackeray was perceptive enough to realize that the fiasco at Strasbourg merely represented a temporary setback in the upward flight of the resurrected Napoleonic eagle. "Who knows," he mused, "how soon [the eagle] may be on the wing again."[27]

In 1837 Louis-Philippe opened the palace of Versailles as a museum devoted to the history of France. In it he set aside several galleries to commemorate the glories of the first empire, secure in his belief that the Bonapartist cause was moribund. As artful a diplomat as he was, though, Louis-Philippe had difficulty hiding his ambivalence toward the emperor. By displaying David's coronation portrait of the ermine-robed emperor, attended by a vast retinue in court finery, he deftly debunked the myth of the Corsican commoner as a simple man of the people. Two other paintings depicting the Eighteenth of Brumaire (when Napoléon seized power) subtly reminded viewers that the emperor's career had been based on deception and the use of military force.

Characteristically Louis-Philippe found tampering with the past far easier than coping with the present. While fending off the specter of the late emperor, he forgot Metternich's warnings about his nephew, who had found an unlikely haven in "perfidious Albion" under the very eyes of his uncle's nemesis, the duke of Wellington. By then, the duke, like Louis-Philippe, considered Bonapartism a dead issue and ignored the young man's presence. Free of surveillance, Louis-Napoléon marshalled his forces for a second invasion of France in August 1840. Shortly before setting out on this would-be coup, he attended a banquet in London where he invited the guests to dine with him at the Tuileries the following year. As it turned out, his landing at Boulogne with an eagle (some say a vulture) on his shoulder ended even more disastrously than his Strasbourg fiasco four years earlier. Grandiose expectations and inadequate preparations, combined with miserable weather, left the invaders floundering in the waters offshore where they were eventually arrested by those whom they had intended to subdue. Although the eagle was comfortably installed in the zoo at the Jardin des Plantes, its foolhardy owner was sentenced to imprisonment in the fortress of Ham—all of which provided the public with a good laugh.

It was at the fortress of Ham, north of Paris, that Louis-Napoléon began corresponding with George Sand. The author, whose father had fought in Napoléon's ill-fated Spanish campaign, was initially awed at addressing a member of the Bonaparte clan. But the prisoner's ties with Mazzini and the Carbonari encouraged her to regard him as a fellow Republican who shared her sentiments. "Noble captive!" she hailed him, "like you, the people are also in chains. Let the Napoléon of today be the personification of the people's sorrow as the other Napoléon personified their glories."[28] She was, of course, doomed to disappointment when her "Republican" prince came to power. By then, however, age had cooled the heat of her politics, and she eventually accepted the vicissitudes of life under an imperial autocrat rather than face the rigors of exile like her colleague, Victor Hugo.

Louis-Napoléon's attempt to overthrow the July monarchy in 1840 was ironically a response to Louis-Philippe's decision that year to negotiate with the English for the return of Napoléon's body to France. Apparently Prince Louis interpreted the king's request as a sign of pro-Bonapartist sentiment in France. On the contrary, it was merely a political maneuver by the prime minister, Adolphe Thiers, to distract the French people from the domestic and international crises that he had caused.

In asking for the return of the emperor's body, both Thiers and Louis-Philippe anticipated resistance from the English. "England cannot say to the world that she wishes to retain a corpse a prisoner," Thiers blustered. "When a condemned man is executed his body is returned to his family.... How indignant I would feel if they didn't return the remains of that illustrious prisoner."[29] To everyone's surprise the English offered no objections. The elderly duke of Wellington may well have summed up his country's attitude when he announced that he didn't give a two-penny damn for the Frenchman's remains. Actually there seems to have been more opposition to the project in France than in England. Alfred de Vigny, for one, felt that the whole enterprise was misguided and refused to take any part in it. Although he had admired Napoléon's capability as a leader, he felt the man had abused his power. Initially even Louis-Philippe harbored some reservations, as did Chateaubriand and the nation's chancellor, Pasquier. After all, such a step went beyond a mere acknowledgment of Napoléon's place in French history: it amounted to a virtual beatification—if not a full-fledged canonization—of the long-worshipped hero.

Although persuading Britain to release the emperor's remains proved easy enough, deciding where to inter them in France posed a more difficult problem. By right of having been a French sovereign, Napoléon was entitled to be buried at Saint-Denis with the nation's other monarchs, but fear of antagonizing the

14.1 A portrait of Napoléon's Marshal Soult in his Grande Army uniform. Later as prime minister of France under the July monarchy, he became a political puppet of Louis-Philippe. In 1840, at the time of the return of Napoléon's remains, Soult once more donned the cherished uniform he had preserved to honor his beloved emperor.

Legitimists made the government reject this option. After some debate it was finally declared that Napoléon's unique position in history deserved unique recognition, and it was decided that he be laid to rest under the dome of the Invalides, one of the city's most impressive historical monuments. Apart from its grandeur and beauty, the Invalides was undoubtedly chosen because of its military associations. Founded in 1670 as a hospital for soldiers wounded in the service of their king, it continued this tradition by housing many veterans of the Napoleonic wars.

Although preparations for this momentous event began early in 1840, the actual Retour des Cendres did not take place until December 15, at the extravagant cost of at least a million francs. In October the Prince de Joinville (the third of Louis-Philippe's five sons) set sail for the island of Saint Helena to recover the remains of the departed emperor. Three months later he was back in the French port of Le Havre, where the casket was transferred to a riverboat that carried it upstream to Paris. Along the route, crowds (often dressed in mourning) gathered on the banks and wept. Aboard the vessel was Napoléon's former marshal, General Soult, who proudly wore his faded Grand Army uniform (fig. 14.1). When the boat finally reached Courbevoie at the outskirts of Paris, a light snow began to fall. There the body would remain until December 15, a date anxiously awaited by every Frenchman in the nation.

14.2 The gaudy four-story-high vehicle that carried Napoléon's remains from the dock at
Courbevoie to the Invalides on December 15, 1840. Ridiculed as a "mountain of gold," it is shown
here at 1:30 in the afternoon as it turned off the quai d'Orsay to ascend the esplanade in front of
the Invalides. Note the gauze-draped fake casket on top of it, the plaster statues (painted to look
like bronze) on either side of the esplanade, and the clouds of smoke billowing out of the urns in
front of the church. Among the soldiers following this ostentatious "hearse" were many of
Chopin's compatriots who once fought in the emperor's campaigns.

The arrival of the great day was, in Victor Hugo's words, "as brilliant as
glory, as cold as the tomb";[30] six inches of snow covered the ground, and giant
blocks of ice floated down the Seine. In spite of the weather, Chopin braved the
bitter cold to be at the Invalides where his friends Pauline Viardot, Louis
Lablache, and Alexis Dupont were to sing the solo parts of Mozart's *Requiem*.
Because he had come mainly for the music, Chopin undoubtedly had a ticket of
admission to the church where the performance was given.

Earlier that day, the emperor's casket had been transferred from the boat at
Courbevoie to the funeral carriage, described by some observers as a "mountain
of gold." Laden with its sacred contents, the ostentatious vehicle plodded slowly
up the hill to the Arc de Triomphe, on top of which gigantic cut-out figures of
Napoléon in a chariot were surrounded by allegorical depictions of Fame, Glory,
and Grandeur. For many present that day, the unparalleled spectacle seemed a
tasteless and pretentious affair. Mme d'Agoult called it disgusting. Even the

Prince de Joinville, who led the procession, was appalled at the tawdriness of what should have been a majestic occasion (fig. 14.2). For one thing, the carriage itself was an enormous vehicle, nearly four stories high, on top of which was an empty sarcophagus, supported by fourteen plaster caryatids and covered by a violet drapery, embroidered with bees. Because of its great weight, the lead casket that actually contained Napoléon's body had been placed down between the wheels of the vehicle where no one could see it. At the front of the carriage, another plaster figure bore a crown against a backdrop of military busts, artillery, and cannon balls. At the rear were more busts and artillery, all but hidden by a cluster of flags, representing the nations conquered by the emperor. With its reams of papier-mâché, plaster gewgaws, and gold paper, the clumsy contraption looked like a monstrous stage prop for some operatic extravaganza. In keeping with its excessive theatricality, this lavish behemoth was surrounded by a colorful cast of "extras." Both in front and behind the bier were endless processions of mounted dignitaries, surrounded by cavalry and foot soldiers. Among them were many of Chopin's fellow Poles, veterans of the emperor's Grand Army.

As the hearse passed under the Arc de Triomphe, it stopped briefly while cannons fired a twenty-one-salvo salute. Above it on the frieze around the monument were names like Poniatowski, Zajączek, and Dambrowski, Polish soldiers who had fought beside Napoléon in his disastrous Russian campaign of 1812. "It was at this moment," the *Journal des Débats* observed, "that France resurrected the glorious martyr of Waterloo from his fatal fall."[31] Subsequently the procession resumed its journey down the Champs Elysées to the place de la Concorde. Flags, alternating with plaster statues of winged victories and imperial eagles (painted to look like bronze), lined the sides of the avenue, where rows of bleachers had been placed to accommodate an estimated crowd of 800,000. Shouts of "Vive l'Empereur!" filled the air as the vehicle passed. Nowhere, though, was anyone heard to cry "Vive le roi!"

While the procession was crossing the Pont de la Concorde, the sun came out, but its rays brought little warmth to the cold, damp day. At approximately 1:30 P.M., the cortege left the quai d'Orsay to begin the gentle ascent up the esplanade to the Invalides. On either side of this grassy expanse were rows of streaming tricolor banners and more faux-bronze and faux-marbre plaster statues, interspersed with flaming urns on gilded pedestals. Behind them rows of grandstands seated still more spectators. Directly in front of the Invalides, a huge tent had been erected and topped with two more urns that billowed clouds of black smoke

14.3 The interior of the chapel of the Invalides, where the royal family and honored guests, including Chopin, witnessed the religious rites accompanying the interment of the emperor. The music chosen for the occasion was Mozart's *Requiem*. It was sung by soloists who would again perform the work at Chopin's funeral in October 1849.

into the frigid air. For the few members of the English colony present that day, the atmosphere seemed particularly chilly due to the Middle East crisis that had brought the British and the French to the brink of war again. Because of this, the English had been warned to stay away from the ceremony. Some like the comtesse de Flahaut (daughter of Admiral Keith who had escorted Napoléon to England on the first step of his journey to Saint Helena) complied and watched the procession from the balcony of her house on the Champs Elysées. Others like Thackeray and Mary Shelley (the poet's widow) showed up anyway, although Mrs. Shelley left before the ceremony because of the intense cold.

At the grill in front of the Invalides's main courtyard, the funeral cart came to a halt. For the next hour and a half, while vendors milled about the crowd selling miniature replicas of Napoléon's casket, a group of sailors removed the real casket and carried it through the gates into the church where it was placed on a catafalque (fig. 14.3). There the archbishop of Paris sprinkled it with holy water in the presence of a select audience, all dressed in mourning. The king then stepped forward to thank his son, the Prince de Joinville, for having returned the emperor's remains, which he received "in the name of France." At this point Marshal Soult presented Louis-Philippe with Napoléon's sword, which the king placed on the coffin while the rest of the royal family watched from a balcony near the altar. After these formalities the religious service began, with the archbishop presiding. From the Seine below, the boom of cannons punctuated Mozart's *Requiem* every fifteen minutes with a thundrous tribute that even Berlioz—who had worshipped the emperor since childhood—could not have rivaled.

Ironically, at this historic moment, no blood relative of Napoléon was present at the ceremonies in honor of him. Considering the law prohibiting the presence of any Bonaparte in France, this was to be expected. There were, however, three illegitimate children of the emperor who (not being officially recognized as Bonapartes) were exempt from this ban. These offspring (two sons and a daughter) had been of special significance to their father because they reassured him of his fertility, which he had come to doubt during his childless marriage to Josephine. Since none of the three had been acknowledged by their father, Louis-Philippe felt he had nothing to fear from these bar sinister descendants, who seemed to have no dynastic ambitions. Of the three, the eldest was Emilie Pellapra, who had seen her father only once and felt little if any attachment to him. At age twenty she had married the Prince de Chimay and divided her time between their Belgian chateaux and a house in Paris on the quai Malaquai. Through her husband's family, who were members of the ancien régime, she had acquired more social status than any Bonaparte connection could ever give her. In her youth the princess took piano lessons but proved to be hopelessly unmusical. Quite the opposite was her talented sister-in-law, Rosalie (also known as the Princesse de Chimay), who claimed to be a pupil of Chopin's and possessed many of his manuscripts at the time of her death. Another member of the Chimay family, Comtesse Jeanne de Caraman, was also said to be one of Chopin's pupils. This claim may well be true as the composer dedicated his Scherzo in E major, opus 54, to her in 1843.

Napoléon's second illegitimate child (and first-born son) was the self-styled "Comte Léon." At birth he had been christened Charles Macon, which he later embellished with the gratuitous title of "comte" followed by the surname of "Léon" derived from the last four letters of "Napoléon." A ne'er-do-well, the frivolous, egotistical, and litigious Comte Léon lived on the fringes of society. Rather than work, he frequented the gaming table, where he suffered enormous losses that he tried to recoup through dubious legal maneuvers. Failing this, the comte resorted to finagling money out of sychophants eager to claim intimacy with a son of the emperor. On hearing that his father's remains were being returned to Paris in 1840, he asked to participate in the ceremonies at the Invalides but was refused.

In contrast to Léon, comte Alexander Walewski, Napoléon's youngest love child, went out of his way to hide his paternity for fear of losing the Walewski fortune that he had inherited. His mother, Maria Walewska (née Łączyńska), had been tutored by Chopin's father during her youth. Since the fall of Warsaw in 1831, the young count lived in Paris intermittently, but in December 1840 he was abroad fighting with Louis-Philippe's troops in Algeria. Although Chopin encountered him on a number of occasions, the two never developed a close rapport.

Despite the government's fear of possible disruptions at the December 15 ceremonies, the affair went smoothly—perhaps because Louis-Napoléon was safely under lock and key in the fortress of Ham. According to Adam Mickiewicz, though, only the intense cold of the day had kept the emotional occasion from turning into a revolution. Whatever the case, Louis-Philippe and his family appeared completely oblivious to any danger as they chatted away throughout the service, paying little attention to the Mozart requiem that was the highlight of the event.

During the following week, the Invalides remained illuminated while crowds (estimated at 200,000 visitors a day) filed past the emperor's coffin to pay their respects. Once the great man had been lowered into the vault beneath the Invalides, Louis-Philippe assumed that the mystique surrounding him had been laid to rest. He was mistaken; the shadow of the legendary hero was to darken the rest of his reign. "After the return of [Napoléon's] remains," Lucas-Dubreton observed, "there were two kings in France; one in the Tuileries and one in the Invalides."[32] Guizot, Louis-Philippe's prime minister from 1840 on, had recognized the dangers inherent in paying such homage to the emperor but felt that a refusal to do so would have brought down the Orleanist monarchy long before it finally collapsed.

From his prison quarters at the fortress of Ham, Prince Louis-Napoléon noted ominously, "The fifteenth of December is a great day for France and for me."[33] Still posing as a Republican, he wrote, "The Napoleonic cause is that of the interest of the people,... sooner or later it will triumph."[34] For the time being, though, most Frenchmen had forgotten all about the prisoner of Ham. Of the few who still remembered him he remained a harmless dreamer, a fanciful young man who had been more impetuous than intelligent in his failed coups against the Orleanist regime. His bumbling attempts, however, had reminded a proud nation of the grandeur it had lost, and this was to pose a serious threat to the lusterless Citizen King.

Typical of the bourgeois mentality that prevailed under the July monarchy was the uproar that took place shortly after the Retour des Cendres, when plans were announced to install a reclining nude sculpture of the emperor in the place Vintimille northeast of the new gare Saint-Lazare. Although public outrage quickly forced the sculpture's removal, Louis-Philippe found it far more difficult to dispel Napoléon's image from the minds of his subjects.

In 1846, Louis-Napoléon, still dismissed as a political clown by most Orleanists, proved himself far more clever than anyone had suspected. That year he regained his freedom by strolling out of the fortress of Ham disguised as a construction worker. Louis-Philippe, one of those who consistently underestimated the prince's intelligence, felt little concern over his escape. At the time he was far more troubled by renewed assassination attempts on his person, a poor grain harvest, and a falling stock market, all of which which were creating unrest among the populace. Less than a year and a half later, the July monarchy was to be only a memory.

Scarcely six months after the 1848 revolution that brought down the house of Orléans, Adolphe Crémieux, the new republic's minister of justice, rescinded the law prohibiting the Bonaparte family from entering France. Eight days later, Louis-Napoléon was back in the country again. Almost immediately he won election to the new constituent assembly from five of its political districts. His next goal was the presidency. In campaigning for this, he took the liberty of publishing a letter from George Sand that he felt would enhance his image among French liberals. By then, however, the novelist had seen through his democratic pose and dashed off an irate response to the editor of a popular left-wing journal in Paris. "Monsieur Louis Bonaparte," she stated (deliberately disregarding his princely title), "is both intellectually and emotionally an enemy of the Republican form of government and has no right whatsoever to present himself as a candidate for the presidency."[35]

But what alternative did the nation have? Among the other presidential candidates was the poet Alphonse Lamartine, who had already proved his political ineptness as president of the provisional government. Apart from him there was only one other viable candidate—General Cavaignac, who had become a national hero for his conquest of Algeria under Louis-Philippe (fig. 14.4). Later,

14.4 General Eugène Cavaignac, who ran against Louis-Napoléon and Alphonse Lamartine for the presidency of the second French republic in 1848. Once a national hero for his role in the conquest of Algeria, Cavaignac antagonized the nation's Republicans by his vigorous repression of the bloody socialist uprising in June of that year. Louis-Napoléon's overwhelming victory at the polls on election day was essentially due to the charisma of the Bonaparte name rather than any shortcomings in his rivals.

though, the general's ferocious suppression of the working-class rebels in the bloody "June Days" of 1848 had alienated French Republicans. From Mme Sand's point of view, the nation's outlook was dismal.

The elections, set for December 10, 1848, occurred only three weeks after Chopin's return from England. Unlike his former mistress, the musician had little interest in politics. His only concern was that the new president (whomever he might be) would provide an environment of order and tranquillity. Neither Chopin's indifference nor Sand's activism, though, were to exert any influence on the nation's fate since the republic's so-called universal suffrage excluded the one as an alien and the other as a woman.

On the night before the French went to the polls, a Napoleonic veteran living in the Invalides claimed to see the emperor's image on the moon. The news spread swiftly among his fellow pensioners, who flocked outdoors to observe the phenomenon (fig. 14.5). All agreed it was an omen of great import; the next day Louis-Napoléon became president of France by a landslide victory.

As George Sand wrote Pauline Viardot a few days later, many of the newly enfranchised peasants voted for Louis-Napoléon in the belief that their immortal emperor lived on in his nephew and would return to them if he were elected. Not all of France, however, had fallen under the sway of the Napoleonic legend. Despite the prince-president's overwhelming majority, many Frenchmen were profoundly unhappy with his election. Among them was the political cartoonist Daumier, who sketched Louis-Napoléon riding in his uncle's bicorn hat, drawn

14.5 Gavarni's sketch of a crusty old Napoleonic veteran like those housed in the Hospital of the Invalides. The caption below reads, "In my time, with all the gunpowder that's wasted today we would have burned Europe and rewritten history."

14.6 A Daumier cartoon entitled "Napoleonic Packet-Boat," showing the future emperor floating in his uncle's bicorn hat, drawn by a scruffy Napoleonic "eagle"—hardly a portrait of imperial dignity.

by a turkey disguised as an eagle. Two decades later, with the nation in shambles after the Franco-Prussian war, most Frenchmen agreed that the turkey had indeed supplanted the eagle (fig. 14.6).

Through a peculiar twist of fate, Chopin was born in "Napoleonic Poland" (the small Duchy of Warsaw established by Napoléon I in 1807) and ended his days in France's second republic, governed by another Napoléon. Although he performed for four European monarchs, Czar Alexander I, King Louis-Philippe, Queen Maria Cristina of Spain, and Queen Victoria of England, he seems to have had no contact with either of the two Napoléons. Chopin was, after all, merely five years old in 1815 when the first Napoléon went into permanent exile on the island of Saint Helena. Years later, in December 1848, when the other became prince-president of France, the musician was far too ill to move in those social circles where he might have encountered him. For the last eleven months of his life, Chopin lived in a republic, an experience few Europeans of his time had

14.7 and 14.8 The Elysée palace is redolent with the history of the Bonapartes. In 1805 it became the home of Napoléon's sister, Caroline Bonaparte, and her husband Joachim Murat (later king and queen of Naples). Subsequently Napoléon settled his ex-empress Josephine there. Shortly after she abandoned the palace for Malmaison, he moved his son l'Aiglon into it. In June 1815 it witnessed the emperor's second abdication prior to his exile on the island of Saint Helena. From 1848–52, during the brief existence of the second French republic, it became the residence of the prince-president Louis-Napoléon Bonaparte. The interior view shows the palace's grand salon during a ball given by the new president.

ever known. Poor health and a fundamental distaste for political matters, however, obscured his perception of the profound ideological clashes that were transforming France as well as the rest of Europe then.

During the summer of 1849, Chopin was fortunate enough to escape the confines of Paris for the semirural atmosphere of Chaillot. There, on a hill to the west of the city, he enjoyed gazing down across the sloping gardens of the suburb to the rooftops of Paris. Among them he could distinguish the Invalides where Napoléon was buried and the empty Tuileries in which Louis-Napoléon would soon enjoy the opulent life of an emperor. After spending most of 1848 in England, Chopin felt relieved to be back among the French, who remained for him as vibrant, elegant, and civilized as ever. Early in September, he moved from his summer retreat to an apartment on the east side of the place Vendôme. Barely a month later, on October 17, 1849, he would take leave of Paris forever, in the very shadow of Napoléon's statue atop the square's famous column (figs. 14.7, 14.8). Just a few blocks to the west, in the Elysée palace, the emperor's diminutive nephew, already known as "le petit Napoléon," was busy contemplating how much height an imperial crown would add to his stature.

Epilogue

Obituary and Funeral of Frédéric Chopin

Revue et Gazette Musicale, Paris, October 21, 1849
Obituary: Frédéric Chopin

"*H*E DEPARTED FROM US on the 17th of this month at two A.M. [*sic*], in the arms of one of his pupils and friends. Since the beginning of his career, this outstanding artist has ranked among the most eminent of his famous contemporaries and has distinguished himself by his unique talent. . . .

During his apprenticeship, the young Chopin preferred to learn by listening to others rather than performing in public himself. Exiled from his native land by the misfortunes and suffering that followed the revolutions, he decided to make a living through his talent. In 1831, he played in public concerts in Vienna and Munich. Preceded by the reputation he gained through these successes, he arrived in Paris toward the end of that year and created a great sensation there. . . .

Probably there has never been any artist whose physical appearance was so similar to his talent. He was as frail in body as his music was delicate in style, almost merging into the impalpable and imperceptible. At the piano he displayed a touch that was unique; in a large concert hall it was all but inaudible; in an intimate setting it was delicious. People came to call him the Aerial of the piano. If Queen Mab ever wanted a pianist for her court, she would surely have chosen Chopin. Only the divine pen that described the fantastic equipage of this Fairy Queen could analyze the infinitely complex web of those musical phrases, thick with notes and yet light as lace, into which the composer has woven his idea.

Chopin was aristocratic both as a man and as an artist. His genius was not subject to any law. Living apart in his own intimate and mysterious world, he . . . seldom played in public. A concert by him with a high-priced admission and limited to a scrupulously screened audience was regarded as an extraordinary favor. It was like being alone—or at the most, having an intimate tête-à-tête with the composer and virtuoso—in his solitary dream world. . . .

1: A view of the rue de la Paix from the boulevards to the Vendôme column topped by the statue of Napoléon Bonaparte: To the left of the column at No. 12 place Vendôme, Chopin was to die under the shadow of the man who had established the duchy of Warsaw where he was born thirty-nine years earlier. At the time of his death, France was governed by another Bonaparte, the former emperor's nephew, President Louis-Napoléon.

Chopin's personality reminds one of those people described by Pope who were so superhumanly sensitive that everything in this world became a torment to them; the least contact was like a wound, the least noise like a clap of thunder, and the slightest whiff of a rose like a fatal poison. For a long time, his thin, pale, and sickly appearance made him seem near death until people began to think he could go on living that way forever. As it was, he departed this life ahead of his time, being only thirty-nine years old when the hour of death struck (fig. 1). His sister had hurried from the far reaches of Poland to ease his last moments with her presence and her prayers.

The mortal remains of the great artist will be embalmed. He had always expressed the wish that Mozart's Requiem be performed at his funeral, which is expected to take place at the church of the Madeleine."

2: One of the deathbed sketches of Chopin by the Polish artist Théofil Kwiatkowski, now in the possession of the author.

Revue et Gazette Musicale, Paris, Nov. 4, 1849

FUNERAL OF FRÉDÉRIC CHOPIN

"Most youthful foreign artists who feel themselves destined for future fame eventually come to Paris for the sake of enjoying a rich and varied intellectual life, full of incessant inspiration. Here they are convinced they will find recognition worthy of them in their lifetime and after their death.

We are aware of the honors bestowed on Grétry at his funeral and more recently to the young Bellini, fallen before his time. Similar honors have now been rendered to Chopin. . . . His genius was especially understood and profoundly felt by women . . . who can discern a special elite, that is, that aristocracy of talent. . . . They loved to hear him lull a small, select audience with his spritely, melodic arabesques and bold, unexpected harmonies, so distinguished, restrained, and pure, with a poignance that suggested a swansong or a hymn to death. Death has now struck him down in the very fullness of his life and talent, forcing him to descend into the tomb as did Raphael, Mozart, Byron, and Weber at the height of their glory (fig. 2).

As a further final proof of the devotion of that sex which offered Chopin so many muses to inspire him, Mme Jendrzejevicz [*sic*], his sister and sole survivor [*sic*] of the great artist's family, invited all the illustrious names of Paris to share in the last tributes arranged for her brother. The ceremony took place last Tuesday, October 30, in the church of the Madeleine (fig. 3). No act of religious devotion, sorrow, and admiration for a great talent was ever carried out with as much dignity, propriety, and profound feeling for the artist and his art. Because of his faith in this noble, great, and time-honored art, Chopin expressed the desire to have Mozart's *Requiem* performed at his funeral. This wish of the great virtuoso

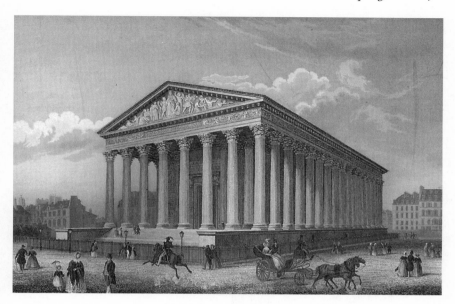

3: The church of the Madeleine, commenced in 1764 but not finished until 1842, was an imposing new landmark on the Paris scene when Chopin's funeral took place there in October 1849.

for the masterpiece of the great composer was fulfilled. Members of the "Society of Concerts" undertook the responsibility of it and accomplished their mission with religious respect, talent, coordination, enthusiasm, and perfection. . . .

Mmes Viardot and Castellane, Messrs. Alexis Dupond [*sic*] and Lablache sang the solo parts with that artistic excellence invariably associated with these skilled interpreters of both modern and classical music. The "Tuba mirum" with its vigorous yet otherworldly ring was performed by Lablache with a powerful sonority and firmness of voice that distinguish this admirable singer. . . . Members of the chorus sang with exactness and coordination, while the orchestra was no less distinguished in its respect for the score and its consistently beautiful execution. . . .

The imposing catafalque on which the body of the deceased rested had been placed at the center of the basilica, where its effect on the mourners was overshadowed by the celebrated pianist's two simple preludes [No. 4 in E minor and No. 6 in B minor], which the Madeleine's organist, M. Louis-James Lefébure-Wély, rendered on the organ in a sedate manner full of mystery and infinite grace . . . with both skill and feeling (fig. 4). Throughout the recurrent slow passages with their splendid cadences and the ethereal flow of the melody, it seemed possible to see

4: Louis-James Lefébure-Wély, the organist at Chopin's funeral, performed several of the composer's piano compositions on the church's new Cavaillé-Coll organ, installed three years earlier and still in use today.

and hear the wandering soul of the great musician, seeking out his place in the firmament. . . . It was as if Chopin were murmuring his farewell to earth, to his pupils, and to his friends in these two charming musical reveries borrowed from his works. A march taken from a sonata of the famous pianist [The "Funeral March" of the Sonata in B-flat minor, opus 35] and arranged for orchestra by M. Reber, served as an *introit* to the mass. Thus did the creator of such pensive melodies and exquisite harmonies make his presence felt by having his spirit come to life through the eloquent interpreters at his funeral. This, no doubt, was a blessing after the long struggles he had endured in life to achieve his fame. Chopin, it seems, was brought into this world to suffer both in body and in soul. The conditions of the times in which we live were not compatible with his nature and caused him constant grief. . . .

Despite this and so many other commonplace and useless regrets, we feel that the world is a better place because Chopin lived among us. And yet, isn't it true that he is still with us? Just sit down at the piano, open up his works, and you will be able to converse with him in the most delightful manner. It is in these works

5: A procession of mourners arriving at the cemetery of Père Lachaise, not unlike those who assembled there in 1849 for Chopin's interment. Today the floral offerings, deposited daily at the composer's grave site, indicate how much posterity still honors Chopin's music and his memory.

that are embodied all the individuality and all the soul of a musician like Chopin, who still speaks a language full of poetry and life to his charmed listeners long after he has left this world.

A great number of private carriages, some draped in mourning, followed the somber hearse as it carried the body of the deceased out to the cemetery in the east known as Père-Lachaise (fig. 5). The artistic elite of Paris were among those who formed the cortege. At the four corners of the funeral carriage were M. Franchomme, our excellent 'cellist who loved Chopin as a brother; M. Eugène Delacroix, the famous painter; Meyerbeer; and Prince Czartoryski, compatriot and friend of Chopin. Several ladies in mourning, his pupils, followed the procession on foot all the way to the resting ground. There the crowd's profound but silent sorrow served as funeral orations worth far more than the vain discourses of any writer or orator."[1]

The Paris Residences of Frédéric Chopin

27 boulevard Poissonière (1831–32)

4 Cité Bergère (1832–33)

5 rue de la Chaussée d'Antin (1833–36)

38 rue de la Chaussée d'Antin (1836–39)

5 rue Tronchet (1839–41)

16 rue Pigalle (1841–42)

9 square d'Orléans (1842–49)

74 Grande rue Chaillot (summer of 1849)

12 place Vendôme (Sept.–Oct. 1849)

Notes

CHAPTER 1.

Paris à la Galignani: An Anglo-Italian Guide to the French Capital for the English-Speaking Tourist

1. Thomas Raikes, *Journal (1831–1847)* (London: Longman, Brown, Green, Longmans, and Roberts, 1856), 1:225.

2. Today Wellington's house is the British embassy in Paris.

3. Jules Janin, *The American in Paris* (London: Longman, Brown, Green, and Longmans, 1843), 144.

4. Théophile Gautier, *Les Maîtres du Théâtre Français* (Paris: Payot, 1929), 208.

5. Paul de Kock, *Scenes of Parisian Life,* tr. E. M. Norris (Boston: Frederic J. Quinby, 1904), 112.

6. *Galignani's New Paris Guide* (Paris: Galignani, 1841), vi.

7. Louis Jacob Frazee, *A Medical Student in Europe* (Cincinnati: H. S. and J. Applegate, 1852), 37.

8. Frédéric Chopin, *Correspondance,* ed. Bronislas Sydow, Suzanne and Denise Chainaye, and Irène Sydow (Paris: Richard-Masse, 1954–60), 2:16.

9. In Chopin's time, the Parc Monceau was the private property of the royal family.

10. Prince de Joinville, *Vieux Souvenirs, 1818–1848* (Paris: Calmann-Lévy, 1894), 4.

11. Janin, *American in Paris,* 64.

12. Ibid., 61.

13. Chopin, *Correspondance,* 2:354.

14. Raikes, *Journal (1831–1847),* 3:39.

15. The rue de Chaillot is today's rue Quentin Bouchart.

16. The Barrière de l'Etoile corresponds to today's place Charles de Gaulle, where the Arc de Triomphe is located.

17. *Galignani's New Paris Guide,* 128.

18. Chopin, *Correspondance,* 2:254.

19. Paul Léon, *Paris, Histoire de la Rue* (Paris: La Taille Douce, 1947), 144.

20. The building called the square d'Orléans still exists, but its entrance is on the rue Taitbout. In Chopin's and Sand's time, it opened onto the rue Saint-Lazare.

21. Honoré de Balzac, *The Wild Ass's Skin,* tr. Herbert J. Hunt (Harmondsworth, Eng.: Penguin, 1986), 22.

22. *La Revue et Gazette Musicale,* Paris, Feb. 20, 1848, p. 58.

23. Chopin, *Correspondance,* 2:83.

24. Ibid., 2:62.

25. Ibid., 2:223.

26. Alexandre Dumas, *The Count of Monte Cristo,* tr. Lowell Blair (New York: Bantam, 1981), 368.

27. J. Culbertson and T. Randall, *Permanent Parisians: An Illustrated Guide to the Cemeteries of Paris* (Chelsea, Vt.: Chelsea Green, 1986), 7.

28. Chopin, *Correspondance,* 2:16.

29. Frances Trollope, *Paris and the Parisians* (New York: Harper and Bros., 1836), 114.

30. Eugène Sue, *The Mysteries of Paris* (New York, Dedalus/Hippocrene, n.d.), 9.

31. Eugène-Emmanuel Viollet-le-Duc, *The Architectural Theory of Viollet-le-Duc,* ed. M. F. Hearn (Cambridge: MIT, 1990), 14.

32. William G. Atwood, *Fryderyk Chopin, Pianist from Warsaw* (New York: Columbia University Press, 1987), 104.

33. Stendhal (Marie-Henri Beyle), *The Red and the Black,* ed. W. Somerset Maugham, tr. Joan Charles (Greenwich, Conn.: Fawcett, 1960), 163.

34. Raikes, *Journal (1831–1847),* 1:249.

35. Both the railroad station and the Grande Chaumière were actually in the eleventh arrondissement but are included here for convenience of discussion.

36. Chopin, *Correspondance,* 2:265.

37. Heinrich Heine, *Mémoires,* ed. G. Karpeles, tr. G. Cannan (London: William Heinemann, 1910), 1:298.

CHAPTER 2.
Polish Parisians: A People in Exile

1. *Album Chopina,* ed. Jerzy Maria Smoter (Warsaw: Polskie Wydawnictwo Muzyczne, 1975), 43–44.

2. News of Warsaw's fall was sent by Chappe's semaphore system of hilltop-to-hilltop transmission, which took seven days.

3. Edward L. Morse, *Samuel F. B. Morse: Letters and Journals* (Boston: Houghton Mifflin, 1914), 1:409.

4. Ibid., 1:408.

5. Michel Sokolnicki, *Les Origines de l'Emigration Polonaise en France, 1831–32* (Paris: Felix Alcan, 1910), 59.

6. Duchesse de Dino, *Chronique de 1831 à 1862* (Paris: Librairie Plon, Plon-Nourrit et Cie, 1909), 8.

7. Angela Pienkos, *The Imperfect Autocrat: Grand Duke Constantine Pavlovich and the Polish Congress Kingdom* (Boulder, Colo.: East European Monographs, 1987), 98.

8. Adam Mickiewicz, *Pan Tadeuz*, tr. K. R. Mackenzie (New York: Hippocrene, 1986), 28.

9. Frédéric Chopin, *Correspondance*, ed. Bronislas Sydow, Suzanne and Denise Chainaye, and Irène Sydow (Paris: Richard-Masse, 1954–60), 2:14.

10. A. Jardin and A-J Tudesq, *Restoration and Reaction: 1815–1848*, tr. E. Forster (Cambridge: Cambridge University Press, 1983), 370.

11. Honoré Balzac, *Cousine Bette*, tr. Marion A. Crawford (Harmondsworth, Eng., Penguin, 1965), 119.

12. Chopin, *Correspondance*, 2:59.

13. Balzac, *Cousine Bette*, 230.

14. Sokolnicki, *Les Origines de l'Emigration Polonaise en France, 1831–32*, 92.

15. Roman Dyboski, *Poland in World Civilization* (New York: J. M. Barrett Corp., 1950), 88.

16. Pienkos, *The Imperfect Autocrat: Grand Duke Constantine Pavlovich and the Polish Congress Kingdom*, 119.

17. In an earlier exile, Niemcewicz fled to the United States, where he visited President Washington at Mount Vernon and took an American wife (whom he later divorced).

18. Sokolnicki, *Les Origines de l'Emigration Polonaise en France, 1831–32*, 60.

19. *Revue et Gazette Musicale*, Mar. 26, 1840.

20. Rodolphe Apponyi, *Journal du Comte Rodolphe Apponyi* (Paris: Plon-Nourrit, 1914–26), 1:227.

21. Fryderyk Chopin, *Korrespondencja Chopina*, ed. Bronislaw Sydow (Warsaw: Panstwowy Instytut Wydawniczy, 1955), 2:191.

22. Hector Berlioz, *Mémoires*, ed. and tr. David Cairns (New York: Norton, 1975), 379.

23. Chopin, *Correspondance*, 3:387.

24. Ibid., 2:326.

25. George Sand, *Correspondance*, ed. Georges Lubin, 9 vols. (Paris: Garnier, 1964–72), 5:610, n. 3.

26. Mickiewicz, *Pan Tadeusz*, 2.

27. Czesław Miłosz, *The History of Polish Literature* (Berkeley: University of California Press, 1983), 226.

28. Jerzy Parvi, *Révolution, Indépendance, Romantisme* (Warsaw: Universytetu Warszawskiego, 1992), 6.

29. W. Szerlecka, *Un Saint des Temps Modernes* (Paris: Charles Amat, 1912), 34–35.

30. Ibid., 37.

31. N. O. Lossky, *Three Chapters from the History of Polish Messianism*, International *Philosophical Library* 2, no. 9 (Prague, Sept. 1936): 14.

32. Miłosz, *History of Polish Literature*, 232.

33. *Cambridge History of Poland, 1697–1935*, ed. W. F. Reddaway, J. H. Penson, O. Halecki, R. Dyboski (Cambridge: Cambridge University Press, 1941), 2:329.

34. Adam Zamoyski, *Chopin* (Garden City, N.Y.: Doubleday, 1980), 162.

35. Eleven of Chopin's twenty or more songs were written to poems by Witwicki and four to works by Zaleski. In addition Chopin dedicated the four mazurkas of his opus 41 to Witwicki.

36. Jeremy Siepmann, *Chopin, the Reluctant Romantic* (Boston: Northeastern University Press, 1995), 178.

37. Edward Hyams, *Pierre-Joseph Proudhon: His Revolutionary Life, Mind and Works* (New York: Taplinger, 1979), 128.

CHAPTER 3.
From Citizen-King to Prince-President: France as a "Bourgeois-cracy"

1. J. Lucas-Dubreton, *La Royauté Bourgeoise* (Paris: Hachette, 1930), 23.

2. Frédéric Chopin, *Correspondance*, ed. Bronislas Sydow, Suzanne and Denise Chainaye, and Irène Sydow (Paris: Richard-Masse, 1954–60), 2:56.

3. Eugène de Mirecourt, *Les Contemporains*, vol. 1: *François Guizot* (Brussels: Alphonse Lebègue, 1854), 54.

4. Lucas-Dubreton, *Royauté Bourgeoise*, 108.

5. Chopin, *Correspondance*, 2:222–23.

6. Lucas-Dubreton, *Royauté Bourgeoise*, 142.

7. Honoré Balzac, *Lost Illusions*, tr. Hubert J. Hunt (Harmondsworth, Eng.: Penguin, 1971), 313.

8. Agnes Stoeckl, *King of the French: A Portrait of Louis-Philippe* (New York: G. P. Putnam's Sons, 1958), 242.

9. Chopin, *Correspondance,* 3:249.

10. Ibid., 3:250.

11. Ibid., 2:56.

12. Arsène Houssaye, *Les Confessions: Souvenirs d'un Demi-Siècle, 1830–1880* (Paris: E. Dentu, 1885), 2:208.

13. Henri d'Alméras, *La Vie Parisienne sous le Règne de Louis-Philippe* (Paris: Albin Michel, 1968), 317.

14. David Thomson, *Europe since Napoléon* (New York: Knopf, 1960), 147.

15. Duchesse de Dino, *Chronique de 1831 à 1862* (Paris: Librairie Plon-Nourrit et Cie, 1909), 82.

16. Beckles Willson, *America's Ambassadors to France (1777–1927)* (New York: Frederick A. Stokes, 1928), 213.

17. Ibid., 217.

18. Ibid., 218.

19. Thomson, *Europe since Napoléon,* 147.

20. Stoeckl, *King of the French,* 64.

21. Ibid.

22. Anka Muhlstein, *Baron James: The Rise of the French Rothschilds* (New York and Paris: Vendôme Press, 1982), 95.

23. Thomas Raikes, *Journal (1831–1847)* (London: Longman, Brown, Green, Longmans, and Roberts, 1856), 2:181.

24. Henri d'Alméras, *La Vie Parisienne sous le Règne de Louis-Philippe* (Paris: Albin Michel, 1968), 321.

25. The duchesse de Berri had given birth precipitously before proper witnesses could be summoned.

26. Raikes, *Journal (1831–1847),* 1:248.

27. Comte de Rambuteau, *Mémoires* (Paris: Calmann-Lévy, 1905), 389.

28. Stoeckl, *King of the French,* 237.

29. Chopin, *Correspondance,* 3:250.

30. Ibid., 3:270.

31. Rosalynd Pflaum, *The Emperor's Talisman: The Life of the Duc de Morny* (New York: Meredith Press, 1968), 80.

32. Chopin, *Correspondance,* 3:329.

33. Ibid., 3:329.

34. Rees Howell Gronow, *The Reminiscences and Recollections of Captain Gronow* (London: Bodley Head, 1964), 297.

35. Ferdinand Denis, *Journal (1829–1848),* "Collectanea Friburgensia," n.s., fasc. 21 (fasc. 30 of the entire collection) (Fribourg, Switz.: University of Fribourg, 1932), 109.

36. Albert D. Vandam, *An Englishman in Paris* (New York: Appleton, 1892), 2:236.

37. Maréchal de Castellane, *Journal (1804–1862)* (Paris: E. Plon, Nourrit et Cie, 1895–97), 4:134.

CHAPTER 4.
Society and Salons: A "Who's Tout" of *le Tout Paris*

1. Frédéric Chopin, *Correspondance,* ed. Bronislas Sydow, Suzanne and Denise Chainaye, and Irène Sydow (Paris: Richard-Masse, 1954–60), 2:15.

2. Ibid., 2:166.

3. Ibid., 2:106.

4. Duchesse de Dino, *Chronique de 1831 à 1862* (Paris: Plon-Nourrit et Cie., 1909–10), 1:10.

5. Ibid., 1:23.

6. Prince Talleyrand became the duchesse de Dino's uncle-in-law when she married his nephew, Edmond de Talleyrand-Périgord, duc de Dino. After the couple's separation, the prince became her lover.

7. Jules Janin, Honoré Balzac, et al., *Pictures of the French* (London: Thomas Tegg, 1841), 101.

8. Chopin, *Correspondance,* 2:85.

9. M-E. Binet, *Un Médecin pas Ordinaire: Le Docteur Véron* (Paris: Editions Albin Michel, 1945), 186.

10. Honoré Balzac, *Cousine Bette,* tr. Marion A. Crawford, (Harmondsworth, Eng.: Penguin, 1965), 117.

11. William G. Atwood, *Fryderyk Chopin, Pianist from Warsaw* (New York: Columbia University Press, 1987), 104–106.

12. Frances Trollope, *Paris and the Parisians* (New York: Harper and Bros., 1836), 48.

13. Jules Janin, *The American in Paris* (London: Longman, Brown, Green, and Longmans, 1843), 151.

14. André Maurois, *Prometheus: The Life of Balzac,* tr. Norman Denny (New York: Avon, 1967), 232.

15. Honoré Balzac, *Père Goriot*, tr. E. K. Brown, Dorothy Walter, and John Watkins (New York: Modern Library, 1950), 81.

16. Rodolphe Apponyi, *Journal du Comte Rodolphe Apponyi* (Paris: Plon-Nourrit, 1914–26), 2:105.

17. Dino, *Chronique de 1831 à 1862*, 1:33.

18. Chopin, *Correspondance*, 2:83.

19. Trollope, *Paris and the Parisians*, 141.

20. Balzac, *Cousin Pons*, 122.

21. Trollope, *Paris and the Parisians*, 229.

22. Prince de Joinville, *Vieux Souvenirs, 1818–1848* (Paris: Calmann-Lévy, 1894), 278.

23. Arsène Houssaye, *Les Confessions: Souvenirs d'un Demi-Siècle, 1830–1880* (Paris: E. Dentu, 1885), 1:383.

24. Apponyi, *Journal du Comte Rodolphe Apponyi*, 2:306.

25. Ibid.

26. Ibid., 2:209.

27. Dino, *Chronique de 1831 à 1862*, 1:290.

28. Maréchal de Castellane, *Journal, 1804–1862* (Paris: E. Plon, Nourrit et Cie, 1895–97), 2:492.

29. Harriet Granville, *Letters of Harriet, Countess of Granville, 1810–1845* (London: Longmans, Green, 1894), 1:433.

30. Philip Ziegler, *The Duchess of Dino* (London: Collins, 1962), 212.

31. Ibid., 194.

32. Maurois, *Prometheus*, 142.

33. Tom Prideaux, *The World of Delacroix, 1798–1863* (New York: Time-Life Books, 1966), 86.

34. Jacques Barzun, "Paris in 1830," from *Paris in the Eighteen Thirties*, vol. 4 of English-French Series: *La Vie Musicale en France au XIXè Siècle*, ed. Peter Bloom (Stuyvesant, N.Y.: Pendragon, 1987), 12.

35. Trollope, *Paris and the Parisians*, 94.

36. Ibid.

37. Alphonse Lamartine, *Portraits et Salons Romantiques* (Paris: Le Goupy, 1927), 75.

38. Ernest Legouvé, *Sixty Years of Recollections*, tr. Albert D. Vandam (London: Eden Remington, 1893), 1:289.

39. Marguerite Louise Virginie Ancelot, *Les Salons de Paris* (Paris: Jules Tardieu, 1858), 185.

40. Balzac, *Cousine Bette*, 228.

41. H. Montgomery Hyde, *Princess Lieven* (Boston: Little Brown, 1938), 215.

42. Ibid., 255.

43. Houssaye, *Les Confessions: Souvenirs d'un Demi-Siècle, 1830–1880*, 1:39.

44. Albert Dresden Vandam, *An Englishman in Paris* (New York: Appleton, 1892), 79.

45. Georges d'Heilly, *Madame de Girardin (Delphine Gay), Sa Vie et ses Oeuvres* (Paris: Bachelin-Deflorene, 1868), 95.

46. Willard Connely, *Count d'Orsay, The Dandy of Dandies* (London: Cassel, 1952), 450. The place Royale is today's place des Vosges.

47. Houssaye, *Les Confessions: Souvenirs d'un Demi-Siècle, 1830–1880*, 1:220.

48. Maurois, *Prometheus*, 179.

49. Ibid., 492.

50. Rees Howell Gronow, *The Reminiscences and Recollections of Captain Gronow* (London: Bodley Head, 1964), 282.

51. Anaïs Bassanville, *Les Salons d'Autrefois* (Paris: A. Broussois, 1897–1901), 3:299.

52. Chopin, *Correspondance*, 2:83.

53. Gronow, *Reminiscences and Recollections of Captain Gronow*, 246.

54. Bassanville, *Salons d'Autrefois*, 2:117.

55. Houssaye, *Les Confessions: Souvenirs d'un Demi-Siècle*, 1:218.

56. Apponyi, *Journal de Comte d'Apponyi*, 2:290.

57. Barzun, *Paris in 1830*, 5.

58. Bassanville, *Salons d'Autrefois*, 2:117.

CHAPTER 5.
Pox Britannica: The Great Epidemic of Anglomania

1. Frédéric Chopin, *Correspondance*, ed. Bronislas Sydow, Suzanne and Denise Chainaye, and Irène Sydow (Paris: Richard-Masse, 1954–60), 2:365–66. Julian Fontana, to whom Chopin wrote this note, was actually Polish rather than English. Because he had lived in London, though, the musician refers to him as an "Englishman" familiar with the latest styles in men's clothing.

2. Honoré Balzac, *Cousin Pons,* tr. Herbert J. Hunt (Harmondsworth, Eng.: Penguin, 1968), 89.

3. Rees Howell Gronow, *The Reminiscences and Recollections of Captain Gronow* (London: Bodley Head, 1964), 196.

4. Hector Berlioz, *Evenings with the Orchestra,* tr. and ed. Jacques Barzun (New York: Knopf, 1956), 77.

5. Stendhal (Marie-Henri Beyle), *The Red and the Black,* tr. J. Charles, ed. Somerset Maugham (Greenwich, Conn.: Fawcett, 1960), 191.

6. Michel Le Bris, *Romantics and Romanticism* (Geneva: Skira, and London: Macmillan, 1981), 132.

7. Alfred de Musset, *Confessions of a Child of the Century* (New York: Current Literary Publishing, 1910), 46.

8. *Galignani's New Paris Guide* (Paris: Galignani, 1841), 555.

9. Arsène Houssaye, *Les Confessions: Souvenirs d'un Demi-Siècle 1830–1880* (Paris: E. Dentu, 1885), 2:302.

10. Lord Henry's elder half-brother, Lord Richard Seymour, the fourth marquis of Hertford, restored the comte d'Artois's eighteenth-century architectural folly, Bagatelle, in the Bois de Boulogne, modeling its gardens after those at Kew. Much of his furniture and art are to be seen now in the famous Wallace collection, left to the city of London by the widow of his illegitimate son, Sir Richard Wallace.

11. Eugène Sue, *The Mysteries of Paris* (New York: Dedalus/Hippocrene, n.d.), 145.

12. Maréchal de Castellane, *Journal (1804–1862)* (Paris: E. Plon, Nourrit et Cie, 1895–97), 3:87.

13. William Makepeace Thackeray, *The Paris Sketch Book* (Boston and New York: Colonial Press, n.d.), 38.

14. Roger Boutet de Monvel, *Eminent English Men and Women,* tr. G. Herring (New York: Charles Scribner's Sons, 1913), 224.

15. Marguerite Louise Virginie Ancelot, *Les Salons de Paris* (Paris: Jules Tardieu, 1858), 236.

16. Chopin, *Correspondance,* 3:378.

17. Ibid., 3:349.

18. Jeffrey L. Sammons, *Heinrich Heine* (Princeton, N.J.: Princeton University Press, 1979), 226.

19. George Sand, *Marianne,* Introduction (quoting from Sand's *Lettres d'un Voyageur,* tr. Sacha Rabinovitch and Patricia Thomson [New York: Penguin, 1987]), 24–25.

CHAPTER 6.

Musical Currents along the Seine: From Concert Halls to Dance Halls

1. Heinrich Heine, *Works of Heinrich Heine*. tr. Chas. Godfrey (New York: Dutton, 1906), 4:332.

2. Richard Wagner, *Wagner Writes from Paris*, ed. and tr. Robert L. Jacob and Geoffrey Skelton (New York: John Day, 1973), 110.

3. Ibid., 7.

4. Frédéric Chopin, *Correspondance*, ed. Bronislas Sydow, Suzanne and Denise Chainaye, and Irène Sydow (Paris: Richard-Masse, 1954–60), 3:273.

5. Heine, *Works*, 4:376.

6. In December 1830 Berlioz left for Italy to study at the Villa Medici after winning the coveted Prix de Rome. He was so unhappy away from Paris, though, that he left before completing his term of residence there.

7. Hector Berlioz, *Evenings with the Orchestra*, tr. and ed. Jacques Barzun (New York: Knopf, 1956), 49.

8. Arthur Hedley, *Selected Correspondence of Fryderyk Chopin*, tr. and ed. Arthur Hedley (London: Heinemann, 1962), 216.

9. *Revue et Gazette Musicale*, Jan. 3, 1841, p. 6.

10. Jacques Barzun, *Berlioz and His Century: An Introduction to the Age of Romanticism* (New York: Meridian, 1956), 138.

11. George Sand, *Correspondance*, ed. Georges Lubin, 9 vols. (Paris: Garnier, 1964–72), 5:799, n.1.

12. Hector Berlioz, *The Mémoires of Hector Berlioz*, ed. and tr. David Cairns (New York: Norton, 1975), 469.

13. *Revue et Gazette Musicale*, May 31, 1835, p. 184.

14. The Salle Pleyel was initially located at No. 9 rue Cadet from 1830 to 1839 and later at No. 22 rue Rochechouart, while the Salle Erard (filled with the owner's handsome collection of art work) still stands at No. 14 rue de Mail. The Salle Herz, at 38 rue de la Victoire, has now disappeared, as has the Salle Pape formerly situated at the corner of the rue Bons Enfans (No. 19) and the rue de Valois (No. 10).

15. Jeffrey L. Sammons, *Heinrich Heine* (Princeton, N.J.: Princeton University Press, 1979), 325.

16. Eugène de Mirecourt, *Les Contemporains*, vol. 17: *Ricord* (Brussels: Lebègue, 1857), 73.

17. Both Berlioz and Paganini were proficient guitarists, while Chopin's mistress, George Sand, studied piano, harp, and guitar and could perform with reasonable facility on each.

18. Arthur Loesser, *Men, Women, and Pianos* (New York: Simon and Schuster, Fireside, 1954), p. viii of introduction by Jacques Barzun.

19. Berlioz, *Mémoires*, 41.

20. Barzun, *Berlioz and His Century*, 258.

21. Ibid.

22. *La France Musicale*, Mar. 1848.

23. *Revue et Gazette Musicale*, June 13, 1841, p. 306.

24. Ibid.

25. The saxhorn and saxophone, often considered the same, were in fact quite different. The saxhorn resembles a bugle and was incorporated into many military bands. The public today knows the saxhorn mainly through the Salvation Army's street musicians, who often play carols on them at Christmastime. The saxophone, of course, is familiar to most people today from its use in popular dance bands. It has a reed mouthpiece as opposed to the saxhorn's brass one.

26. The work was a revision of Berlioz's "Prayer" from *Herminie*.

27. Chopin, *Correspondance*, 2:307.

28. Ibid.

29. *Revue et Gazette Musicale*, Sept. 5, 1841, p. 406.

30. *Revue et Gazette Musicale*, Oct. 10, 1841, p. 447.

31. *Revue et Gazette Musicale*, Nov. 16, 1834.

32. *Le Ménestrel*, Feb. 18, 1838.

33. Louis Maigron, *Le Romantisme et la Mode* (Paris: Librairie Ancienne Honoré Champion, 1911), 194.

34. Barzun, *Berlioz and His Century*, 30.

35. *Revue et Gazette Musicale*, Apr. 19, 1840, p. 274.

36. Léon Guichard, *La Musique et les Lettres au Temps du Romantisme* (Paris: Presses Universitaires de France, 1955), 48.

37. Berlioz, *Evenings with the Orchestra*, 47.

38. Marcel Bouteron, *Danse et Musique Romantique* (Paris: Le Goupy, 1927), 161.

39. *Revue et Gazette Musicale*, June 13, 1841, p. 305.

40. Berlioz, *Evenings with the Orchestra*, 188.

41. *Le Ménestrel*, Mar. 4, 1838.

42. Berlioz, *Mémoires*, 361.

43. Ibid.

44. Julien Tiersot, *La Musique aux Temps Romantiques* (Paris: Felix Alcan, 1930), 73.

45. *Revue et Gazette Musicale,* Jan. 21, 1836, p. 39.

46. Frederick Dorian, *The History of Music in Performance* (New York: Norton, 1966), 251.

47. Arsène Houssaye, *Les Confessions: Souvenirs d'un Demi-Siècle, 1830–1880* (Paris: E. Dentu, 1885), 2:282.

48. Dorian, *History of Music in Performance,* 233.

49. *Le Ménestrel,* Apr. 21, 1844.

50. Heine, *Works,* 4:415.

51. *Revue et Gazette Musicale,* Mar. 30, 1834, p. 107.

52. Heine, *Works,* 4:387.

53. Ibid., 389.

54. *Revue et Gazette Musicale,* Apr. 1, 1841, pp. 204–205.

55. Wagner, *Wagner Writes from Paris,* pp. 124–25.

56. John Chancellor, *Wagner* (Boston: Little Brown, 1978), 72.

57. *Revue et Gazette Musicale,* Jan. 28, 1841, p. 60.

58. Chopin, *Correspondance,* 3:27.

59. *Revue et Gazette Musicale,* Dec. 21, 1834, p. 410.

60. George Sand, *Spiridion* (Paris: Editions Aujourd'hui, 1976), 190.

61. *Galignani's New Paris Guide* (Paris: Galignani, 1841), 231.

62. Adam Carse, *The Life of Jullien* (Cambridge: W. Heffer and Sons, 1951), 114.

63. Offenbach's talent impressed Cherubini enough that he broke his long-standing rule against accepting foreign-born students.

CHAPTER 7.
Opera: Vocal Art and Social Spectacle

1. Louis Huart, *Galerie de la Presse de la Littérature et des Beaux-Arts,* "Marie Taglioni," *La Presse* (Paris) 1839–40, pages not numbered.

2. Stendhal (Marie-Henri Beyle), *The Charterhouse of Parma,* tr. Margaret R. B. Shaw (London: Penguin, 1958), 427.

3. Imbert de Saint-Amand, *Marie-Amélie et la Cour des Tuileries* (Paris: Librairie de la Société des Gens de Lettres, 1893), 19.

4. *Galignani's New Paris Guide* (Paris: Galignani, 1841), 466.

5. From the beginning of the Louis-Philippe era until it burned in January of 1838, the Théâtre des Italiens was located in the Salle Favart, the site of today's Opéra-Comique on the place Boïeldieu. Following the fire, it finished out the season in the Salle Ventadour on the rue Marsollier. From 1838 until 1841 it was housed in the Left Bank's Odéon, after which it returned to the Salle Ventadour for the rest of its existence. The Opéra-Comique's migrations between 1830 and 1850 went in a reverse direction, from the Salle Ventadour (1829–32) to the Théâtre des Nouveautés at the southwest corner of the Bourse (1832–40), and finally to the Salle Favart from 1840 on.

6. Joseph-Marc Bailbé, *Le Roman et la Musique en France sous la Monarchie de Juillet* (Paris: Minard, 1969), 31.

7. Ibid., 30, quoting from La Brière's novel *Deux Etoiles.*

8. Charles de Boigne, *Petits Mémoires de l'Opéra* (Paris: Librairie Nouvelle, 1857), 106.

9. Ibid., 9.

10. M. Binet, *Un Médecin pas Ordinaire: Le Docteur Véron* (Paris: Editions Albin Michel, 1945), 141.

11. Ibid.

12. *Gazette Musicale,* Mar. 23, 1834, p. 97.

13. Jean Gourret, *Ces Hommes qui on fait l'Opéra* (Paris: Albatros, 1984), 122.

14. Jacques Barzun, *Berlioz and His Century: An Introduction to the Age of Romanticism* (New York: Meridian, 1956), 148.

15. *Gazette Musicale,* Jan. 18, 1835, pp. 22–23.

16. Frances Trollope, *Paris and the Parisians* (New York, Harper and Bros., 1836), 288. Her remark was actually a quote from Rossini's "Barber of Seville."

17. Ibid.

18. Ibid., 287.

19. *Gazette Musicale,* July 3, 1836, p. 233.

20. Hector Berlioz, *Evenings with the Orchestra,* tr. and ed. Jacques Barzun (New York: Knopf, 1956), 116.

21. William L. Crosten, *French Grand Opera: An Art and a Business* (New York: Da Capo, 1972), 67.

22. Frédéric Chopin, *Correspondance,* ed. Bronislas Sydow, Suzanne and Denise Chainaye, and Irène Sydow (Paris: Richard-Masse, 1954–60), 2:25–26.

23. Eugène de Mirecourt, *Les Contemporains,* vol. 4: *Meyerbeer* (Brussels: Alphonse Lebègue, 1854), 58.

24. Jeffrey L. Sammons, *Heinrich Heine* (Princeton, N.J.: Princeton University Press, 1979), 246.

25. Chopin, *Correspondance*, 3:409.

26. Ibid.

27. Mirecourt, *Les Contemporains*, vol. 4: *Meyerbeer*, 65.

28. Patrick Smith, *The Tenth Muse: A Historical Study of the Opera Libretto* (New York: Knopf, 1970), 231.

29. Crosten, *French Grand Opera*, 100.

30. Barzun, *Berlioz and His Century*, 183.

31. Smith, *The Tenth Muse*, 221.

32. Crosten, *French Grand Opera*, 105.

33. De Boigne, *Petits Mémoires de l'Opéra*, 80.

34. Huart, *Galerie de la Presse et de la Littérature et des Beaux-Arts*, "Marie Taglione," pages not numbered.

35. Gautier's mistress, Ernesta, and her sister, Carlotta, were cousins of the Italian opera's prima donnas, Giulia and Giudetta Grisi.

36. Sammons, *Heinrich Heine*, 289.

37. "Robert" [Louis Castel], *Mémoires d'un Claqueur* (Paris: Constant-Chantpie, 1829), 106.

38. De Boigne, *Petits Mémoires de l'Opéra*, 86.

39. R. A. Barrows, *The Parisian Claque and George Sand's "Grand Soirée des Pomme Cuites,"* read at the Eighth International George Sand Conference, l'Université François Rabelais (Tours, France), July 6, 1989.

40. Richard Wagner, *Wagner Writes from Paris*, ed. and tr. Robert L. Jacob and Geoffrey Skelton (New York: John Day, 1973), 115.

41. Ernest Legouvé, *Sixty Years of Recollections*, tr. Albert D. Vandam (London: Eden Remington, 1893), 1:212.

42. Bailbé, *Le Roman et la Musique en France sous la Monarchie de Juillet*, 101.

43. Lablache, who was actually the son of a French father and an Irish mother, grew up in Italy and became imbued with the cultural heritage of that country. For this reason he is generally considered "Italian" despite his hereditary background.

44. It was not until late in life that Wagner came to appreciate Auber. During his early years in Paris, he once remarked that the act of composing for Auber was "as much a habit as soaping to a barber" (Wagner, *Wagner Writes from Paris*, 123).

45. Hector Berlioz, *Mémoires*, ed. and tr. David Cairns (New York: Norton, 1975), 416.

CHAPTER 8.
Bohemia and the Demimonde: Two Operas in the Making

1. Philip Carr, *Days with the French Romantics in the Paris of 1830* (London: Methuen, 1932), xxii.

2. Marius Boisson, *Les Compagnons de la Vie de Bohème* (Paris: Tallandier, 1929), 18.

3. Joanna Richardson, *Théophile Gautier: His Life and Times* (London: Max Reinhardt, 1958), 79 (quoting Charles Monselet).

4. In spite of much speculation, the origin of the word "bousingot" has remained a mystery. Some claim it was an English word once used to describe the broad-brimmed, glazed hats worn by British sailors. Others attribute its derivation to the French word *bousin*, meaning a tavern catering to a noisy lower-class crowd. Still others regard it as a corruption of the English word "boozing." Certainly the Bousingots were intoxicated with their mission of reform, if nothing else.

5. Théophile Gautier, *Les Jeunes France* (Paris: Flammarion, 1974), 30.

6. Honoré Balzac, *Cousine Bette*, tr. Marion A. Crawford (Harmondsworth, Eng.: Penguin, 1965), 60.

7. Ibid.

8. Ibid., 61.

9. Théophile Gautier, *Mademoiselle de Maupin* (Paris: Garnier-Flammarion, 1966), 210.

10. Ibid., preface, 45.

11. Ibid., 294.

12. Ibid., 211.

13. *La Presse*, June 7, 1841.

14. Théophile Gautier, *Complete Works*, vol. 3: *Portraits of the Day*, tr. and ed. S. C. de Sumichrast (London: Atheneum, n.d.), 177.

15. Joanna Richardson, *The Bohemians: La Vie de Bohème in Paris, 1830–1914* (South Brunswick and New York: A. S. Barnes and Co., 1971), 58.

16. Joanna Richardson, *The Courtesans: The Demi-Monde in Nineteenth-Century France* (Cleveland and New York: The World, 1967), 173.

17. Richardson, *The Bohemians: La Vie de Bohème in Paris, 1830–1914*, 111.

18. A. Moss and E. Marvel, *The Legend of the Latin Quarter: Henry Murger and the Birth of Bohemia* (New York: Beechhurst, 1946), 50.

19. Eugène de Mirecourt, *Les Contemporains*, vol. 8: *Gozlan- Champfleury* (Brussels: Alphonse Lebègue, 1854), 77.

20. Robert Baldick, *The First Bohemian* (London: Hamish Hamilton, 1961), 66.

21. Boisson, *Les Compagnons de la Vie de Bohème*, 38.

22. Ibid., 38.

23. Baldick, *First Bohemian*, 114.

24. Ibid., 84.

25. Henri Murger, *Scènes de la Vie de Bohème* (Paris: Gallimard, 1988), 218.

26. Baldick, *First Bohemian*, 81.

27. An earlier unsuccessful opera by Leoncavallo was also based on Murger's story.

28. Gautier, *Complete Works*, vol. 3: *Portraits of the Day*, 301.

29. Although Dumas *fils* wrote *Le Demi-Monde* in 1853, it was set in 1846 and describes the social world of the July monarchy.

30. Murger, *Scènes de la Vie de Bohème*, 311.

31. Balzac, *Cousine Bette*, 427.

32. Gautier, *Complete Works*, vol. 3: *Portraits of the Day*, 296.

33. Balzac, *Cousine Bette*, 371.

34. Murger, *Scènes de la Vie de Bohème*, 311.

35. Gautier, *Complete Works*, vol. 3: *Portraits of the Day*, 296.

36. Frédéric Chopin, *Correspondance*, ed. Bronislas Sydow, Suzanne and Denise Chainaye, and Irène Sydow (Paris: Richard-Masse, 1954–60), 3:203.

37. Théophile Gautier, *Lettres à la Présidente* (Paris: Cercle du Livre Précieux, 1940), 197.

38. Olympe Pélissier served as the models for the unfeeling Foedora in Balzac's *Peau de Chagrin* and the ambitious Sarah M'Gregor in Sue's *The Mysteries of Paris*.

39. Wallace Brockway and Herbert Weinstock, *Men of Music* (New York: Simon and Schuster, 1950), 243.

40. Chopin, *Correspondance*, 3:284.

41. Ibid., 3:285.

42. Edmond and Jules de Goncourt, *Pages from the Goncourt Journal*, ed. and tr. Robert Baldick (London: Oxford University Press, 1962), 98.

43. Chopin, *Correspondance*, 3:284.

44. Balzac, *Cousine Bette*, 23.

45. Mme Judith, *My Autobiography* (London: Eveleigh Nash, 1912), 237.

46. Alexandre Dumas *fils*, *La Dame aux Camélias*, tr. Edmund Gosse (New York: Heritage, 1955), viii.

47. Mme Judith, *My Autobiography*, 240.

48. Jean Prasteau, *The Lady of the Camellias: The Story of Marie Duplessis,* tr. Stella Rochway (London: Hutchinson, 1965), 225.

49. Gustave Claudin, *Mes Souvenirs: Les Boulevards de 1840–70* (Paris: Calmann Lévy, 1884), 42.

CHAPTER 9.
Penning a Profit: Literature Becomes Lucrative

1. Charles Baudelaire, *Selected Letters,* tr. and ed. Rosemary Lloyd (Chicago: University of Chicago Press, 1986), 32.

2. Eugène de Mirecourt, *Les Contemporains,* vol. 4: *Paul de Kock* (Brussels: Alphonse Lebègue, 1854), 88.

3. Théophile Gautier, *Complete Works,* vol. 3: *Portraits of the Day,* tr. and ed. S. C. de Sumichrast (London: Atheneum Press, n.d.), 197.

4. Ibid., 88.

5. Andre Maurois, *Olympio: The Life of Victor Hugo,* tr. Gerard Hopkins (New York: Harper and Row, Pyramid, 1968), 87.

6. Heinrich Heine, *Mémoires,* tr. G. Carman, ed. G. Karpeles (London: Heinemann, 1910), 2:114.

7. Ibid.

8. Honoré Balzac, *Cousine Bette,* tr. Marion A. Crawford (Harmondsworth Eng.: Penguin, 1965), 305.

9. Honoré Balzac, *Lost Illusions,* tr. Hubert J. Hunt (Harmondsworth, Eng.: Penguin, 1971), 285.

10. Ibid., 185.

11. Eugène Sue, *The Wandering Jew* (New York: Dedalus/Hippocrene, 1990), 329.

12. Jacques Barzun, *Berlioz and His Century: An Introduction to the Age of Romanticism* (New York: Meridian, 1956), 55.

13. W. M. Thackeray, *The Paris Sketch Book* (Boston and New York: Colonial Press., n.d.), 204.

14. Ibid., 261.

15. Jeffrey Sammons, *Heinrich Heine* (Princeton, N.J.: Princeton University Press, 1979), 282.

16. Samuel Edwards, *Victor Hugo: A Tumultuous Life* (New York: David McKay, 1971), 7.

17. G. L. Strachey, *Landmarks in French Literature* (New York: Henry Holt, 1912), 203.

18. Frédéric Chopin, *Correspondance*, ed. Bronislas Sydow, Suzanne and Denise Chainaye, and Irène Sydow (Paris: Richard-Masse, 1954–60), 3:203.

19. Edwards, *Victor Hugo*, 7.

20. Mme Judith, *My Autobiography* (London: Eveleigh Nash, 1912), 217.

21. Charles-Augustin Sainte-Beuve, *Monday Chats*, tr. and ed. William Matthews (Chicago: S. C. Griggs, 1878), introduction, p. xxiii.

22. Frances Winwar, *George Sand and Her Times* (New York and London: Harper, 1945), 185.

23. Sainte-Beuve, *Monday Chats*, introduction, p. xviii.

24. César Grana, *Bohemian vs. Bourgeois* (New York: Basic Books, 1964), 80.

25. Ibid.

26. Sammons, *Heinrich Heine*, 171.

27. A feuilleton was the lower portion of the front page of a French newspaper. Separated from the upper half of the page (devoted to major news items) by a horizontal line, it was usually reserved for installments of a fictional work and articles of literary or artistic criticism.

28. Rees Howell Gronow, *The Reminiscences and Recollections of Captain Gronow* (London: Bodley Head, 1964), 186.

29. Thomas Raikes, *Journal (1831–1847)* (London: Longman, Brown, Green, Longmans, and Roberts, 1856), 2:174.

30. Ibid., 2:175.

31. Frances Trollope, *Paris and the Parisians* (New York: Harper, 1836), 97.

32. Ibid.

33. Grana, *Bohemian vs. Bourgeois*, 26.

34. Balzac, *Lost Illusions*, 314.

35. Honoré Balzac, *Wild Ass's Skin*, tr. Herbert J. Hunt (Harmondsworth, Eng.: Penguin, 1986), 160.

36. *Almanach Populaire de la France* (Paris: n.p., 1843), 116.

37. Ibid.

38. Hector Berlioz, *Mémoires*, ed. and tr. David Cairns (New York: Norton, 1975), 357.

39. Barzun, *Berlioz and His Century*, 140.

40. The snide and condescending review of Chopin's concert at the Salle Pleyel on April

26, 1841, was actually written for the most part by Liszt's mistress, the comtesse d'Agoult, although Liszt himself undoubtedly edited and contributed to it.

41. Théophile Gautier, *Maîtres du Théâtre Français* (Paris: Payot, 1929), 5.

42. Alphonse Lamartine, *Portraits et Salons Romantiques* (Paris: Le Goupy, 1927), 10.

43. Edmond and Jules de Goncourt, *Pages from the Goncourt Journal*, ed. and tr. Robert Baldick (London: Oxford University Press, 1962), 202.

44. Elizabeth Gilmore Holt, *The Triumph of Art for the Public: 1785–1848* (Princeton, N.J.: Princeton University Press, 1979), 336.

45. Balzac, *Lost Illusions*, 373.

46. Ibid., 229.

47. Ibid.

48. Ibid., 246.

49. Ibid., 275.

50. Ibid., 249.

51. Ibid., 314.

52. Balzac, *Wild Ass's Skin*, 57.

53. Gautier, *Complete Works*, vol. 3: *Portraits of the Day*, 178.

54. Mme Sand had had earlier novels published by installments in Buloz's biweekly journal, the *Revue des Deux Mondes*, and her own monthly *Revue Indépendante*. These, however, were not the new Girardin-styled dailies with their front page feuilletons, which reached a far greater public.

55. Curtis Cate, *George Sand* (New York: Houghton Mifflin, 1975), 533.

56. Théophile Gautier, *Artistes et Ecrivains* (Paris: Librairie Plon), 120.

57. Mirecourt, *Les Contemporains*, vol. 8: *Léon Gozlan*, 47.

58. Albert Dresden Vandam, *An Englishman in Paris* (New York: Appleton, 1892), 1:56.

59. André Maurois, *The Titans: The Extraordinary Lives of the Three Dumas* (New York: Pyramid, 1967), 181.

60. Balzac, *Wild Ass's Skin*, 29.

61. George Sand, *Leone Leoni*, tr. George Burnham Ives (Chicago: Academy Press, 1978), 291.

62. Ibid., 301.

63. Eugène Sue, *The Mysteries of Paris* (New York: Dedalus/Hippocrene, n.d.), 295.

64. Ibid., 317.

65. George Sand, *Correspondance,* ed. Georges Lubin, 9 vols. (Paris: Garnier, 1964–72), 1:823.

CHAPTER 10.
Stage by Stage: The Evolution of Theatrical Taste from the Battle of "Hernani" to the Reign of Rachel

1. Charles-Valentin Morhange, known as Alkan, was a pianist and composer as well as a friend and neighbor of Chopin in Paris's square d'Orléans.

2. Frédéric Chopin, *Correspondance,* ed. Bronislas Sydow, Suzanne and Denise Chainaye, and Irène Sydow (Paris: Richard-Masse, 1954–60), 3:272.

3. Heinrich Heine, *Works of Heinrich Heine,* tr. Chas. Godfrey (New York: Dutton, 1906), 4:225.

4. Gérard de Nerval, *Petits Chateaux de Bohème* (Paris: Librairie Ancienne Honoré Champion, 1926), 267.

5. Brander Matthews, *French Dramatists of the Nineteenth Century* (New York and London: Benjamin Blom, 1968), 94.

6. Théophile Gautier, *Maîtres du Théâtre Français* (Paris: Payot, 1929), 248.

7. Ibid., 245.

8. Ibid., 245–46.

9. Paul Foucher, *Entre Cour et Jardin* (Paris: Amyot, 1867), 530.

10. Ibid., 525.

11. Ibid.

12. Jean Prasteau, *The Lady of the Camellias: A Story of Marie Duplessis,* tr. Stella Rochway (London: Hutchinson, 1965), 144.

13. Louis Huart, *Galerie de la Presse de la Littérature et des Beaux-Arts,* 1st ser. (Paris: *La Presse,* 1839), pages not numbered.

14. Frederick Brown, *Theater and Revolution: The Culture of the French Stage* (New York: Viking, 1980), 90.

15. Robert Baldick, *The Life and Times of Frederick Lemaître* (London: Hamish Hamilton, 1959), 36.

16. Gérard de Nerval, *Oeuvres Complètes* (Paris: Librairie Ancienne Honoré Champion, 1926), 2:302.

17. Foucher, *Entre Cour et Jardin,* 555.

18. Janet Seligman, *Figures of Fun* (London: Oxford University Press, 1957), 110.

19. Brown, *Theater and Revolution: The Culture of the French Stage*, 120.

20. Baldick, *Life and Times of Frederick Lemaître*, 37.

21. Brown, *Theater and Revolution: The Culture of the French Stage*, 90.

22. William Makepeace Thackeray, *The Paris Sketch Book* (Boston and New York: Colonial Press, n.d.), 269.

23. Victor Hugo, *Hernani*, "Preface" (Paris: Librairie Larousse, 1965), 31.

24. Alexandre Dumas *père*, *Mlle. de Belle-Isle*, in *Théâtre Complet* (Paris: Michel Lévy, 1864), 4:96.

25. *Prefaces and Prologues to Famous Books*, ed. Charles W. Eliot (Danbury Conn.: Grolier, 1980), 358.

26. Matthews, *French Dramatists of the Nineteenth Century*, 3.

27. *Prefaces and Prologues to Famous Books*, 372.

28. Ibid., 375.

29. Malcolm Easton, *Artists and Writers in Paris* (London: Edward Arnold, 1964), 53.

30. Ernest Legouvé, *Sixty Years of Recollections*, tr. Albert D. Vandam (London: Eden Remington, 1893), 2:139.

31. Gautier, *Maîtres du Théâtre Francais*, 153.

32. Matthews, *French Dramatists of the Nineteenth Century*, 42.

33. Thackeray, *Paris Sketch Book*, 259.

34. Matthews, *French Dramatists of the Nineteenth Century*, 36–37.

35. Patrick J. Smith, *The Tenth Muse* (New York: Knopf, 1970), 234.

36. Imbert Saint-Amand, *Marie-Amélie et la Cour des Tuileries* (Paris: Librairie de la Société des Gens de Lettres, 1893), 87.

37. George Sand, *Correspondance*, ed. Georges Lubin (Paris: Garnier, 1964–72), 2:807.

38. Ibid., 2:898.

39. André Maurois, *The Titans: The Extraordinary Lives of the Three Dumas* (New York: Harper and Row [Pyramid ed.], 1967), 86.

40. Matthews, *French Dramatists of the Nineteenth Century*, 64.

41. Chopin, *Correspondance*, 2:15–16.

42. Foucher, *Entre Cour et Jardin*, 542.

43. Chopin, *Correspondance*, 2:78.

44. Richard Wagner, *Wagner Writes from Paris*, ed. and tr. Robert L. Jacob and Geoffrey Skelton (New York: John Day, 1973), 118.

45. Théophile Gautier, *Complete Works,* vol. 3: *Portraits of the Day,* tr. and ed. S. C. de Sumichrast (London: Atheneum, n.d.), 325.

46. Heine, *Works,* 4:232.

47. Nerval, *Petits Chateaux de Bohème,* 261.

48. Eugène de Mirecourt, *Les Contemporains,* vol. 7: *Rose Cheri* (Brussels: Alphonse Lebègue, 1855), 45.

49. Sand, *Correspondance,* 4:789.

50. Marie Dorval, *Marie Dorval, 1798–1849, Documents inédits* (Paris: Librairie Internationale, 1868), 46.

51. Ibid., 66.

52. Victor Hugo, *Dramas,* vol. 4: *Marion Delorme* (Boston: Estes and Laureat, n.d.), *passim,* 176–254.

53. Chopin, *Correspondance,* 3:226.

54. When George Sand's grandmother died, she left the author a house, the Hôtel Narbonne (now demolished), on the Left Bank's rue de la Harpe. Sand never lived in the house but instead rented it out for income.

55. Sand, *Correspondance,* 4:768. *The Mississippians* never reached the stage but was published as a *roman dialogué,* a novel in dialogue form.

56. Sand, *Correspondance,* 4:753.

57. Ibid., 5:37.

58. Ibid., 5:46–47.

59. Ibid., 5:47.

60. *Journal des Débats,* Sept. 10, 1838.

61. Gautier, *Les Maîtres du Théâtre Français,* 27.

62. Ibid., 109.

63. Gautier, *Complete Works,* 3:338.

64. Ibid., 337.

65. Ibid., 339.

66. Gautier, *Les Maîtres du Théâtre Français,* 173.

67. Chopin, *Correspondance,* 3:289.

68. Eugène de Mirecourt, *Les Contemporains,* vol. 6: *Brohan* (Brussels: Alphonse Lebègue, 1855), 72.

69. Mme Récamier, *Mémoires and Correspondance*, tr. I. M. Luyster (Boston: Knight and Millet, 1867; AMS ed., New York, 1975), 380.

70. Heine, *Works*, 4:267.

71. James Agate, *Rachel* (London: Gerald Howe, 1928), 45.

72. Sand, *Correspondance*, 9:172.

73. Joanna Richardson, *Rachel* (London: Max Reinhardt, 1956), 106.

74. Thackeray, *Paris Sketch Book*, 258.

75. Gautier, *Complete Works*, vol. 3: *Portraits of the Day*, 339.

76. Ibid., 342.

CHAPTER 11.

Delacroix, Daumier, and Daguerre: A "3-D" View of Art

1. Eugène Delacroix, *The Journal of Eugène Delacroix*, ed. H. Wellington, tr. L. Norton (London: Phaidon, 1951), 321.

2. *La Presse*, Mar. 28, 1854.

3. Eugène Delacroix, *Lettres Intimes de Delacroix, Correspondance inédite* (Paris: Gallimard, 1954), 161.

4. Delacroix, *Journal*, 131–32.

5. Elizabeth Gilmore Holt, *The Triumph of Art for the Public, 1785–1848* (Princeton, N.J.: Princeton University Press, 373).

6. Tom Prideaux, *The World of Delacroix, 1798–1863* (New York: Time-Life Books, 1966), 70.

7. Charles Baudelaire, *Art in Paris, 1845–1862: Salons and Other Exhibitions*, tr. Jonathan Mayne (London: Phaidon, 1965), 3.

8. Charles Baudelaire, *Eugène Delacroix: His Life and Work*, tr. Jos. M. Bernstein (New York: Lear, 1947), 56.

9. Holt, *Triumph of Art for the Public, 1785–1848*, 368.

10. Frédéric Chopin, *Correspondance*, ed. Bronislas Sydow, Suzanne and Denise Chainaye, and Irène Sydow (Paris: Richard-Masse, 1954–60), 3:204.

11. William Makepeace Thackeray, *The Paris Sketch Book* (Boston and New York: Colonial Press, n.d.), 48.

12. Ibid.

13. George Sand, *Correspondance.* ed. Georges Lubin (Paris: Garnier Frères, 1968), 4:408.

14. Théophile Gautier, *Complete Works,* vol. 3: *Portraits of the Day,* tr. and ed. S. C. de Sumichrast (London: Atheneum, n.d.), 282.

15. Delacroix, *Journal,* 110.

16. Ibid., 46.

17. Ibid., 169.

18. Ibid., 303.

19. Ibid., 292.

20. Baudelaire, *Eugène Delacroix: His Life and Work,* 62–64.

21. Maurice Serullaz, *Eugène Delacroix* (New York: Harry N. Abrams, n.d.), 158.

22. Delacroix, *Journal,* 274.

23. Ibid., 382.

24. Ibid., 267, 110, 98, 71.

25. Ibid., 173

26. Ibid., 172.

27. Chopin, *Correspondance,* 3:112–13.

28. Ibid., 3:113.

29. Delacroix, *Journal,* 223.

30. Oddly enough, neither Sand nor Chopin ever dedicated any of their works to the other.

31. Delacroix, *Journal,* 106–107.

32. Ibid., 108.

33. While Philipon sketched Louis-Philippe's body in the shape of a pear, Daumier distorted his face in the same manner. Daumier's version seems to have become the more popular of the two caricatures.

34. Roger Passeron, *Daumier* (Secaucus, N.J.: Poplar, 1979), 118.

35. Thackeray, *Paris Sketch Book,* 159–60.

36. Gavarni's real name was Sulpice-Guillaume Chevalier. "Gavarni" was the name of the street on which he lived.

37. *The Daguerreotype,* ed. John Wood (London: Duckworth, 1989), p. 1.

38. William L. Crosten, *French Grand Opera, an Art and a Business* (New York: Da Capo, 1972), 56.

39. Delacroix, *Lettres Intimes,* Sept. 4, 1822.

40. Chopin, *Correspondance,* 2:46.

41. Erla Zwingle, "Seizing the Light," *National Geographic* 176, no. 4 (Oct. 1989): 536; Stefan Richter, *Art of the Daguerreotype* (New York: Viking Penguin, 1989), 9.

42. Ibid., 10.

43. Idzikowski and Sydow report two other photographs taken in 1846 that are possibly of Chopin.

CHAPTER 12.

"A Votre Santé!": Coping with Poultices, Purges, and the Parisian Medical Profession

1. Frédéric Chopin, *Correspondance,* ed. Bronislas Sydow, Suzanne and Denise Chainaye, and Irène Sydow (Paris: Richard-Masse, 1954–60), 3:449.

2. Frederick Niecks, *Frederick Chopin as a Man and Musician* (London and New York: Novello, Ewer and Co., 1888), 2:321.

3. Anaïs Bassanville, *Les Salons d'Autrefois* (Paris: 1863), 4:227.

4. Chopin, *Correspondance,* 2:14.

5. Ibid., 2:16.

6. Ibid.

7. Chopin's youngest sister, Emilia, died of tuberculosis at age fourteen, and the first symptoms of the disease appeared in Frédéric himself around age sixteen.

8. Chopin, *Correspondance,* 2:98.

9. Ibid., 2:131.

10. Ibid.

11. George Sand, *Correspondance,* ed. Georges Lubin (Paris: Garnier Frères, 1969), 5:647.

12. Bassanville, *Les Salons d'Autrefois,* 2:243.

13. Eugène Sue, *The Mysteries of Paris* (New York: Dedalus/Hippocrene, n.d.), 341.

14. *Revue et Gazette Musicale,* Sept. 27, 1840.

15. Ibid., Oct. 4, 1840, p. 482.

16. Ibid., May 2, 1841, 251.

17. Hector Berlioz, *Mémoires,* ed and tr. David Cairns (New York: Norton, 1975), 46.

18. Louis Jacob Frazee, *A Medical Student in Europe* (Cincinnati: H. S. and J. Applegate, 1852), 116.

19. Ibid.

20. A. S. Lyons and R. J. Petrucelli, *Medicine, An Illustrated History* (New York: Harry N. Abrams, 1978), 515.

21. Ibid., 524.

22. Roberto Margotta, *The Story of Medicine* (New York: Golden, 1968), 250.

23. George Sand, *Lettres d'un Voyageur,* tr. Sacha Rabinovitch and Patricia Thomson (New York: Penguin, 1987), 193.

24. Ibid., 198.

25. Ibid., 207.

26. Chopin, *Correspondance,* 3:288.

27. Rosa W. Hobhouse, *Life of Christian Samuel Hahnemann* (London: C. W. Daniel, 1933), 268.

28. Chopin, *Correspondance,* 3:407.

29. Ibid., 3:416.

30. Ibid., 3:418.

31. Ibid., 3:422.

32. I am well aware of conflicting medical opinions suggesting that Chopin's death was due to conditions such as cystic fibrosis, bronchiectasis, mitral stenosis, pulmonary aspergillosis, emphysema, or certain rare genetic enzyme defects. But as a physician, I feel that a form of disseminated tuberculosis with relative sparing of the lungs best fits the clinical history of the musician's disease and the autopsy findings at his death.

33. Esmond R. Long, *A History of the Therapy of Tuberculosis and the Case of Frédéric Chopin* (Lawrence: University of Kansas Press, 1956), 18.

34. *Almanach Populaire de la France* (Paris: n.p., 1843), 90.

35. Heinrich Heine, *Works of Heinrich Heine,* tr. Charles Godfrey Leland (New York: Dutton, 1906), 1:272.

36. Ibid., 1:273.

37. M. Binet, *Un Médecin pas Ordinaire: Le Docteur Véron* (Paris: Editions Albin Michel, 1945), 63.

38. Rodolphe Apponyi, *Journal du Comte Rodolphe Apponyi* (Paris: Plon-Nourrit, 1914–26), 3:172.

39. Henri Mondor, *Doctors and Medicine in the Works of Daumier* (New York, Leon Amiel, n.d.), 13.

40. Hector Berlioz, *Evenings with the Orchestra,* tr. and ed. Jacques Barzun (New York: Knopf, 1956), 55.

41. Honoré Balzac, *Cousin Pons,* tr. Herbert J. Hunt (Harmondsworth, Eng.: Penguin, 1968), 173.

CHAPTER 13.

Visions of a Better World: Searching for Utopia from Menilmontant to the Rue Vanneau

1. George Sand, *Lettres d'un Voyageur,* tr. Sacha Rabinovitch and Patricia Thomson (New York: Penguin, 1987), 219.

2. Joseph Barry, *Infamous Woman: The Life of George Sand* (Garden City, N.Y.: Doubleday, 1977), 47.

3. In contrast to married women, single women who had reached their majority were granted legal autonomy over their own lives and fortunes by the Napoleonic code.

4. Sand, *Lettres d'un Voyageur,* 123.

5. George Sand, *Correspondance,* ed. Georges Lubin, 9 vols. (Paris: Garnier, 1964–72), 2:120.

6. Sand, *Correspondance,* 4:435.

7. Ibid.

8. When Mallefille learned of his mistress's duplicity, he stationed himself outside Chopin's apartment with a pistol in hand, intent on murdering the new lovers. When his opportunity finally arrived, a large wagon passing down the street fortuitously blocked his aim and allowed the couple to escape.

9. Sand, *Correspondance,* 3:285.

10. Ibid., 4:437.

11. The building at No. 6 rue Monsigny was known as the Hôtel de Gèvres. On Christmas Day in 1834, Chopin performed there at a concert organized by a German music teacher, Franz Stoepel.

12. Frédéric Chopin, *Correspondance,* ed. Bronislas Sydow, Suzanne and Denise Chainaye, and Irène Sydow (Paris: Richard-Masse, 1954–60), 2:57.

13. Henry Raynor, *Music and Society since 1815* (New York: Schocken, 1976), 9.

14. Sand, *Lettres d'un Voyageur,* 218.

15. Sand, *Correspondance,* 7:257.

16. Chopin, *Correspondance,* 3:269.

17. Sand, *Correspondance,* 8:595.

18. Honoré Balzac, *Lost Illusions,* tr. Hubert J. Hunt (Harmondsworth, Eng.: Penguin, 1971), 375.

19. Fourier worked for years in the Parisian branch of a wholesale firm owned by Messrs. Curtis and Lamb of New York.

20. Sand, *Correspondance,* 7:256.

21. Curtis Cate, *George Sand: A Biography* (New York: Houghton Mifflin, 1975), 493.

22. Eugène de Mirecourt, *Les Contemporains,* vol. 1: *Lamennais* (Brussels, Alphonse Lebègue, 1854), 70.

23. Ibid., p. 81. Some years later Pope Gregory XVI was to blacklist a number of George Sand's novels. In many of these works she had expressed Lamennais's views.

24. Sand, *Correspondance,* 3:622.

25. Sand, *Lettres d'un Voyageur,* 176.

26. Sand, *Correspondance,* 6:68.

27. William Makepeace Thackeray, *Paris Sketch Book* (Boston and New York, Colonial Press., n.d.), 218.

28. George Sand, *Histoire de ma Vie* (Paris: n.p., 1928), 4:356; Sand, *Correspondance,* 5:757.

29. Heinrich Heine, *Mémoires,* ed. G. Karpeles, tr. G. Carman (London: Heinemann, 1910), 115.

30. David Owen Evans, *Social Romanticism in France, 1830–1848* (Oxford: Clarendon, 1951), 13.

31. Ibid. p. 115.

32. J-P Lacassagne, *Histoire d'un Amitié: Pierre Leroux et George Sand* (Paris: Klincksieck, 1973), 36.

33. Chopin, *Correspondance,* 3:211.

34. Lacassagne, *Histoire d'un Amitié,* 83.

35. Francine Du Plessix Gray, *Rage and Fire: A Life of Louise Colet* (New York: Simon and Schuster, 1994), 70, 75.

36. Renée Winegarten, *The Double Life of George Sand, Woman and Writer* (New York: Basic Books, 1978), 181.

37. Sand, *Correspondance,* 5:507.

38. Ibid., 6:805.

39. Gray, *Rage and Fire,* 381.

40. Sandra Dijkstra, *Flora Tristan: Feminism in the Age of George Sand* (London and Concord, Mass.: Pluto, 1991), 167.

41. Ibid., 174.

42. Sand, *Correspondance,* 6:789–90.

43. Ibid., 6:329.

44. André Maurois, *Prometheus: The Life of Balzac,* tr. Norman Denny (New York: Avon, 1967), 477.

45. Ibid.

46. Lacassagne, *Histoire d'un Amitié*, 69.

47. Dijkstra, *Flora Tristan*, 136.

48. Jeffrey L. Sammons, *Heinrich Heine* (Princeton, N.J.: Princeton University Press, 1979), 250.

49. Ibid., 327.

50. Eugène Sue, *The Wandering Jew* (New York: Dedalus/Hippocrene, 1990), 537.

51. *George Sand in Her Own Words*, ed. Joseph Barry (Garden City, N.Y.: Anchor, 1979), 388.

52. Sand, *Correspondance*, 8:407.

53. Frances Winwar, *George Sand and Her Times* (New York and London: Harper and Bros., 1945), 293.

CHAPTER 14.
The Big Shadow of the Little Corporal: Napoléon Becomes a Legend

1. Alfred de Musset, *Confessions of a Child of the Century* (New York: Current Literary Publishing, 1910), 2–8.

2. Ibid., 15.

3. Ibid., 17.

4. Stendhal (Marie-Henri Beyle), *A Life of Napoléon* (London: Rodale, 1956), 4.

5. Honoré Balzac, *La Recherche de l'Absolu*, quoted in *The Anchor Book of French Quotations*, ed. Norbert Guterman (New York: Anchor, Doubleday, 1990), 278.

6. Duff Cooper, *Talleyrand* (New York: Fromm International, 1986), 176.

7. A. L. Guerard, *Reflections on the Napoleonic Legend* (New York: Charles Scribner's Sons, 1924), 131.

8. Jean Lucas-Dubreton, *Le Culte de Napoléon, 1815–1848* (Paris: Editions Albin Michel, 1960), 397.

9. William Makepeace Thackeray, *The Paris Sketch Book* (Boston and New York: Colonial Press, n.d.), 122.

10. A curious insight into Napoléon's concept of equality is revealed in one of the coins that he had minted during his reign. On it is a portrait of himself with the oxymoronic title, "Emperor of the French republic."

11. Napoléon had two illegitimate sons, the comte Waleswski, a dashing dandy, and the comte Léon, an incorrigible wastrel, neither of whom the Bonapartists ever regarded as acceptable successors to their father's throne.

12. André Maurois, *Prometheus: The Life of Balzac,* tr. Norman Denny (New York: Avon, 1967), 381.

13. Ibid.

14. Eugène Delacroix, *Journal,* ed. H. Wellington, tr. L. Norton (London: Phaidon, 1951), 39.

15. André Maurois, *The Titans: The Extraordinary Lives of the Three Dumas* (New York: Pyramid, 1967), 99.

16. George Sand, *Correspondance,* ed. Georges Lubin (Paris: Garnier Frères, 1964), 1:789.

17. Nicholas Brazier, *Chroniques des Petits Théâtres de Paris* (Paris: Rouveyre et G. Blond, 1883), 1:164–65.

18. Michel Le Bris, *Romantics and Romanticism* (London: Macmillan, 1981), 130.

19. Eugène Sue, *The Wandering Jew* (New York: Dedalus/Hippocrene, 1990), 494.

20. Ibid., 574.

21. Czesław Miłosz, *The History of Polish Literature* (Berkeley: University of California Press, 1983), 198.

22. Jeffrey L. Sammons, *Heinrich Heine* (Princeton, N.J.: Princeton University Press, 1979), 33.

23. Ibid., 141.

24. Guerard, *Reflections on the Napoleonic Legend,* 209.

25. Lucas-Dubreton, *Culte de Napoléon,* 310.

26. Ibid., 349.

27. Thackeray, *Paris Sketch Book,* 123.

28. Sand, *Correspondance,* 6:710.

29. Stanley Mellon, "The July Monarchy and the Napoleonic Myth," *Yale French Studies,* no. 26 (fall–winter 1960–61): 74.

30. Guerard, *Reflections on the Napoleonic Legend,* 144.

31. *Journal des Débats,* Dec. 16, 1840.

32. Lucas-Dubreton, *Culte de Napoléon,* 387.

33. Ibid.

34. Ibid., 388.

35. Sand, *Correspondance,* 8:718.

Epilogue: Obituary and Funeral of Frédéric Chopin

1. The names of the pallbearers at Chopin's funeral have been subject to debate. This account, published only five days after the event and written by a member of the staff of the *Revue et Gazette Musicale* (most of whom knew Chopin well), is probably correct.

Index